Honda Civic Automotive Repair Manual

Alec J Jones

T Eng (CEI), AMIMI

Models covered

UK: Honda Civic 1300 Hatchback, 1335 cc
USA: Honda Civic Hatchback, Sedan and Wagon, 81.4 cu in
(1335 cc) & 90.8 cu in (1488 cc)

Covers manual, semi-automatic and fully automatic transmission versions

ISBN 1 85010 074 8

© **Haynes North America, Inc. 1982, 1984**

With permission from J. H. Haynes & Co. Ltd.

Printed in the USA   *(633 – 7U2)*

Haynes Publishing Group
Sparkford Nr Yeovil
Somerset BA22 7JJ England

Haynes North America, Inc
861 Lawrence Drive
Newbury Park
California 91320 USA

Acknowledgements

Thanks are due to Honda (UK) Ltd for their assistance in supplying technical material and certain illustrations, Castrol Limited who supplied the lubrication data, and the Champion Sparking Plug Company, who provided the illustrations showing the various spark plug conditions. The bodywork repair photographs used in this manual were provided by Holt Lloyd Limited who supply 'Turtle Wax', 'Dupli-Color Holts', and other Holts range products, and Sykes-Pickavant Limited provided some of the workshop tools.

About this manual

Its aim

The aim of this manual is to help you get the best value from your car. It can do so in several ways. It can help you decide what work must be done (even should you choose to get it done by a garage), provide information on routine maintenance and servicing, and give a logical course of action and diagnosis when random faults occur. However, it is hoped that you will use the manual by tackling the work yourself. On simpler jobs it may even be quicker than booking the car into a garage and going there twice to leave and collect it. Perhaps most important, a lot of money can be saved by avoiding the costs the garage must charge to cover its labour and overheads.

The manual has drawings and descriptions to show the function of the various components so that their layout can be understood. Then the tasks are described and photographed in a step-by-step sequence so that even a novice can do the work.

Its arrangement

The manual is divided into thirteen Chapters, each covering a logical sub-division of the vehicle. The Chapters are each divided into Sections, numbered with single figures, eg 5; and the Sections into paragraphs (or sub-sections), with decimal numbers following on from the Section they are in, eg 5.1, 5.2, 5.3 etc.

It is freely illustrated, especially in those parts where there is a detailed sequence of operations to be carried out. There are two forms of illustration: figures and photographs. The figures are numbered in sequence with decimal numbers, according to their position in the Chapter -- eg Fig. 6.4 is the fourth drawing/illustration in Chapter 6. Photographs carry the same number (either individually or in related groups) as the Section or sub-section to which they relate.

There is an alphabetical index at the back of the manual as well as a contents list at the front. Each Chapter is also preceded by its own individual contents list.

References to the 'left' or 'right' of the vehicle are in the sense of a person in the driver's seat facing forwards.

Unless otherwise stated, nuts and bolts are removed by turning anti-clockwise, and tightened by turning clockwise.

Vehicle manufacturers continually make changes to specifications and recommendations, and these, when notified, are incorporated into our manuals at the earliest opportunity.

Whilst every care is taken to ensure that the information in this manual is correct, no liability can be accepted by the authors or publishers for loss, damage or injury caused by any errors in, or omissions from, the information given.

Introduction to the Honda Civic

The new models of the Honda Civic with a redesigned bodyshell and 1335 cc engine were introduced to the UK in January 1980. Although in many ways similar to the Honda Civic 1500 they incorporate several modifications.

In the USA the Civic is fitted with a 1335 cc or 1488 cc CVCC (Compound Vortex Controlled Combustion) engine. This engine produces very low exhaust emission levels, considerably reducing the complexity of the emission control equipment necessary. The oper-

ation of the CVCC engine is described fully in Chapter 1.

According to production date and territory, transmission may be four- or five-speed manual, two-speed semi-automatic, or three-speed fully automatic. Drive is to the front wheels.

The Honda Civic is proving to be very popular and is selling in large numbers worldwide. Its success is probably due to its excellent performance and driveability and to the number of model variants which are available.

Contents

UK model Honda Civic 1300 Hatchback

US model Honda Civic DX Hatchback

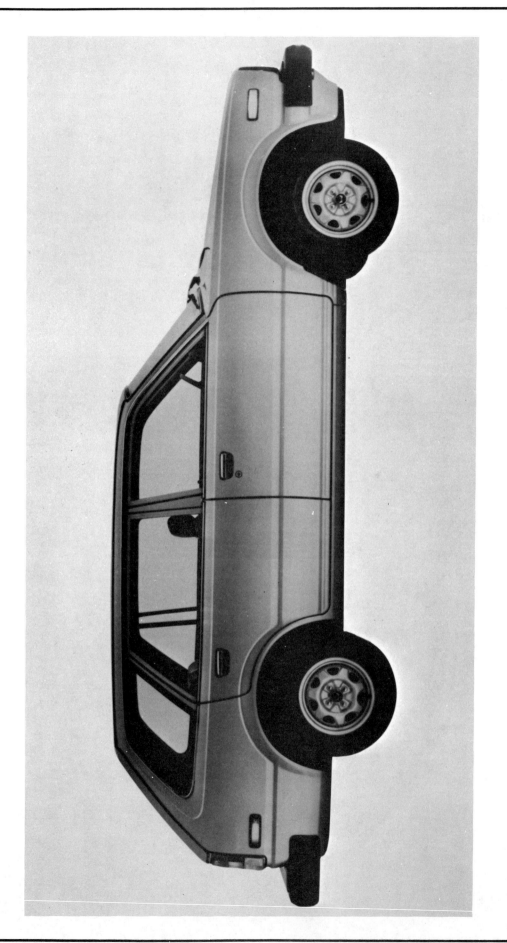

US model Honda Civic Wagon

General dimensions, weights and capacities

Refer to Chapter 13 for specifications related to 1982 and 1983 US models

UK models
Dimensions
Overall length:
    2-door Hatchback .... 148.0 in (3760 mm)
    4-door Hatchback .... 150.8 in (3830 mm)
Overall width .... 62.2 in (1580 mm))
Overall height .... 52.6 in (1335 mm)
Wheelbase:
    2-door Hatchback .... 88.6 in (2250 mm)
    4-door Hatchback .... 91.3 in (2320 mm)
Ground clearance .... 6.4 in (165 mm)
Front track .... 53.5 in (1360 mm)
Rear track .... 53.9 in (1370 mm)

Kerb weights
2-door Hatchback:
    2-speed .... 1653 lb (750 kg)
    4-speed .... 1609 lb (730 kg)
    5-speed .... 1653 lb (750 kg)
4-door Hatchback:
    2-speed .... 1731 lb (785 kg)
    4-speed .... 1664 lb (755 kg)
    5-speed .... 1731 lb (785 kg)

Capacities
Engine oil:
    Drain and refill .... 2.6 Imp qt (3.0 litres)
    Initial fill .... 3.2 Imp qt (3.6 litres)
Manual transmission oil:
    Drain and refill .... 2.2 Imp qt (2.5 litres)
    Initial fill .... 2.3 Imp qt (2.6 litres)
Hydraulic fluid:
    Transmission only .... 2.2 Imp qt (2.5 litres)
    Complete system .... 3.7 Imp qt (4.2 litres)
Fuel tank .... 9.0 Imp gall (41 litres)
Cooling system:
    Initial fill .... 0.9 Imp gall (4.0 litres)
    Drain and refill .... 0.8 Imp gall (3.4 litres)

US models
    The figures given are for 1981 models. There are slight differences in some of the figures for 1980 models and on 1981 Californian models.

Dimensions
Overall length:
    Hatchback .... 148.0 in (3760 mm)
    Wagon .... 160.8 in (4085 mm)
Overall width .... 62.2 in (1580 mm)
Overall height:
    Hatchback .... 53.0 in (1345 mm)
    Wagon .... 54.1 in (1375 mm)
Wheelbase:
    Hatchback .... 88.6 in (2250 mm)
    Wagon .... 91.3 in (2320 mm)
Ground clearance .... 6.5 in (165 mm)
Front track .... 53.5 in (1360 mm)
Rear track .... 54.3 in (1380 mm)

Curb weights
1300 Hatchback:
    3-speed .... 1797 lb (815 kg)
    4-speed .... 1747 lb (792 kg)
    5-speed .... 1753 lb (795 kg)
1500 Hatchback:
    3-speed .... 1841 lb (835 kg)
    5-speed .... 1812 lb (822 kg)
Wagon:
    3-speed .... 1989 lb (902 kg)
    5-speed .... 1978 lb (897 kg)

Capacities
Engine oil (drain and refill):
    Without filter .... 3.2 US qt (3.0 litres)
    With filter .... 3.6 US qt (3.4 litres)
Transmission oil:
    Drain and refill .... 2.6 US qt (2.5 litres))
    Initial fill .... 2.81 US qt (2.65 litres)
Automatic transmission:
    Transmission alone .... 2.6 US qt (2.5 litres)
    Complete system .... 5.2 US qt (4.9 litres)
Fuel tank .... 10.8 US gall (41 litres)
Cooling system:
    Initial fill:
        1300 Hatchback .... 1.3 US gall (5.0 litres)
        1500 Hatchback .... 1.5 US gall (5.5 litres)
        Wagon .... 1.5 US gall (5.5 litres)
    Drain and refill .... 1.2 US gall (4.5 litres)

Use of English

As this book has been written in England, it uses the appropriate English component names, phrases, and spelling. Some of these differ from those used in America. Normally, these cause no difficulty, but to make sure, a glossary is printed below. In ordering spare parts remember the parts list may use some of these words:

English	American	English	American
Accelerator	Gas pedal	Locks	Latches
Aerial	Antenna	Methylated spirit	Denatured alcohol
Anti-roll bar	Stabiliser or sway bar	Motorway	Freeway, turnpike etc
Big-end bearing	Rod bearing	Number plate	License plate
Bonnet (engine cover)	Hood	Paraffin	Kerosene
Boot (luggage compartment)	Trunk	Petrol	Gasoline (gas)
Bulkhead	Firewall	Petrol tank	Gas tank
Bush	Bushing	'Pinking'	'Pinging'
Cam follower or tappet	Valve lifter or tappet	Prise (force apart)	Pry
Carburettor	Carburetor	Propeller shaft	Driveshaft
Catch	Latch	Quarterlight	Quarter window
Choke/venturi	Barrel	Retread	Recap
Circlip	Snap-ring	Reverse	Back-up
Clearance	Lash	Rocker cover	Valve cover
Crownwheel	Ring gear (of differential)	Saloon	Sedan
Damper	Shock absorber, shock	Seized	Frozen
Disc (brake)	Rotor/disk	Sidelight	Parking light
Distance piece	Spacer	Silencer	Muffler
Drop arm	Pitman arm	Sill panel (beneath doors)	Rocker panel
Drop head coupe	Convertible	Small end, little end	Piston pin or wrist pin
Dynamo	Generator (DC)	Spanner	Wrench
Earth (electrical)	Ground	Split cotter (for valve spring cap)	Lock (for valve spring retainer)
Engineer's blue	Prussian blue	Split pin	Cotter pin
Estate car	Station wagon	Steering arm	Spindle arm
Exhaust manifold	Header	Sump	Oil pan
Fault finding/diagnosis	Troubleshooting	Swarf	Metal chips or debris
Float chamber	Float bowl	Tab washer	Tang or lock
Free-play	Lash	Tappet	Valve lifter
Freewheel	Coast	Thrust bearing	Throw-out bearing
Gearbox	Transmission	Top gear	High
Gearchange	Shift	Torch	Flashlight
Grub screw	Setscrew, Allen screw	Trackrod (of steering)	Tie-rod (or connecting rod)
Gudgeon pin	Piston pin or wrist pin	Trailing shoe (of brake)	Secondary shoe
Halfshaft	Axleshaft	Transmission	Whole drive line
Handbrake	Parking brake	Tyre	Tire
Hood	Soft top	Van	Panel wagon/van
Hot spot	Heat riser	Vice	Vise
Indicator	Turn signal	Wheel nut	Lug nut
Interior light	Dome lamp	Windscreen	Windshield
Layshaft (of gearbox)	Countershaft	Wing/mudguard	Fender
Leading shoe (of brake)	Primary shoe		

Buying spare parts
and vehicle identification numbers

Buying spare parts

Replacement parts are available from many sources, which generally fall into one of two categories – authorized dealer parts departments and independent retail auto parts stores. Our advice concerning these parts is as follows:

Retail auto parts stores: Good auto parts stores will stock frequently needed components which wear out relatively fast, such as clutch components, exhaust systems, brake parts, tune-up parts, etc. These stores often supply new or reconditioned parts on an exchange basis, which can save a considerable amount of money. Discount auto parts stores are often very good places to buy materials and parts needed for general vehicle maintenance such as oil, grease, filters, spark plugs, belts, touch-up paint, bulbs, etc. They also usually sell tools and general accessories, have convenient hours, charge lower prices and can often be found not far from home.

Authorized dealer parts department: This is the best source for parts which are unique to the vehicle and not generally available elsewhere (such as major engine parts, transmission parts, trim pieces, etc.).

Warranty information: If the vehicle is still covered under warranty, be sure that any replacement parts purchased – regardless of the source – do not invalidate the warranty!

To be sure of obtaining the correct parts, have engine and chassis numbers available and, if possible, take the old parts along for positive identification.

Vehicle identification numbers (except North America)

The *chassis number* is stamped on a plate attached to the engine compartment bulkhead on the top left side.

The *engine number* is stamped on the cylinder block casting, adjacent to the starter motor.

Engine and chassis numbers are repeated on the vehicle identification plate attached to the engine compartment front frame.

Vehicle identification numbers (North America)

The *chassis number* is located inside the windscreen on the upper surface of the facia panel. It is repeated together with the engine number on a plate attached to the firewall.

The *engine number* is located on a machined face of the cylinder block (right side).

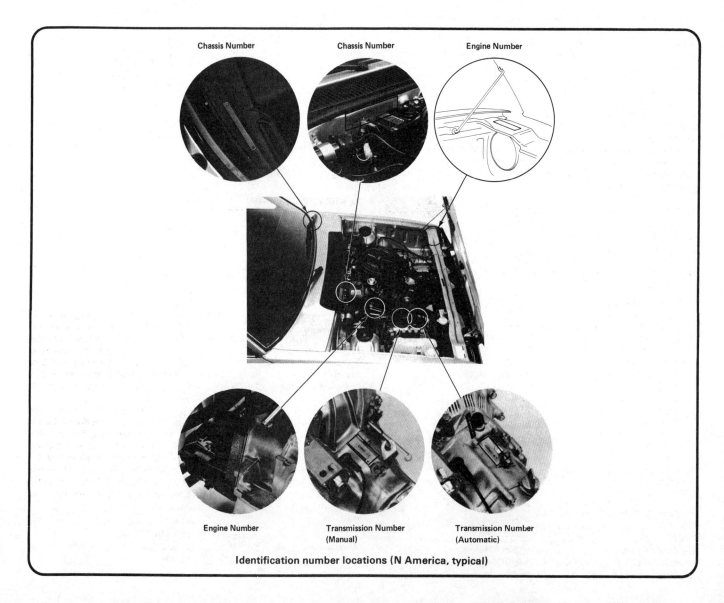

Chassis Number   Chassis Number   Engine Number

Engine Number   Transmission Number (Manual)   Transmission Number (Automatic)

Identification number locations (N America, typical)

Tools and working facilities

Introduction

A selection of good tools is a fundamental requirement for anyone contemplating the maintenance and repair of a motor vehicle. For the owner who does not possess any, their purchase will prove a considerable expense, offsetting some of the savings made by doing-it-yourself. However, provided that the tools purchased meet the relevant national safety standards and are of good quality, they will last for many years and prove an extremely worthwhile investment.

To help the average owner to decide which tools are needed to carry out the various tasks detailed in this manual, we have compiled three lists of tools under the following headings: *Maintenance and minor repair*, *Repair and overhaul*, and *Special*. The newcomer to practical mechanics should start off with the *Maintenance and minor repair* tool kit and confine himself to the simpler jobs around the vehicle. Then, as his confidence and experience grow, he can undertake more difficult tasks, buying extra tools as, and when, they are needed. In this way, a *Maintenance and minor repair* tool kit can be built-up into a *Repair and overhaul* tool kit over a considerable period of time without any major cash outlays. The experienced do-it-yourselfer will have a tool kit good enough for most repair and overhaul procedures and will add tools from the *Special* category when he feels the expense is justified by the amount of use these tools will be put to.

It is obviously not possible to cover the subject of tools fully here. For those who wish to learn more about tools and their use there is a book entitled *How to Choose and Use Car Tools* available from the publishers of this manual.

Maintenance and minor repair tool kit

The tools given in this list should be considered as a minimum requirement if routine maintenance, servicing and minor repair operations are to be undertaken. We recommend the purchase of combination spanners (ring one end, open-ended the other); although more expensive than open-ended ones, they do give the advantages of both types of spanner.

Combination spanners - 8, 10, 11, 12, 13, 14 & 17 mm
Adjustable spanner - 9 inch
Spark plug spanner (with rubber insert)
Spark plug gap adjustment tool
Set of feeler gauges
Brake bleed nipple spanner
Screwdriver - 4 in long x $\frac{1}{4}$ in dia (flat blade)
Screwdriver - 4 in long x $\frac{1}{4}$ in dia (cross blade)
Combination pliers - 6 inch
Hacksaw (junior)
Tyre pump
Tyre pressure gauge
Grease gun
Oil can
Fine emery cloth (1 sheet)
Wire brush (small)
Funnel (medium size)

Repair and overhaul tool kit

These tools are virtually essential for anyone undertaking any major repairs to a motor vehicle, and are additional to those given in the *Maintenance and minor repair* list. Included in this list is a comprehensive set of sockets. Although these are expensive they will be found invaluable as they are so versatile - particularly if various

drives are included in the set. We recommend the $\frac{1}{2}$ in square-drive type, as this can be used with most proprietary torque spanners. If you cannot afford a socket set, even bought piecemeal, then inexpensive tubular box wrenches are a useful alternative.

The tools in this list will occasionally need to be supplemented by tools from the *Special* list.

Sockets (or box spanners) to cover range in previous list
Reversible ratchet drive (for use with sockets)
Extension piece, 10 inch (for use with sockets)
Universal joint (for use with sockets)
Torque wrench (for use with sockets)
Mole wrench - 8 inch
Ball pein hammer
Soft-faced hammer, plastic or rubber
Screwdriver - 6 in long x $\frac{5}{16}$ in dia (flat blade)
Screwdriver - 2 in long x $\frac{5}{16}$ in square (flat blade)
Screwdriver - 1$\frac{1}{2}$ in long x $\frac{1}{4}$ in dia (cross blade)
Screwdriver - 3 in long x $\frac{1}{8}$ in dia (electricians)
Pliers - electricians side cutters
Pliers - needle nosed
Pliers - circlip (internal and external)
Cold chisel - $\frac{1}{2}$ inch
Scriber
Scraper
Centre punch
Pin punch
Hacksaw
Valve grinding tool
Steel rule/straight-edge
Allen keys
Selection of files
Wire brush (large)
Axle-stands
Jack (strong scissor or hydraulic type)

Special tools

The tools in this list are those which are not used regularly, are expensive to buy, or which need to be used in accordance with their manufacturers' instructions. Unless relatively difficult mechanical jobs are undertaken frequently, it will not be economic to buy many of these tools. Where this is the case, you could consider clubbing together with friends (or joining a motorists' club) to make a joint purchase, or borrowing the tools against a deposit from a local garage or tool hire specialist.

The following list contains only those tools and instruments freely available to the public, and not those special tools produced by the vehicle manufacturer specifically for its dealer network. You will find occasional references to these manufacturers' special tools in the text of this manual. Generally, an alternative method of doing the job without the vehicle manufacturers' special tool is given. However, sometimes, there is no alternative to using them. Where this is the case and the relevant tool cannot be bought or borrowed you will have to entrust the work to a franchised garage.

Valve spring compressor (where applicable)
Piston ring compressor
Balljoint separator
Universal hub/bearing puller
Impact screwdriver

Micrometer and/or vernier gauge
Dial gauge
Stroboscopic timing light
Dwell angle meter/tachometer
Universal electrical multi-meter
Cylinder compression gauge
Lifting tackle (photo)
Trolley jack
Light with extension lead

Buying tools

For practically all tools, a tool factor is the best source since he will have a very comprehensive range compared with the average garage or accessory shop. Having said that, accessory shops often offer excellent quality tools at discount prices, so it pays to shop around.

There are plenty of good tools around at reasonable prices, but always aim to purchase items which meet the relevant national safety standards. If in doubt, ask the proprietor or manager of the shop for advice before making a purchase.

Care and maintenance of tools

Having purchased a reasonable tool kit, it is necessary to keep the tools in a clean serviceable condition. After use, always wipe off any dirt, grease and metal particles using a clean, dry cloth, before putting the tools away. Never leave them lying around after they have been used. A simple tool rack on the garage or workshop wall, for items such as screwdrivers and pliers is a good idea. Store all normal wrenches and sockets in a metal box. Any measuring instruments, gauges, meters, etc, must be carefully stored where they cannot be damaged or become rusty.

Take a little care when tools are used. Hammer heads inevitably become marked and screwdrivers lose the keen edge on their blades from time to time. A little timely attention with emery cloth or a file will soon restore items like this to a good serviceable finish.

Working facilities

Not to be forgotten when discussing tools, is the workshop itself. If anything more than routine maintenance is to be carried out, some form of suitable working area becomes essential.

It is appreciated that many an owner mechanic is forced by circumstances to remove an engine or similar item, without the benefit of a garage or workshop. Having done this, any repairs should always be done under the cover of a roof.

Wherever possible, any dismantling should be done on a clean flat workbench or table at a suitable working height.

Any workbench needs a vise: one with a jaw opening of 4 in (100 mm) is suitable for most jobs. As mentioned previously, some clean dry storage space is also required for tools, as well as the lubricants, cleaning fluids, touch-up paints and so on which become necessary.

Another item which may be required, and which has a much more general usage, is an electric drill with a chuck capacity of at least $\frac{5}{16}$ in (8 mm). This, together with a good range of twist drills, is virtually essential for fitting accessories such as wing mirrors and reversing lights.

Last, but not least, always keep a supply of old newspapers and clean, lint-free rags available, and try to keep any working area as clean as possible.

Spanner jaw gap comparison table

Jaw gap (in)	Spanner size
0.250	$\frac{1}{4}$ in AF
0.276	7 mm
0.313	$\frac{5}{16}$ in AF
0.315	8 mm
0.344	$\frac{11}{32}$ in AF; $\frac{1}{8}$ in Whitworth
0.354	9 mm
0.375	$\frac{3}{8}$ in AF
0.394	10 mm
0.433	11 mm
0.438	$\frac{7}{16}$ in AF
0.445	$\frac{3}{16}$ in Whitworth; $\frac{1}{4}$ in BSF
0.472	12 mm
0.500	$\frac{1}{2}$ in AF
0.512	13 mm
0.525	$\frac{1}{4}$ in Whitworth; $\frac{5}{16}$ in BSF
0.551	14 mm
0.563	$\frac{9}{16}$ in AF
0.591	15 mm
0.600	$\frac{5}{16}$ in Whitworth; $\frac{3}{8}$ in BSF
0.625	$\frac{5}{8}$ in AF
0.630	16 mm
0.669	17 mm
0.686	$\frac{11}{16}$ in AF
0.709	18 mm
0.710	$\frac{3}{8}$ in Whitworth, $\frac{7}{16}$ in BSF
0.748	19 mm
0.750	$\frac{3}{4}$ in AF
0.813	$\frac{13}{16}$ in AF
0.820	$\frac{7}{16}$ in Whitworth; $\frac{1}{2}$ in BSF
0.866	22 mm
0.875	$\frac{7}{8}$ in AF
0.920	$\frac{1}{2}$ in Whitworth; $\frac{9}{16}$ in BSF
0.938	$\frac{15}{16}$ in AF
0.945	24 mm
1.000	1 in AF
1.010	$\frac{9}{16}$ in Whitworth; $\frac{5}{8}$ in BSF
1.024	26 mm
1.063	$1\frac{1}{16}$ in AF; 27 mm
1.100	$\frac{5}{8}$ in Whitworth; $\frac{11}{16}$ in BSF
1.125	$1\frac{1}{8}$ in AF
1.181	30 mm
1.200	$\frac{11}{16}$ in Whitworth; $\frac{3}{4}$ in BSF
1.250	$1\frac{1}{4}$ in AF
1.260	32 mm
1.300	$\frac{3}{4}$ in Whitworth; $\frac{7}{8}$ in BSF
1.313	$1\frac{5}{16}$ in AF
1.390	$\frac{13}{16}$ in Whitworth; $\frac{15}{16}$ in BSF
1.417	36 mm
1.438	$1\frac{7}{16}$ in AF
1.480	$\frac{7}{8}$ in Whitworth; 1 in BSF
1.500	$1\frac{1}{2}$ in AF
1.575	40 mm; $\frac{15}{16}$ in Whitworth
1.614	41 mm
1.625	$1\frac{5}{8}$ in AF
1.670	1 in Whitworth; $1\frac{1}{8}$ in BSF
1.688	$1\frac{11}{16}$ in AF
1.811	46 mm
1.813	$1\frac{13}{16}$ in AF
1.860	$1\frac{1}{8}$ in Whitworth; $1\frac{1}{4}$ in BSF
1.875	$1\frac{7}{8}$ in AF
1.969	50 mm

Jacking and towing

Jacking

The jack supplied with the vehicle should only be used for changing a roadwheel (photos). Always chock the wheels on the side opposite that being worked on, and engage a gear or apply the handbrake as appropriate.

When repairs or overhaul operations are being carried out, always supplement the jack with axle stands placed under the sill support points. If a trolley jack is used, only jack up at the points illustrated.

Towing

In the event of a roadside breakdown, the vehicle may be towed using the front towing hook (photo), but the following precautions must be observed:

(a) The wheels and axle must not be touching the body or frame
(b) The ignition key must be turned to positon I, so that the steering is unlocked, and the steering wheel must turn freely
(c) The transmission must be in neutral
(d) The parking brake must be fully released
(e) Towing speed must not exceeed 35 mph (55 kph) and towing distance must not exceed 50 miles (80 km)

If the above conditions cannot be met, the vehicle must be towed with its front wheels clear of the ground (suspended tow).

If the vehicle is to be used to tow another car in an emergency, do not attach the tow rope to any part of the vehicle except the rear towing eye (photo).

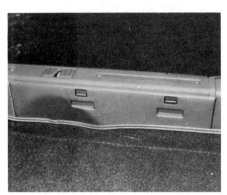

Trim panel covering jack stowage

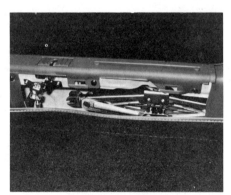

Jack when stowed

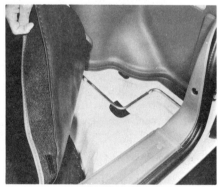

Jack handle location

Correct position for jack

Front towing eye

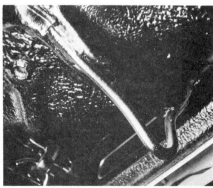

Rear towing eye

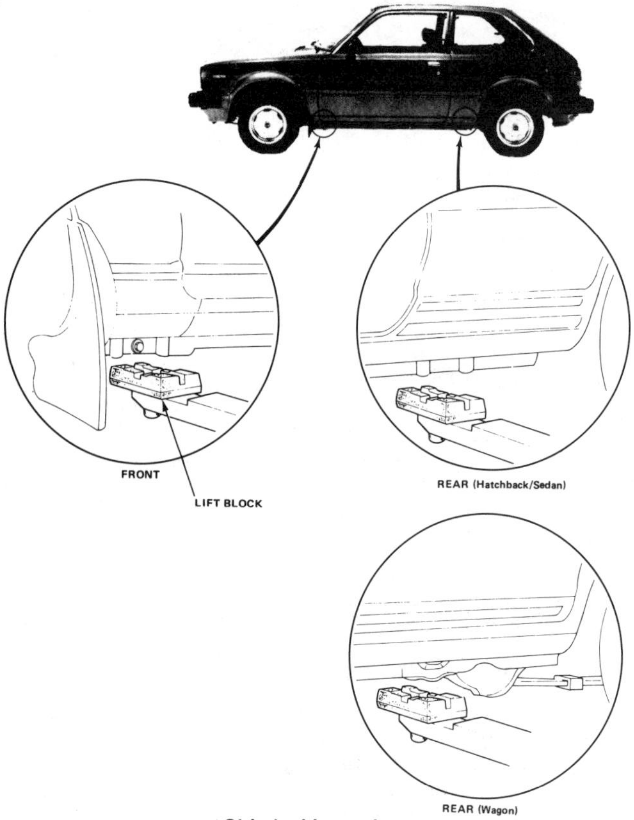

14

FRONT

LIFT BLOCK

REAR (Hatchback/Sedan)

REAR (Wagon)

Side jacking points

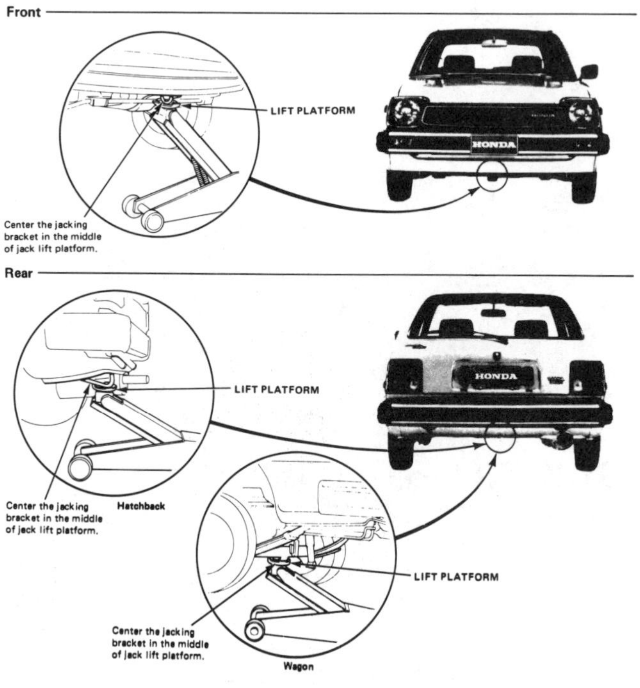

Front

LIFT PLATFORM

Center the jacking bracket in the middle of jack lift platform.

Rear

LIFT PLATFORM

Center the jacking bracket in the middle of jack lift platform.

Hatchback

LIFT PLATFORM

Center the jacking bracket in the middle of jack lift platform.

Wagon

Centre jacking points

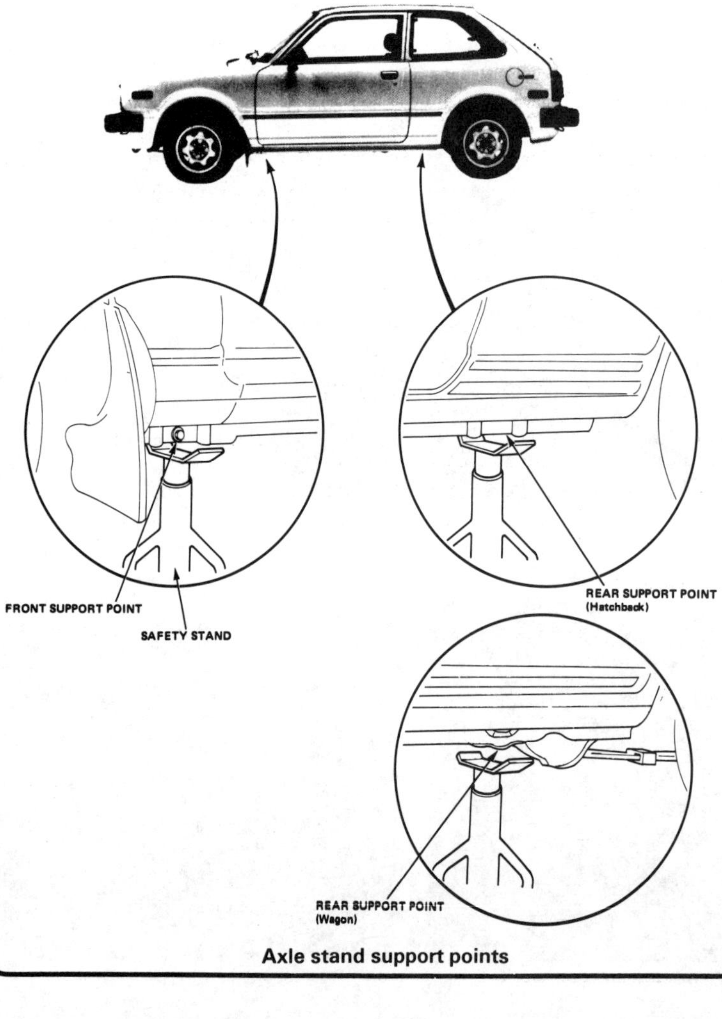

FRONT SUPPORT POINT

SAFETY STAND

REAR SUPPORT POINT (Hatchback)

REAR SUPPORT POINT (Wagon)

Axle stand support points

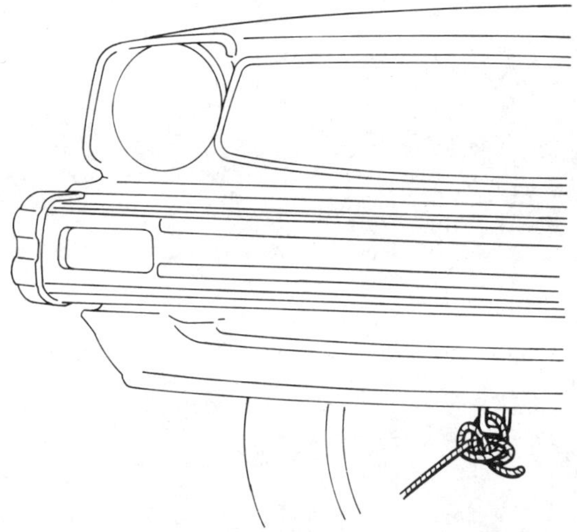

Towing point

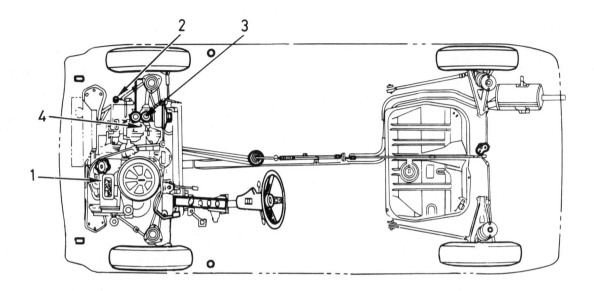

Recommended lubricants and fluids

Component or system	Lubricant type or specification	Castrol product
1 Engine	Multigrade engine oil SAE 10W/40 or 20W/50	GTX
2A Manual transmission	Multigrade engine oil SAE 10W/30 or 10W/40	Castrolite
2B Automatic transmission	Dexron R type ATF	Dexron R II
3 Brake hydraulic system	Hydraulic fluid to DOT 3 or DOT 4	Universal brake and Clutch Fluid
4 Constant velocity joints	Molybdenum disulphide grease	MS3 Grease
Steering gear	Multi-purpose grease	LM Grease
Wheel bearings	Multi-purpose grease	LM Grease

Note: *Lubrication requirements may vary from territory to territory and according to vehicle usage. Consult the operator's handbook supplied with your car.*

Safety first!

Regardless of how enthusiastic you may be about getting on with the job at hand, take the time to ensure that your safety is not jeopardized. A moment's lack of attention can result in an accident, as can failure to observe certain simple safety precautions. The possibility of an accident will always exist, and the following points should not be considered a comprehensive list of all dangers. Rather, they are intended to make you aware of the risks and to encourage a safety conscious approach to all work you carry out on your vehicle.

Essential DOs and DON'Ts

DON'T rely on a jack when working under the vehicle. Always use approved jackstands to support the weight of the vehicle and place them under the recommended lift or support points.

DON'T attempt to loosen extremely tight fasteners (i.e. wheel lug nuts) while the vehicle is on a jack — it may fall.

DON'T start the engine without first making sure that the transmission is in Neutral (or Park where applicable) and the parking brake is set.

DON'T remove the radiator cap from a hot cooling system — let it cool or cover it with a cloth and release the pressure gradually.

DON'T attempt to drain the engine oil until you are sure it has cooled to the point that it will not burn you.

DON'T touch any part of the engine or exhaust system until it has cooled sufficiently to avoid burns.

DON'T siphon toxic liquids such as gasoline, antifreeze and brake fluid by mouth, or allow them to remain on your skin.

DON'T inhale brake lining dust — it is potentially hazardous (see *Asbestos* below)

DON'T allow spilled oil or grease to remain on the floor — wipe it up before someone slips on it.

DON'T use loose fitting wrenches or other tools which may slip and cause injury.

DON'T push on wrenches when loosening or tightening nuts or bolts. Always try to pull the wrench toward you. If the situation calls for pushing the wrench away, push with an open hand to avoid scraped knuckles if the wrench should slip.

DON'T attempt to lift a heavy component alone — get someone to help you.

DON'T rush or take unsafe shortcuts to finish a job.

DON'T allow children or animals in or around the vehicle while you are working on it.

DO wear eye protection when using power tools such as a drill, sander, bench grinder, etc. and when working under a vehicle.

DO keep loose clothing and long hair well out of the way of moving parts.

DO make sure that any hoist used has a safe working load rating adequate for the job.

DO get someone to check on you periodically when working alone on a vehicle.

DO carry out work in a logical sequence and make sure that everything is correctly assembled and tightened.

DO keep chemicals and fluids tightly capped and out of the reach of children and pets.

DO remember that your vehicle's safety affects that of yourself and others. If in doubt on any point, get professional advice.

Asbestos

Certain friction, insulating, sealing, and other products — such as brake linings, brake bands, clutch linings, torque converters, gaskets, etc. — contain asbestos. *Extreme care must be taken to avoid inhalation of dust from such products since it is hazardous to health.* If in doubt, assume that they *do* contain asbestos.

Fire

Remember at all times that gasoline is highly flammable. Never smoke or have any kind of open flame around when working on a vehicle. But the risk does not end there. A spark caused by an electrical short circuit, by two metal surfaces contacting each other, or even by static electricity built up in your body under certain conditions, can ignite gasoline vapors, which in a confined space are highly explosive. Do not, under any circumstances, use gasoline for cleaning parts. Use an approved safety solvent.

Always disconnect the battery ground (–) cable *at the battery* before working on any part of the fuel system or electrical system. Never risk spilling fuel on a hot engine or exhaust component.

It is strongly recommended that a fire extinguisher suitable for use on fuel and electrical fires be kept handy in the garage or workshop at all times. Never try to extinguish a fuel or electrical fire with water.

Torch (flashlight in the US)

Any reference to a "torch" appearing in this manual should always be taken to mean a hand-held, battery-operated electric light or flashlight. It DOES NOT mean a welding or propane torch or blowtorch.

Fumes

Certain fumes are highly toxic and can quickly cause unconsciousness and even death if inhaled to any extent. Gasoline vapor falls into this category, as do the vapors from some cleaning solvents. Any draining or pouring of such volatile fluids should be done in a well ventilated area.

When using cleaning fluids and solvents, read the instructions on the container carefully. Never use materials from unmarked containers.

Never run the engine in an enclosed space, such as a garage. Exhaust fumes contain carbon monoxide, which is extremely poisonous. If you need to run the engine, always do so in the open air, or at least have the rear of the vehicle outside the work area.

If you are fortunate enough to have the use of an inspection pit, never drain or pour gasoline and never run the engine while the vehicle is over the pit. The fumes, being heavier than air, will concentrate in the pit with possibly lethal results.

The battery

Never create a spark or allow a bare light bulb near a battery. They normally give off a certain amount of hydrogen gas, which is highly explosive.

Always disconnect the battery ground (–) cable *at the battery* before working on the fuel or electrical systems.

If possible, loosen the filler caps or cover when charging the battery from an external source (this does not apply to sealed or maintenance-free batteries). Do not charge at an excessive rate or the battery may burst.

Take care when adding water to a non maintenance-free battery and when carrying a battery. The electrolyte, even when diluted, is very corrosive and should not be allowed to contact clothing or skin.

Always wear eye protection when cleaning the battery to prevent the caustic deposits from entering your eyes.

Mains electricity (household current in the US)

When using an electric power tool, inspection light, etc., which operates on household current, always make sure that the tool is correctly connected to its plug and that, where necessary, it is properly grounded. Do not use such items in damp conditions and, again, do not create a spark or apply excessive heat in the vicinity of fuel or fuel vapor.

Secondary ignition system voltage

A severe electric shock can result from touching certain parts of the ignition system (such as the spark plug wires) when the engine is running or being cranked, particularly if components are damp or the insulation is defective. In the case of an electronic ignition system, the secondary system voltage is much higher and could prove fatal.

Routine maintenance

Refer to Chapter 13 for information related to 1982 and 1983 US models

Maintenance is essential for ensuring safety and desirable for the purpose of getting the best in terms of performance and economy from the car. Over the years the need for periodic lubrication — oiling, greasing and so on — has been drastically reduced if not totally eliminated. This has unfortunately tended to lead some owners to think that because no such action is required the items either no longer exist or will last for ever. This is a serious delusion. It follows therefore that the largest initial element of maintenance is visual examination. This may lead to repairs or renewals.

Every 250 miles (400 km) or weekly

Check and top up the engine oil level (photos)
Check automatic transmission fluid level and top up if necessary
Check the coolant level in the expansion tank (photo)
Check the battery electrolyte level (photos)
Check the brake fluid level (photos)
Check the tyre pressures (including the spare) (photos)
Check lights for bulb failure
Top up the windscreen washer reservoir

Every 5000 miles (8000 km)

Check idle speed and CO level

Every 7500 miles (12 000 km)

Change engine oil and renew oil filter (photo). More frequent changing may be advisable in severe operating conditions
Inspect brake pipes and hoses
Check handbrake operation
Check manual transmission oil level and top up if necessary (photo)
Check clutch free play
Check exhaust system for leaks and security
Check the tightness of the engine and transmission mounting bolts
Inspect spark plugs, clean and reset gap
Check for play in the steering rack and steering balljoints

Every 15 000 miles (24 000 km)

In addition to, or instead of, the work specified for the 7500 mile service
Check alternator drivebelt tension and condition (photo)
Check condition and security of coolant hoses
Clean all dirt and debris from the radiator core
Renew the air cleaner element (more frequent renewal may be necessary in dusty conditions)
Check the operation of the intake air temperature system

Check the operation of the throttle controller (US)
Check the operation of the automatic choke mechanism (US)
Check the evaporative emission control system (US)
Renew the spark plugs
Check the crankcase emission control system
Check the condition of the front brake pads and caliper
Check the front and rear wheel alignment

Every 30 000 miles (48 000 km)

In addition to, or instead of, the work specified for the previous services
Renew manual transmission oil or automatic transmission fluid
Renew the fuel filter (photo)
Inspect condition and security of fuel hoses
Renew the charcoal canister (evaporative fuel control system)
Check ignition timing and adjust if necessary
Inspect distributor cap and HT leads and renew as necessary
Inspect rear brake shoes and renew as necessary

Every 30 000 miles (48 000 km) or two years, whichever comes first

Drain cooling system and refill with fresh fluid
Renew brake hydraulic fluid by bleeding

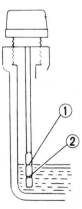

Automatic transmission fluid level checking. Dipstick must not be screwed in for check

1   Upper level   *2   Lower level*

Engine oil dipstick

Topping up the engine oil

Transmission filler/level plug (arrowed)

Coolant expansion tank

Battery electrolyte level must be between marks

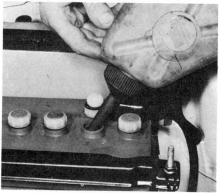
Topping the battery

Checking tyre pressures

Location of spare wheel

Checking brake fluid level

Engine oil drain plug

Checking alternator drivebelt tension

Fuel filter. Arrow on filter shows direction of flow

Fault diagnosis

Introduction

The car owner who does his or her own maintenance according to the recommended schedules should not have to use this section of the manual very often. Modern component reliability is such that, provided those items subject to wear or deterioration are inspected or renewed at the specified intervals, sudden failure is comparatively rare. Faults do not usually just happen as a result of sudden failure, but develop over a period of time. Major mechanical failures in particular are usually preceded by characteristic symptoms over hundreds or even thousands of miles. Those components which do occasionally fail without warning are often small and easily carried in the car.

With any fault finding, the first step is to decide where to begin investigations. Sometimes this is obvious, but on other occasions a little detective work will be necessary. The owner who makes half a dozen haphazard adjustments or replacements may be successful in curing a fault (or its symptoms), but he will be none the wiser if the fault recurs and he may well have spent more time and money than was necessary. A calm and logical approach will be found to be more satisfactory in the long run. Always take into account any warning signs or abnormalities that may have been noticed in the period preceding the fault – power loss, high or low gauge readings, unusual noises or smells, etc – and remember that failure of components such as fuses or spark plugs may only be pointers to some underlying fault.

The pages which follow here are intended to help in cases of failure to start or breakdown on the road. There is also a Fault Diagnosis Section at the end of each Chapter which should be consulted if the preliminary checks prove unfruitful. Whatever the fault, certain basic principles apply. These are as follows:

Verify the fault. This is simply a matter of being sure that you know what the symptoms are before starting work. This is particularly important if you are investigating a fault for someone else who may not have described it very accurately.

Don't overlook the obvious: For example, if the car won't start, is there petrol in the tank? (Don't take anyone else's word on this particular point, and don't trust the fuel gauge either!). If an electrical fault is indicated, look for loose or broken wires before digging out the test gear.

Cure the disease, not the symptom. Substituting a flat battery with a fully charged one will get you off the hard shoulder, but if the underlying cause is not attended to, the new battery will go the same way. Similarly, changing oil-fouled spark plugs for a new set will get you moving again, but remember that the reason for the fouling (if it wasn't simply an incorrect grade of plug) will have to be established and corrected.

Don't take anything for granted. Particularly, don't forget that a 'new' component may itself be defective (especially if it's been rattling round in the boot for months), and don't leave components out of a fault diagnosis sequence just because they are new or recently fitted. When you do finally diagnose a difficult fault, you'll probably realise that all the evidence was there from the start.

Electrical faults

Electrical faults can be more puzzling than straightforward mechanical failures, but they are no less susceptible to logical analysis if the basic principles of operation are understood. Car electrical wiring exists in extremely unfavourable conditions – heat, vibration and chemical attack – and the first things to look for are loose or corroded connections and broken or chafed wires, especially where the wires pass through holes in the bodywork or are subject to vibration.

All metal-bodied cars in current production have one pole of the battery 'earthed', ie connected to the car bodywork, and in nearly all modern cars it is the negative (–) terminal. The various electrical components – motors, bulb holders etc – are also connected to earth, either by means of a lead or directly by their mountings. Electric current flows through the component and then back to the battery via the car bodywork. If the component mounting is loose or corroded, or if a good path back to the battery is not available, the circuit will be incomplete and malfunction will result. The engine and/or gearbox are also earthed by means of flexible metal straps to the body or subframe; if these straps are loose or missing, starter motor, generator and ignition trouble may result.

Assuming the earth return to be satisfactory, electrical faults will be due either to component malfunction or to defects in the current supply. Individual components are dealt with in Chapter 10. If supply wires are broken or cracked internally this results in an open-circuit, and the easiest way to check for this is to bypass the suspect wire temporarily with a length of wire having a crocodile clip or suitable connector at each end. Alternatively, a 12V test lamp can be used to verify the presence of supply voltage at various points along the wire and the break can be thus isolated.

If a bare portion of a live wire touches the car bodywork or other earthed metal part, the electricity will take the low-resistance patch thus formed back to the battery: this is known as a short-circuit. Hopefully a short-circuit will blow a fuse, but otherwise it may cause burning of the insulation (and possible further short-circuits) or even a fire. This is why it is inadvisable to bypass persistently blowing fuses with silver foil or wire.

Spares and tool kit

Most cars are only supplied with sufficient tools for wheel changing; the *Maintenance and minor repair* tool kit detailed in *Tools and working facilities*, with the addition of a hammer, is probably sufficient for those repairs that most motorists would consider attempting at the roadside. In addition a few items which can be fitted without too much trouble in the event of a breakdown should be carried. Experience and available space will modify the list below, but the following may save having to call on professional assistance:

Spark plugs, clean and correctly gapped
HT lead and plug cap – long enough to reach the plug furthest from the distributor
Distributor rotor
Drivebelt – emergency type may suffice
Spare fuses
Set of principal light bulbs
Tin of radiator sealer and hose bandage
Exhaust bandage
Roll of insulating tape
Length of soft iron wire
Length of electrical flex
Torch or inspection lamp (can double as test lamp)
Battery jump leads
Tow rope
Tyre valve core
Ignition waterproofing aerosol
Litre of engine oil
Sealed can of hydraulic fluid
Emergency windscreen

If spare fuel is carried, a can designed for the purpose should be used to minimise the risks of leakage and collision damage. A first aid kit and a warning triangle, whilst not at present compulsory in the UK, are obviously sensible items to carry in addition to the above.

When touring abroad it may be advisable to carry additional

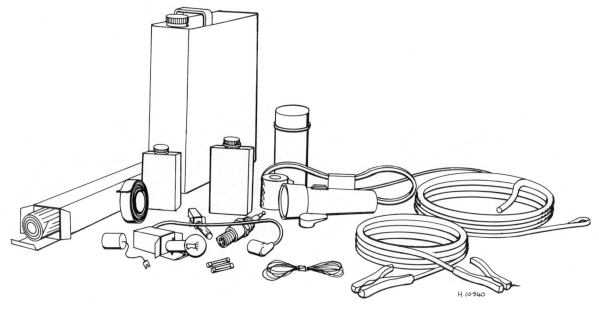

Carrying a few spares can save you a long walk!

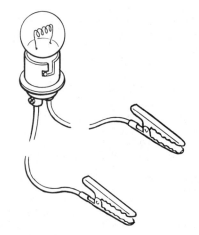

A simple test lamp is useful for tracing electrical faults

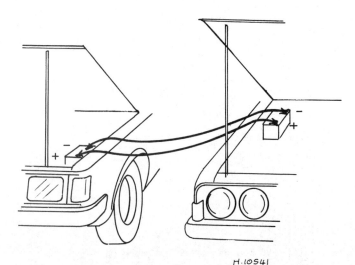

Correct way to connect jump leads. Do not allow car bodies to touch!

spares which, even if you cannot fit them yourself, could save having to wait while parts are obtained. The items below may be worth considering:

Clutch and throttle cables
Cylinder head gasket
Alternator brushes
Spare fuel pump

One of the motoring organisations will be able to advise on availability of fuel etc in foreign countries.

Engine will not start

Engine fails to turn when starter operated
Flat battery (recharge, use jump leads, or push start)
Battery terminals loose or corroded
Battery earth to body defective
Engine earth strap loose or broken
Starter motor (or solenoid) wiring loose or broken
Ignition/starter switch faulty
Major mechanical failure (seizure) or long disuse (piston rings rusted to bores)
Starter or solenoid internal fault (see Chapter 10)

Starter motor turns engine slowly
Partially discharged battery (recharge, use jump leads, or push start)
Battery terminals loose or corroded
Battery earth to body defective
Engine earth strap loose
Starter motor (or solenoid) wiring loose
Starter motor internal fault (see Chapter 10)

Starter motor spins without turning engine
Flywheel gear teeth damaged or worn
Starter motor mounting bolts loose

Engine turns normally but fails to start
Damp or dirty HT leads and distributor cap (crank engine and check for spark)
No fuel in tank (check for delivery at carburettor) (photo)
Excessive choke (hot engine) or insufficient choke (cold engine)
Fouled or incorrectly gapped spark plugs (remove, clean and regap)

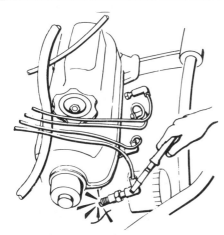

Crank engine and check for spark. Note use of insulated tool!

Other ignition system fault (see Chapter 4)
Other fuel system fault (see Chapter 3)
Poor compression (see Chapter 1)
Major mechanical failure (eg camshaft drive)

Engine fires but will not run

Insufficient choke (cold engine) – check adjustment
Air leaks at carburettor or inlet manifold
Fuel starvation (see Chapter 3)
Ignition fault (see Chapter 4)

Engine cuts out and will not restart

Engine cuts out suddenly – ignition fault

Loose or disconnected LT wires
Wet HT leads or distributor cap (after traversing water splash)
Coil or condenser failure (check for spark)
Other ignition fault (see Chapter 4)

Engine misfires before cutting out – fuel fault

Fuel tank empty
Fuel pump defective or filter blocked (check for delivery)
Fuel tank filler vent blocked (suction will be evident on releasing cap)
Carburettor needle valve sticking
Carburettor jets blocked (fuel contamination)
Other fuel system fault (see Chapter 3)

Engine cuts out – other causes

Serious overheating
Major mechanical failure (eg camshaft drive)

Engine overheats

Ignition (no-charge) warning light illuminated

Slack or broken drivebelt – retension or renew (Chapter 2)

Ignition warning light not illuminated

Coolant loss due to internal or external leakage (see Chapter 2)
Thermostat defective
Low oil level
Brakes binding
Radiator clogged externally or internally
Electric cooling fan not operating correctly
Engine waterways clogged
Ignition timing incorrect or automatic advance malfunctioning
Mixture too weak

Note: *Do not add cold water to an overheated engine or damage may result*

Remove fuel pipe from carburettor to check delivery

Low engine oil pressure

Warning light illuminated with engine running

Oil level low or incorrect grade
Defective sender unit
Wire to sender unit earthed
Engine overheating
Oil filter clogged or bypass valve defective
Oil pressure relief valve defective
Oil pick-up strainer clogged
Oil pump worn or mountings loose
Worn main or big-end bearings

Note: *Low oil pressure in a high-mileage engine at tickover is not necessarily a cause for concern. Sudden pressure loss at speed is far more significant. In any event, check the warning light sender before condemning the engine.*

Engine noises

Pre-ignition (pinking) on acceleration

Incorrect grade of fuel
Ignition timing incorrect
Distributor faulty or worn
Worn or maladjusted carburettor
Excessive carbon build-up in engine

Whistling or wheezing noises

Leaking vacuum hose
Leaking carburettor or manifold gasket
Blowing head gasket

Tapping or rattling

Incorrect valve clearance
Worn valve gear
Worn timing belt
Broken piston ring (ticking noise)

Knocking or thumping

Unintentional mechanical contact (eg fan blades)
Worn fanbelt
Peripheral component fault (generator, water pump etc)
Worn big-end bearings (regular heavy knocking, perhaps less under load)
Worn main bearings (rumbling and knocking, perhaps worsening under load)
Piston slap (most noticeable when cold)

Chapter 1 Engine

Refer to Chapter 13 for specifications and information related to 1982 and 1983 US models

Contents

Specifications

General

Engine type	4-stroke, 4-cylinder, water cooled, ohc; CVCC head on US models
Bore:	
1300	2.83 in (72.0 mm)
1500	2.91 in (74.0 mm)
Stroke:	
1300	3.23 in (82.0 mm)
1500	3.41 in (86.5 mm)
Displacement:	
1300	81.4 cu in (1335 cc)
1500	90.8 cu in (1488 cc)
Compression ratio	8.8 : 1

Compression ratio (300 rpm, throttle wide open):

	Nominal	Minimum
UK models	171 lbf/in² (12 kgf/cm²)	142 lbf/in² (10 kgf/cm²)
US models. 1980, 1300	156 lbf/in² (11 kgf/cm²)	128 lbf/in² (9 kgf/cm²)
US models, 1980, 1500, and all 1981 models	185 lbf/in² (13 kgf/cm²)	156 lbf/in² (11 kgf/cm²)
Maximum variation between cylinders (all models)	28 lbf/in² (2 kgf/cm²)	

Cylinder head

Warpage service limit	0.002 in (0.05 mm)
Height, new:	
Standard engine	3.35 in (85.0 mm)
CVCC engine	3.56 in (90.5 mm)
Height, minimum after refinishing:	
Standard engine	3.34 in (84.95 mm)
CVCC engine	3.55 in (90.3 mm)

Cylinder block

Warpage of top surface:	
New	0.003 in (0.08 mm) maximum
Service limit	0.004 in (0.10 mm)

	1300	1500
Bore diameter:		
Standard (new)	2.834 to 2.835 in (72.00 to 72.02 mm)	2.913 to 2.914 in (74.00 to 74.02 mm)
Service limit	2.839 in (72.10 mm)	2.917 in (74.10 mm)
Rebore limit	+0.010 in (0.25 mm)	+0.010 in (0.25 mm)
Bore taper:		
Standard (new)	0.0003 to 0.0005 in (0.007 to 0.012 mm)	
Service limit	0.002 in (0.05 mm)	

Pistons

	1300	1500
Skirt outside diameter:		
Standard (new)	2.833 to 2.835 in (71.97 to 72.00 mm)	2.912 to 2.913 in (73.96 to 73.99 mm)
Service limit	2.832 in (71.95 mm)	2.911 in (73.95 mm)
Clearance in cylinder:		
Standard (new)	0.0004 to 0.0020 in (0.01 to 0.05 mm)	0.0004 to 0.0024 in (0.01 to 0.06 mm)
Service limit	0.004 in (0.10 mm)	0.004 in (0.10 mm)

Piston rings

Piston-to-ring clearance (compression rings):
Standard (new) .... 0.0008 to 0.0018 in (0.020 to 0.045 mm)
Service limit .... 0.005 in (0.13 mm)
Ring end gap (compression rings):
Standard (new) .... 0.006 to 0.014 in (0.15 to 0.35 mm)
Service limit .... 0.022 in (0.55 mm)
Ring end gap (oil control ring):
Standard (new) .... 0.012 to 0.035 in (0.30 to 0.90 mm)
Service limit .... 0.043 in (1.10 mm)

Connecting rods and piston pins

Piston pin diameter:
Standard (new) .... 0.6691 to 0.6693 in (16.994 to 17.000 mm)
Oversize available (blue mark) .... 0.6692 to 0.6694 in (16.997 to 17.003 mm)
Pin to rod interference:
Standard (new) .... 0.0006 to 0.0016 in (0.016 to 0.040 mm)
Service limit .... 0.0005 in (0.014 mm)
Big-end bore diameter (nominal):
1300 .... 1.69 in (43 mm)
1500 .... 1.77 in (45 mm)
Endfloat, installed on crankshaft:
Standard (new) .... 0.006 to 0.012 in (0.15 to 0.30 mm)
Service limit .... 0.016 in (0.40 mm)

Crankshaft

Main journal diameter (nominal, see text):
UK and 1980 US models .... 1.9687 to 1.9697 in (50.006 to 50.030 mm)
1981 US models .... 1.9676 to 1.9685 in (49.976 to 50.000 mm)
Connecting rod journal diameter (nominal, see text):
1300 .... 1.5739 to 1.5748 in (39.976 to 40.000 mm)
1500 .... 1.6526 to 1.6535 in (41.976 to 42.000 mm)
Taper/out-of-round, all journals:
Standard (new) .... 0.0002 in (0.005 mm) maximum
Service limit .... 0.0004 in (0.010 mm)
Endfloat:
Standard (new) .... 0.004 to 0.014 in (0.10 to 0.35 mm)
Service limit .... 0.018 in (0.45 mm)
Run-out:
Standard (new) .... 0.0012 in (0.030 mm) maximum
Service limit .... 0.0024 in (0.060 mm)

Crankshaft bearings

Main bearing oil clearance:
Standard (new) – 1300 .... 0.0009 to 0.0017 in (0.024 to 0.042 mm)
Standard (new) – 1500 .... 0.0010 to 0.0022 in (0.026 to 0.055 mm)
Service limit – all models .... 0.003 in (0.07 mm)
Connecting rod bearing oil clearance:
Standard (new) .... 0.0008 to 0.0015 in (0.020 to 0.038 mm)
Service limit .... 0.003 in (0.07 mm)

Camshaft

Endfloat:
Standard (new) .... 0.002 to 0.006 in (0.05 to 0.15 mm)
Service limit .... 0.020 in (0.5 mm)

Oil clearance:
    Standard (new) .... 0.002 to 0.004 in (0.05 to 0.09 mm)
    Service limit .... 0.006 in (0.15 mm)
Run-out:
    Standard (new) .... 0.0012 in (0.03 mm) maximum
    Service limit .... 0.0024 in (0.06 mm)

Valve clearances (cold)
Inlet .... 0.005 to 0.007 in (0.12 to 0.17 mm)
Exhaust .... 0.007 to 0.009 in (0.17 to 0.22 mm)
Auxiliary (CVCC engines) .... 0.005 to 0.007 in (0.12 to 0.17 mm)

Valves

	Standard (new)	Service limit
Valve stem diameter:		
Auxiliary inlet, 1300 CVCC	0.2154 to 0.2160 in (5.472 to 5.487 mm)	0.215 in (5.45 mm)
Auxiliary inlet, 1500 CVCC	0.2587 to 0.2593 in (6.572 to 6.587 mm)	0.258 in (6.55 mm)
Main inlet, all models	0.2591 to 0.2594 in (6.580 to 6.590 mm)	0.258 in (6.55 mm)
Exhaust	0.2574 to 0.2578 in (6.537 to 6.560 mm)	0.257 in (6.52 mm)

	Standard (new)	Service limit
Valve stem installed height above cylinder head:		
UK models	1.681 to 1.720 in (42.7 to 43.7 mm)	1.730 in (43.95 mm)
US models, 1980	1.701 in (43.2 mm)	1.730 in (43.95 mm)
US models, 1981	1.380 to 1.429 in (35.05 to 36.30 mm)	1.439 in (36.55 mm)
Valve stem-to-guide clearance:		
Auxiliary inlet (CVCC engines)	0.0009 to 0.0023 in (0.023 to 0.058 mm)	0.003 in (0.08 mm)
Main inlet	0.0008 to 0.0020 in (0.02 to 0.05 mm)	0.003 in (0.08 mm)
Exhaust, UK models	0.0020 to 0.0031 in (0.05 to 0.08 mm)	0.0047 in (0.12 mm)
Exhaust, US models	0.0025 to 0.0037 in (0.063 to 0.093 mm)	0.0047 in (0.12 mm)
Valve seat width:		
Auxiliary inlet (CVCC engines)	0.0139 to 0.0194 in (0.353 to 0.494 mm)	0.04 in (1.0 mm)
Main inlet and exhaust	0.055 to 0.061 in (1.40 to 1.55 mm)	0.08 in (2.0 mm)

Valve springs
Free length:
    Auxiliary inlet – 1980 .... 1.120 in (28.5 mm)
    Auxiliary inlet – 1981 .... 1.169 in (29.7 mm)
    Main inlet and exhaust:
      Inner – UK models .... 2.047 in (52.0 mm)
      Outer – UK models .... 2.118 in (53.8 mm)
      Inner and outer – US models .... 1.665 in (42.3 mm)

Valve guides

	Standard (new)	Service limit
Internal diameter:		
Auxiliary inlet – 1300 models	0.217 to 0.218 in (5.51 to 5.53 mm)	0.219 in (5.55 mm)
Auxiliary inlet – 1500 models	0.260 to 0.261 in (6.61 to 6.63 mm)	0.262 in (6.65 mm)
Main inlet and exhaust	0.260 to 0.261 in (6.61 to 6.63 mm)	0.262 in (6.65 mm)

Oil pump

	Standard (new)	Service limit
Inner to outer rotor radial clearance	0.006 in (0.15 mm)	0.008 in (0.20 mm)
Body to rotor radial clearance	0.004 to 0.007 in (0.10 to 0.18 mm)	0.008 in (0.20 mm)
Body to rotor side clearance	0.001 to 0.004 in (0.003 to 0.100 mm)	0.006 in (0.15 mm)
Backlash in pump drivegear	0.002 to 0.004 in (0.04 to 0.10 mm)	
Drivegear side clearance	0.002 to 0.012 in (0.05 to 0.30 mm)	
Pump delivery (minimum)	7.71 Imp gal (9.25 US gal, 35 litres) per minute at 3000 rpm	
Pressure relief valve setting:		
Standard (new)	48 to 60 lbf/in^2 (3.4 to 4.2 kgf/cm^2)	
Service limit	21 lbf/in^2 (1.5 kgf/cm^2)	

Torque wrench settings

	lbf ft	Nm
Sump drain plug	33	45
Transmission drain plug	29	40
Transmission filler plug	33	45
Oil cooler banjo bolt (A/T)	21	29
Air conditioner compressor bolts	31	43
Tie-rod end balljoint locknut	32	44
Lower arm balljoint locknut	25	35
Exhaust manifold-to-header pipe nuts	36	50
Alternator adjuster bolt	19	26
Auxiliary valve locknut	58	80
Rocker assembly bolts (M6)	7	10
Rocker assembly bolts (M8)	16	22
Camshaft sprocket bolt	22	30
Manifold nuts	16	22
Manifold bolts	18	25
Water pump pulley bolts	9	12
Crankshaft pulley centre bolt:		
All UK models and 1980 US models	61	85
1981 US models	80	110
Timing belt tensioner bolts	32	43
Inlet and exhaust valve adjuster locknuts	14	20
Auxiliary inlet valve adjuster locknuts	10	14
Main bearing cap bolts (1300 engine)	29	40
Main bearing cap bolts (1500 engine)	33	45
Flywheel mounting bolts	36	50
Connecting rod bearing caps	21	29
Oil pump mounting bolts	9	12
Oil pump gear cover bolts	9	12
Oil sump nuts and bolts	9	12
Cylinder head bolts	43	60
Engine mountings	See Fig. 1.9	

1 General description

The engine is of the four-cylinder, in-line, overhead camshaft type. It is mounted integrally with the transmission and final drive and is installed transversely across the engine compartment. The drive is to the front roadwheels through open driveshafts.

The cylinder block is of light alloy, with pressed in cast iron sleeves for the cylinders. The cylinder head is also of light alloy. The design of cylinder head differs between the conventional head used on UK models and the Compound Vortex Controlled Combustion (CVCC) head used on US models. On UK models the cylinder head is of the crossflow type, with the inlet and exhaust valves mounted diametrically opposite each other. On US models the normal inlet and exhaust valves are mounted adjacent to each other on the same side of the camshaft and a third (auxiliary inlet) valve is mounted on the opposite side.

The camshaft and the valve operating gear are incorporated in the cylinder head. The camshaft drive is from the crankshaft through a toothed belt and sprockets.

The CVCC engine is designed to reduce the quantity of carbon monoxide, oxides of nitrogen and unburnt hydrocarbons in the exhaust gas. Each cylinder has two combustion chambers, a main chamber and a pre-chamber. On the inlet stroke a rich fuel/air mixture enters the pre-chamber through a small auxiliary inlet valve and at the same time a very lean mixture enters the main chamber through an inlet valve of normal size. The spark plug ignites the rich mixture and once combustion has started, it proceeds and ignites the leaner main charge. This system of progressive ignition produces a high exhaust gas temperature which reduces pollution.

The engine is water-cooled and circulation is assisted by a centrifugal pump. The radiator is front mounted and has a cooling fan which is electrically driven and thermostatically controlled.

All moving parts of the engine are lubricated by pressure feed from an oil pump installed in the sump, the oil being filtered continuously by a full flow filter.

2 Operations possible with the engine installed

1 Removal and installation of the cylinder head assembly and the engine ancillaries can be carried out without removing the engine. The sump, oil pump, piston and connecting rod assemblies can be removed. The water pump can be removed and the timing belt renewed.

2 Any other major operations, such as crankshaft removal, necessitate removal of the engine.

3 Method of engine removal

1 It is recommended that the engine is removed from the vehicle complete with the transmission for later separation.

2 It should be noted that the transmission can be removed from the vehicle leaving the engine in position (see Chapter 6).

3 On vehicles equipped with air conditioning, have the air conditioning system depressurised before attempting to disconnect any parts of it. Disconnection is not necessary if the engine is removed as described in Section 4.

4 Engine and transmission – removal and installation

1 Disconnect both battery cables (photo).

2 Remove the battery clamp, battery and tray (photo).

3 Remove the four bolts from the battery mount and remove the mount (photo).

4 Remove the two screws from each headlight trim and unhook the trim (Fig. 1.1). On Sedan models the three screws must first be removed from the grille and then the grille pulled forward (Fig. 1.2).

5 Remove the front bumper apron and grille (Fig. 1.3).

6 Remove the screws from the bonnet hinges and lift the bonnet off (photo).

7 Unscrew and remove the radiator cap. If the engine is hot, cover the cap with a cloth before attempting to unscrew the cap and unscrew it slowly.

8 Place a clean container beneath the radiator drain plug, remove the plug and drain the coolant. If the coolant is re-usable store it. Place a clean container beneath the cylinder block drain plug, remove the plug and drain the coolant. After draining install the drain plug using a new washer; also install the radiator cap and drain plug.

9 Remove the oil filler cap. Place a suitable container beneath the sump drain plug, remove the plug and allow the oil to drain out. Re-install the drain plug, using a new washer.

HEADLIGHT TRIM (4 screws)

Fig. 1.1 Headlight trim screw positions (Hatchback & Wagon) (Sec 4)

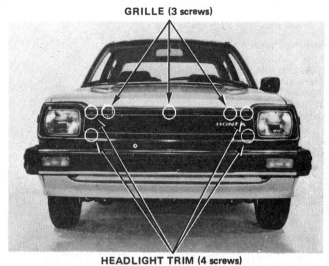

GRILLE (3 screws)

HEADLIGHT TRIM (4 screws)

Fig. 1.2 Headlight trim and grille screw positions (Sedan) (Sec 4)

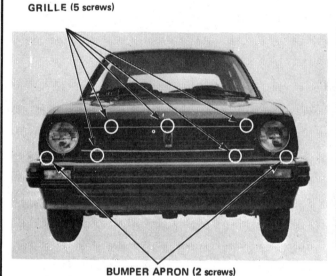

GRILLE (5 screws)

BUMPER APRON (2 screws)

Fig. 1.3 Grille and bumper apron screw positions (Hatchback and Wagon) (Sec 4)

T-FITTING   **FUEL HOSE**

Fig. 1.4 Fuel hose T-piece (US models) (Sec 4)

#1 CONTROL BOX

CONNECTOR   **VACUUM HOSE**

Fig. 1.5 No 1 control box (US models) (Sec 4)

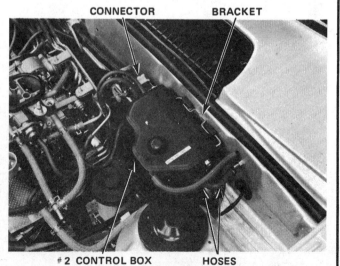

CONNECTOR   **BRACKET**

#2 CONTROL BOX   **HOSES**

Fig. 1.6 No 2 control box (later US models) (Sec 4)

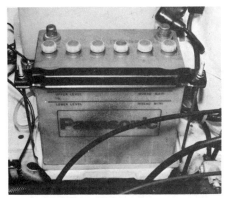
4.1 Disconnect the battery cable

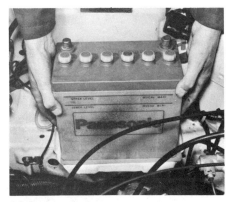
4.2 Remove the battery

4.3 Remove the battery mount bolts

4.6 Bonnet hinge screws

4.11 Removing the air cleaner cover and filter element

4.13 Air cleaner removed showing air bleed valve hose

4.14 Brake booster hose (arrowed)

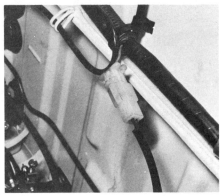
4.15a Distributor connector ...

4.15b ... and condenser wire

4.16a Disconnect the alternator wires ...

4.16b ... starter solenoid wires ...

4.16c ... reversing light switch wires ...

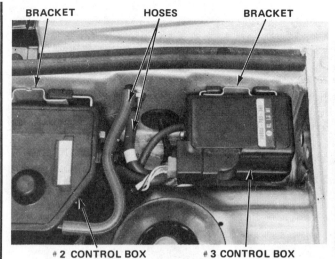

BRACKET   HOSES   BRACKET

2 CONTROL BOX   # 3 CONTROL BOX

Fig. 1.7 Nos 2 and 3 control boxes (later California models)
(Sec 4)

AIR JET CONTROLLER
HOSES

Fig. 1.8 Air jet controller and hoses (US models) (Sec 4)

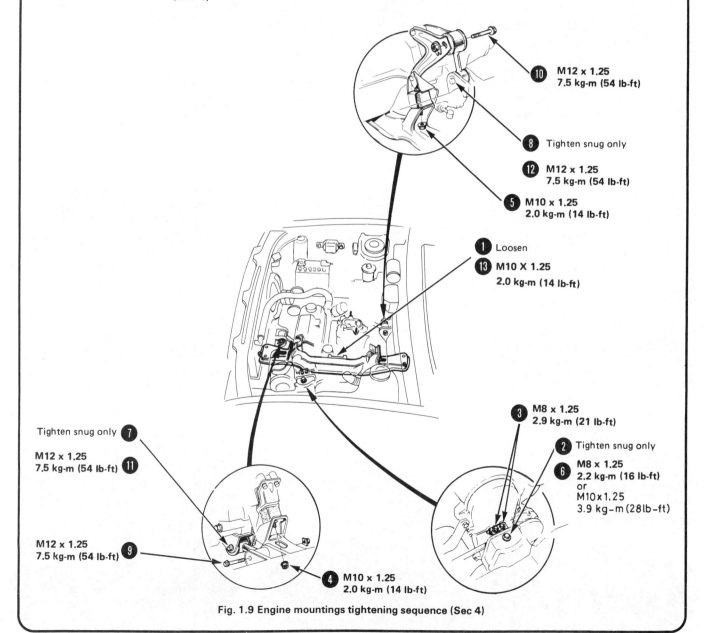

10 M12 x 1.25
7.5 kg-m (54 lb-ft)

8 Tighten snug only

12 M12 x 1.25
7.5 kg-m (54 lb-ft)

5 M10 x 1.25
2.0 kg-m (14 lb-ft)

1 Loosen

13 M10 X 1.25
2.0 kg-m (14 lb-ft)

3 M8 x 1.25
2.9 kg-m (21 lb-ft)

2 Tighten snug only

6 M8 x 1.25
2.2 kg-m (16 lb-ft)
or
M10 x 1.25
3.9 kg-m (28 lb-ft)

Tighten snug only 7

M12 x 1.25
7.5 kg-m (54 lb-ft) 11

M12 x 1.25
7.5 kg-m (54 lb-ft) 9

4 M10 x 1.25
2.0 kg-m (14 lb-ft)

Fig. 1.9 Engine mountings tightening sequence (Sec 4)

4.16d ... coolant temperature sender ...

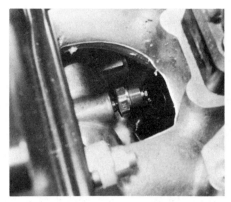
4.16e ... and oil pressure sender

4.19 Disconnect the fuel hoses from the pump

4.21 Disconnect the throttle and choke cables (as applicable)

4.25 Tachometer cable connection

4.27 Disconnect the clutch cable from the release arm

4.34a Balljoint separator

4.34b Bolt securing brake hose to suspension strut

4.34c Steering knuckle clamp bolts

4.34d Steering knuckle separated from suspension strut

4.36a Gearshift coupling retainer

4.36b Shift coupling retainer spring pin

4.36c Disconnecting the shift lever torque rod

4.38 Exhaust pipe header disconnected

4.40 Engine top mounting

4.41a Removing the engine front mounting nut

4.41b Engine rear mounting nut

4.42 Engine front torque rod

4.43a Remove bolt from engine end of rear torque rod and ...

4.43b ... swing the rod up out of the way

4.45 Removing the engine and transmission

4.49 Cooling system bleed screw (arrowed)

4.50 Refilling the engine with oil

10 Remove the filler plug (or dipstick – automatic models) from the transmission. Place a suitable container beneath the drain plug, then remove the plug and drain the oil (or automatic transmission fluid) from the transmission. Re-install the drain plug with a new washer and re-install the filler plug.

11 Remove the cover from the air cleaner and take out the air filter element (photo).

12 Disconnect the cold and warm air ducts from the air cleaner and disconnect the vacuum hose from the air control diaphragm. On US models, disconnect the three wires from the intake air temperature sensor at their connectors.

13 Remove the air cleaner securing screws. Lift the air cleaner so that the hose to the air bleed valve can be disconnected and remove the air cleaner (photo). On US models so equipped, the hose to the anti-afterburn valve must also be disconnected.

14 Disconnect the vacuum hose from the brake booster (UK models), or from the elbow (US models) (photo).

15 Disconnect the engine compartment sub-wire harness connector, distributor connector, coil high tension wire and condenser wire (photos).

16 Disconnect the alternator wires, starter solenoid wires, reversing light switch wires, and the wires to the coolant temperature and oil pressure senders (photos).

17 On US models, also disconnect the automatic choke wires, the fuel cut-off solenoid valve wire and (on vehicles with air conditioning) the compressor clutch wire.

18 Disconnect the engine earth strap.

19 Disconnect the fuel hoses from the fuel pump (UK models) (photo) or at the T-piece (US models) (Fig. 1.4).

20 On cars with air conditioning, disconnect the vacuum hoses from the idle control solenoid valve.

21 Disconnect the throttle cable from the carburettor. On UK models also disconnect the choke cable (photo).

22 Disconnect the charcoal canister hose from the carburettor.

23 On US models, remove the anti-tampering band (if so equipped) and disconnect No 1 control box connector (Fig. 1.5). Lift the control box off its bracket and let it hang next to the engine. Similarly disconnect the wires and hoses from the EGR control box or from boxes Nos 2 and 3, as applicable, and let the boxes hang against the engine.

24 On Californian and High Altitude models, disconnect the hoses to the air jet controller (Fig. 1.8).

25 On models having a tachometer, unscrew the knurled ring from the cable connection to the cylinder head (photo).

26 Disconnect the radiator and heater hoses from the engine. Disconnect the heater hose with the water valve cable attached.

27 On cars with manual transmission, loosen the clutch cable adjusting nut and disconnect the clutch cable from the release arm (photo).

28 On cars with automatic transmission, disconnect the oil cooler hoses from the transmission. Drain its fluid from the hoses, then plug the hoses and tie them up out of the way near the radiator.

29 Remove the clip from the speedometer cable and pull the cable out of its housing. **Do not** remove the gear holder because this may allow the gear to fall into the transmission housing.

30 On US models so equipped, remove the anti-afterburn valve. If this is not done the valve may be damaged when the engine is lifted.

31 On vehicles with air conditioning, remove the compressor belt cover and loosen the belt adjusting nut. Slacken the bolt on the compressor hose bracket at the radiator. Remove the compressor mounting bolts and lift the compressor out of its bracket with the hoses still attached to the compressor. Wire the compressor to the bulkhead so that the hoses are not under strain. If the compressor is removed in this way, it is not necessary to have the air conditioning system depressurised. Remove the compressor bracket.

32 On vehicles with a headlight washer, remove the headlight washer tank.

33 Loosen the front wheel nuts slightly, jack up the front of the car and support it on firmly based stands under the recommended body support points. Apply the handbrake and chock the rear wheels, then remove the front wheels.

34 Use a balljoint separator to remove the tie-rod ends (photo). Either separate the lower arm balljoints, or remove the bolt securing the brake hose to the suspension strut (photo) and remove the clamp bolt securing the steering knuckle to the suspension strut (photo). Tap the knuckle off the end of the strut (photos). If a balljoint separator is not available, remove the pivot bolt from the lower control arm and pull the suspension strut assembly outwards as far as possible.

35 Turn the steering knuckle outwards as far as it will go. With a screwdriver against the inboard CV joint, prise the driveshaft out of its housing about $\frac{1}{2}$ in (12 mm), to force the spring clip on the driveshaft out of its groove inside the differential. Pull the driveshaft out of the transmission. Tie plastic bags over the shaft ends to keep them free from dirt and tie the shafts up out of the way.

36 On vehicles with manual transmission, slide back the retainer of the gear shift to transmission coupling, drive out the spring pin and disconnect the shift rod from the transmission. Disconnect the shift lever torque rod from the clutch housing (photos).

37 On vehicles with automatic transmission, remove the centre console, place the shift lever in reverse and remove the lockpin from the shift cable (see Chapter 7).

38 Squirt penetrating oil on the exhaust manifold studs, unscrew and remove the nuts using a socket spanner and disconnect the exhaust pipe header from the manifold (photo). On some models the exhaust pipe clamp must be removed before the header can be disconnected from the manifold.

39 Attach lifting slings to the cylinder head and to the bracket on the transmission and hoist the engine just enough to take the weight off its mountings.

40 Remove the bolts from the engine top mounting (photo) and push the mounting into the mounting tower.

41 Remove the nut from the engine front mounting and from the engine rear mounting (photos).

42 Remove the bolt from the engine end of the front torque rod (photo). Slacken the bolt at the chassis end and swing the rod down out of the way.

43 Remove the bolt from the engine end of the rear torque rod. Slacken the bolt at the chassis end and swing the rod up out of the way (photos).

44 Check that there is no wire or pipe still connected to the engine or transmission. Raise the engine about 6 in and again check that it is free.

45 Raise the engine clear of the engine compartment and remove it from the vehicle (photo).

46 Installation is the reverse of removal, but the following points should be noted.

47 Check that the bushings of the engine mountings and torque rods are not twisted or offset and then tighten the bolts in the sequence shown in Fig. 1.9. If the bolts are not tightened in this sequence it may reduce the life of the mountings and cause excessive noise and vibration.

48 When inserting the driveshafts into the transmission, ensure that the spring clip of the driveshaft clicks into the differential.

49 Fill the cooling system and then with the heater wide open, bleed the system at the bleed screw (photo). Tighten the bleed screw and check that the radiator and engine drain plugs have been tightened.

50 Refill the engine and transmission with oil and ensure that the drain plugs have been tightened (photo).

51 Adjust the throttle cable, and the choke cable on manual choke models, and check for correct operation.

52 Check the free movement of the clutch pedal.

53 Check that all gears can be selected smoothly.

54 Check that all wires and pipes have been connected correctly and that all hose clips have been tightened.

55 After installing the speedometer cable and clip, pull the cable to ensure that the clip has engaged in the groove and that the cable is secure.

5 Engine – separation from manual transmission

1 Unscrew and remove the bolts which secure the clutch bellhousing to the engine crankcase.

2 Support the engine and transmission, then withdraw the transmission in a straight line so that at no time does the weight of the transmission hang on the end of the gearbox mainshaft. When the mainshaft is clear of the clutch driven plate, lower the transmission.

6 Engine – separation from automatic transmission

1 Remove the cover plate from the bottom of the engine-facing side

of the torque converter housing and unscrew and remove the eight bolts which secure the torque converter housing to the driveplate.

2 When the cover plate has been removed the bolts are accessible one at a time by turning the crankshaft pulley to bring the bolts into view successively. To turn the crankshaft, use a ring spanner on the securing bolt of the crankshaft pulley.

3 It is important that only the eight bolts which secure the torque converter to the driveplate are removed. The bolts which are accessible through the holes in the driveplate secure the torque converter cover to the torque converter housing and should **not** be disturbed.

4 Unscrew and remove the bolts which secure the torque converter housing to the block. While supporting the weight of the transmission, pull it away from the engine until it is clear of the dowel pins, then remove the transmission, taking care to ensure that the torque converter does not fall out of its housing.

7 Engine ancillary components – removal

1 With the engine removed and separated from the transmission, remove the ancillary components before dismantling the engine.

2 Detailed removal procedures are given in the appropriate Chapters, as indicated in parenthesis.

3 Unbolt and remove the alternator and drivebelt (Chapter 10).

4 Unbolt and remove the inlet manifold with the carburettor attached. Also remove the exhaust manifold (Chapter 3).

5 Remove the water pump and header pipe (Chapter 2).

6 Unscrew and remove the oil filter cartridge and discard it.

8 Engine dismantling – preparation

1 It is best to mount the engine on a dismantling stand, but if one is not available stand the engine on a strong bench, to be at a comfortable working height.

2 During the dismantling process great care should be taken to keep the exposed parts free from dirt. As an aid to achieving this, thoroughly clean down the outside of the engine, removing all traces of oil and congealed dirt.

3 To clean the exterior of the engine use paraffin or water-soluble solvent; the latter compound will make the job much easier, for after the solvent has been applied and allowed to stand for a time, a vigorous jet of water will wash off the solvent with all the grease and dirt. If the dirt is thick and deeply embedded, work the solvent into it with a stiff brush.

4 Finally wipe down the exterior of the engine with a rag and only then, when it is quite clean, should the dismantling process begin. As the engine is stripped, clean each part in a bath of paraffin.

5 **Never** immerse parts with oilways (for example the crankshaft) in paraffin, but to clean, wipe down carefully with a petrol dampened cloth. Oilways can be cleaned out with wire. If an air line is available, all parts can be blown dry and the oilways blown through as an added precaution.

6 Re-use of the old engine gaskets is false economy and will lead to oil and water leaks, if nothing worse. Always use new gaskets throughout.

7 Do not throw the old gasket away for it sometimes happens that an immediate replacement cannot be found and the old gasket is then very useful as a template. Hang up old gaskets as they are removed.

8 To strip the engine it is best to start from the top down. The underside of the crankcase when supported on wooden blocks acts as a firm base. When the stage is reached, where the crankshaft and connecting rods have to be removed, the engine can be turned on its side, and all other work carried out in this position.

9 Whenever possible, refit nuts, bolts and washers finger tight from wherever they are removed. This helps to avoid loss and muddle later. If they cannot be refitted, lay them out in such a fashion that it is clear from whence they came.

9 Rocker gear and camshaft – removal

1 Remove the distributor cap. Remove the bolt securing the distributor, make alignment marks on the engine and mounting plate and remove the distributor (photos).

9.1a Remove the distributor cap screw

9.1b Distributor with cap removed

9.1c Removing the distributor

9.2a Cylinder head cover nut (front)

9.2b Cylinder head cover nut (rear)

2   Remove the two domed nuts from the cylinder head cover and remove the cover (photos).
3   Remove the two bolts from the timing belt upper cover and remove the cover.
4   Slacken the timing belt pivot and adjusting bolts and slip the timing belt off the camshaft sprocket. If the camshaft is being removed without the engine being dismantled, first turn the camshaft until the timing marks on the sprocket are aligned with the valve cover surface (1300 models) or until the mark on the sprocket is aligned with the arrow on the cylinder head (1500 models). The cutaway in the sprocket (US models) or the keyway (UK models) should be uppermost. **Do not** rotate the camshaft or crankshaft whilst the timing belt is removed, as there is a risk of piston-valve contact and subsequent damage.
5   If the camshaft sprocket is to be removed, jam the sprocket to prevent it rotating and then unscrew and remove the securing bolt and washer. Use a puller to draw the sprocket off the camshaft.
6   Remove the bolt from the oil pump gear cover, remove the cover and pull the oil pump shaft out of the cylinder head.
7   Unscrew the rocker arm bolts two turns at a time in a criss-cross pattern, to prevent damage to the valves or rocker assembly, then remove the bolts and lift the rocker assembly off the cylinder head.
8   Lift the camshaft out of the cylinder head.

10 Rocker gear – dismantling, inspection and reassembly

1   Use a pair of side cutting pliers to grip and prise up the spring pin from either of the end pedestals.
2   Remove the end pedestal and then dismantle the rocker assembly, taking care to lay the parts out so that they can be reinstalled in their original positions (Fig. 1.10 or 1.11).
3   Examine the shafts for damage and wear. If the shaft is bent, or if it has steps on it caused by rocker arm movement, renew the shaft.
4   Inspect the springs for damage and distortion, renewing any that are defective.
5   Inspect the rocker arm bores for wear, checking that they are not unduly slack on the rocker shaft. Examine the rocker pads, which should have a slightly curved surface. Renew any rocker arm which has a pad which is grooved, or flat. Check that the threads of the rocker arms, the adjuster screws and the locknuts are in good condition and renew any parts which are not satisfactory.
6   Installation is the reverse of removal, but take care to ensure that all re-used parts are in their original locations.

11 Cylinder head – removal

Note: *The cylinder head must only be removed with the engine cold (less than 100°F/38°C).*
1   If the cylinder head is to be removed with the engine still in the vehicle, the following preparatory work is necessary.
2   Disconnect the battery leads.
3   Drain the cooling system.
4   Remove the air cleaner after labelling all the hoses connected to it so that they can be re-installed correctly.
5   Disconnect the electrical wires from the temperature gauge sender, fuel cut-off solenoid valve (US models), automatic choke (US models) and idle cut-off solenoid valve (vehicles with air conditioning).
6   Disconnect the fuel lines and throttle cable from the carburettor. On models with manual choke, also disconnect the choke cable.
7   Label all hoses connected to the carburettor, disconnect them and remove the carburettor.
8   Disconnect the condenser wire from the distributor. Also disconnect the low tension and high tension cables.
9   Disconnect the radiator top hose, heater inlet hose and bypass inlet hose from the cylinder head (photos).
10 Remove the exhaust header pipe clamp (when fitted) (photo). Squirt penetrating oil onto the three nuts securing the header pipe to the manifold and remove the nuts using a socket spanner. Disconnect the header pipe from the manifold.
11 On cars without air conditioning, remove the bolt holding the alternator bracket to the cylinder head. Loosen the alternator adjusting bolt and slide the bracket away from the cylinder head.
12 On cars with air conditioning, remove the drivebelt cover and loosen the drivebelt adjusting nut. Remove the compressor mounting bolts, loosen the bolt in the hose bracket at the radiator, then lift the compressor out and wire it to the front bulkhead, ensuring that the hoses are not strained. If the compressor is removed in this way, it is not necessary to have the air conditioning system depressurised. Remove the compressor bracket.
13 On US models so equipped, disconnect the air jet controller hoses from the carburettor. Also remove the anti-afterburn valve (when fitted) and its bracket from the cylinder head.
14 On models having a tachometer, unscrew the knurled ring from the cable connection to the cylinder head and withdraw the cable.
15 Remove the two domed bolts from the cylinder head cover and remove the cover.
16 Remove the two bolts from the timing belt upper cover and remove the cover.

1

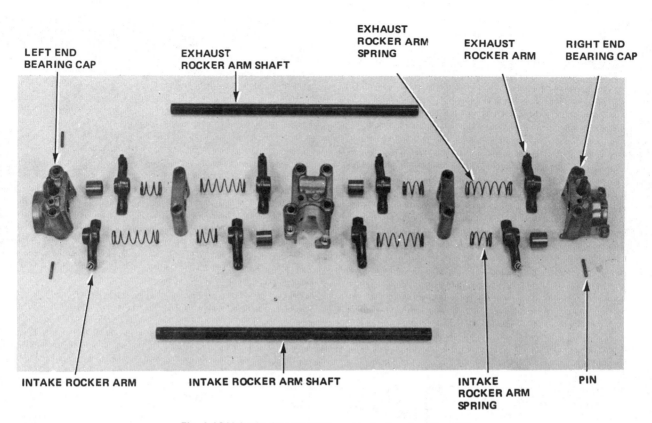

LEFT END
BEARING CAP

EXHAUST
ROCKER ARM SHAFT

EXHAUST
ROCKER ARM
SPRING

EXHAUST
ROCKER ARM

RIGHT END
BEARING CAP

INTAKE ROCKER ARM

INTAKE ROCKER ARM SHAFT

INTAKE
ROCKER ARM
SPRING

PIN

Fig. 1.10 Valve rocker assembly – standard engine (Sec 10)

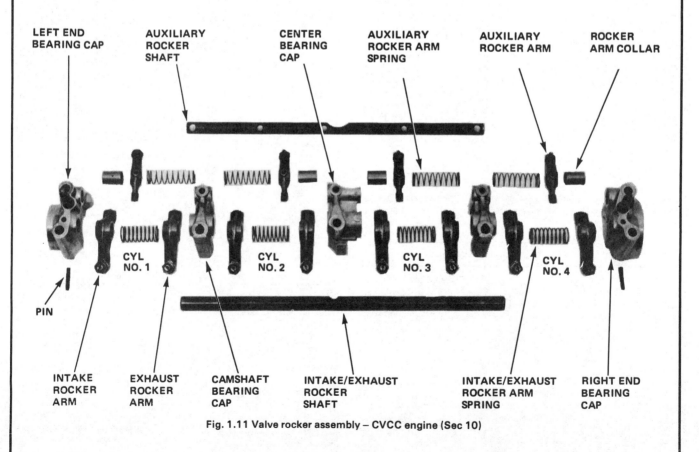

LEFT END
BEARING CAP

AUXILIARY
ROCKER
SHAFT

CENTER
BEARING
CAP

AUXILIARY
ROCKER ARM
SPRING

AUXILIARY
ROCKER ARM

ROCKER
ARM COLLAR

CYL
NO. 1

CYL
NO. 2

CYL
NO. 3

CYL
NO. 4

PIN

INTAKE
ROCKER
ARM

EXHAUST
ROCKER
ARM

CAMSHAFT
BEARING
CAP

INTAKE/EXHAUST
ROCKER
SHAFT

INTAKE/EXHAUST
ROCKER ARM
SPRING

RIGHT END
BEARING
CAP

Fig. 1.11 Valve rocker assembly – CVCC engine (Sec 10)

11.9a Radiator top hose

11.9b Heater inlet and bypass inlet hoses

11.10 Exhaust pipe header clamp

11.17 Timing belt pivot and adjusting bolts. Pivot bolt is on the left

17 Slacken the timing belt pivot and adjusting bolts (photo). Align the camshaft sprocket as described in Section 9, paragraph 4, and slip the timing belt off the camshaft sprocket.

18 If preferred, the cylinder head can be removed as an assembly complete with camshaft, rocker gear assembly and distributor. Otherwise remove the rocker gear and camshaft as described in Section 9. In either case, remove the oil pump driveshaft (Section 9, paragraph 6).

19 Unscrew the cylinder head bolts $\frac{1}{3}$ turn at a time in the sequence shown in Fig. 1.12, until the bolts are no longer in tension. This is to prevent the cylinder head from warping. Remove the bolts, lift the cylinder head clear of the dowels and remove it. If necessary tap the cylinder head with a soft-headed hammer to release it, but do not attempt to prise it off.

12 Cylinder head – dismantling

1 Unless previously done, remove the rocker gear and camshaft.

2 Using a suitable valve spring compressor, compress each valve spring in turn and extract the split cotters (photo). Release the compressor and remove the spring retainer, the outer and inner valve springs, the spring seat and the valve.

3 If the valve spring compressor fails to move the spring retainer, do

not continue to apply pressure as there is a risk of damage. Release the compressor, tap the top of the valve smartly with a wooden or plastic mallet to free the retainer, then try again.

4 Identify each valve and associated components so that they can be re-installed in the same position in the cylinder head. A compartmented box is ideal for this.

13 Auxiliary valve assembly (CVCC engine) – removal and dismantling

1 Remove the auxiliary valve holder nuts and withdraw the auxiliary valves complete with holders. A long box spanner or deep socket will be needed to undo the valve holder nuts. The auxiliary valve assemblies can then be dismantled using a normal valve spring compressor.

2 As with the main inlet and exhaust valves, the auxiliary valve components must not be interchanged if they are to be re-used.

3 If it is wished to remove the pre-combustion chambers from the cylinder head, special Honda tools will be required. These consist of a slide hammer and a special attachment which engages in a hole in the chamber. It is probably best to have this work done by an authorised Honda agent, since the cost of the tools is unlikely to justify their purchase for the home mechanic.

Fig. 1.12 Cylinder head bolt removal sequence (Sec 11)

12.2 Valve split cotters exposed by compressor

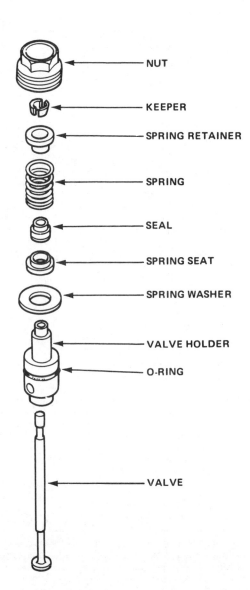

— NUT

— KEEPER

— SPRING RETAINER

— SPRING

— SEAL

— SPRING SEAT

— SPRING WASHER

— VALVE HOLDER

— O-RING

— VALVE

Fig. 1.13 CVCC auxiliary inlet valve assembly (Sec 13)

14 Timing belt, tensioner and drive sprocket – removal

Engine in vehicle

1   Jack up the front left-hand side of the vehicle and support it securely. Remove the left-hand front wheel.
2   Through the hole in the inner wing thus exposed, apply a socket wrench to the crankshaft pulley bolt. Turn the crankshaft anti-clockwise until the TDC mark on the pulley (UK models) or flywheel/driveplate (US models) is opposite the pointer on the timing case or crankcase. Pass a bar or thick screwdriver through one of the cut-outs on the pulley and hold the pulley still by levering against the crankcase while the pulley bolt is unscrewed and removed in an anticlockwise direction.
3   Remove the rocker cover.
4   Remove the alternator drivebelt, and air conditioning compressor drivebelt (if applicable).
5   Remove the timing belt upper cover and mark the direction of rotation on the belt if being used again.
6   Unbolt and remove the water pump pulley.
7   Unbolt and remove the sealing plate which fits between the water pump and the timing belt lower cover.
8   From the front face of the timing belt lower cover, unscrew the two belt tensioner bolts two or three turns only. Prise out the two rubber sealing rings from behind the bolt heads.
9   Pull off the crankshaft pulley.
10 Remove the timing belt lower cover by unbolting it and pulling it downwards.
11 Disconnect the left-hand engine mounting from the engine bracket and push the outer member as far as possible into the housing on the inner wing. No support for the engine is required.
12 Extract the dished belt-retaining washer from the front of the crankshaft drive sprocket, prise the belt tensioner's pulley upwards to release its tension and then slide the belt from the crankshaft and camshaft sprockets, pressing the belt out through the gap in the engine mounting bracket components. Avoid turning the crankshaft or camshaft sprocket whilst the belt is removed or the valve heads may impinge or jam in the piston crowns.
13 To remove the belt tensioner, unscrew the pivot and adjustment bolts and remove the tensioner and spring noting the spring location.
14 Withdraw the timing belt drive sprocket and dished washers from the crankshaft, noting the respective washer positions.

Engine out of vehicle

15 The procedure is identical to that just described except that the ancillary components such as the alternator and water pump will probably have been completely removed and also the transmission separated from the engine, in which case, the starter ring gear can be jammed with a cold chisel or large screwdriver to prevent the crankshaft rotating while the crankshaft pulley bolt is unscrewed.

15 Pistons and connecting rods – removal and dismantling

1   Remove the cylinder head as described in Section 11.
2   Unscrew and remove the sump securing bolts, withdraw the sump and gasket from the crankcase. The rear two sump bolts secure the engine rear plate which can also be removed.
3   Examine the tops of the cylinder bores. If a severe wear ridge is evident then this must be scraped or ground carefully before the pistons are removed from the top of the cylinder block, otherwise damage may be caused to the pistons rings, pistons or gudgeon pins.
4   Unbolt and remove the oil pump assembly from within the crankcase. One bolt is located under the filter screen and the screen must be carefully prised out to gain access to it. Avoid distorting the filter screen.
5   Note that the connecting rod big-ends and their caps are not numbered in respect of their position in the cylinder block. Any numbers found indicate big-end bore tolerances, see Section 21. Dot punch the rods and caps 1 to 4 at adjacent points starting at the crankshaft pulley end of the engine and note to which side of the engine the punch marks face. Note that this may already have been done if the engine has previously been dismantled.
6   Turn the crankshaft by means of the flywheel until No 1 piston (nearest crankshaft pulley) is at the lowest point of travel in its bore. Unscrew and remove the big-end bearing cap nuts and remove the cap.
7   Using the wooden handle of a hammer applied to the end of the connecting rod, drive the piston/rod assembly from the cylinder bore. Take care that the big-end bolt threads do not score the bores.
8   If for any reason the bearing shells are to be used again, identify them in respect of connecting rod and cap using a piece of adhesive tape or a spirit marker.
9   Repeat the foregoing operations on the remaining three pistons/connecting rod assemblies.
10   A press and special adaptors are required to remove and refit the piston to the connecting rod as the gudgeon pin is an interference fit in the rod. It is recommended that this work is left to your Honda dealer. When correctly assembled, the dot on the piston crown should be nearest the oil drilling in the connecting rod.
11   To remove the rings from a piston, slide two or three old feeler blades behind the top ring and then remove the ring using a twisting motion. Remove the second compression ring and the oil control ring in a similar way. The feeler blades will prevent the lower rings dropping into the higher vacant grooves as they are withdrawn.

16 Clutch, flywheel (or driveplate), crankshaft and main bearings – removal

1   Mark the clutch pressure plate in relation to the flywheel if they are not already marked.
2   Lock the flywheel by jamming the ring gear teeth with a bar or screwdriver and unscrew evenly and progressively the eight pressure plate bolts. Remove the pressure plate and clutch disc from the flywheel.
3   Unbolt and remove the flywheel (or driveplate – auto transmission) from the crankshaft.
4   On engines with individual main bearing caps, check that a number indicating its position is cast onto the bearing cap. If not, mark them so that they can be identified and re-installed in their original positions.
5   Unbolt and remove the main bearing caps and their bearings. If the bearing shells are to be used again, identify them in respect of their main bearing cap using adhesive tape or a spirit marker.
6   Lift the crankshaft from the crankcase. Remove the oil seals.
7   Extract the bearing shells from the crankcase and again place them with their respective main bearing caps if they are to be used again. Note the semi-circular thrust washers located either side of the No 4 main bearing (numbering from the crankshaft pulley end).

17 Engine lubrication system – description

1   The oil pump is of rotor type mounted within the crankcase and driven by a gear on the upper end of its shaft from the camshaft.
2   Oil from the sump is picked up through the oil pump intake screen

17.4 Cartridge oil filter

and pumped under pressure to the engine bearings. Splash lubrication is used for the cylinder bores, and spray jets at the top of the connecting rods provide additional lubrication for the top of the cylinder bores.
3   A pressure relief valve is incorporated in the oil pump body. Its operating pressure is given in the Specifications.
4   A cartridge type full flow oil filter is mounted on the forward facing side of the engine crankcase and is easily accessible for renewal at the specified service intervals (photo).

18 Crankcase ventilation system – maintenance

1   The emission of fumes from the engine crankcase is controlled by a closed type ventilation system.
2   Maintenance consists of occasionally checking the security of the system hoses and at intervals cleaning the fixed orifice in the system using a 1.1 mm diameter twist drill.
3   Detach the condensation chamber from the air cleaner and tilt it to inspect its interior. Clean out any condensation or deposits from it, and also from the connecting tubes.
4   Check that the gasket which fits between the chamber and the air cleaner is in good condition and then refit the chamber to the air cleaner body and reconnect the drain hose.

19 Engine components – examination and renovation (general)

1   With the engine completely dismantled, every component should be thoroughly cleaned and then examined for wear and renovated, as described in the following Sections.
2   Many of the measurements required will need the use of feeler blades or a micrometer but in many instances wear will be visually evident or the old component can be compared with a new one.
3   If in doubt as to whether or not to renew a component, bear in mind the trouble and effort which will be caused if it fails at a relatively early date. Consider also the expected life remaining to the vehicle as a whole. Less reconditioning is possible on this engine than on 'traditional' engines – for example, the crankshaft cannot be reground if worn.
4   Always renew oil seals and gaskets as a matter of course. Big-end and main bearing shells should also be renewed, unless they are known to be in perfect condition.
5   When selecting big-end and main bearing shells (see Sections 20 and 21), it may be possible to compensate for **even** crankshaft wear by using a shell one size below that indicated by the relevant code letters and numbers. However, this should only be attempted if some means exists of checking the oil clearance with the shells installed (see Specifications). A proprietary product such as Plastigage may be used

1

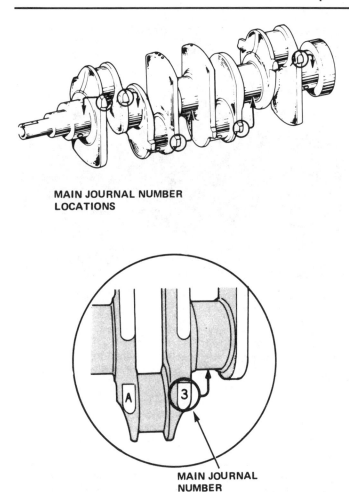

MAIN JOURNAL NUMBER
LOCATIONS

MAIN JOURNAL
NUMBER

Fig. 1.14 Crankshaft main journal identification (Sec 20)

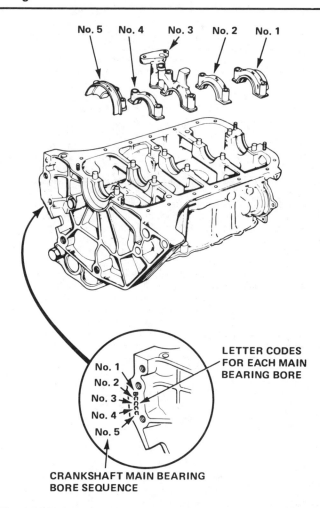

LETTER CODES
FOR EACH MAIN
BEARING BORE

CRANKSHAFT MAIN BEARING
BORE SEQUENCE

Fig. 1.16 Main bearing bore identification – 1500 engines (Sec 20)

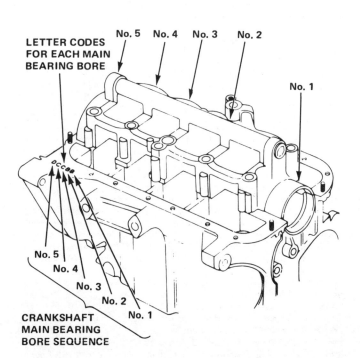

LETTER CODES
FOR EACH MAIN
BEARING BORE

CRANKSHAFT
MAIN BEARING
BORE SEQUENCE

Fig. 1.15 Main bearing bore identification – 1300 engines (Sec 20)

for checking the clearance. Instructions for use are supplied with Plastigage, which should be available from your Honda dealer.

20 Crankshaft and main bearings – examination and renovation

1   Examine the surfaces of the crankpins and journals for scoring. Using a micrometer, check that any taper or eccentricity of the crankpins and journals is within the limits given in the Specifications. If outside the limits, the crankshaft must be renewed, it cannot be reground.

2   The main bearing shells are colour coded. If the shells are to be renewed, ensure that each shell is replaced by one of the same colour.

3   The method of identifying the bearing tolerances is as follows. The crankshaft is stamped with numbers which indicate the diameter of the main journals (Fig. 1.14). The numbers used are 1 to 4 and represent deviation from the nominal diameter. Each journal is measured separately and a crankshaft may have any combination of the numbers 1, 2, 3 and 4.

4   The parent bores in the crankcase are measured individually and are stamped with the letter A, B, C, or D to indicate the deviation of the bore from standard. The position of the letters and the bores to which they refer are shown in Figs. 1.15 and 1.16.

5   Having noted the crankcase bore letter and the crankshaft main journal number of each bearing, the correct size of bearing is determined from the table (Fig. 1.17).

Crankshaft Main Journal Numbers	Crankshaft Bore Letters			
	A	B	C	D
	Bearing Color			
1	Red	Pink	Yellow	Green
2	Pink	Yellow	Green	Brown
3	Yellow	Green	Brown	Black
4	Green	Brown	Black	Blue

Fig. 1.17 Crankshaft main bearing selection table (Sec 20)

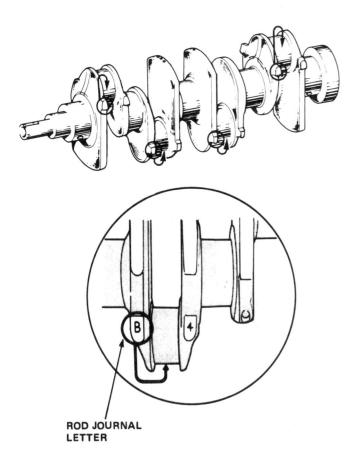

ROD JOURNAL LETTER

Fig. 1.18 Connecting rod journal identification (Sec 21)

Connecting Rod Bearing Identification

Crankshaft Rod Journal Letters	Connecting Rod Numbers			
	1	2	3	4
	Bearing Color			
A	Red	Pink	Yellow	Green
B	Pink	Yellow	Green	Brown
C	Yellow	Green	Brown	Black
D	Green	Brown	Black	Blue

Fig. 1.19 Connecting rod bearing selection table (Sec 21)

21 Big-end bearings and connecting rods – examination and renovation

1   Inspect the connecting rods for cracks and heat damage and if any rod is defective renew it. Note that a number is stamped across the joint on one side of the connecting rod. This is a connecting rod bore tolerance code number and does **not** refer to the cylinder number for which the connecting rod is intended. If a connecting rod is renewed, make sure that the new one has the same tolerance code number stamped on it.

2   Examine the bearing shells for damage and wear and if any bearing needs renewing, use one having the same colour code.

3   The method of identifying the bearing tolerance is as follows. The crankshaft is stamped with letters which indicate the diameter of the crankpins (Fig. 1.18). The letters used are A, B, C and D and each represent a deviation from the nominal diameter. Each crankpin is measured separately and a crankshaft may have any combination of the letters A, B, C and D.

4   The big-end bores of the connecting rods are measured individually. As mentioned above, the rods are stamped across their joint faces with a number 1, 2, 3 or 4 to indicate the deviation of the bore from standard.

5   Having noted the crankpin letter and the big-end bore number, the correct size of bearing is determined from the table (Fig. 1.19).

22 Cylinder bores – examination and renovation

1   Examine the cylinder bores for scoring and scratches. If the bore has slight damage and is not significantly worn, it can be honed by a Honda dealer or specialist workshop provided their honing does not go beyond the service limit given in the Specifications.

2   Measure the diameter of the bore about $\frac{1}{4}$ in (6 mm) from the top, about $\frac{1}{4}$ in (6 mm) from the bottom and at a point midway between. If either the bore size or the bore taper (which is the difference between the top and bottom measurements) exceeds the service limit given in the Specifications, the cylinder block may be rebored if of standard size. A block which has been rebored and has reached its service limit must be renewed. Reboring will necessitate the fitting of oversize pistons and rings.

3   If no micrometer is available, a rough guide to the amount of wear can be gained by removing the piston rings from the bore's piston and inserting the piston about halfway down the bore. If the piston to bore clearance, measured with a feeler gauge, does not exceed the specified service limit, the piston and bore can still be regarded as serviceable.

4   If the bores have worn slightly and oil consumption is high, but the cost of reboring and the fitting of new oversize pistons is not justified, an improvement may be obtained by using one of the brands of special oil control rings. These rings, which should be installed in accordance with their manufacturer's instructions, usually include a compression ring which has a step in it. This ring is installed in the top piston ring groove and the step in the ring should be uppermost so that if there is a ridge at the top of the cylinder bore, the ring will not be damaged.

23 Pistons and piston rings – examination and renovation

1   If the old pistons are to be re-installed, carefully remove the piston rings, noting their positions so that the rings when re-installed will be the same way up and in the same groove as before removal.

2   Clean the rings thoroughly, and clean out the ring grooves of the pistons using a ring groove cleaner of the correct width, or the squared off end of a piece of broken piston ring. Protect your fingers – piston rings are sharp! Do not use a wire brush and take care not to cut away either the base or the sides of the ring grooves with the cleaning tool.

3   Install the piston rings as shown in Fig. 1.20 and measure the clearance between the piston ring and the side of the ring groove (Fig. 1.21). If this exceeds the dimension given in the Specifications, install new rings and re-check. If still outside the specified limits, renew the piston.

1

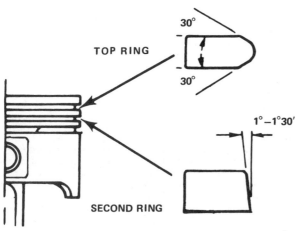

Fig. 1.20 Identification of piston rings (Sec 23)

Fig. 1.21 Measuring piston ring clearance (Sec 23)

24 Oil pump – inspection

1   Extract the split pin from the end of the pressure relief valve and gently tap out the collar, spring and pressure relief valve (photos).
2   Remove the four bolts securing the cover and filter assembly from the pump body and dismantle the pump (photos).
3   Clean all the components and then install the pump shaft, inner rotor and outer rotor in the pump body. Measure the clearance between the outer rotor and the bore of the pump housing, using a feeler gauge (photo).
4   Use a feeler gauge to measure the clearance between the tips of the lobes on the inner rotor and the outer rotor (photo).
5   With a new gasket installed on the joint face of the pump body, place a straight-edge across the pump body and measure the clearance between the straight edge and the end face of the inner rotor.

6   Compare the clearances with those given in the Specifications.
7   If any measurements are outside the permitted tolerance, or if any part of the pump is scored or damaged, a new pump assembly must be installed.
8   Check that the relief valve seating is undamaged and that the plunger slides freely in its bore. Examine the spring for distortion and check that it is not weak or damaged.
9   Reasssemble the pump and tighten the bolts to the specified torque. If the bolts are not tightened as specified, the pump rotor and clearance will not be correct and the gasket may be damaged.
10 With the pump installed and the valve rocker gear also installed,

24.1a Pressure relief valve split pin

24.1b Collar, spring and pressure relief valve plunger

24.2a Separating the pump cover and body

24.2b Pump body dismantled

24.3 Measuring rotor to bore clearance

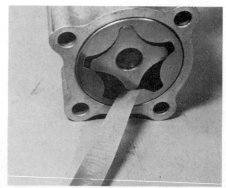

24.4 Measuring rotor tip clearance

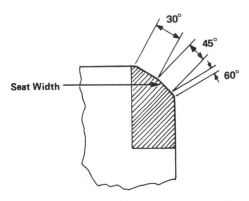

Fig. 1.22 Correct valve seat profile (Sec 26)

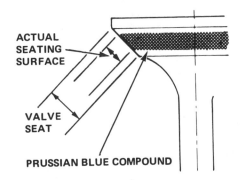

Fig. 1.23 Checking valve seat position (Sec 26)

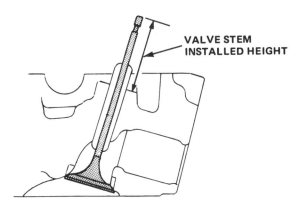

Fig. 1.24 Checking valve stem installed height (Sec 26)

bolt the drivegear cover on to the cylinder head and then use a feeler gauge to measure the clearance between the gear and its cover. Install a new cover if the clearance exceeds that given in the Specifications.

25 Timing components – examination and renovation

1   Check the camshaft and camshaft sprocket for wear in the teeth and if evident, renew as required.
2   Check the belt tensioner, if it rotates noisily or has a tendency to shake due to wear, renew it.
3   The timing belt should be renewed if it is oil stained or the right-angled corners of the teeth are deformed. Always renew the belt if it has been in use for 30 000 miles (48 000 km) or more at the time of major overhaul. Always renew the belt cover sealing strips.

26 Inlet and exhaust valves – examination and renovation

1   Clean the valves with a wire brush and then examine them for signs of pitting and burning. The valves are not intended to be reground and if unsuitable for re-use, must be discarded.
2   Measure the diameter of the valve stems. If they are worn beyond the service limit given in the Specifications, discard the valves.
3   Examine the valve seats in the cylinder head. If the seats are pitted or burned, they may be re-cut either using a hand reamer, or preferably by grinding carried out by a Honda authorised agent or specialist workshop. If you have the equipment and are skilled in its use, proceed as follows. (An unskilled operator can quickly render the head scrap!).
4   Using a cutter to give a 45° seat angle, remove just enough material to give a smooth concentric seat, then bevel the upper edge of the seat to a 30° angle and the lower edge to a 60° angle (Fig. 1.22).
5   After resurfacing the valve seat, apply engineer's blue to the valve face and insert the valve in its original position in the cylinder head. Lift the valve and snap it closed several times to transfer some of the engineer's blue to the valve seating, then remove the valve and examine the ring of blue round the valve seating surface.
6   If the ring of blue is not in the centre of the valve seat (Fig. 1.23), correct its position by the following action. If the seating is too near the valve stem, make a second cut to the 30° upper bevel and then a second cut to restore the width of the 45° section of the seat. If the seating is too near the head of the valve, take a second cut to the 60° bevel of the lower edge and then a second cut to restore the width of the 45° section of the seat.
7   When the seat is satisfactory, insert the valve and measure the projection of the stem from the cylinder head (Fig. 1.24). If the projection is more than the limit given in the Specifications, the valve seat is too deep and the cylinder head must be renewed.
8   On CVCC engines, if the auxiliary valve seat width exceeds the maximum specified, both valve and holder must be renewed. Otherwise, the same considerations apply as for the main inlet and exhaust valves.

27 Inlet and exhaust valve guides – examination and renovation

1   The only satisfactory method of assessing valve guide wear is to measure the diameter inside the valve guide and the external diameter of the valve to see whether the clearance exceeds that specified.
2   In the absence of measuring equipment, insert the valve in the guide and judge whether it is a loose fit and test to see if the valve stem has side play in the guide.
3   Valve guides can be renewed by driving out the old ones and installing new, but a special tool is required to ensure that the guides are installed to the correct depth and after installation the guides must be reamed to size. It is therefore recommended that new valve guides are installed by a Honda authorised agent or a specialist workshop.

28 Valve springs – examination and renovation

1   Examine the valve springs for damage and distortion. Measure their free length and renew them if they are shorter than the length given in the Specifications.
2   An old spring may have lost strength even if its free length is satisfactory, and if springs have been in use for more than 50 000 miles it is advisable to have them checked by a Honda authorised agent who will be able to measure the force which they exert when installed and when compressed. Alternatively, renew all the springs regardless of condition if the engine has done a high mileage.

29 Cylinder head – decarbonising and examination

1   With modern fuels, routine decarbonising is no longer necessary, but if the cylinder head is removed for any reason, any build-up of carbon should be removed. Use a wire brush and a blunt scraper to remove all traces of carbon and other deposits from the combustion chambers and the ports in the cylinder head. Remove the valves and clean all carbon from the valves and valve stems. Using a blunt knife, carefully clean the joint face of the cylinder head.
2   Clean the pistons and top of the cylinder bores. If the pistons are still in the cylinder bores then it is essential that great care is taken to

ensure that no carbon gets into the cylinder bores as this could scratch the cylinder walls or cause damage to the piston and rings. To ensure that this does not happen first turn the crankshaft so that two of the pistons are at the top of the bores. Place clean non-fluffy rag into the other two bores or seal them off with paper and masking tape. The waterways and oilways should always be covered with a small piece of masking tape to prevent particles of carbon entering the cooling system and damaging the water pump or entering the lubrication system and damaging the oil pump or bearings.

3   Press some grease into the gap between the cylinder walls and the two pistons which are being worked upon. With a blunt scraper carefully scrape away the carbon from the piston crowns taking care not to score the aluminium surface. Also scrape the carbon ring from the top of the bores.

4   Remove the rags and masking tape and wipe away the rings of grease which will now be mixed with carbon particles.

5   The crankshaft can now be turned to bring the other two pistons to the top of their strokes and the operations previously described can be repeated.

6   Wipe away every trace of carbon and pour a little thin oil round the pistons to lubricate the rings and to help flush out any remaining carbon particles from the piston grooves.

7   Clean out any holes in the cylinder head and examine for cracks.

8   Using a precision straight-edge and feeler gauges, check the cylinder head for distortion with the straight-edge parallel to each side in turn and then across the two diagonals. If the warpage exceeds the limit given in the Specifications, have the cylinder head re-faced, provided that this will not reduce its overall height below the specified limit.

30 Oil seals and gaskets – renewal

1   If any oil seal, O-ring or gasket is disturbed, do not re-install it, but replace it by a new one.

2   Make sure that joint faces are scraped clean of all old gasket material and sealing compound before installing a new gasket, and that oil seal and O-ring recesses are clean and undamaged.

3   Make sure that the lips of all seals face the correct way when installed. The concave side of the seal should be towards the source of oil or grease which the seal is intended to restrain. Some seals are marked with an arrow to show the direction of rotation to which they may be subjected.

31 Engine reassembly – suggested sequence

1   It is recommended that the following sequence is used during engine reassembly:

> (a) Crankshaft and main bearings
> (b) Flywheel (or driveplate – automatic transmission)
> (c) Piston/connecting rod assemblies
> (d) Oil pump
> (e) Sump
> (f) Crankshaft sprocket
> (g) Timing belt tensioner, belt and lower cover
> (h) Cylinder head (reassembled) with or without manifold
> (j) Timing belt (connection to camshaft and tensioning)
> (k) Water pump (see Chapter 2)
> (m) Valve clearance adjustment
> (n) Oil pump drive gear and shaft
> (p) Water distribution tube
> (q) Water pump pulley, crankshaft pulley
> (r) Inlet and exhaust manifolds (if not previously installed with cylinder head)
> (s) Camshaft rocker cover
> (t) Alternator and drivebelt

2   Make sure that absolute cleanliness is observed and lubricate all internal components before reassembly using clean engine oil.

32 Crankshaft and main bearings – installation

1   If the original bearing shells are being re-used, install them in their original positions in the crankcase.

2   If new shells are being installed, ensure that these have been selected as described in Section 20. In both cases ensure that the backs of the bearings and their seatings in the crankcase are wiped clean.

3   Install the bearings so that their tangs engage in the recess in the crankcase (photo). Install the two semi-circular thrust washers, one on each side of the main bearing web in front of No 4 cylinder, using a small quantity of grease to retain them. The grooved surfaces of the washers should face outwards (photo). Lower the crankshaft into the crankcase (photo).

4   Install the main bearing halves and thrust washers to the bearing caps and install the bearing caps (photo). On engines with individual bearing caps, make sure that each cap is installed in its original position.

5   Install the main bearing cap bolts and tighten them to the specified torque (photo).

6   Check the crankshaft endfloat by prising the crankshaft first in one direction, then in the other. Measure the endfloat either with a dial gauge against the nose of the crankshaft, or by inserting a feeler gauge between the thrust washers and the crankshaft. If the endfloat exceeds the specified limits, install new thrust washers. If the endfloat is still excessive, the crankshaft must be renewed. If the endfloat is too small, do not reduce the thickness of the thrust washer by filing or grinding, but check that the main bearing caps are installed correctly and that the crankshaft is not distorted.

7   Check that the crankshaft rotates freely. If it does not, check that the bearing shells have not been mixed up. On engines with individual bearing caps also check that the bearing caps have not been mixed up. (A certain amount of stiffness with new shells is normal, but there should be no binding).

8   Smear a small quantity of non-hardening sealant over the joints in the seal recesses.

9   Smear oil onto the lips of the crankshaft oil seals and also onto the surfaces of the crankshaft with which they come into contact. Install the seals with their flat faces outwards and drive the seals in until they bottom in their recesses (photos).

33 Flywheel (or driveshaft) – installation

1   Install the flywheel on the crankshaft flange, aligning the hole in the flywheel with the dowel in the crankshaft.

2   Install the six bolts and tighten them in diagonal pairs to the specified torque (photo).

3   Installation of the driveplate for automatic transmission models is similar.

34 Pistons and connecting rods – assembly and installation

1   If new piston rings are being installed, first check the piston ring gap by inserting the new ring in the top of its cylinder bore and then using the piston to push the ring down the bore until it is about $\frac{3}{4}$ in (20 mm) from the bottom of the cylinder.

2   Withdraw the piston and then measure the gap between the ends of the piston ring, using feeler gauges, and compare it with the gap given in the Specifications. If the gap is too small, check that you have the correct rings for your engine. If the gap is too large, also re-check that the cylinder has not exceeded its wear limit. If the bore is over the limit, the cylinder block must be rebored or renewed – see Section 22.

3   Using two or three old feeler gauges placed across the top piston ring grooves, install the piston rings. Start with the lower oil ring, followed by the spacer and then the upper oil ring.

4   Identify the top and second piston rings (see Fig. 1.20). The second ring has a chamfer on one edge only and the top ring has a rounded edge.

5   Install the second ring so that the face of it which is marked is uppermost and then install the top ring with its marked face uppermost (Fig. 1.25) (photo).

6   Check that the rings are free to rotate in their grooves and check the side clearance of the top and second rings as described in Section 23.

7   Slide the rings round so that the gaps in their ends are positioned as shown in Fig. 1.26.

8   Lubricate the piston rings liberally and clamp a piston ring compressor to the piston and connecting rod assembly which is to be

32.3a Installing a crankcase bearing shell

32.3b No 4 main bearing thrust washers

32.3c Installing the crankshaft

32.4 Installing the main bearing caps

32.5 Tightening the main bearing cap bolts

32.9a Crankshaft front oil seal

32.9b Crankshaft rear oil seal

32.9c Driving in an oil seal

33.2 Flywheel and bolts installed

installed in No 1 cylinder bore. Lubricate the cylinder bore.

9   Align the piston so that the connecting rod bearing is square with its crankpin journal and the dot on the piston crown is towards the inlet manifold side of the engine (photo). Slide short pieces of rubber hose over the threaded ends of the big-end bolts to prevent scratching the crankpin as the connecting rod is inserted, then lower the piston into the bore until the piston ring compressor contacts the cylinder head (photos).

10   Tap the piston in, using the wooden handle of a hammer. When the ring compressor is free, stop and check that the connecting rod bearing and crankpin journal are still correctly aligned before pushing the piston down fully and engaging the bearing and crankpin.

11   Remove the protective rubber sleeves and install the big-end cap complete with bearing shell, making certain that the cap is the correct way round as marked before removal (see Section 15) (photo).

12   Install and tighten the bearing cap nuts to the specified torque (photo).

13   Repeat the operations for the other three positions and then rotate the crankshaft to ensure that nothing is binding.

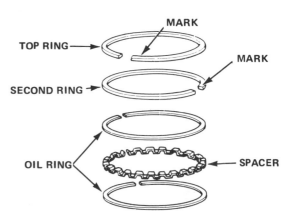

Fig. 1.25 Piston ring installation sequence (Sec 34)

34.5 Piston with rings installed

34.9a Dot on piston crown goes towards inlet manifold

34.9b Inserting a connecting rod

34.9c Inserting a piston

34.11 Installing a connecting rod bearing cap

34.12 Tightening a connecting rod bearing nut

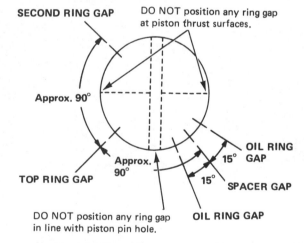
Fig. 1.26 Piston ring gap spacing (Sec 34)

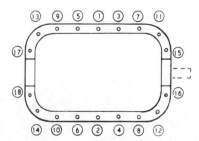
Fig. 1.27 Oil sump bolt tightening sequence (Sec 35)

14 Use feeler gauges to check that the play between the crankshaft web and the cap of the connecting rod big-end bearing cap is within the limits given in the Specifications. If any are out of tolerance, a new connecting rod should be installed.

35 Oil pump and sump – installation

1 Install the pump and (if appropriate) bypass tube, using new gaskets or O-rings as necessary (photo).
2 Install and tighten the pump securing bolts (photo).
3 Position a new gasket in position on the flange of the crankcase and over the caps of the crankshaft end bearings (photo).
4 Lower the sump onto the crankcase (photo). Install the nuts and screws and tighten them to the prescribed torque in the sequence shown in Fig. 1.27. It is important that the nuts and screws are not overtightened, because this may distort the gasket and tend to cause oil leaks.

36 Timing components – installation

1 To the front of the crankshaft install the plain timing sprocket flange, with its convex side towards the crankcase. Install the sprocket and then the perforated flange with its convex side away from the engine (photos).
2 Install the belt tensioner, but only install the pivot and adjustment bolts finger tight. Connect the belt tensioner spring (photo).
3 Engage the timing belt on the crankshaft sprocket, making sure that if a directional arrow was marked on to the belt before removal, the arrow will point in the direction of belt rotation after installation. (The belt rotates anti-clockwise when viewed from the timing pulley end of the engine). If a new timing belt is being installed, the lettering on it should be the right way up when viewed from the front of the engine.
4 Install the water pump and then install the timing belt lower cover using new seals (photos).

35.1 Installing the oil pump and bypass block

35.2 Oil pump installed

35.3 Crankcase gasket over bearing cap

35.4 Lowering the sump

36.1a Crankshaft sprocket plain flange ...

36.1b ... sprocket ...

36.1c ... and perforated flange

36.2 Belt tensioner installed

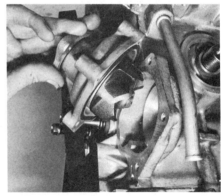
36.4a Installing the water pump

36.4b Install the timing belt lower cover

36.6 Crankshaft pulley, bolt and washer

36.7 Water pump pulley and bolts

1

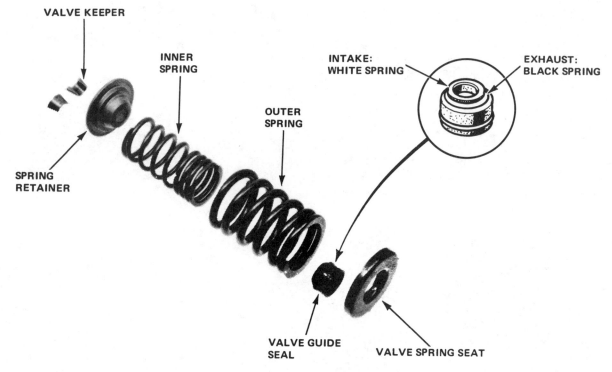

Fig. 1.28 Valve components installation sequence (Sec 37)

Align dowel pin with
cylinder head groove

Fig. 1.29 Auxiliary inlet valve assembly (Sec 37)

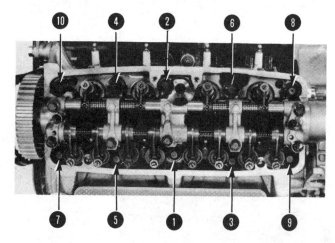

Fig. 1.30 Cylinder head bolt tightening sequence (Sec 37)

5   If the cylinder head has been installed, engage the timing belt
round the camshaft pulley (see Section 38). Otherwise retain the belt
by draping it over the top of the belt cover until it can be connected to
the camshaft sprocket. Do not kink or pinch the belt.
6   Install the crankshaft pulley, insert its retaining bolt and tighten it
to the specified torque (photo).
7   Install the water pump pulley, insert its three bolts and tighten
them (photo).

37 Cylinder head – reassembly and installation

1   With the gasket head resting on its side, insert the valves into their
guides after first lubricating the valve stems with engine oil (photo). If

valves are being re-used, they must be installed in the same position
as they occupied before removal.
2   Install the valve spring seats over the tops of the valve guides and
then install the valve guide seals, taking care not to damage the lips of
the seals when pushing them over the valve stems (photo). Note that
inlet valve guide seals and exhaust valve guide seals are different and
are not interchangeable (Fig. 1.28). Also note that some engines do
not have seals on the exhaust valve guides.
3   Install the inner and outer valve springs onto the spring seat
(photo), with the end of the spring which has the more closely wound
coils towards the cylinder head. If valve springs are being re-used, they
should be installed on the valve from which they were removed.
4   Install the valve spring cap and use a valve spring compressor to
compress the valve spring sufficiently for the split collet retainers to be
inserted in the groove machined in the top of the valve stem.
5   Release the valve spring compressor and tap the top of the valve
stem with a plastic mallet to ensure that the split collets have seated
properly.

37.1 Inserting a valve

37.2 Valve spring seat and valve guide seal

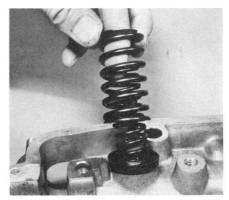
37.4 Installing the valve springs

37.10a Cylinder head gasket installed

37.10b Installing the cylinder head

37.10c Insert the cylinder head bolts

37.10d Install the oil pump drivegear

37.11 Install the camshaft

37.12 Install the rocker assembly

37.13a Tightening the rocker assembly bolts

37.13b Oil pump drivegear cover

37.15 Driving in the camshaft oil seal

1

Fig. 1.31 Rocker arm assembly bolt tightening sequence (standard engine) (Sec 37)

Fig. 1.32 Rocker arm assembly bolt tightening sequence (CVCC engine) (Sec 37)

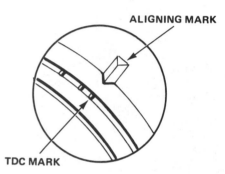

Fig. 1.33 No 1 piston TDC mark (standard engine) (Sec 38)

6   On CVCC engines, the auxiliary combustion chambers must be re-inserted in the cylinder head if they have been removed. Use a new gasket beneath the chamber and on top of it, and use a suitable round bar to align the hole in the side of the auxiliary chamber with the spark plug hole in the cylinder head.

7   Install the auxiliary valves into their valve holders in the same manner as the installing of the inlet and exhaust valves into the cylinder head. Install a new O-ring on the outside of the valve holder and lubricate the ring with a molybdenum disulphide oil.

8   Insert the auxiliary valve assembly into the cylinder head, aligning its dowel pin with the cylinder head groove (Fig. 1.29). Lubricate the threads of the locknut with a molybdenum disulphide oil, screw the locknut in and tighten it to the specified torque.

9   The cylinder head may be installed at this stage as in the following description, or the camshaft and rocker gear may be assembled before the cylinder head is installed.

10 Install the cylinder head dowels and a new gasket (photo), then lower the cylinder head onto the crankcase (photo). Insert the cylinder head bolts (photo) and tighten them in the order shown in Fig. 1.30 to a torque of about 22 lbf ft (30 Nm). Using the same sequence retighten the bolts to the final torque given in the Specifications. Insert the oil pump drivegear (photo).

11 Wipe the camshaft and its journals in the cylinder head. Lubricate the cams and journals and install the camshaft in the cylinder head (photo). Turn the camshaft until the keyway at the pulley end is vertically upwards.

12 Slacken the locknuts on the adjusting screws of the valve rockers and back the screws off several turns. Install the rocker arm assembly on the cylinder head (photo). Check that the rockers are all aligned with their valves and install the bolts, noting that there are three different types of bolt on the CVCC engine. Of the smaller bolts, No 2 (Fig. 1.32) is the longer.

13 Tighten the bolts two turns at a time in the sequence shown in Fig. 1.31 or 1.32. Install the cover on the oil pump drivegear (photos). Check the drivegear clearance (Section 24).

14 Apply a small amount of non-hardening sealant to the joint faces in the recesses in the two end caps of the camshaft.

15 In the front recess, install a new seal with its flat face towards the camshaft pulley. Lubricate the camshaft spindle and the seal lip with engine oil and drive the seal in until it bottoms.

16 If applicable, install the tachometer drive housing into the recess in the camshaft rear end cap and drive in its spring pin to retain it (photos).

17 Install the camshaft sprocket with its bolt and special washer. The recessed face of the sprocket must be towards the front of the engine. Tighten the camshaft bolt to the specfied torque (photos).

38 Timing belt – installation and adjustment

1   Set No 1 piston to TDC. On normal engines, this is when the non-coloured notch in the crankshaft pulley aligns with the mark on the timing belt cover ((Fig. 1.33). On CVCC engines the pointer on the crankcase aligns with the TDC mark on the flywheel, or driveplate (Fig. 1.34).

2   Turn the camshaft sprocket until the two marks on it are aligned with the cylinder head surface (1300 engine) (Fig. 1.35) or until the mark is aligned with the arrow on the cylinder head surface (1500 engines) (Fig. 1.36). It is important that the camshaft sprocket has its keyway uppermost. This corresponds with the lobe on the boss behind the sprocket washer (UK models) or the notch in one of the sprocket cut-outs (US models).

3   Slip the belt over the camshaft sprocket with the left-hand side of the belt as tight as possible and any slack in the belt on the right-hand side (photo).

4   Slacken the timing belt tensioner pivot end and adjusting bolts and with a socket spanner on the crankshaft pulley nut, turn the pulley anti-clockwise about a quarter of a turn. This will cause the tensioner to take up the slack.

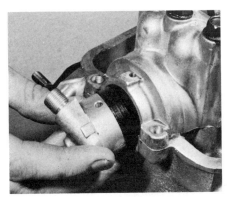
37.16a Installing the tachometer drive

37.16b Drive in the spring pin

37.17a Camshaft sprocket ...

37.17b ... bolt and special washer

38.3 Camshaft sprocket and belt installed. Note timing marks

38.6 Timing belt upper cover

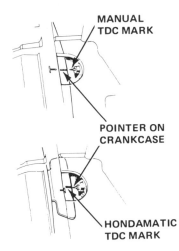
MANUAL TDC MARK

POINTER ON CRANKCASE

HONDAMATIC TDC MARK

Fig. 1.34 No 1 piston TDC mark (CVCC engine) (Sec 38)

Timing mark aligned with valve cover surface.

Fig. 1.35 Camshaft pulley timing mark position (1300) (Sec 38)

5   Tighten the adjusting bolt (Fig. 1.37 or 1.38), then tighten the pivot bolt. If the flywheel pulley bolt becomes loosened while turning the crankshaft, re-tighten the bolt to the specified torque.
6   Install the upper part of the timing belt cover (photo).

39 Valve clearances – adjusting

1   Remove the valve rocker cover if it is not already off.
2   Valves should only be adjusted when the engine is cold. The cylinder head temperature should be less than 100°F (38°C).
3   The method of adjusting valve clearances is the same for inlet, exhaust and auxiliary valves, but the exhaust valve clearance is different from that of the inlet and auxiliary valves (see Specifications).
4   Turn the crankshaft until No 1 piston is at TDC and the cam lobes operating the valves of No 1 cylinder are not in contact with the rockers. Align the camshaft pulley marks for No 1 cylinder piston at TDC as shown for the engine being adjusted (Fig. 1.39 or 1.40). (On UK engines the lobe on the boss behind the sprocket washer corresponds with the cut-out shown in Fig. 1.39.)
5   Slacken the adjuster screw locknut if it has not been released previously and turn the adjuster screw until a feeler gauge of the appropriate thickness will just slide between the top of the valve stem and the end of the adjuster screw (photo).

Timing mark aligned with arrow on cylinder head surface.

Fig. 1.36 Camshaft pulley timing mark position (1500) (Sec 38)

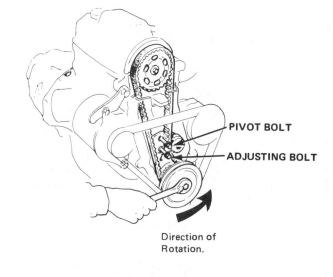

PIVOT BOLT

ADJUSTING BOLT

Direction of Rotation.

Fig. 1.38 Timing belt pivot and adjustment bolts (CVCC engine) (Sec 38)

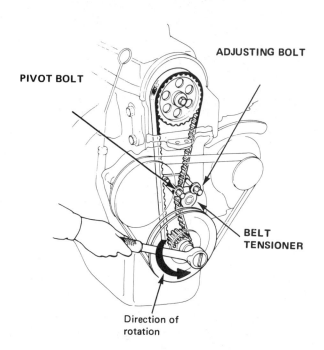

ADJUSTING BOLT

PIVOT BOLT

BELT TENSIONER

Direction of rotation

Fig. 1.37 Timing belt pivot and adjustment bolts (standard engine) (Sec 38)

39.5 Adjusting valve clearance

6　Withdraw the feeler gauge, hold a screwdriver in the slot of the adjuster screw to prevent the screw from rotating and tighten the locknut.

7　Check that the clearance has not altered and readjust if necessary.

8　Rotate the crankshaft pulley 180° anti-clockwise. The camshaft will rotate 90° and take up the position for No 3 piston at TDC. Adjust the valve clearances of No 3 cylinder.

9　Repeat the operations of turning the crankshaft 180° and adjusting the valve clearances for No 4 cylinder and finally No 2 cylinder.

40 Ancillary components – installation

1　Install the distributor, the inlet and exhaust manifolds, the carburettor, alternator and drivebelt. (photos).

2　Adjust the tension of the alternator drivebelt (see Chapter 2).

3　Install the water pump header pipe (photos).

4　Smear oil on the seal of a new cartridge oil filter. Screw the filter onto the cylinder block until the seal just contacts the block and then tighten the filter by hand a further half turn. **Do not** use a wrench to tighten the filter.

5　On manual transmission models, install the clutch friction and pressure plates, taking care to centralise the friction plate before tightening the pressure plate screws (see Chapter 5).

6　Install the fuel pump (mechanical type) (photo).

41 Engine to transmission – reconnection

1　Connect the engine and transmission by reversing the operations described in Section 5 or 6, as appropriate.

2　When a manual transmission is being connected to the engine, take care that the transmission mainshaft is not strained by the weight

Number 1 Piston at TDC

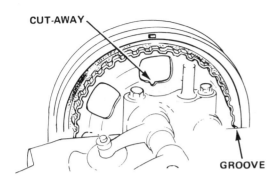

Number 1 Piston at TDC

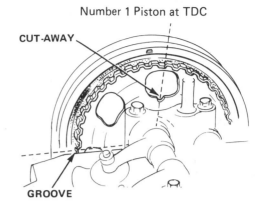

Number 3 Piston at TDC

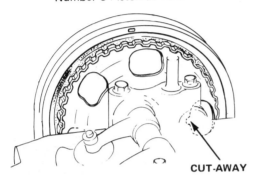

Number 3 Piston at TDC

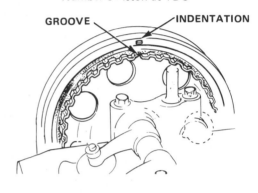

Number 4 Piston at TDC

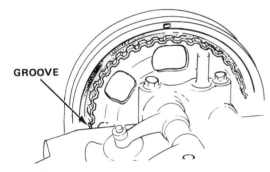

Number 4 Piston at TDC

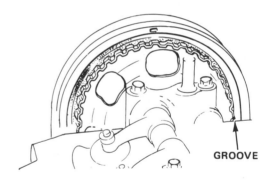

Number 2 Piston at TDC

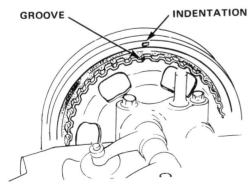

Number 2 Piston at TDC

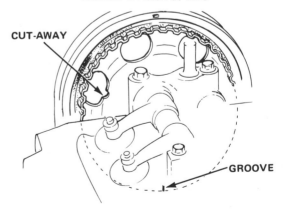

Fig. 1.39 Valve adjusting sequence – 1300 models. Pulley differs on UK models (Sec 39)

Fig. 1.40 Valve adjusting sequence (1500 CVCC) (Sec 39)

1

40.1a Inlet manifold gasket

40.1b Installing the inlet manifold and carburettor

40.1c Note bracket on inlet manifold front stud

40.1d Exhaust manifold gaskets

40.1e Installing the exhaust manifold

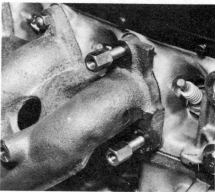

40.1f Note thick nuts on exhaust manifold front studs

40.1g Exhaust manifold cover

40.3a Header pipe connection to water pump

40.3b Header pipe retaining screw

40.6a Installing the fuel pump

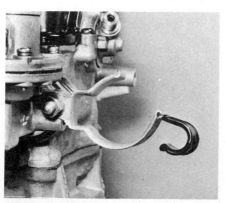

40.6b Note bracket on fuel pump right-hand stud

41.2 Installing the manual transmission

41.3 Installing the starter motor

4.14a Engine front mounting

41.4b Engine rear mounting

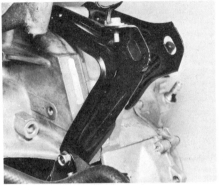

41.4c Rear torque arm bracket

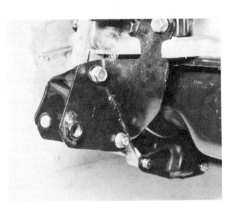

41.4d Front torque arm bracket

41.4e Transmission guard plate

of the transmission bearing on the shaft (photo).

3   Install the starter motor (photo).

4   Check that all the engine mounting brackets are installed correctly (photos). Refer to Fig. 1.9 for the correct tightening sequence. Do not forget to install the transmission guard plate (photo).

42 Engine start-up after major overhaul

1   After re-installing the engine as described in Section 4, check that the lubricants and coolant have been replenished and that all cables and hoses are correctly installed.

2   Check that no tools or cloths have been left in the engine compartment.

3   Start the engine and leave it running at no more than fast idling speed until it attains normal working temperature. During this time look for oil and coolant leaks and also check for leaks in the exhaust system.

4   Stop the engine and again look for oil and coolant leaks.

5   Road test the car. If new bearings and/or new pistons and rings have been installed, follow the manufacturer's instructions for running in. After 500 miles (800 km) or so have been covered, change the engine oil and filter, check the tightness of the cylinder head bolts and readjust the valve clearances if necessary.

43 Fault diagnosis – engine

When investigating engine faults, do not be tempted into snap diagnosis. Adopt a logical procedure and follow it through – it will take less time in the long run.

Symptom	Reason(s)
Engine fails to turn when starter operated	Flat or defective battery
	Battery connections loose or corroded
	Earth strap(s) loose, broken or missing
	Automatic transmission inhibitor switch faulty or maladjusted
	Broken wire or loose connection in starter circuit
	Ignition/starter switch defective
	Starter motor or solenoid defective (see Chapter 10)
	Major mechanical failure (seizure)

Symptom	Reason(s)
Engine turns but will not start	Partly discharged battery HT leads damp or dirty Fuel tank empty Insufficient or excessive choke Ignition system fault (see Chapter 4) Fuel system fault (see Chapter 3) Valve clearances incorrect Ignition timing incorrect Incorrect valve timing (after rebuild) Serious overheating
Engine stalls and will not restart	Excessive choke Fuel tank empty or fuel contaminated Fuel cut-off solenoid defective or disconnected (if applicable) Overheating Ignition system fault (see Chapter 4) Fuel system fault (see Chapter 3) Major mechanical failure (eg timing belt broken)
Engine misfires or idles unevenly	Ignition system fault (see Chapter 4) Fuel system fault (see Chapter 3) Valve clearances incorrect Air leak at manifold(s) or carburettor Burnt or leaking valve(s) Weak or broken valve spring(s) Sticking valves Head gasket blowing
Engine lacks power	Ignition timing incorrect or auto advance malfunctioning Valve clearances incorrect Air cleaner clogged Valve(s) burnt or leaking Valve spring(s) weak or broken Head gasket blown Overheating Incorrect valve timing (after rebuild) Carburation defect (see Chapter 3) Fuel pump delivery inadequate Brakes binding (see Chapter 9)
Excessive oil consumption	Overfilling! External leakage Worn valve guides or defective seals Worn pistons, rings and/or bores Crankcase breather clogged Head gasket blown
Unusual mechanical noises	Unintentional mechanical contact (eg fan blades) Peripheral component fault (eg water pump) Pinking (pre-ignition) Valve clearances too big Piston ring(s) broken (ticking noise) Small end(s) worn (light tapping noise) Piston slap (worst when cold) Big-end bearing(s) worn (knocking noise, perhaps, lessening under load) Main bearing(s) worn (knocking and rumbling, perhaps worsening under load) Piston/valve contact (valve timing incorrect) Camshaft bearings worn Timing belt tensioner worn
Low oil pressure	Oil level low or incorrect grade Pressure warning switch defective Oil filter clogged Pick-up strainer clogged or mountings loose Oil pump worn or mountings loose Crankshaft bearings worn

Chapter 2 Cooling system

Refer to Chapter 13 for specifications related to 1982 and 1983 US models

Contents

Specifications

General
System type .... Pressurised, thermo-syphon, pump-assisted
Cooling fan .... Electric, thermostatically controlled
Radiator cap blow-off pressure .... 11 to 15 lbf/in² (0.75 to 1.05 kgf/cm²)

Thermostat
Standard type:
  Starts opening .... 176° to 183°F (80° to 84°C)
  Fully open .... 203°F (95°C)
  Lift height .... 0.32 in (8 mm)
Optional (cold climate) type:
  Starts opening .... 187° to 194°F (86° to 90°C)
  Fully open .... 212°F (100°C)
  Lift height .... 0.32 in (8 mm)

Fan thermoswitch
Cuts in .... 191° to 197° (88.5° to 91.5°C)
Cuts out .... 9°F (5°C) below cut-in temperature

Coolant capacity (excluding reservoir)

	Drain and refill	From dry
UK models	0.8 Imp gal (3.4 litres)	0.9 Imp gal (4 litres)
US models, 1980:		
1300	0.9 US gal (3.4 litres)	1.3 US gal (5 litres)
1500	0.9 US gal (3.4 litres)	1.6 US gal (6 litres)
US models, 1981:		
1300	1.1 US gal (4 litres)	1.3 US gal (5 litres)
1500	1.2 US gal (4.5 litres)	1.5 US gal (5.5 litres)

Torque wrench settings

	lbf ft	Nm
Fan thermoswitch	16	22
Temperature gauge sender unit	16	22
Water pump pulley bolts	9	12
Water pump mounting bolts	9	12
Thermostat housing bolts	9	12
Water distribution pipe clamp bolt	9	12
Alternator adjusting clamp bolt	18	25
Alternator pivot bolt:		
M8	18	25
M10	33	45
Engine drain plug	24	32

1 General description

The engine cooling system is of the thermo-syphon water pump assisted type, the pump being driven by a belt from the crankshaft pulley.

The front-mounted radiator is of the sealed type, having an expansion tank, and it is cooled by a thermostatically controlled electric fan (photo).

A thermostat is mounted towards the front of the cylinder head (UK) or on the distributor housing bolted to the end of the cylinder head (US). A temperature sender unit is screwed into the housing.

The car interior heater works from coolant applied from the engine cooling system.

2 Cooling system – draining

1   Place the heater control to maximum heat.
2   Remove the radiator cap. If the engine is hot remove the cap very slowly, having first covered it with a cloth, to prevent escaping steam or coolant, which is under pressure, from causing injury.
3   If the coolant is to be used again, place a container of sufficient capacity under the radiator drain plug.
4   Unscrew and remove the plug (photo) and drain the coolant into the container.
5   Remove the expansion tank and empty the contents into the container.
6   If the system requires flushing, proceed as described in the next Section.

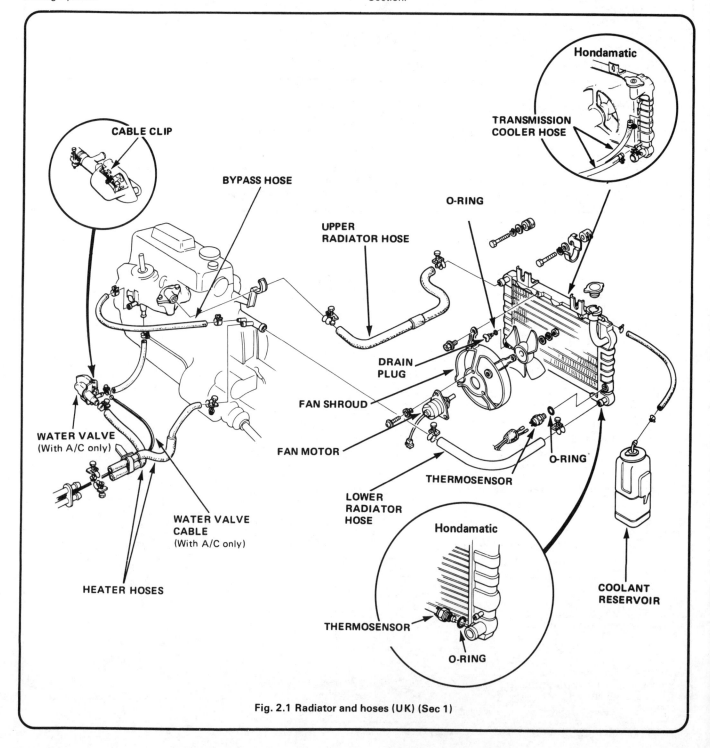

Fig. 2.1 Radiator and hoses (UK) (Sec 1)

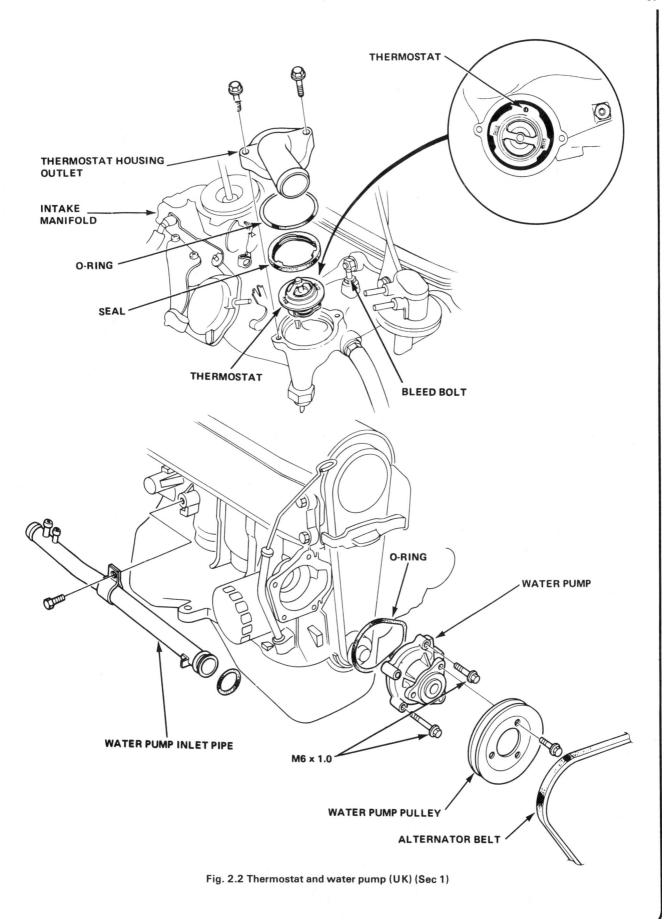

THERMOSTAT

THERMOSTAT HOUSING OUTLET

INTAKE MANIFOLD

O-RING

SEAL

THERMOSTAT

BLEED BOLT

O-RING

WATER PUMP

WATER PUMP INLET PIPE

M6 x 1.0

WATER PUMP PULLEY

ALTERNATOR BELT

2

Fig. 2.2 Thermostat and water pump (UK) (Sec 1)

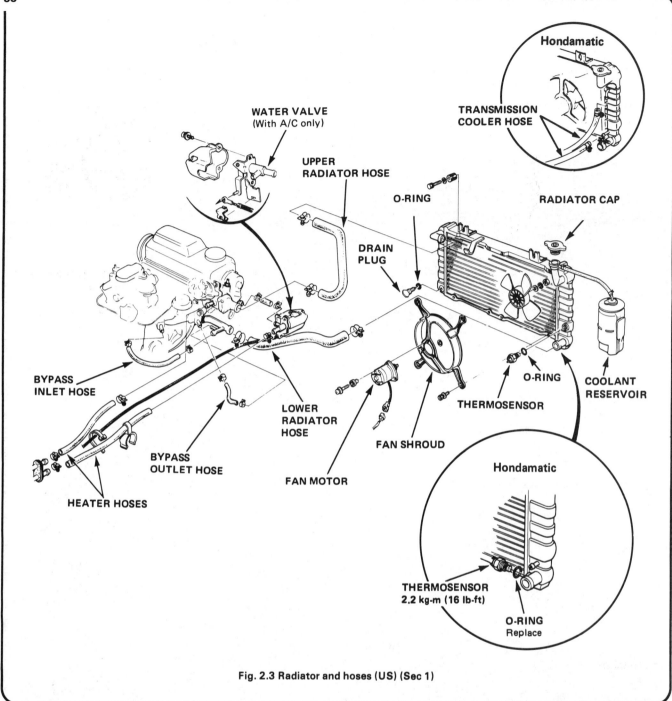

WATER VALVE
(With A/C only)

UPPER
RADIATOR HOSE

O-RING

Hondamatic

TRANSMISSION
COOLER HOSE

RADIATOR CAP

DRAIN
PLUG

BYPASS
INLET HOSE

LOWER
RADIATOR
HOSE

BYPASS
OUTLET HOSE

FAN SHROUD

FAN MOTOR

HEATER HOSES

O-RING

THERMOSENSOR

COOLANT
RESERVOIR

Hondamatic

THERMOSENSOR
2.2 kg-m (16 lb-ft)

O-RING
Replace

Fig. 2.3 Radiator and hoses (US) (Sec 1)

1.0 Radiator and fan assembly

2.4 Radiator drain plug

4.1 Cooling system bleed screw (US shown, UK similar)

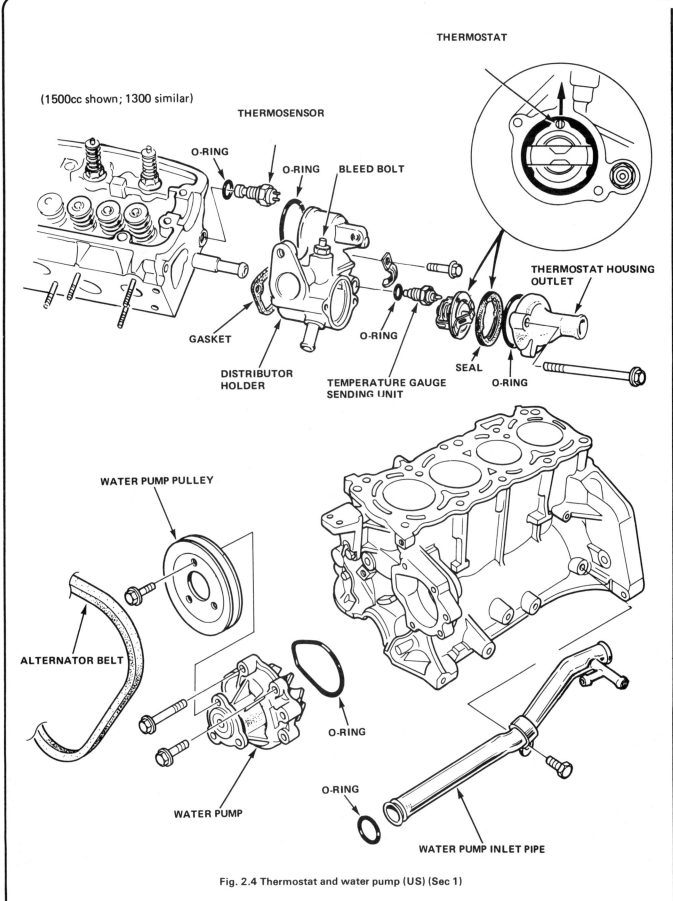

THERMOSTAT

(1500cc shown; 1300 similar)

THERMOSENSOR

O-RING

O-RING

BLEED BOLT

THERMOSTAT HOUSING OUTLET

GASKET

DISTRIBUTOR HOLDER

TEMPERATURE GAUGE SENDING UNIT

O-RING

SEAL

O-RING

WATER PUMP PULLEY

ALTERNATOR BELT

WATER PUMP

O-RING

O-RING

WATER PUMP INLET PIPE

2

Fig. 2.4 Thermostat and water pump (US) (Sec 1)

7 If the system is in good condition and does not require flushing, refit the radiator drain plug and refer to Section 4.

3 Cooling system – flushing

1 If the coolant has not been renewed at the recommended mileage intervals, or if due to leakage the antifreeze mixture used has become diluted, the system should be flushed with clean water before refilling.
2 Unbolt the thermostat housing cover and extract the thermostat.
3 Refit the radiator drain plug and radiator cap.
4 Insert a cold water hose into the thermostat opening in the cylinder head and reverse flush the cooling system until clean water is seen to flow from the hose which is normally attached to the thermostat housing cover. Make sure that the heater control is set to maximum heat during the flushing operation.
5 Remove the radiator cap and drain plug and drain the system.
6 Refit the thermostat with a new gasket, the expansion tank and radiator drain plug.

4 Cooling system – filling

1 Release the bleed screw (photo) and refill the system by pouring coolant slowly through the radiator filler cap. Also half fill the expansion tank.
2 When air ceases to escape from the bleed nipple and coolant is seen to emerge, tighten the bleed screw.
3 With the radiator cap still removed, start the engine and run it to normal operating temperature until the electric cooling fan cuts in.
4 Switch off the engine, top up the radiator to the base of the filler neck and refit the cap.
5 Top up the expansion tank to the 'FULL' mark.

5 Antifreeze mixture

1 In order to maintain the correct antifreeze and anti-corrosive properties of the coolant it is recommended that an antifreeze product suitable for use with aluminium is used in a proportion of 50% with soft water when refilling the cooling system in temperate zones.
2 In more severe climatic conditions, increase the ratio of antifreeze to water to 60% and 40% for temperatures between -34° and -62°F, and 70% and 30% for temperatures below -62°F.
3 If topping-up is necessary due to leakage losses, use coolant mixed in similar proportions to the original.
4 Modern glycol-based antifreeze mixtures can normally be left in the cooling system for two years. Renewal after this period is necessary because even if the frost protection properties of the antifreeze are maintained, the corrosion inhibitors will have deteriorated.
5 It is advisable to check the concentration of the antifreeze after the first year of use. Hydrometers are available for this purpose, or your dealer can do it for you.
6 In areas where antifreeze protection is not necessary, a corrosion inhibitor suitable for use in aluminium engines should be added to the coolant.

6 Radiator/fan assembly – removal and installation

1 Drain the cooling system as previously described.
2 Disconnect the hoses from the radiator, including the overflow hose to the expansion tank. On automatic transmission models, disconnect and plug the ATF cooler hoses.
3 Disconnect the electrical leads from the thermoswitch and the electrically-operated radiator fan.
4 Unscrew and remove the radiator securing bolts (photo).
5 Lift the radiator assembly from the engine compartment (photo).
6 Installation is a reversal of removal.

7 Radiator – inspection and cleaning

1 With the radiator out of the car any leaks can be soldered up or repaired with a suitable filler. Clean out the radiator by flushing as described in Section 3. It should be mentioned that solder repairs are best completed professionally; it is too easy to damage other parts of the radiator by excessive heating.
2 When the radiator is out of the car, it is advantageous to turn it upside-down for reverse flushing. Clean the exterior of the radiator by hosing down the radiator matrix with a strong jet of water to clean away road dirt, dead flies, etc.
3 Inspect the radiator hoses for cracks (internal and external), perishing and damage caused by over-tightening of the hose clips. Renew the hoses as necessary.
4 Examine the hose clips and renew them if they are rusted or distorted. The drain plugs and washers should be renewed if leaking.

8 Radiator fan thermoswitch – testing and renewal

1 The radiator cooling fan motor is actuated by a thermoswitch located in the radiator bottom tank (photo). If the cooling system is overheating due to non-operation of the fan, check the switch in the following way.
2 Run the engine until the coolant temperature is between 191 and 197°F (88.5 and 91.5°C). This temperature range can be checked by inserting a thermometer in the radiator filler neck.
3 If the fan motor does not cut in, switch off the engine and disconnect the black/yellow and blue leads from the thermoswitch and join their ends together.
4 Turn the ignition switch on, when the motor should start running. If it does, renew the thermoswitch which must be faulty. To do this, drain the system and unscrew the switch from the radiator bottom tank.
5 If the motor does not operate, check the motor leads and connections and the fuse. If these are in order, remove the motor as described in the following Section.

6.4 Radiator securing bolt

6.5 Radiator bottom mounting

8.1 Radiator thermoswitch

10.2a Removing the thermostat cover (UK)

10.2b Thermostat cover on distributor housing (US)

10.3a Thermostat removed from housing (UK)

10.3b Thermostat refitted (note location of air release pin at top) (US)

9 Fan and motor – removal, inspection and installation

1   Disconnect the leads from the fan motor.
2   Unscrew and remove the bolts which secure the fan cage and motor to the radiator and then lift the fan/motor assembly from the engine compartment. The fan motor is mounted on the cage with three bolts and bushes. The fan itself is retained on the motor shaft by a single nut.
3   It will be necessary to remove the fan before the motor can be detached. Hold the fan, whilst the motor shaft nut is undone, then jolt the fan off the shaft.
4   If the fan motor shaft bearings are sloppy or the motor does not run, or runs unevenly, the only remedy is to renew the motor.
5   The motor unit has no facility for repair.
6   The fan itself is of moulded nylon and is not repairable.
7   Reassembly of the fan unit follows the reversal of the dismantling procedure.
8   Install the fan assembly to the radiator and connect the leads.

10 Thermostat – removal, testing and installation

1   Drain the cooling system as previously described.
2   Unbolt and remove the thermostat cover from the cylinder head (photos).
3   Extract the thermostat (photos).
4   The thermostat may be tested for correct functioning by suspending it together with a thermometer in a saucepan of cold water. Heat the water and note the temperature at which the thermostat begins to open. This temperature should be as given in the specifications. Discard the thermostat if it is open too early. Continue heating the water until the thermostat is fully open and note that temperature, again comparing it with the specifications. Turn off the heat to allow the thermostat to cool down. If the thermostat does not open fully in near boiling water, or close completely when cooled, the unit must be discarded and a new thermostat fitted.
5   Install the thermostat and the cover using a new gasket and refill the cooling system.

11.5 Removing the water pump

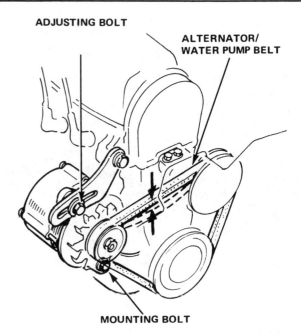

Fig. 2.6 Drivebelt adjustment (US) (Sec 12)

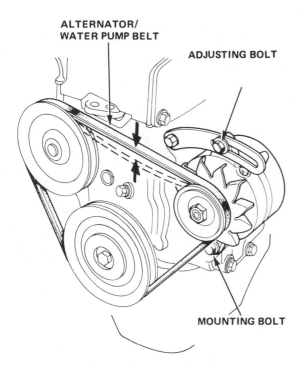

Fig. 2.5 Drivebelt adjustment (UK) (Sec 12)

11 Water pump – removal and installation

1   The water pump is mounted on the front face of the cylinder block and is driven by a belt from the crankshaft pulley which also drives the alternator.
2   To remove the water pump, drain the cooling system.
3   Slacken the alternator mounting and adjustment strap bolts, push the alternator in towards the engine and slip the drivebelt from the water pump pulley.
4   Unscrew and remove the water pump securing bolts.
5   Extract the water pump from the cylinder block. Part of the pump body passes between the timing belt cover and engine block. The pump should be removed with the rubber dust seal which sits between pump and timing belt cover (photo). Once the pump has been removed and it has been found to be faulty, the only action is to discard it and fit a new pump.

6   Before installing the pump, check that the seal is in good condition and not cracked or broken. Clean the joint faces of the pump and cylinder block.
7   Position the timing belt cover seal on the pump body and offer the pump into position. Once the impeller has entered the pump housing in the cylinder block the pump can be slid into position. Ensure that the timing cover seal is properly seated.
8   Insert the four pump bolts and tighten to the specified torque.
9   Reconnect the drivebelt and adjust it, as described in the next Section.

12 Drivebelt – adjusting tension

1   It is important to keep the drivebelt co rrectly adjusted: it should be checked at the specified intervals. If the belt is slack, it will slip, wear rapidly and cause water pump and/or alternator malfunction. If the belt is too tight, the alternator and water pump bearings will wear rapidly.
2   The belt tension is correct when there is just $\frac{1}{2}$ in (12.7 mm) of vertical movement at the mid-point position between water pump and alternator pulleys.
3   To adjust the belt tension, slacken the alternator pivot and slot arm bolts, just sufficiently for the unit to be moved away from the engine. Once the new position of the alternator has been obtained for the correct belt tension, the unit's bolts can be tightened (Fig. 2.5 or 2.6).
4   Do not lever against the body of the alternator with anything other than a piece of wood, and even then, proceed carefully. The alternator is fragile and expensive!
5   A new belt should be rechecked, and adjusted if necessary, after a couple of hundred miles have been covered.

13 Water temperature gauge and sender unit – testing

1   If the water temperature gauge reads incorrectly according to the known engine condition, first check the gauge.
2   To do this, disconnect the yellow/green lead from the sender unit and earth the end of the lead.
3   Turn the ignition switch on and observe the needle of the gauge which should move to the maximum 'H' position. If this is not the case and the wires are intact, renew the gauge.
4   If the foregoing test proves satisfactory check the sender unit, but an ohmmeter will be required and unless one is already owned, the

cheaper alternative may be to substitute a new sender unit.

5 To test the sender unit, disconnect the yellow/green lead from it and having applied the ohmmeter lead to the sender unit terminal, take a reading with the engine cold. Start the engine and take further readings as the engine warms up. The resistances at various temperature levels should approximate to those shown in the following table. Use a thermometer inserted in the radiator filler neck to establish the temperature levels.

Temperature	122°F (50°C)	176°F (80°C)	212°F (100°C)
Resistance (ohms)	154	48 to 56	26 to 29

6 If the sender unit fails to meet the resistance test, drain the cooling system and unscrew it from the cylinder head and renew it.

14 Fault diagnosis – cooling system

Symptom	Reason(s)
Overheating	Low coolant level
	Low oil level
	Slack drivebelt to pump
	Thermostat not operating
	Radiator pressure cap faulty, or wrong type
	Defective water pump
	Cylinder head gasket blowing
	Radiator core clogged with flies or dirt
	Radiator blocked internally
	New engine not run-in
	Ignition retarded
	Mixture too weak
	Binding brakes
	Bottom hose or tank frozen
Engine running too cool	Defective or incorrect thermostat
	Faulty water temperature gauge or sender
Loss of coolant	Leaking radiator or hose
	Cylinder head gasket leaking
	Leaking cylinder block core plugs
	Faulty radiator filler cap, or wrong type fitted

2

Chapter 3 Fuel, exhaust and emission control systems

Refer to Chapter 13 for specifications and information related to 1982 and 1983 US models

Contents

Specifications

General

System type	Rear-mounted fuel tank, electric or mechanical fuel pump, fixed jet downdraught carburettor
Emission control equipment	Various, according to model and territory
Fuel tank capacity:	
1981 US Sedan	12.2 US gallons (46 litres)
All other models	9.0 Imp gallons (10.8 US gallons, 41 litres)
Fuel type:	
UK models	91 RON minimum (2-star)
US models	Unleaded gasoline

Fuel pump

Delivery pressure	2 to 3 lbf/in^2 (0.15 to 0.20 kgf/cm^2)
Delivery rate:	
Mechanical pump	750 cc/min at 3000 rpm
Electrical pump	500 cc/min at 12 volts

Idle speed

1981 US 1300 models	800 ± 50 rpm
All other models	750 ± 50 rpm
Automatic and Hondamatic transmission	750 ± 50 rpm in gear

Carburettor adjustment data – UK models

Float level (from gasket)	1.39 to 1.47 in (35.4 to 37.4 mm)
Float needle clearance	0 to 0.004 in (0 to 0.1 mm)
Accelerator pump lever travel	0.39 in (10 mm)

Carburettor adjustment data – US models

Float level	See text (Section 20)
Accelerator pump lever travel:	
1980 models	9/16 to 19/32 in (14.5 to 15.0 mm)
1981 models	29/64 to 31/64 in (11.5 to 12.0 mm)
Fast idle speed:	
All 1980 models	3000 ± 500 rpm
1981 models:	
All manual, except California	3000 rpm
Manual, California	3200 rpm
Automatic, except California	2800 rpm
Automatic, California	2700 rpm

Fuel gauge sender calibration

Float position:	Resistance (ohms)
Empty	105 to 110
Half-full	25.5 to 39.5
Full	2 to 5

Torque wrench settings

	lbf ft	Nm
Carburettor flange nuts	14	20
Fuel tank bolts	16	22
Fuel tank drain plug	36	50
Fuel pump (electric) mounting bolts	7	10
Fuel pump (mechanical) mounting nuts	16	22
Inlet manifold nuts	16	22
Exhaust manifold nuts	16	22
Exhaust manifold-to-exhaust pipe flange nuts	36	50
Exhaust pipe-to-silencer flange nuts	16	22
Catalytic converter flange nuts	25	34
Exhaust manifold shroud bolts	7	10

1 General description

The fuel system consists of a rear-mounted fuel tank, a fuel pump and carburettor. On UK models the fuel pump is mounted on the cylinder head and is operated by the camshaft, whilst on US models the pump is electrically operated and is positioned beneath the vehicle at the rear.

The carburettors of the UK and US models are entirely different, and on US models the fuel system has additional features for exhaust emission control. Several different emission control devices can be installed, to make up a very comprehensive system, but the actual combination depends upon the market for which the vehicle is intended.

2 Air cleaner – servicing, removal and installation

1 Before the air enters the carburettor it passes through a cartridge filter with a dry paper element. The filter element should be renewed at the specified intervals, or more frequently if the vehicle is used in unusually dusty conditions.

2 To remove the filter element, undo the wing nut in the centre of the air cleaner cover, release the clips, if fitted, and remove the cover. Lift out the element and discard it (photos).

3 Wipe the inside of the air cleaner and its cover with a damp cloth to remove dust and dirt, and check that the sealing rings in the cleaner and its cover are in good condition and are properly installed.

4 Install a new paper element, ensuring that it is positioned centrally and contacts the lower sealing gasket properly. Install the cover.

5 A dirty or clogged air filter can result in bad starting and high fuel consumption and it is advisable to examine the filter between the specified renewal intervals to check its condition.

6 The air intake to the cleaner has a flap valve operated by an air temperature sensor. When the outside air temperature is low, the flap valve ensures that the intake air is drawn from around the exhaust manifold. At a preset temperature the flap valve operates to close this pre-heated air intake and open an intake which draws air from behind the front grille.

7 To remove the air cleaner assembly, disconnect the two air hoses connected to it and also the pipe to the air intake control diaphragm. On models so equipped, unplug the electrical lead from the air temperature sensor.

8 Remove the air cleaner cover and element and then remove the two nuts and washers securing the air cleaner to the carburettor.

9 Installation is a reversal of removal. Renew the gasket between the air cleaner and the carburettor and take care that this gasket is properly installed before installing the air cleaner.

3 Fuel filter – renewal

1 A fuel filter is installed in the line from the fuel tank to the pump and is located adjacent to the fuel tank (photo). This filter should be renewed at the specified intervals.

2 Ensure that the vehicle is in a well-ventilated area, free from naked flames or other sources of ignition. Do not smoke. Changing the filter should **not** be carried out with the vehicle over an inspection pit.

4 Chock the front wheels securely, raise the rear of the vehicle and support it on blocks, or firmly based stands. On Hatchback models, remove the rear left wheel.

5 Clamp the fuel hoses and slide back the clips from the hose attachments to the filter. Note which way round the filter is installed and then remove the hoses by twisting them. Do not attempt to pull the hoses off the filter without twisting, because this will damage the hoses.

6 On Wagon models, detach the filter from its mounting bracket.

7 Install a new filter, ensuring that it is connected the same way round as the one which was removed. On some filters there is an arrow to indicate the direction of fuel flow. Install the fuel hoses and clips and remove the clamps from the hoses.

2.2a Air cleaner wing nut

2.2b Air cleaner cover clip

3.1 Fuel filter (arrowed)

4 Fuel pump – removal and installation

Mechanical pump

1 Ensure that the vehicle is in a well-ventilated area, free from naked flames or other sources of ignition. Do not smoke. Removal of the fuel pump should **not** be carried out with the vehicle over an inspection pit.
2 Mark the hoses to ensure that they are reconnected to the correct port of the pump, then clamp the hoses. Release the hose clips and disconnect the hoses by twisting them and then pulling them. Do not attempt to remove the hoses by pulling without twisting, because this will damage them. Be prepared for a small spillage of fuel when the hoses are disconnected (photo).
3 Remove the two nuts and washers and the bracket secured by the right-hand nut, then pull the pump off the cylinder head.
4 When installing the pump, use a new gasket on each side of the heat insulator and ensure that the pump operating lever is inserted below the cam.

Electric pump

5 Observe the precautions detailed in paragraph 1. Disconnect the battery ground lead.
6 Chock the front wheels securely, raise the rear of the vehicle and support it on blocks, or firmly based stands. On Hatchback models remove the rear left wheel (Fig. 3.1).
7 Clamp the fuel lines and remove the fuel filter.
8 Disconnect the electrical leads from the pump.
9 Remove the bolts from the pump mounting bracket and remove the pump on its mounting. On Wagon models, do not remove the fuel tank bracket (Fig. 3.2).
10 Remove the pump mounting bolts and detach the pump from its mounting.
11 Installation is the reverse of removal.

5 Fuel pump – testing

Mechanical pump

1 Ensure that the vehicle is in a well-ventilated area, free from naked flames or other sources of ignition. Do not smoke. Testing of the fuel pump should **not** be carried out with the vehicle over an inspection pit.
2 Connect a pressure gauge with a range up to 5 lbf/in^2 (0.35 kgf/cm^2) into the line between the pump and the carburettor, using a T-piece and rubber hose (Fig.3.3).
3 Start the engine and run it at varying speeds, noting the pressure reading. If the reading is outside the range given in the Specifications, install a new pump.
4 Stop the engine, remove the pressure gauge and hold the open end of the hose over a graduated container.
5 Start the engine, run it for 60 seconds at 3000 rpm, then stop the engine and measure the amount of fuel in the container.
6 If the fuel flow is equal to or greater than the minimum given in the Specifications, disconnect the T-piece and reconnect the fuel pipe from the fuel pump to the carburettor.
7 If the fuel flow is below the limit, install a new fuel pump and re-test.

Electric pump

8 Observe the precautions given in paragraph 1.
9 Remove the fuse box cover and withdraw the fuel cut-off relay, then connect a jumper wire between the two black/yellow wires at the relay socket (Fig. 3.4).
10 Disconnect the fuel line from the carburettor and connect the line to a pressure gauge with a range up to 5 lbf/in^2 (0.35 kgf/cm^2).
11 Turn the ignition key on and when the pressure is steady, note the gauge reading and then turn the ignition off. If the reading is outside the range given in the Specifications, install a new pump.
12 If the pressure is satisfactory, disconnect the pressure gauge and hold the open end of the fuel line over a graduated container.
13 Turn the ignition on for 60 seconds and then turn the ignition off. Measure the amount of fuel in the container and if it is less than the value given in the Specifications, install a new pump.
14 If the measured quantity of fuel is adequate, reconnect the fuel line, remove the jumper wire and re-install the fuel cut-off relay.

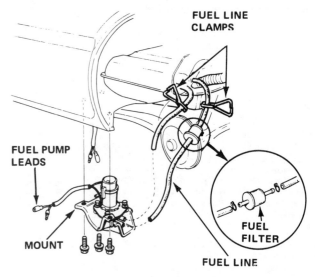

Fig. 3.1 Electric fuel pump removal (Hatchback) (Sec 4)

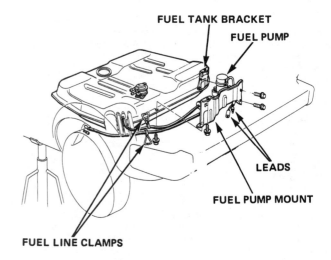

Fig. 3.2 Electric fuel pump removal (Wagon) (Sec 4)

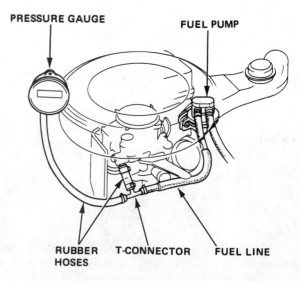

Fig. 3.3 Testing a mechanical fuel pump (Sec 5)

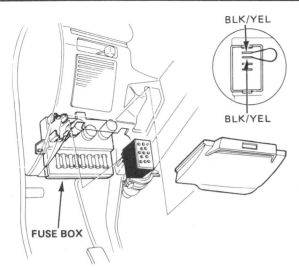

Fig. 3.4 Fuel cut-off relay bypassing (Sec 5)

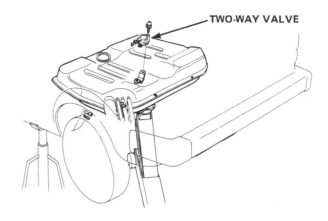

Fig. 3.5 Fuel system two-way valve (Sec 7)

6 Fuel tank – removal and installation

1   Ensure that the vehicle is in a well-venlitated area, free from naked flames, or other sources of ignition. Do not smoke. Removal of the fuel tank should **not** be carried out with the vehicle over an inspection pit.
2   For safety, disconnect the battery leads.
3   Chock the front wheels securely. Raise the rear of the vehicle and support it on blocks, or firmly based stands.
4   Remove the drain plug from the tank and drain the fuel into a metal container which is suitable for the storage of petrol (photo).
5   Disconnect the wires from the fuel gauge sender unit.
6   Mark the hoses to show the pipes to which each of them is connected, slide back the hose clips and twist and pull the hoses to disconnect them. Do not attempt to pull the hoses off without twisting them, because this will damage the hoses.
7   Position a jack beneath the fuel tank, Place a piece of flat wood on the head of the jack to prevent damage to the tank and then raise the jack until the wood is just in contact with the tank.
8   On models having a mechanical fuel pump, remove the four bolts securing the fuel tank.
9   On models with an electric fuel pump, the procedure for Hatchback models is the same as for models with a mechanical pump.
10 On Wagon models with an electric pump, remove the fuel pump

mount and fuel pump, the fuel tank bracket at the right rear corner of the fuel tank and the two bolts holding the front edge of the fuel tank to the chassis.
11 After removing the tank fixings, lower the jack and remove the tank, taking care not to let the tank foul the handbrake cable.
12 Take care to store the tank safely, so that there is no possibility of the vapour inside it becoming ignited. **Do not** attempt to solder or weld a leaking tank.
13 Installation is the reverse of removal.

7 Two-way valve – removal and installation

1   A two-way valve is mounted on the top of the fuel tank (Fig. 3.5) and it controls the venting of the fuel tank. When the temperature of the tank increases, the pressure relief part of the valve allows fuel vapour to escape to the charcoal canister. When the temperature of the tank decreases, the vacuum part of the valve allows air to enter the tank to relieve the vacuum.
2   To remove the valve, remove the fuel tank as previously described, except that the tank need only be partially lowered to give access to the valve.
3   When the valve is accessible, mark the positions of the two hoses so that they will be reconnected correctly, then disconnect them.
4   Either remove the two screws securing the valve to the tank, or pull the valve from its retaining clip.
5   Installation is the reverse of removal.

4.2 Fuel pump hose connections. Arrows on pump show direction of flow

6.4 Fuel tank drain plug

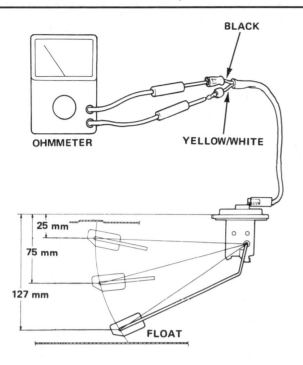

Fig. 3.6 Testing the fuel gauge sender unit (Sec 8)

Fig. 3.7 Fuel sender wrench (Sec 9)

6   Connect an ohmmeter to the two wires of the sender unit and note the resistance reading with the float in the three positions shown in Fig. 3.6. These positions correspond to the FULL, HALF and EMPTY markings on the gauge and the readings should be as given in the Specifications. If the readings are outside the specified limits, install a new sender unit.

8   Fuel tank gauge – testing

1   Chock the front wheels securely. Raise the rear of the vehicle, support it on blocks or firmly based stands, and remove the rear wheels.
2   Check that the ignition switch is off.
3   Disconnect the fuel gauge sender unit at its connection to the wiring harness and then connect together the black and yellow/white wires of the harness.
4   Turn the ignition switch on and watch the fuel gauge. As soon as the needle stops moving, turn the ignition off. If the gauge is satisfactory, the needle will stop at the FULL mark. Do not leave the ignition switched on for longer than 5 seconds, because this will damage the fuel gauge.
5   If the gauge is satisfactory, remove the sender unit (Section 9) and test it as follows.

9   Fuel gauge sender unit – removal and installation

1   Remove the fuel tank, as described in Section 6.
2   Turn the locking ring of the tank sender using a special wrench (Fig. 3.7). Alternatively, turn the ring using a plastic-headed hammer and a drift of non-sparking material.
3   After removing the locking ring, lift the sender unit out of the tank, taking care not to bend the float arm.
4   Installation is the reverse of removal, but use a new sealing gasket and ensure that the mating surfaces for the gasket are clean and undamaged.

10   Carburettor (UK) – removal and installation

1   Remove the air cleaner as described in Section 2 (photo).
2   Disconnect the throttle and choke linkage from the carburettor.
3   Disconnect and plug the fuel hoses and evaporation control hoses from the carburettor.
4   Disconnect the vacuum pipe and the fuel cut-off solenoid connections from the carburettor.
5   Unscrew and remove the carburettor flange mounting nuts and lift the carburettor off the inlet manifold.
6   Remove the carburettor insulator.
7   Installation is the reverse of removal. Use a new gasket between the manifold and the insulator and a new O-ring between the insulator and the carburettor flange. After installing the carburettor, install the spring washers over the plain washers, the concave side of the spring washers facing down. Check the throttle and choke cables for correct operation.

11   Carburettor (UK) – dismantling and reassembly

1   Dismantling of the carburettor is not recommended and should not normally be necessary. If it is dismantled (Fig. 3.8) the following points should be noted.
2   Take great care to ensure that any hand tools used are of exactly the right size for the fasteners to be used.
3   Dismantle the carburettor systematically and keep the components separated into the groups to which they belong.
4   Use compressed air to clean the jet orifices and fuel passages. **Do not** use wire, and do not attempt to dismantle the throttle and choke valves from their shafts.

10.1 Removing the air cleaner from the carburettor (UK models)

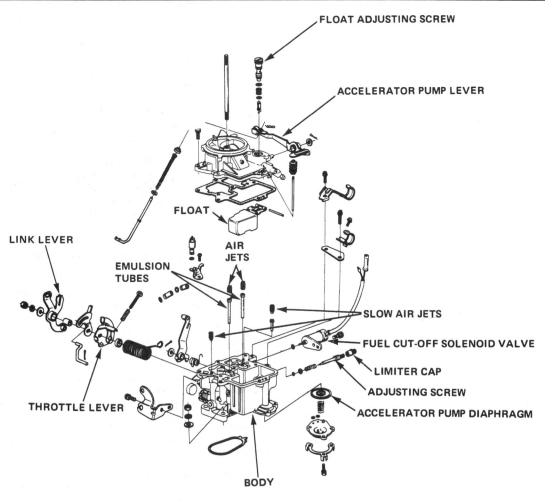

Fig. 3.8 Carburettor (UK) components (Sec 11)

5   Dismantle the carburettor in a clean area and use only petrol, or a proprietary carburettor cleaning fluid, for cleaning.
6   When reassembling, use new gaskets and renew any parts as sets if so required in the parts list.

12.12 Throttle stop (idle speed) screw (arrowed)

12 Carburettor (UK) – adjustments

Float level adjustment
1   Remove the air cleaner, disconnect the pipes from the carburettor upper part and disconnect the accelerator pump lever.
2   Remove the screws from the carburettor upper part and remove the upper part and its gasket.
3   Hold the upper part so that the float hangs vertically and measure the clearance between the float tab and the end of the needle valve.
4   If the clearance is outside the limit shown in Fig. 3.9 when the distance from the gasket to the centre of the float is as given in the Specifications, adjust the clearance by turning the adjusting screw in, or out.
5   After making the adjustment, use paint to lock the screw in position.

Accelerator pump adjustment
6   Measure the clearance between the tang on the accelerator pump lever and the stop on the carburettor body (Fig. 3.10).
7   If the clearance is not as given in the Specifications, bend the tang to obtain the correct clearance.

Choke relief valve adjustment
8   If the engine is difficult to start in cold weather, or if it is impossible to drive the car when the choke is operating, increase the tension of the relief spring.
9   To do this, unhook the end of the spring from the choke lever and install the hook of the spring in its next strongest position (Fig. 3.11). Restore the original setting when the weather improves.

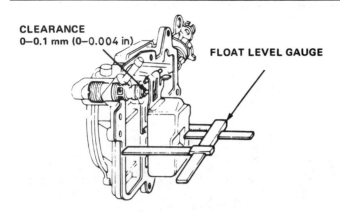

Fig. 3.9 Float level adjustment (UK) (Sec 12)

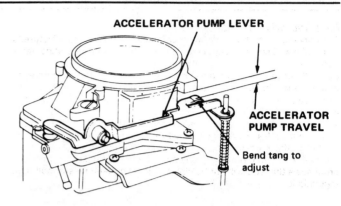

Fig. 3.10 Accelerator pump adjustment (UK) (Sec 12)

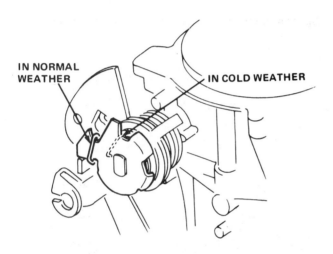

Fig. 3.11 Choke adjustment (UK) (Sec 12)

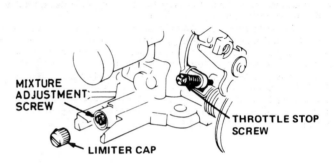

Fig. 3.12 Idle speed and mixture adjustment (UK) (Sec 12)

Idle speed and mixture adjustment

10 Ensure that the ignition timing and valve clearances are correct and that the engine is at normal operating temperature.

CO meter method

11 The most satisfactory way of making the adjustment is with a CO meter. Connect the CO meter in accordance with its manufacturer's instructions.

12 Start the engine and check that the idle speed is as given in the Specifications. If necessary adjust the idle speed by turning the throttle stop screw (photo).

13 Remove the limiter cap from the mixture adjustment screw and turn the screw until the CO level is at a minimum, or complies with local regulations.

14 When the adjustment is satisfactory, check the idle speed and refit the limiter cap.

Idle drop method

15 To adjust idle speed and mixture without a CO meter, start the engine and run it to normal operating temperature.

16 Remove the limiter cap and turn the mixture adjustment screw and the throttle adjusting screw a few degrees at a time until the smoothest idle is obtained under the following conditions. The headlights and the cooling fan must be switched off and the engine running at 800 rpm in neutral for manual transmission, and at 770 rpm in gear for Hondamatic transmission.

17 Having obtained the best idle, turn the mixture adjusting screw clockwise until the engine idle speed drops to 750 rpm.

18 Replace the limiter cap.

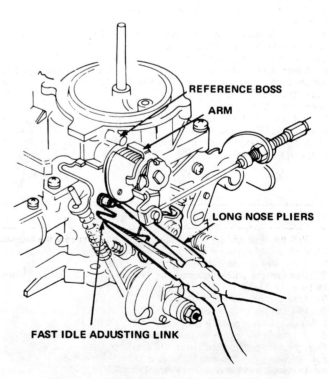

Fig. 3.13 Fast idle adjustment (UK) (Sec 12)

Fast idle adjustment

19 Connect a tachometer in accordance with its manufacturer's instructions. Start the engine and run it to normal operating temperature.

20 Pull out the choke knob to its full detent. Check that the reference arm on the choke lever lines up with the reference boss on the carburettor and if necessary operate the choke knob to achieve alignment (Fig. 3.13).

21 Note the fast idle speed, which should be between 1600 and cial equipment and any adjustments which the owner makes should be limited to those described.

Check also before making any adjustment or breaking any tamper-proof seals that you will not be violating local or national anti-pollution regulations.

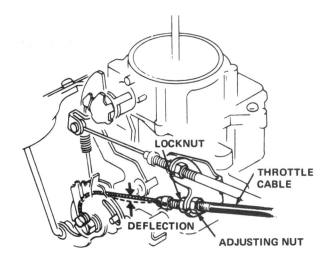

Fig. 3.14 Throttle cable adjustment. UK shown, US models are similar (Sec 13)

13 Throttle cable – adjustment

1   Remove the air cleaner to give better access to the cable adjuster and also to be able to see the movement of the throttle valve.

2   Press the throttle pedal to ensure that the cable operates smoothly and without sticking throughout its range.

3   Check the cable free play at the throttle linkage. It should be possible to deflect the cable $\frac{3}{16}$ to $\frac{3}{8}$ in (4 to 10 mm) without the throttle valve moving (Fig. 3.14). If the deflection is not within this range, loosen the locknut and turn the adjusting nut until the correct deflection is obtained. Tighten the locknut when adjustment is correct.

4   After making the adjustment, have an assistant press the accelerator pedal to the floor and then release it several times. Check that the throttle valve opens fully when the pedal is depressed and that it returns to its idling stop when the pedal is released.

14 Choke cable (UK) – adjustment

1   Remove the air cleaner to give better access to the cable adjuster and also to be able to see the movement of the choke valve.

2   Check that the choke cable operates smoothly and without sticking throughout its range.

3   Push the choke knob in fully and check that the choke butterfly valve is fully open.

4   If the butterfly valve does not open fully, slacken the locknut and turn the cable adjusting nut (Fig. 3.15) until the butterfly touches the positioning stop tab (Fig. 3.16).

5   When the butterfly fully open position is correct, turn the adjusting nut until the cable has no deflection and then loosen the nut until the cable deflects 0.20 to 0.24 in (5 to 6 mm). Tighten the locknut when adjustment is correct.

6   Pull the choke knob out fully and check that the choke butterfly valve closes fully. If the valve does not close fully, check that the valve shaft is not binding and also check that the butterfly valve return spring is operating properly.

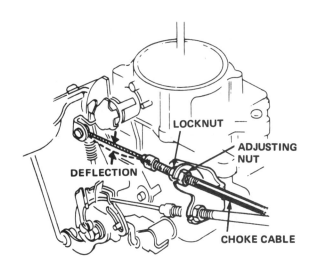

Fig. 3.15 Choke cable adjustment (UK) (Sec 14)

15 Throttle cable – removal and installation

1   Pull the boot off the end of the outer cable. Unscrew the locknut from the end of the outer cable and then pull the outer cable back until the cable can be slid out of the throttle bracket.

2   Release the cable end from its hole in the throttle link on the carburettor (Fig. 3.17).

3   Free the cable from the bracket on the valve cover.

4   Release the other end of the cable from the hole in the upper end of the accelerator pedal lever.

5   At the point in the engine compartment where the cable goes through the front bulkhead, turn the grommet through 90° and then pull the cable through into the engine compartment.

6   Installation is the reverse of removal. Apply sealant to the mating surface of the grommet before inserting it into the bulkhead. On completion of installation, adjust the cable.

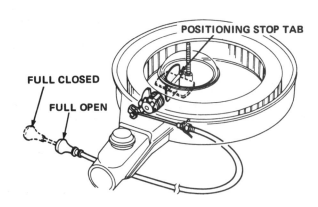

Fig. 3.16 Choke opening stop (UK) (Sec 14)

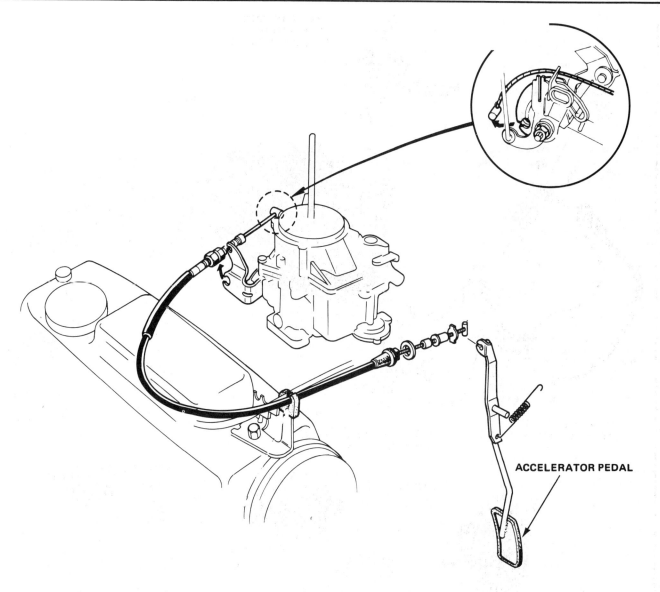

Fig. 3.17 Typical throttle cable installation (Sec 15)

ACCELERATOR PEDAL

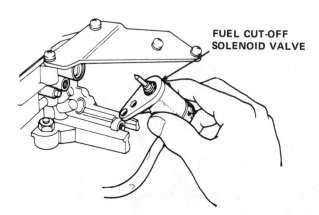

FUEL CUT-OFF
SOLENOID VALVE

Fig. 3.18 Fuel cut-off solenoid valve removal (Sec 16)

16 Fuel cut-off solenoid valve – testing

1   The fuel cut-off solenoid valve on UK models blocks fuel to the idle circuit when the engine is switched off and so prevents the engine from running on. US model carburettors have two such valves, one (mixture cut-off) blocking the primary idle circuit and the other (main fuel cut-off) blocking the primary main jet (Fig. 3.19). The procedure below applies to all valves.
2   If the engine runs roughly or erratically at idling, or if the engine runs on after it has been switched off, the valve may be defective.
3   To test the valve, remove the screw(s) securing the valve to the carburettor and pull it off its mounting peg (Fig. 3.18).
4   Hold the casing of the valve against a clean part of the engine to obtain a good earth connection and then have an assistant turn the ignition key on. *It is important that the valve is earthed effectively before the ignition is turned on, otherwise there is a danger of sparking and fire.* When the valve is energized, the needle should be seen to retract.
5   If the valve is satisfactory, check the valve seat and the carburettor passage for blockage.

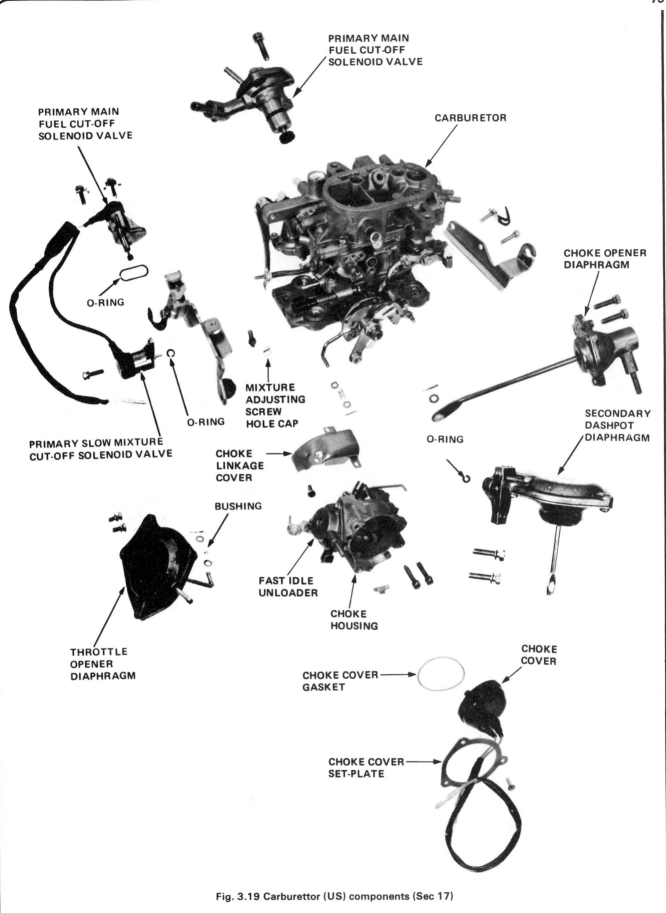

PRIMARY MAIN
FUEL CUT-OFF
SOLENOID VALVE

PRIMARY MAIN
FUEL CUT-OFF
SOLENOID VALVE

CARBURETOR

O-RING

CHOKE OPENER
DIAPHRAGM

MIXTURE
ADJUSTING
SCREW
HOLE CAP

O-RING

O-RING

SECONDARY
DASHPOT
DIAPHRAGM

PRIMARY SLOW MIXTURE
CUT-OFF SOLENOID VALVE

CHOKE
LINKAGE
COVER

BUSHING

FAST IDLE
UNLOADER

CHOKE
HOUSING

THROTTLE
OPENER
DIAPHRAGM

CHOKE
COVER

CHOKE COVER
GASKET

CHOKE COVER
SET-PLATE

3

Fig. 3.19 Carburettor (US) components (Sec 17)

6   If the valve does not operate, connect a 12 volt test lamp between its connecting wire and chassis earth and see if the lamp lights when the ignition is turned on. If the lamp lights, the valve is defective and a new one must be installed.

17 Carburettor (US) – general

To comply with emission control regulations, the carburettor used on US models is complex (Fig. 3.19). Although specific sub-assemblies which are suspected of being defective may be removed, general dismantling is not recommended. The majority of carburettor adjustments require special equipment and any adjustments which the owner makes should be limited to those described.

Check also before making any adjustment or breaking any tamper-proof seals that you will not be violating local or national anti-pollution regulations.

18 Automatic choke (US) – general description

1   The automatic choke mechanism controls both the position of the choke valve and the fast idle speed during warm-up. The mechanism comprises a bi-metal coil and heater, a choke opener, thermovalve and fast idle unloader and associated components.
2   The bi-metal coil, heater and controlling thermistor are mounted in the choke cover. The choke opener and fast idle unloader diaphragms are on the outside of the carburettor and the intake air sensor is in the air cleaner, with an associated resistor on the front bulkhead. A thermovalve, which controls the choke opener, is installed in the distributor housing.
3   When the engine is started, the choke opener pulls the choke open a small amount. Progressive opening of the choke is achieved by the voltage applied to the heater which affects the bi-metal coil, causing it to unwind and open the valve. The amount of opening is initially controlled by the heater temperature which, in turn, is controlled by a thermistor responding to air temperature.
4   Choke position is also affected by a thermovalve which increases the vacuum applied to the opener diaphragm as engine coolant temperature rises.
5   An additional variation to the rate of the bi-metal spring heating is produced by an air intake sensor, which switches an additional resistor into the heater circuit whenever the intake air is cooler than about 49°F (9°C). By reducing the rate of bi-metal spring heating in this way, choke opening time is increased.
6   When the engine coolant reaches its normal temperature, the engine thermosensor switches vacuum to the fast idle unloader and pulls the engine off fast idle.

19 Automatic choke (US) – testing

Choke tension and linkage

1   With the engine cold, remove the air cleaner and open and close the throttle fully to let the choke close.
2   Inspect the choke valve to see if it has closed. If the air temperature is below about 82°F (28°C) the choke should close completely. Above this temperature there will be a small amount of choke opening, but it should not be more than $\frac{1}{8}$ in (3 mm).
3   If the choke does not close completely, the choke spring or linkage may be defective. The covers of the choke mechanism and linkage are retained by rivets on later models. To remove such covers, drive the mandrel out of the centre of the rivets using a very thin punch and then carefully drill the rivets out.

Fast idle unloader — cold

4   With the engine cold, open and close the throttle fully to let the choke close and then start the engine.
5   If the engine does not run at fast idle, disconnect the fast idle unloader hose and check for vacuum, by putting a finger over the end of the hose. With the engine cold there should not be vacuum.
6   If the foregoing test indicates no vacuum, check the operation of the fast idle cam.
7   If vacuum is present with the engine cold, check that the thermostat has continuity between its terminals (Fig. 3.20). If it does not, renew the thermosensor.

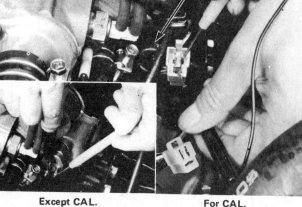

Except CAL.   For CAL.

Fig. 3.20 Checking adjustment continuity (Sec 19)

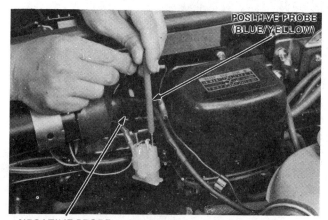

Fig. 3.21 Checking for voltage at the unloader solenoid valve (Sec 19)

Clean orifice with
0.5 mm (0.020 in.) drill

Fig. 3.22 Cleaning the choke opener orifice (Sec 19)

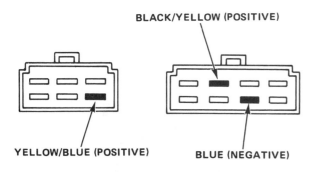

BLACK/YELLOW (POSITIVE)

YELLOW/BLUE (POSITIVE)   BLUE (NEGATIVE)

Fig. 3.23 Emission control box connector test points for fast idle unloader – 49 States and High Altitude (left), California (right) (Sec 19)

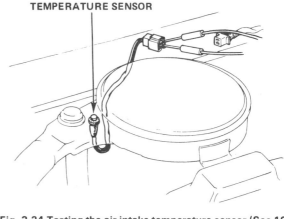

INTAKE AIR TEMPERATURE SENSOR

Fig. 3.24 Testing the air intake temperature sensor (Sec 19)

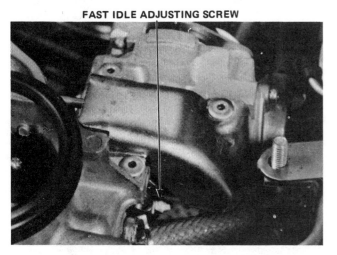

FAST IDLE ADJUSTING SCREW

Fig. 3.25 Fast idle adjusting screw (Sec 20)

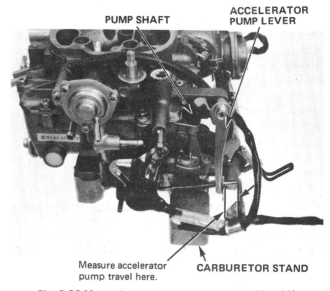

PUMP SHAFT   ACCELERATOR PUMP LEVER

Measure accelerator pump travel here.   CARBURETOR STAND

Fig. 3.26 Measuring accelerator pump travel (Sec 20)

3

8   If the thermosensor has continuity, check for voltage at the unloader solenoid valve (Fig. 3.21). If there is no voltage, check the wiring. If voltage is present, renew the unloader solenoid valve.

Choke opener
9   With the engine cold, open and close the throttle fully to let the choke close and then start the engine.
10   The choke should open partially. If it does not, the choke opener diaphragm is suspect and should be tested as follows.
11   Remove the two screws securing the choke opener to the carburettor and remove it. While holding a finger over the orifice in the choke opener, apply vacuum to its hose fitting until the opener rod comes to the end of its stroke. Hold the vacuum to see if the rod remains stationary, indicating that the diaphragm is satisfactory. If the diaphragm is perforated, install a new unit.
12   Release the vacuum and check that the rod is released. If it is not, clean the opener orifice.
13   If the choke opener is satisfactory and the choke does open partially, check the position of the tab on the choke lever. If the coolant temperature is below 52°F (11°C) the tab should not be in contact with the carburettor. If it is, disconnect the choke opener hose and if the tab still does not come off its stop, press down on the choke lever until it does. If it does not then remain off, clean the orifice in the choke opener with a 0.020 in (0.5 mm) drill (Fig. 3.22). If this does not cure the problem, renew the choke opener.
14   If, with the coolant temperature below 52°F (11°C) the tab is initially in contact, but comes off its stop when the choke opener hose is disconnected, clean the thermovalve filter. If this is not effective, renew the thermovalve.

Choke coil heater
15   With the engine cold, remove the air cleaner so that the operation of the choke valve is visible. Start the engine and allow it to run, observing whether or not the choke valve opens fully when the engine achieves normal operating temperature.
16   If it does not, check the linkage and if the choke still does not open, disconnect the air temperature sensor connector and check that there is battery voltage between the blue/white wire on the choke cover and vehicle ground. If there is battery voltage between the blue/white choke cover wire and ground, check that there is 2 to 4 volts between the choke cover red wire and ground. If there is not, the choke heater is open-circuited and the choke cover must be renewed.
17   If there is no voltage between the blue/white wire on the choke cover and ground, check the voltage regulator, fuse and wiring.

Fast idle unloader — hot
18   When the engine warms up, its speed should drop below 1400 rpm as the unloader pulls the internal choke linkage off the fast idle cam.
19   If the fast idle speed does not drop when the engine warms up, disconnect the hose from the unloader and check that vacuum is present, If there is no vacuum, check that voltage is being applied to the unloader solenoid valve by testing at the emission control box connector (Fig. 3.23). If voltage is present, the solenoid is defective and must be renewed.

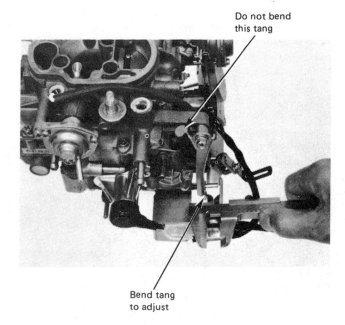

Do not bend
this tang

Bend tang
to adjust

Fig. 3.27 Adjusting accelerator pump travel (Sec 20)

20 If vacuum is present at the end of the vacuum pipe, check the
unloader for leaks. Also check the unloader rod and linkage for free
movement.

Intake air temperature sensor
21 Disconnect the intake air sensor connector and check for continuity between its terminals (Fig. 3.24).
22 If the air temperature is above about 73°F (23°C) there should be
continuity. There should not be continuity below 40°F (4.5°C).
23 If the operation of the sensor is not as specified, renew the sensor.

20 Carburettor (US) – adjustments

Float level adjustment
1 Float level adjustment is carried out with the engine running and
using special equipment.
2 If it is suspected that the float setting is incorrect, consult a Honda
authorised dealer.

Idle speed and mixture adjustment
3 The correct idle speeds are given in the Specifications. The
adjustment of idle speed and mixture requires the use of a propane
enrichment kit and should only be done by a Honda authorised dealer.

Fast idle adjustment
4 Run the engine until it attains normal operating temperature, then
stop the engine and connect a tachometer in accordance with its
manufacturer's instructions.
5 Disconnect the vacuum pipe from the fast idle unloader and plug
the pipe.
6 While holding the choke butterfly in the closed position, fully open
the throttle and then close it, so that the fast idle cam is engaged.
7 Start the engine, note the fast idle speed and compare it with the
Specifications.
8 If it is necessary to adjust the speed, turn the adjusting screw (Fig.
3.25). Reconnect the vacuum pipe on completion.

Accelerator pump adjustment
9 Before measuring the accelerator pump linkage travel, check that
the pump travels freely over its entire stroke and that the pump lever
is in contact with the pump shaft (Fig. 3.26).

10 Measure the gap between the tang on the bottom end of the
pump lever and its stop. If it is outside the specified limits, bend the
tang to achieve the correct setting (Fig. 3.27).

21 Emission control systems – general

1 The purpose of an emission control system is threefold.
2 Firstly the emission of fumes from the engine crankcase must be
controlled (see Chapter 1).
3 The evaporation of fumes from the fuel tank and carburettor must
be contained.
4 The elimination, as far as is possible, of noxious gases emitted
from the exhaust pipe must be arranged. This last condition is the most
complex and according to vehicle model and operating territory may
consist of some or all of the various systems described later.

22 Evaporative control system – description and testing

1 There are a number of features which prevent the escape to
atmosphere of fuel vapour.
2 The venting of the fuel tank is controlled by a two-way valve
described in Section 7. A liquid/vapour separator allows any liquid fuel
to return to the tank. The vapour passes to a canister of activated
charcoal, where it is absorbed temporarily and later drawn into the
carburettor and burned in the engine (Fig. 3.28).
3 An air vent cut-off diaphragm operates a valve which blocks the air
vent passages of the carburettor when the engine is not running. The
fuel vapour in the float chambers is vented to the charcoal canister.
4 A purge control valve, which is solenoid-operated and is controlled
by a thermosensor, causes the charcoal canister to be purged when
engine temperature reaches a preset level.
5 Solenoid valves incorporated in the carburettor cut off the main
and slow primary fuel metering systems when the engine is not
running and prevent any fuel from entering the carburettor bore.
6 On later Californian models an additional solenoid valve controls a
vacuum supply to the power valve to close the power valve and cut off
the fuel passages when the ignition is switched off.
7 Periodically inspect the condition and security of all the hoses of
the system.
8 To test the system the engine must be cold so that the
thermosensor has continuity. Disconnect the upper hose from the
purge control diaphragm (Fig. 3.29), start the engine and allow it to
idle. Test for vacuum at the end of the hose which has been
disconnected. If no vacuum can be felt, the system is satisfactory. If
vacuum is present, check the purge control valve.

23 Air intake control – description and testing

1 The system maintains a uniform temperature of about 100°F
(38°C) inside the air cleaner so that the carburettor receives air of
almost constant temperature regardless of outside temperature.
2 To test the system, remove the air cleaner cover and filter element.
With the engine cold, crank the engine for about 5 seconds. The air
control door (Fig. 3.30) should rise during cranking and remain fully
open for at least 3 seconds after cranking.
3 If the door does not operate as above, disconnect and plug the
hose to the air bleed valve. Check that the door is not binding and then
repeat the test. If the door operates correctly, renew the air bleed
valve.
4 To check the air control diaphragm, remove the deflector plate and
disconnect the hose from the diaphragm. Raise the air control door
manually, block the inlet pipe of the diaphragm unit and release the
door. If the diaphragm is satisfactory, the door will stay up for as long
as the inlet pipe is blocked.

24 Exhaust emission control system – general

1 Exhaust emissions are controlled by the design of the CVCC
engine and by additional systems. A total of six additional systems are
available, the systems actually installed depending upon production
data and the market for which the vehicle was intended.

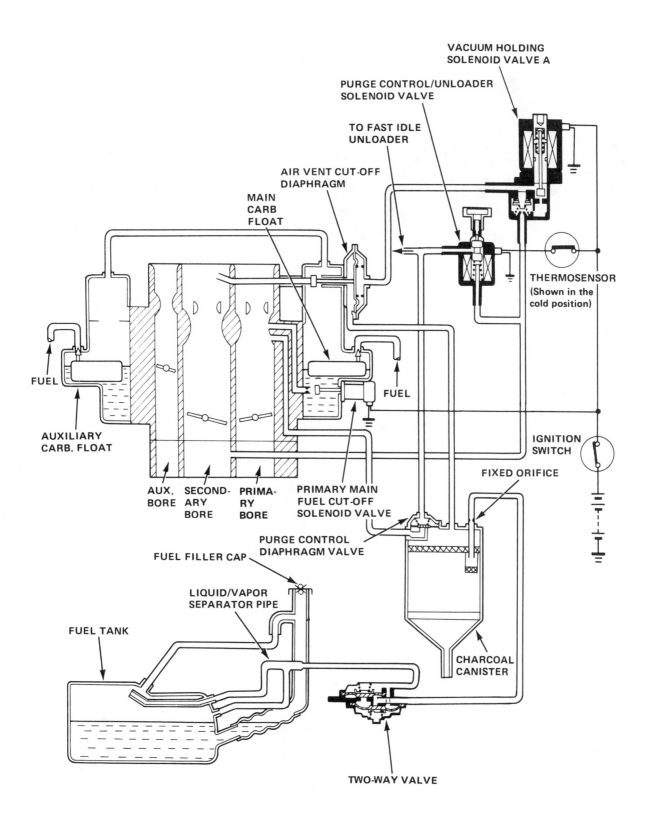

Fig. 3.28 Evaporative control system schematic (Sec 22)

3

Fig. 3.29 Purge control diaphragm valve (Sec 22)

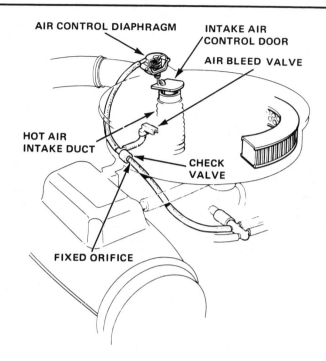

Fig. 3.30 Air intake control system (Sec 23)

2   The CVCC engine has two combustion chambers for each cylinder. On intake, a rich fuel/air mixture enters a pre-combustion chamber, which is to one side of the main combustion chamber. At the same time a very lean mixture enters the main chamber in the conventional way. Under compression, a moderate fuel/air mixture forms at the boundary between the pre-combustion chamber and the main chamber. The spark plug, which is in the pre-combustion chamber, ignites the rich mixture, which in turn ignites the moderate mixture and then the lean main charge.

3   The additional systems available are:

  (a) *Ignition control*
  (b) *Throttle controls*
  (c) *Anti-afterburn valve*
  (d) *Air jet control*
  (e) *Exhaust gas recirculation*
  (f) *Catalytic converter*

Further details of these are given in the following Sections.

25 Ignition control system – description and testing

Description

1   The ignition control system supplements the centrifugal advance mechanism of the distributor by a vacuum control system which responds to engine speed, load and (on some models) coolant temperature. On all except certain Californian models, vacuum is applied regardless of temperature, and may be drawn from the intake manifold or from a tapping above the primary throttle butterfly.

2   On 1981 1300 Californian models with manual transmission, vacuum is applied via a solenoid valve which is only energised when engine speed is above a certain level, **or** when engine coolant is below a certain temperature. When **both** of these conditions are not met (low speed, high temperature) the valve is de-energised and vacuum advance is not applied.

3   On 1981 1300 Californian models with automatic transmission, and on 1980 1300 Californian manual models, the system has no speed sensor. Vacuum advance is applied only when the engine coolant is below a certain temperature.

4   On 1981 1500 Californian models with automatic transmission, the distributor is equipped with a vacuum unit having both advance and retard connections. Vacuum is applied to the advance side of the unit from above the primary throttle butterfly at all times. Vacuum to the retard side of the unit is derived from the carburettor insulator, and is only applied when the engine coolant is above a certain tem-

perature. The overall effect is to retard ignition timing at idle when the engine has warmed up.

Testing

5   Testing of the distributor vacuum unit is covered in Chapter 4.

6   On Californian models with temperature dependent components, the thermosensor should show continuity when the engine is cold, and open-circuit when it is hot.

7   If a speed sensor is installed, this should produce a 12 volt signal at the control box blue/white wire when indicated road speed is above 15 mph. Below 10 mph there should be no signal.

8   The solenoid valve, when present, may be tested by applying vacuum and voltage to the appropriate connections and checking that a change of state occurs.

9   Before condemning expensive components, make sure that all vacuum hoses are in good condition and securely connected, and that vacuum ports are clear.

26 Throttle control systems – description and testing

1   Two interrelated systems are used to control excessive emissions of exhaust gas hydrocarbons during periods of deceleration, or when shifting gears and the throttle is closed.

2   The first system is essentially a throttle positioner in which a speed sensor in the speedometer head signals (at roadspeeds above approximately 15 mph/24 kph) a solenoid valve which opens and applies vacuum to the throttle control valve. When this vacuum pressure exceeds a preset value during deceleration, the throttle control valve opens and in turn the throttle controller diaphragm opens the throttle into the carburettor a fixed amount to improve combustion.

3   When the vehicle speed drops to 10 mph (16 kph) or the vacuum pressure drops below the preset value of the throttle control valve, this valve closes and the residual vacuum in the system is destroyed by the entry of air at atmospheric pressure through the valve orifice.

4   The second system incorporates a dashpot to restrict the closing speed of the throttle. The dashpot solenoid valve actuated by the manifold vacuum displaces air from the rear of the throttle controller diaphragm and so prevents the throttle plate closing too quickly.

5   During the period of throttle closure, the flow of air is restricted by the dashpot solenoid valve orifice and flows to both the carburettor

and the throttle controller diaphragm. When the throttle valve plate finally closes, and blocks the carburettor vacuum port then air flows only to the throttle controller diaphragm.

6   Any malfunction in the system may be due to loose hoses or electrical connections. Testing of individual components cannot be carried out without special equipment.

27 Anti-afterburn valve – description and testing

1   When the manifold vacuum increases suddenly, such as during acceleration, the anti-afterburn valve admits fresh air to the inlet manifold. The valve is installed on 1980 1300 models, and on all 1981 Californian models.

2   The increase in vacuum pulls the diaphragm in the valve downwards (Fig. 3.31). Airflow from the air chamber to the sensing chamber is restricted by an orifice creating a pressure differential on the diaphragm until after a few seconds the pressure is equalised, the spring overcomes the force on the diaphragm and the valve closes.

3   To test the valve, remove the air cleaner cover and element. Start the engine and allow it to idle.

4   Place a finger over the air inlet tube (Fig. 3.32) and feel for vacuum. No vacuum should be present when the engine is idling and if there is, the valve is defective and must be renewed.

5   Quickly raise engine speed to about 3500 rpm and close the throttle suddenly. Vacuum should be felt at the air inlet pipe during acceleration and for a few seconds afterwards. If there is no vacuum, check for blockages. If there are no blockages, it indicates that the valve is defective and must be renewed.

28 Air jet control – description and testing

1   The air jet controller, fitted to Californian and High Altitude models, varies the amount of air flow to the air jets of the carburettor according to the atmospheric pressure.

2   As altitude increases, the atmospheric pressure drops and the bellows expand to open the air jet controller (Fig. 3.33). This allows additional air to pass to the air jets, to maintain optimum airflow.

3   Testing the valve is not possible without special equipment.

29 Exhaust gas recirculation system – description and testing

1   The exhaust gas recirculation (EGR) system is designed to reduce the oxides of nitrogen in the exhaust, by recirculating exhaust gas through the inlet manifold.

2   Oxides of nitrogen in the exhaust gas are greatest when the engine is at normal operating temperature and is accelerating or cruising, and the EGR valve has an associated control system (Fig. 3.34) which ensures that exhaust gas is only recirculated during these conditions and not when the engine is cold, idling or decelerating.

3   The EGR control valve is operated by vacuum from the carburettor port, so that the volume of gas recirculated is proportional to engine load. The vacuum signal is ported above the idle throttle valve position so that there is no operating signal when the engine is idling.

4   A thermosensor in the coolant system controls the vacuum signal to the EGR valve via a solenoid valve. When the engine is cold, the thermosensor energises the solenoid valve and cuts off the vacuum supply which operates the EGR valve.

5   The vacuum supply is further controlled by a second valve, which is normally closed and opens only when manifold vacuum reaches a preset level. A vacuum-operated switch, which is operated when inlet manifold rises during deceleration, also controls the electrical supply to the solenoid valve. The solenoid valve is thereby energised during deceleration and the EGR valve is cut off.

6   On later Californian models a barometric switch is also incorporated so that the EGR valve is closed at high altitudes.

7   The testing of individual components of the EGR system requires speical equipment, but the operation of the system can be checked in the following way if a vacuum gauge and voltmeter are available.

8   Ensure that the engine is at normal operating temperature. Disconnect the vacuum hose from the EGR valve and connect a vacuum gauge to the hose (Fig. 3.35). Connect the positive probe of the voltmeter to the blue/white terminal of the control box connector and connect the negative probe to chassis earth.

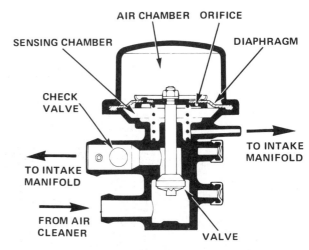

Fig. 3.31 Anti-afterburn valve (Sec 27)

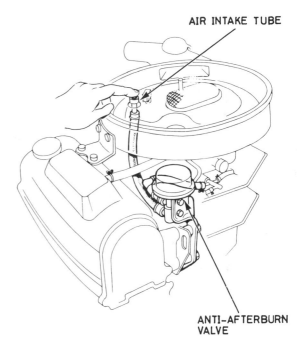

Fig. 3.32 Anti-afterburn valve testing (Sec 27)

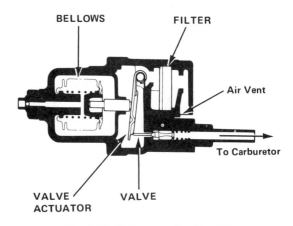

Fig. 3.33 Air jet controller (Sec 28)

3

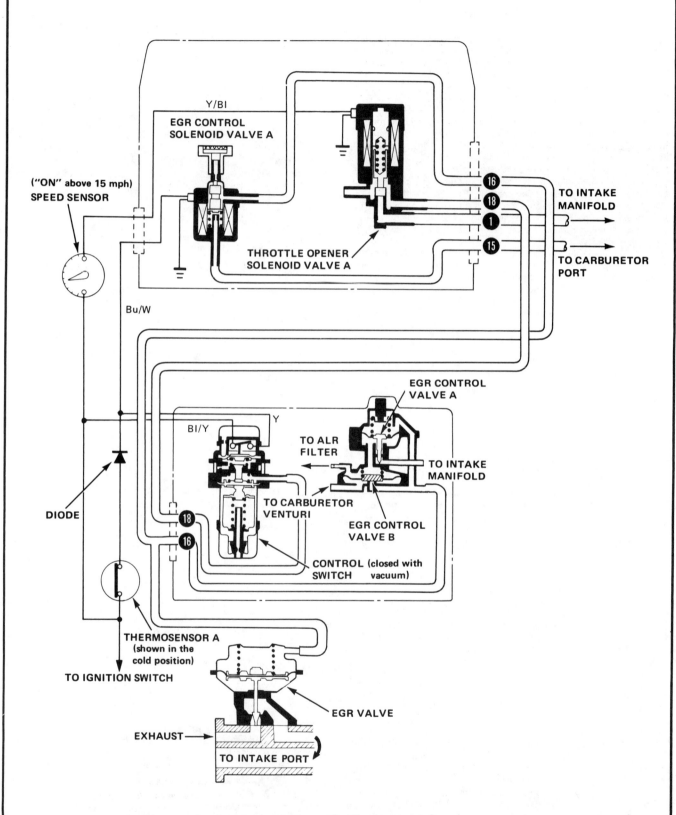

80

Fig. 3.34 Typical EGR control system schematic (Sec 29)

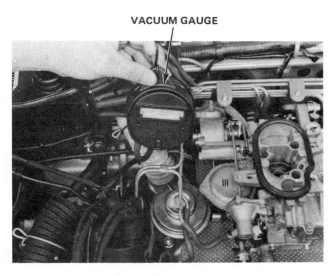

Fig. 3.35 EGR system testing (Sec 29)

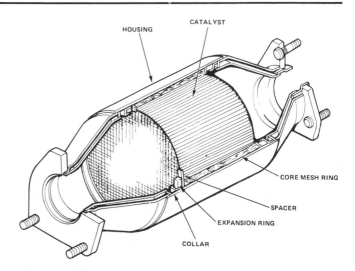

Fig. 3.36 Catalytic converter sectional view (Sec 30)

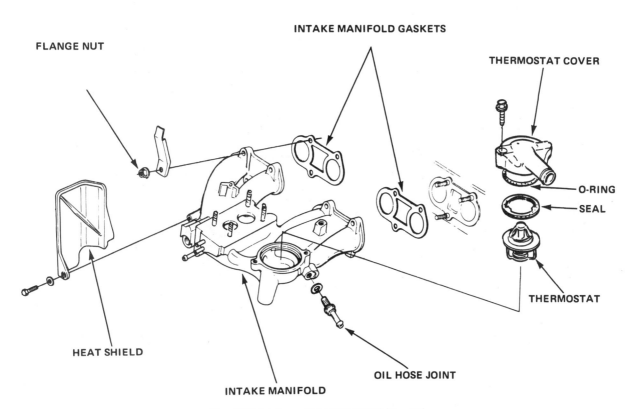

Fig. 3.37 Inlet manifold (UK 1300) (Sec 31)

9   Jack up the front of the car and support it on firmly based stands, chock the rear wheels and apply the handbrake firmly.

10 Start the engine and allow it to run until the cooling fan comes on, then check the vacuum and voltage according to the following table:

Condition	Vacuum at EGR hose	Voltage at blue/white wire
Idle	*No*	*No*
4500 rpm	*Yes*	*No*
Rapid acceleration above 15 mph*	*Yes*	*No*
Deceleration above 15 mph*	*No*	*Yes*

*Car in 2nd gear (manual transmission) or 2 (automatic transmission).

11 If the readings are not correct, have the system examined by a Honda authorised dealer.

30 Catalytic converter – description and testing

1   The catalytic converter is inserted in the exhaust system and oxidises any unburned hydrocarbons in the exhaust gas. It is fitted to all except 1980 1300 models.

2   If a catalytic converter is installed it is important that only unleaded fuel is used, because lead will poison the catalyst and render it useless.

3   A converter will only act effectively if the carburettor and ignition systems are adjusted correctly.

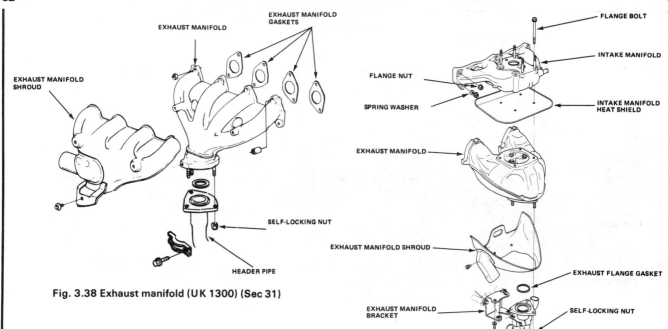

Fig. 3.38 Exhaust manifold (UK 1300) (Sec 31)

Fig. 3.41 Manifold assembly (US 1300). Non-EGR type shown (Sec 31)

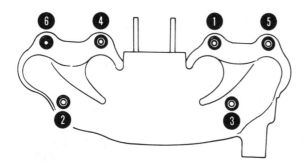

Fig. 3.39 Inlet manifold tightening sequence (UK 1300) (Sec 31)

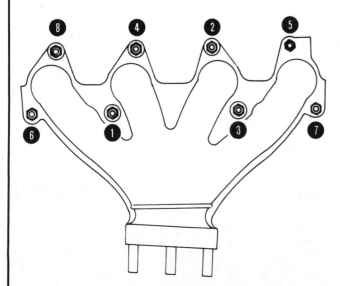

Fig. 3.40 Exhaust manifold tightening sequence (UK 1300) (Sec 31)

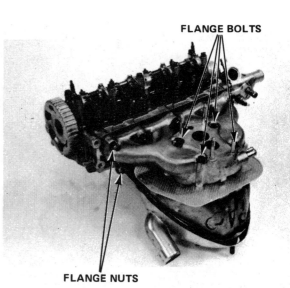

FLANGE BOLTS

FLANGE NUTS

Fig. 3.42 Manifold tightening sequence (US 1300) (Sec 31)

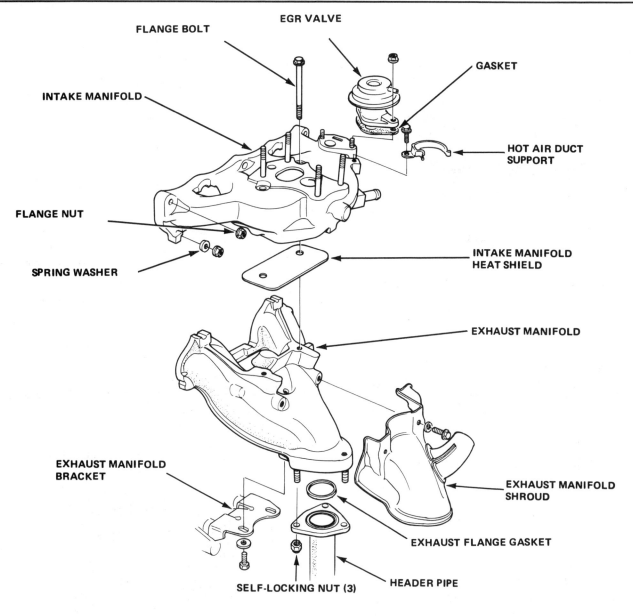

FLANGE BOLT

EGR VALVE

INTAKE MANIFOLD

GASKET

HOT AIR DUCT SUPPORT

FLANGE NUT

SPRING WASHER

INTAKE MANIFOLD HEAT SHIELD

EXHAUST MANIFOLD

EXHAUST MANIFOLD BRACKET

EXHAUST MANIFOLD SHROUD

EXHAUST FLANGE GASKET

SELF-LOCKING NUT (3)

HEADER PIPE

Fig. 3.43 Manifold assembly (US 1500). EGR type shown (Sec 31)

4 Carburettors can easily be damaged by mechanical shocks and it is important to avoid hitting them on ground projections, or dropping them if they are removed from the vehicle. It is also important to note that their casings achieve a very high temperature which can cause severe burns if the casing is touched and can lead to a fire if the vehicle is driven on long dry grass.

5 To test the effectiveness of a converter requires special equipment, but it may be removed from the vehicle and inspected visually for signs of clogging of the element, cracks, or other damage. If the converter is in bad condition, install a new one.

31 Manifolds and exhaust system – removal and installation

Manifolds

1 The inlet and exhaust manifolds are conventional and can be removed independently of each other. After removing the manifolds, check them for cracks and damage and renew if necessary.

2 When installing, ensure that the mating surfaces are clean and free from damage, and use new gaskets. Tighten the bolts to the specified torque in the sequence shown (Figs. 3.39 and 3.40).

1300 US models

3 The inlet and exhaust manifolds are combined and must be removed as an assembly and then separated.

4 Because the nuts between the middle runners of the inlet manifold are difficult to reach, it may not be possible to remove them without the use of a special tool (Honda tool No 83023), or without first removing the cylinder head with the manifold attached.

5 When installing the manifolds, the following procedure must be used so that the risk of leakage is minimised.

6 Assemble the manifolds, using a new heat shield between them, and install the flange bolts finger tight.

7 Check that the cylinder head studs are clean and straight and that the nuts open freely on them and then install new gaskets onto the studs.

8 Install the manifold assembly and retain it with the end nuts and washers. The dished side of the washers should be towards the cylinder head and the nuts should be screwed on finger tight.

3

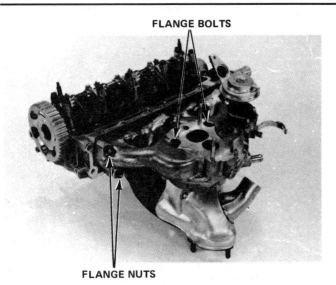

FLANGE BOLTS

FLANGE NUTS

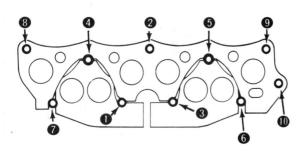

Fig. 3.44 Manifold tightening sequence (US 1500) (Sec 31)

9   Install the remaining washers by suspending them on a wire hook and pushing them on to the studs with a screwdriver.
10 Install the nuts in a similar manner and start them on the threads by turning them with a screwdriver.
11 Tighten all nuts to 7 lbf ft (10 Nm) in the sequence shown (Fig. 3.42) and then, using the same sequence, tighten them to the specified torque.
12 Tighten the flange bolts to the specified torque, in diagonal pairs.
1500 US models
13 Although the manifolds are different (Fig. 3.43), the procedure is essentially the same as for the 1300 models.
14 Installation is also similar to the procedure for the 1300 models except that there are only two flange bolts (Fig. 3.44).

Exhaust system
15 Although the exhaust system of all models is basically similar, there are several constructional differences in the systems of different models.
16 Except on systems which include a catalytic converter, the exhaust system is in two pieces with a front pipe which incorporates a small expansion chamber, and a combined tailpipe and main silencer.
17 The exhaust pipe and silencer should be examined at regular intervals because a defective system can allow poisonous exhaust gases to enter the car, besides causing excessive noise. Engine efficiency is also impaired by a choked or leaking exhaust.
18 Small defects can be repaired by using a proprietary exhaust repair putty, or by welding. Alternatively, either part of the system can be renewed after disconnecting the flange joints and flexible supports.
19 Before attempting to undo the flange joint of the exhaust manifold, saturate the studs and nuts in penetrating oil, or a proprietary dismantling fluid. Use a correctly fitting socket spanner on the nuts, but **do not** attempt to release the nuts by using an impact spanner.
20 When installing an exhaust system, install the complete system with all nuts finger tight. After checking that the system is free from strain and has adequate clearance from the body at all points, tighten all the nuts, starting at the manifold flange and working towards the tailpipe. Check the tightness of the flange nuts and the mountings after the engine has been run and the exhaust has warmed up.
21 On systems including a catalytic converter, refer to Figs. 3.48 and 3.49 for installation details.

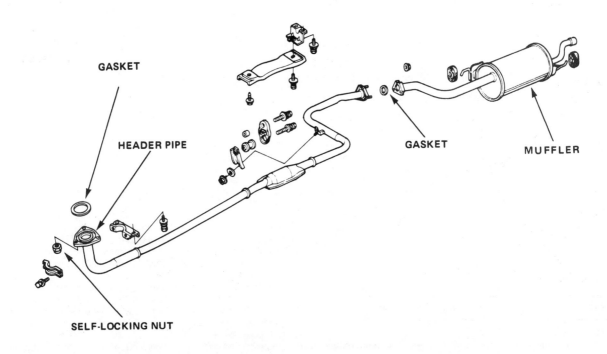

GASKET

HEADER PIPE

GASKET   MUFFLER

SELF-LOCKING NUT

Fig. 3.45 Exhaust system (UK 1300) (Sec 31)

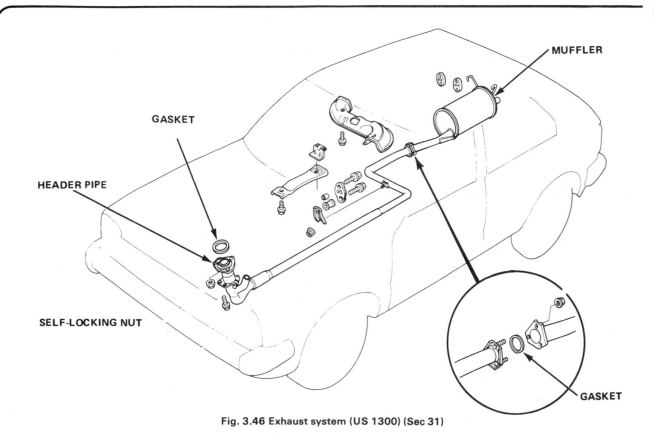

Fig. 3.46 Exhaust system (US 1300) (Sec 31)

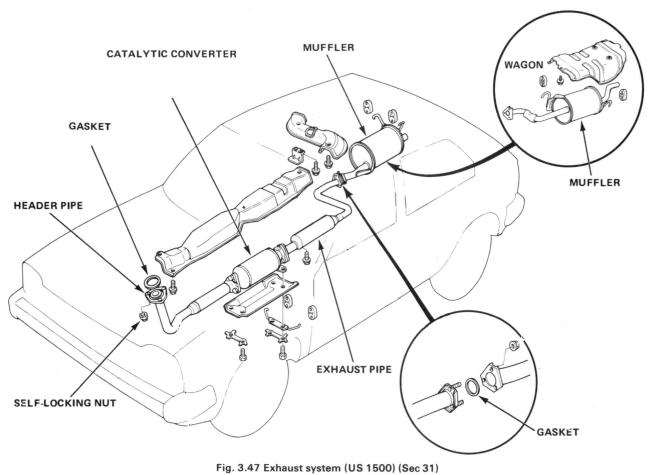

Fig. 3.47 Exhaust system (US 1500) (Sec 31)

3

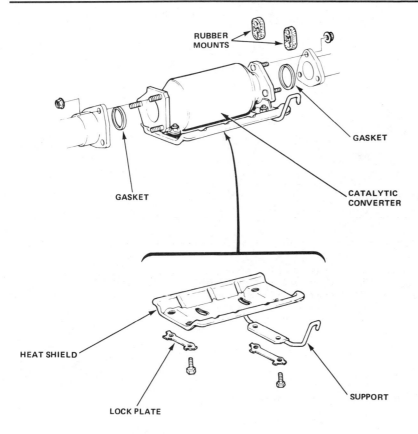

RUBBER MOUNTS

GASKET

GASKET

CATALYTIC CONVERTER

HEAT SHIELD

LOCK PLATE

SUPPORT

Fig. 3.48 Catalytic converter installation (Sec 31)

TOP

RIGHT SIDE

LEFT SIDE

①　②　③

Fig. 3.49 Catalytic converter tightening sequence (Sec 31)

---

32 Fault diagnosis – fuel system

Unsatisfactory engine performance and excessive fuel consumption are not necessarily the fault of the fuel system or carburettor. In fact they more commonly occur as a result of ignition and timing faults. Before acting on the following it is necessary to check the ignition system first. Even though a fault may lie in the fuel system it will be difficult to trace unless the ignition is correct. The faults below, therefore, assume that this has been attended to first (where appropriate).

Symptom	Reason(s)
Smell of petrol when engine is stopped	Leaking fuel lines or unions Leaking fuel tank
Smell of petrol when engine is idling	Leaking fuel lines unions between pump and carburettor Overflow of fuel from float chamber due to wrong level setting, ineffective needle valve or punctured float
Excessive fuel consumption for reasons not covered by leaks or float chamber faults	Worn jets Incorrect jets Sticking mechanism on choke
Difficult starting, uneven running, lack of power, cutting out	One or more jets blocked or restricted Float chamber fuel level too low or needle valve sticking Fuel pump not delivering sufficient fuel

Chapter 4 Ignition system

Contents

Specifications

General

System type	Breakerless distributor, 12 volt coil
Firing order	1,3,4,2
Location of No 1 cylinder	Nearest crankshaft pulley

Distributor
Make and type:

UK models	Hitachi or Toyodenso, with separate igniter
US models	Hitachi, with integral igniter
Direction of rotation	Anti-clockwise

Ignition timing
UK models:

Manual transmission	2° BTDC (red mark) at 750 ± 50 rpm
Hondamatic transmission	8° BTDC (yellow mark) at 750 ± 50 rpm

US models, 1980:

All California and High Altitude models	0° BTDC (white mark) at 750 ± 50 rpm
49 States, 1300 models	2° BTDC (red mark) at 750 ± 50 rpm
49 States, 1500 Hondamatic models	0° BTDC (white mark) at 750 ± 50 rpm
49 States, 1500 Hatchback, manual	15° BTDC (red mark) at 750 ± 50 rpm
49 States, 1500 Wagon, manual	10° BTDC (red mark) at 750 ± 50 rpm

US models, 1981*:

All 1300 models	2° BTDC (red mark) at 800 ± 50 rpm (manual) or 750 ± 50 rpm (automatic)
1500 models, California	2° ATDC (red mark) at 750 ± 50 rpm
1500 models, 49 States, automatic	2° ATDC (red mark) at 750 ± 50 rpm
1500 Hatchback, 49 States, manual	10° BTDC (red mark) at 750 ± 50 rpm
1500 Wagon, 49 States, manual	4° BTDC (red mark) at 750 ± 50 rpm

*All ± 2°

Ignition coil

Primary (LT) winding resistance	1.0 to 1.3 ohms at 70°F (20°C)
Secondary (HT) winding resistance	7400 to 11 000 ohms at 70°F (20°C)

Spark plugs
Type:

UK models, normal driving	NGK BPR 5ES, ND W16 EXR-U, or equivalent
UK models, extensive high speed driving	NGK BPR 6ES, ND W20 EXR-U, or equivalent
US models, 1980, 1300	ND W20 ES-L11, or equivalent
US models, 1980, 1500	NGK B7EB-11, or equivalent
US models, 1981	NGK B6EB-11, ND W20 ES-L11, or equivalent

Electrode gap:

UK models	0.028 to 0.031 in (0.7 to 0.8 mm)
US models	0.039 to 0.043 in (1.0 to 1.1 mm)

4

HT leads
Resistance .... 25 000 ohms (per lead) maximum

Torque wrench settings

	lbf ft	Nm
Distributor clamp bolt	10	14
Spark plugs	13	18

1   General description

The ignition system is responsible for providing a spark at the spark plugs to ignite the compressed fuel/air mixture in the cylinders. On all Honda Civic models covered by this manual, the system is of the breakerless type, the function of the contact breaker points in a 'conventional' system being undertaken by an electronic pulse generator and a transistorised igniter unit. On UK models the igniter unit is external to the distributor; on US models the igniter unit is contained within the distributor.

The distributor is similar in appearance to a conventional distributor. Its shaft, driven at half crankshaft speed, rotates a four-toothed reluctor. Each time a reluctor tooth passes a stator pole, a magnetic pulse is generated, which is converted by the igniter unit into a switching current through the coil primary (LT) winding. Each time the current through the coil primary winding is interrupted, a high voltage pulse is generated in the secondary (HT) winding. This HT voltage is fed via the HT leads and distributor rotor arm to the correct spark plug, where it jumps across the plug electrodes, creating the spark which ignites the mixture.

The precise timing of the spark is varied according to engine speed (centrifugal advance) and load (vacuum advance) in the same way as in a conventional system.

The breakerless ignition system is potentially much more reliable than systems using mechanical contact breakers. Variations in ignition timing due to mechanical wear of contact breaker points, and reduction in efficiency due to deterioration of the point faces, are both eliminated. Nevertheless, the correct functioning of the system is still vital for engine efficiency, and what little maintenance remains must not be neglected.

Before undertaking any work on the ignition system, refer to the cautions in Section 11.

2   Reluctor air gap – adjustment

1   Unlike contact breaker gap adjustment, the reluctor air gap does not require periodic adjustment, but the efficiency of the spark depends upon the gap being set correctly.
2   On Hitachi distributors (Fig. 4.1), slacken the two clamp screws of the stator plate and move the plate sideways until the gap between

the stator and the teeth of the reluctor is the same on both sides. Clamp the screws and recheck.
3   On Toyodenso distributors (Fig. 4.2), slacken the three clamp screws and move the stator plate until the gap between each of the four teeth of the reluctor and its adjacent stator tooth is the same. Clamp the screws and recheck.

3   Distributor – removal and installation

1   Remove the HT leads from the spark plugs.
2   Disconnect the hose from the vacuum advance diaphragm (photo).
3   Disconnect the earth lead from the condenser.
4   Disconnect the two wires from the igniter unit or coil, as applicable.
5   Mark the distributor plate and the engine mounting surface so that the plate can be reinstalled without altering the timing, then remove the distributor clamp bolt and remove the distributor.
6   To re-install, first turn the crankshaft until No 1 piston is at TDC on its compression stroke. The crankshaft can be turned either by applying a socket wrench to the crankshaft pulley bolt, or by jacking up the front of the vehicle, selecting a gear and turning a front roadwheel (on vehicles with manual transmission). It is easier to turn the crankshaft if the spark plugs are removed. To check that No 1 piston is on its compression stroke, place a finger over the spark plug hole until compression is felt as the engine is turned. On UK models, TDC is when the TDC mark on the crankshaft pulley is aligned with the pointer on the timing belt cover. On US models it is necessary to remove the rubber plug from the rear of the cylinder block and align the pointer on the cylinder block with the TDC mark on the flywheel, or driveplate.
7   Install a new O-ring on the distributor housing.
8   Line up the mark on the distributor gear with the mark on the housing (Fig. 4.3).
9   Install the distributor. As it is inserted, the rotor will turn itself to No 1 firing position.
10 Install the clamp bolt, line up the marks on the plate and engine mounting which were made before removal and tighten the bolt.
11 Install the distributor cap. The No 1 cylinder mark on the cap (Fig. 4.4 or 4.5) should be in line with the firing end of the rotor.
12 Check and if necessary adjust the timing as described in Section 4.

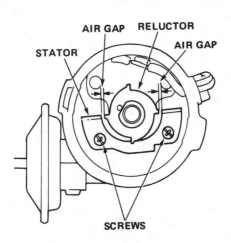

Fig. 4.1 Reluctor air gap adjustment (Hitachi) (Sec 2)

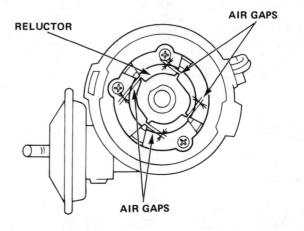

Fig. 4.2 Reluctor air gap adjustment (Toyodenso) (Sec 2)

3.2 Ignition leads and (arrowed) distributor vacuum hose

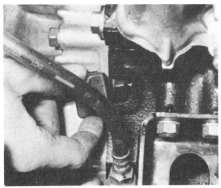

4.4a Rubber plug and timing marks (US models)

4.4b Timing marks (UK models) – TDC mark is aligned

Toyodenso Type   **Hitachi Type**

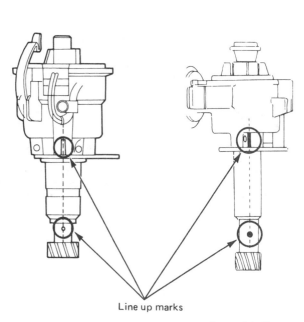

Line up marks

Fig. 4.3 Distributor lining up marks (Secs 3 & 6)

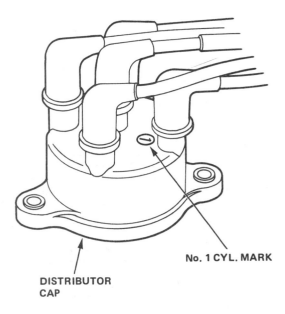

No. 1 CYL. MARK

DISTRIBUTOR CAP

Fig. 4.5 Distributor cap No 1 cylinder mark (Toyodenso) (Sec 3)

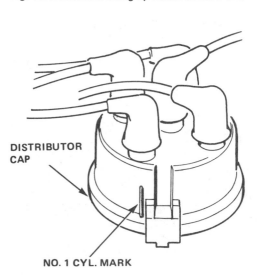

DISTRIBUTOR CAP

NO. 1 CYL. MARK

Fig. 4.4 Distributor cap No 1 cylinder (Hitachi) (Sec 3)

4   Ignition timing – checking and adjusting

1   Whenever the distributor has been removed and re-installed, and as part of periodic maintenance checks, the ignition timing should be checked and if necessary adjusted..

2   Static timing, as carried out on conventional (contact breaker) ignition systems, is not possible on this vehicle. If the distributor is installed as described in Section 3, the timing should be sufficiently accurate to enable the engine to be run, enabling dynamic timing to be carried out as follows.

3   Run the engine until it has reached normal operating temperature, then switch it off. Connect a timing light (strobe) to the engine in accordance with the manufacturer's instructions. One connection must be to No 1 spark plug lead; depending on the type of light, connections to the car battery or to a mains power source may also be necessary. Ideally, an independent tachometer (rev-counter) should also be connected so that the engine idle speed can be checked.

4   Start the engine and allow it to idle. Shine the timing light onto the timing marks. On UK models, the timing marks will be found on the crankshaft pulley; on US models, the marks are visible on the flywheel/driveplate after removing the rubber plug from the inspection window in the cylinder block (photos).

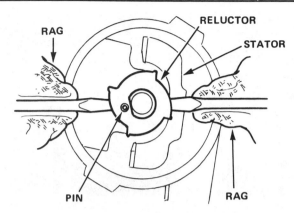

Fig. 4.6 Prising off the reluctor (Sec 6)

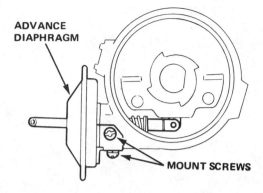

Fig. 4.7 Vacuum diaphragm mounting (Sec 6)

5   The timing marks will appear to be stationary and, if the timing is correct, the relevant mark will be aligned with the pointer on the timing cover or cylinder block. Refer to the Specifications or to the under-bonnet decal for the correct timing mark for your model.

6   If adjustment is necessary, stop the engine and slacken the distributor clamp bolt. Rotate the distributor body clockwise to advance the timing, or anti-clockwise to retard it. Tighten the bolt, start the engine again and re-check.

7   When the timing is correct, remove the timing light (and tachometer, if used), re-make the ignition system connections and (on US models) re-install the rubber plug in the cylinder block.

5   Automatic advance mechanism – checking

1   To check the centrifugal advance, disconnect and plug the vacuum hose from the distributor and connect a timing light as when checking the ignition timing.

2   Increase the engine speed from idling, and the timing mark should advance past the fixed reference mark on the timing belt cover (UK) or cylinder block (US). If this does not occur, the centrifugal advance mechanism is sticking or binding, and the distributor should be dismantled, cleaned and lubricated.

3   To check the vacuum advance, remove the distributor cap and disconnect the vacuum hose from the distributor advance diaphragm.

4   Either connect a vacuum pump, or suck by mouth on the pipe of the vacuum diaphragm, while watching the movement of the breaker plate. Check for the smooth operation of the plate with no evidence of binding, and also check that there is no leakage of suction. If there is leakage, the diaphragm unit must be renewed.

6   Distributor – dismantling and reassembly

1   Remove the distributor from the engine, remove its cap and rotor.

2   Using rag to protect the edges of the distributor body, use two screwdrivers to prise off the reluctor (Fig. 4.6). Take care not to damage the reluctor or stator.

3   Remove the mounting screws of the vacuum unit, lift the diaphragm unit arm off the pin of the breaker plate assembly and remove the vacuum unit (Fig. 4.7).

4   Remove the screws securing the breaker assembly and lift it out complete with pulse generator or igniter unit and stator.

5   Prise the plug out of the top of the rotor shaft. Remove the screw beneath and lift out the rotor shaft.

6   Drive out the roll pin from the distributor shaft (Fig. 4.10). Remove the gear, washers and shaft assembly.

7   Mark the positions of the centrifugal weights and springs and remove them.

8   Thoroughly clean all parts and inspect them for damage and wear. Renew as necessary.

9   Grease the distributor and rotor shafts and lightly oil the pivots of the centrifugal weights.

10 Reassembly is the reverse of dismantling, but care is needed to

ensure that assembly is correct. Begin by reassembling the centrifugal weights and springs on the shaft.

11 Insert the shaft into the body. On the Hitachi distributor the thrust plate and two thrust washers must be threaded on the shaft before it is inserted.

12 Install the thrust washers (if applicable) and the gear to the base of the shaft.

13 Line up the mark on the gear with the mark on the distributor housing (Fig. 4.3). Line up the hole in the shaft with the hole in the gear and drive in a new roll pin.

14 With the gear and housing marks still aligned, install the rotor shaft. Make sure that the rotor shaft engages with the centrifugal weight pins, and note the alignment of the flat on the rotor shaft (Fig. 4.12 or 4.13).

15 Secure the rotor shaft by installing and tightening its screw, then install the plug over the screw.

16 Install the pick-up base (Toyodenso) or breaker plate assembly (Hitachi). Check that the upper plate of the breaker plate assembly moves freely and make sure that the diaphragm arm attachment pin does not rotate past the slot in the lower plate (Fig. 4.14).

17 Install the reluctor and secure it with a new roll pin, ensuring that the joint in the roll pin is away from the shaft. Check the rotor air gap and adjust it if necessary (Section 2).

7   Condenser – testing

1   Unlike a conventional ignition system in which the condenser influences the strength of the spark, the condenser of the breakerless

7.1 Ignition coil and condenser

CARBON DEPOSITS

Symptoms: Dry sooty deposits indicate a rich mixture or weak ignition. Causes misfiring, hard starting and hesitation.

Recommendation: Check for a clogged air cleaner, high float level, sticky choke and worn ignition points. Use a spark plug with a longer core nose for greater anti-fouling protection.

OIL DEPOSITS

Symptoms: Oily coating caused by poor oil control. Oil is leaking past worn valve guides or piston rings into the combustion chamber. Causes hard starting, misfiring and hesition.

Recommendation: Correct the mechanical condition with necessary repairs and install new plugs.

TOO HOT

Symptoms: Blistered, white insulator, eroded electrode and absence of deposits. Results in shortened plug life.

Recommendation: Check for the correct plug heat range, over-advanced ignition timing, lean fuel mixture, intake manifold vacuum leaks and sticking valves. Check the coolant level and make sure the radiator is not clogged.

PREIGNITION

Symptoms: Melted electrodes. Insulators are white, but may be dirty due to misfiring or flying debris in the combustion chamber. Can lead to engine damage.

Recommendation: Check for the correct plug heat range, over-advanced ignition timing, lean fuel mixture, clogged cooling system and lack of lubrication.

HIGH SPEED GLAZING

Symptoms: Insulator has yellowish, glazed appearance. Indicates that combustion chamber temperatures have risen suddenly during hard acceleration. Normal deposits melt to form a conductive coating. Causes misfiring at high speeds.

Recommendation: Install new plugs. Consider using a colder plug if driving habits warrant.

GAP BRIDGING

Symptoms: Combustion deposits lodge between the electrodes. Heavy deposits accumulate and bridge the electrode gap. The plug ceases to fire, resulting in a dead cylinder.

Recommendation: Locate the faulty plug and remove the deposits from between the electrodes.

NORMAL

Symptoms: Brown to grayish-tan color and slight electrode wear. Correct heat range for engine and operating conditions.

Recommendation: When new spark plugs are installed, replace with plugs of the same heat range.

ASH DEPOSITS

Symptoms: Light brown deposits encrusted on the side or center electrodes or both. Derived from oil and/or fuel additives. Excessive amounts may mask the spark, causing misfiring and hesitation during acceleration.

Recommendation: If excessive deposits accumulate over a short time or low mileage, install new valve guide seals to prevent seepage of oil into the combustion chambers. Also try changing gasoline brands.

WORN

Symptoms: Rounded electrodes with a small amount of deposits on the firing end. Normal color. Causes hard starting in damp or cold weather and poor fuel economy.

Recommendation: Replace with new plugs of the same heat range.

DETONATION

Symptoms: Insulators may be cracked or chipped. Improper gap setting techniques can also result in a fractured insulator tip. Can lead to piston damage.

Recommendation: Make sure the fuel anti-knock values meet engine requirements. Use care when setting the gaps on new plugs. Avoid lugging the engine.

4

SPLASHED DEPOSITS

Symptoms: After long periods of misfiring, deposits can loosen when normal combustion temperature is restored by an overdue tune-up. At high speeds, deposits flake off the piston and are thrown against the hot insulator, causing misfiring.

Recommendation: Replace the plugs with new ones or clean and reinstall the originals.

MECHANICAL DAMAGE

Symptoms: May be caused by a foreign object in the combustion chamber or the piston striking an incorrect reach (too long) plug. Causes a dead cylinder and could result in piston damage.

Recommendation: Remove the foreign object from the engine and/or install the correct reach plug.

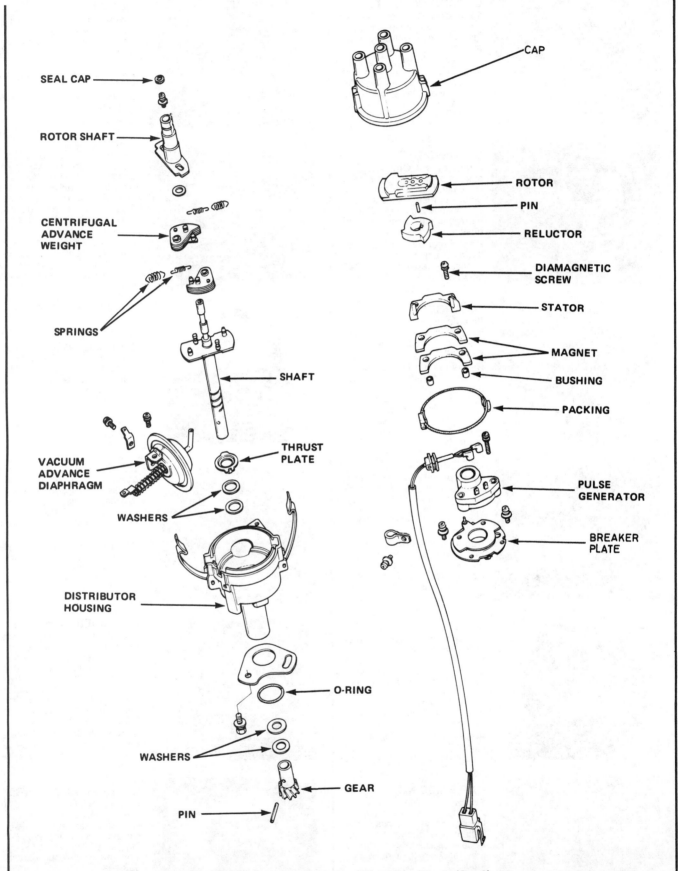

SEAL CAP

ROTOR SHAFT

CENTRIFUGAL
ADVANCE
WEIGHT

SPRINGS

SHAFT

VACUUM
ADVANCE
DIAPHRAGM

THRUST
PLATE

WASHERS

DISTRIBUTOR
HOUSING

O-RING

WASHERS

GEAR

PIN

CAP

ROTOR

PIN

RELUCTOR

DIAMAGNETIC
SCREW

STATOR

MAGNET

BUSHING

PACKING

PULSE
GENERATOR

BREAKER
PLATE

Fig. 4.8 Distributor components – UK models, Hitachi (Sec 6)

93

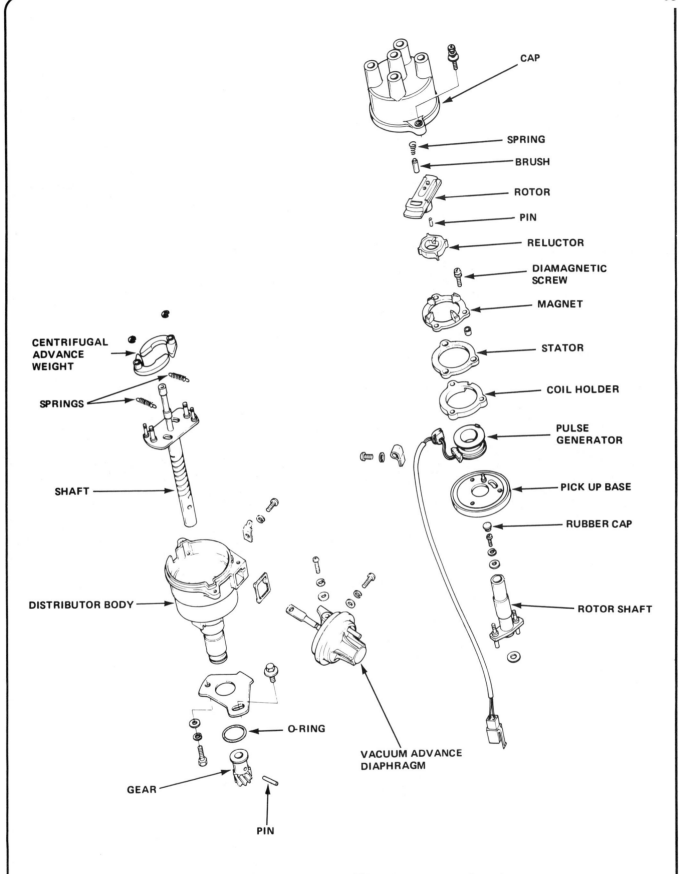

CAP

SPRING

BRUSH

ROTOR

PIN

RELUCTOR

DIAMAGNETIC SCREW

MAGNET

STATOR

COIL HOLDER

PULSE GENERATOR

PICK UP BASE

RUBBER CAP

ROTOR SHAFT

CENTRIFUGAL ADVANCE WEIGHT

SPRINGS

SHAFT

DISTRIBUTOR BODY

O-RING

GEAR

PIN

VACUUM ADVANCE DIAPHRAGM

4

Fig. 4.9 Distributor components – UK models, Toyodenso (Sec 6)

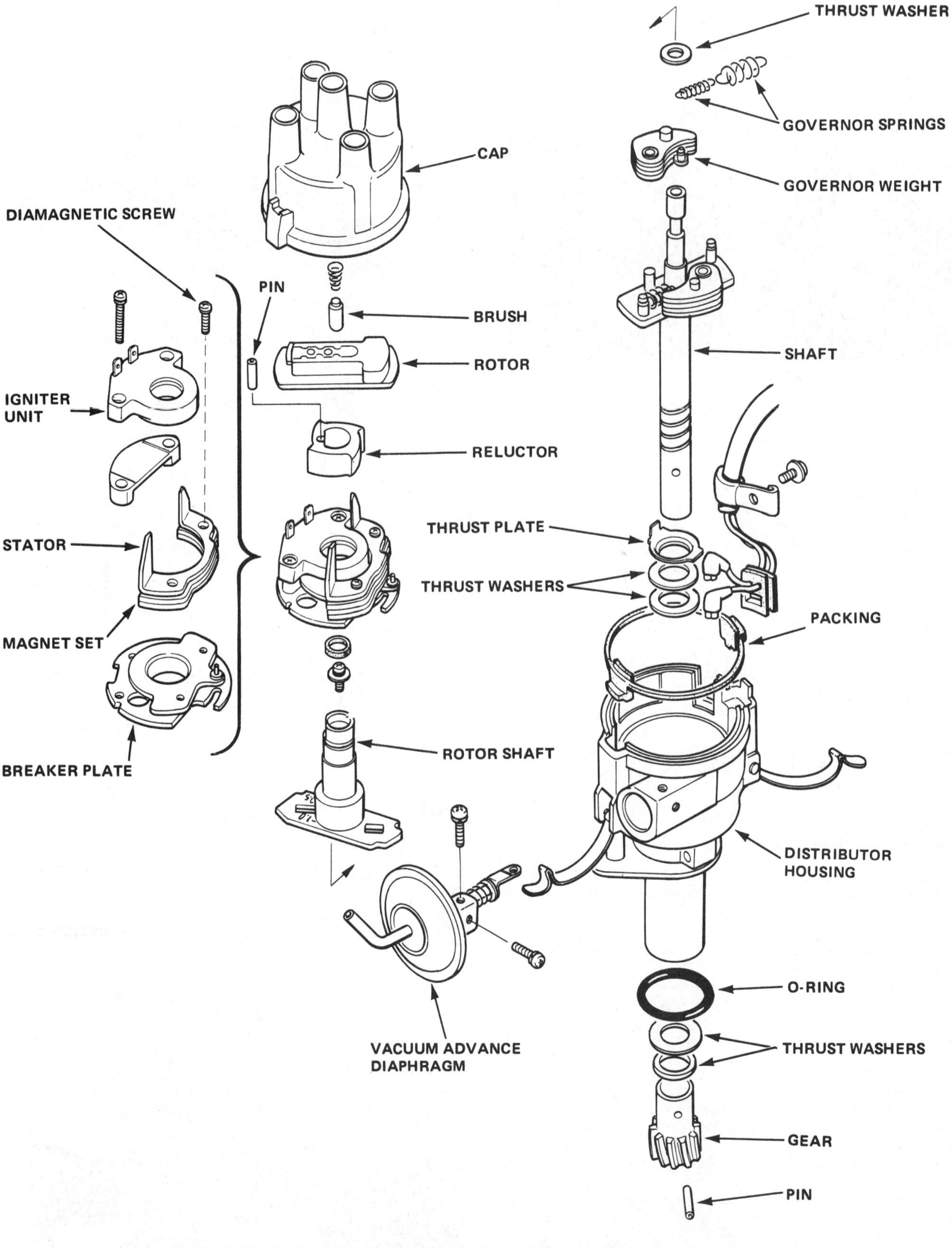

THRUST WASHER

GOVERNOR SPRINGS

GOVERNOR WEIGHT

DIAMAGNETIC SCREW

PIN

CAP

BRUSH

ROTOR

SHAFT

IGNITER UNIT

RELUCTOR

STATOR

THRUST PLATE

THRUST WASHERS

MAGNET SET

PACKING

BREAKER PLATE

ROTOR SHAFT

DISTRIBUTOR HOUSING

VACUUM ADVANCE DIAPHRAGM

O-RING

THRUST WASHERS

GEAR

PIN

Fig. 4.10 Distributor components – US models, Hitachi with integral igniter (Sec 6)

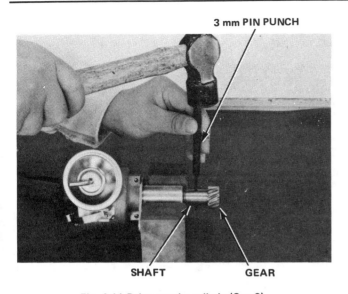

3 mm PIN PUNCH

SHAFT   **GEAR**

Fig. 4.11 Drive out the roll pin (Sec 6)

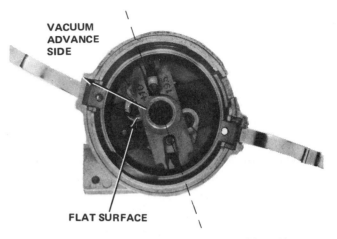

VACUUM ADVANCE SIDE

FLAT SURFACE

Fig. 4.12 Rotor shaft alignment (Hitachi) (Sec 6)

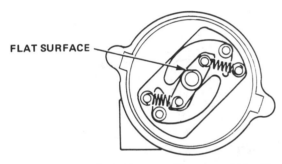

FLAT SURFACE

Fig. 4.13 Rotor shaft alignment (Toyodenso) (Sec 6)

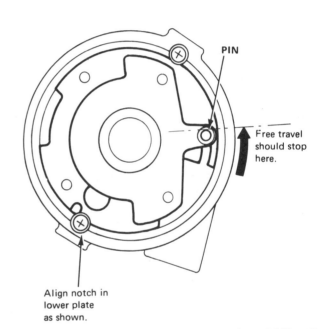

PIN

Free travel should stop here.

Align notch in lower plate as shown.

Fig. 4.14 Correct installation of breaker plate (Hitachi) (Sec 6)

ignition system is only to suppress radio interference (photo).

2   If a condenser becomes short-circuited it will prevent the ignition system from operating. If it becomes open-circuited, or its capacitance decreases, the ignition circuit will continue to function, but there will be increased radio interference.

3   A suspect condenser can be checked on a condenser tester, but it is usually easier to change the condenser for one known to be good. A short-circuited condenser can be disconnected temporarily, when the engine should run.

8   Ignition coil – testing

1   Ignition coils are usually trouble-free, but if it is suspected that the coil is malfunctioning, it may be checked as follows.

2   With the ignition switch off, disconnect the coil and connect an ohmmeter across the two low tension terminals of the coil. Note the resistance reading and compare it with the value given in the Specifications.

3   Connect the ohmmeter to the centre (high voltage) terminal of the coil and to the positive terminal of the primary winding. Note the resistance and compare it with the value given in the Specifications.

4   The resistance values obtained will vary according to the temperature of the coil, and a value which is only slightly outside that specified does not necessarily indicate that the coil is defective. Further testing should be by substitution of a known good unit.

9   Igniter unit – testing

1   Disconnect the plug connection (photo) and turn the ignition switch on. (On US models, disconnect the plug at the distributor).

9.1 Igniter unit on UK models is separate from distributor

4

2   Check the voltage between the blue wire and chassis earth and between the black/yellow wire and chassis earth. There should be battery voltage in both cases.

3   With the wires to the igniter disconnected check continuity between the igniter unit terminals using an ohmmeter switched to its X100 range. With the ohmmeter connected to the igniter terminals which receive the black/yellow and blue wires, there should be continuity in one direction but not in the other (ie with the ohmmeter probes reversed). If there is the same meter reading in both directions – continuity or open-circuit – the igniter unit is defective and must be renewed.

10 Pulse generator – testing

1   On distributors which have an externally mounted igniter unit, with only the pulse generator installed inside the distributor, the pulse generator may be tested as follows.

2   Disconnect the cable connector from the distributor and connect the probes of an ohmmeter between the blue and red terminals.

3   If the resistance reading is in the range 600 to 800 ohms, the pulse generator is satisfactory. If it is outside these limits the pulse generator must be renewed.

11 Ignition system – precautions

1   In addition to taking the normal precautions to guard against electric shock from the high voltages of the ignition system, the breakerless ignition system requires additional precautions.

2   Take care not to connect the battery + and – terminals wrongly because this will damage the semiconductor components of the system.

3   Do not disconnect the battery while the engine is running.

4   Make certain that all wires and cables are connected correctly.

5   Do not bring pulse generator wires into contact with the HT leads because this may produce pulses which will cause the ignition system to malfunction.

6   Take care not to produce stray electrical pulses. For example, do not disconnect the wire from the B terminal of the alternator and use it to produce sparks as a means of checking that the alternator is charging.

7   When connecting a pulse type tachometer, check its manufacturer's instructions to see that it is suitable for breakerless ignition systems.

12 Spark plugs and HT leads – general

1   The good condition of the spark plugs and HT leads is vital for the performance and efficiency of the engine. Maintenance is simple but must not be neglected.

2   At the specified intervals, remove the spark plugs and inspect them. If they are in good condition, clean and regap them. Renew the plugs if they are badly worn, or at the specified mileage intervals; not to do so is false economy.

3   If the insulator nose of the spark plug is clean and white, with no deposits, this is indicative of a weak mixture, or too hot a plug. (A hot plug transfers heat away from the electrode slowly – a cold plug transfers heat away quickly). The plugs fitted as standard are specified at the beginning of this Chapter.

4   If the top and insulator nose are covered with hard black-looking deposits, then this is indicative that the mixture is too rich. Should the plug be black and oily, then it is likely that the engine is fairly worn, as well as the mixture being too rich.

5   If the insulator nose is covered with light tan to greyish brown deposits, then the mixture is correct and it is likely that the engine is in good condition. Note however that on CVCC engines, as fitted to US models, the plug may show signs of working with a rich mixture, ie darker than normal. This is because the mixture in the pre-combustion chamber is richer than the mixture in the main combustion chamber. No corrective action is necessary.

6   If there are any traces of long brown tapering stains on the outside of the white portion of the plug, then the plug will have to be renewed, as this shows that there is a faulty joint between the plug body and the

insulator, and compression is being allowed to leak away.

7   Plugs should be cleaned by a sand blasting machine, which will free them from carbon more than cleaning by hand. The machine will also test the condition of the plugs under compression. Any plug that fails to spark at the recommended pressure should be renewed.

8   The spark plug gap is of considerable importance, if it is too large, or too small, the size of the spark and its efficiency will be seriously impaired. For the best results the spark plug gap should be set in accordance with the Specifications at the beginning of this Chapter.

9   To set it, measure the gap with a feeler gauge, and then bend open, or close, the outer plug electrode until the correct gap is achieved. The centre electrode should never be bent as this may crack the insulation and cause plug failure if nothing worse.

10   Apply a small quantity of anti-seize compound to the plug threads before installing them, and do not tighten the plugs beyond the recommended torque. Take care that the plug leads from the distributor are installed to give the correct firing order.

11   The plug leads require no routine attention other than being kept clean, but they should be checked periodically to ensure that they are in good condition and that their terminals are not broken or corroded.

Fig. 4.15 Checking the ignition switch (Sec 13)

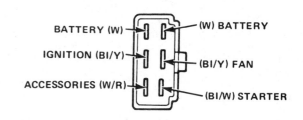

	TERMINAL				
POSITION	ACC	BAT	IG	ST	FAN
O (LOCK)					
I (ACC)	o———o				
II (ON)	o———o		o		o
III (START)		o	o	o	o
COLOR	W/R	W	BI/Y	BI/W	BI/Y

Fig. 4.16 Ignition switch continuity (Sec 13)

12 To check that the leads are satisfactory, connect the probes of an ohmmeter to the two ends of the wire and measure the resistance. If it is outside the value given in the Specifications, renew the lead.
13 When removing HT leads care is needed, and they should only be disconnected by pulling on the rubber boots. Do not bend the leads sharply, because this may break the conductor wire.

13 Ignition switch – testing

1 The ignition switch may be tested without removing it. Remove the steering column shroud (Chapter 11) and disconnect the wiring harness plug from the switch.
2 Use an ohmmeter, or a battery and test lamp, to check the continuity of the switch in all switch positions. The correct continuity is given in Fig. 4.16. Renew the switch if it is defective.

14 Fault diagnosis – ignition system

Engine fails to start
1 If the engine fails to start and the car was running normally when it was last used, first check there is fuel in the tank. If the engine turns normally on the starter motor and the battery is evidently well charged, then the fault may be in either the high or low tension circuits. First check the secondary high tension (HT) circuit. **Note:** If the battery is known to be fully charged; the ignition light comes on, and the starter motor fails to turn the engine, **check the tightness of the leads on the battery terminals** and also the secureness of the earth lead to its **connection to the body.** It is quite common for the leads to have worked loose, even if they look and feel secure. If one of the battery terminal posts gets very hot when trying to work the starter motor this is a sure indication of a faulty connection to that terminal.
2 One of the commonest reasons for bad starting is wet or damp spark plug leads and distributor. Remove the distributor cap. If condensation is visible internally, dry the cap with a rag and also wipe over the leads. Re-install the cap.
3 If the engine still fails to start, check that current is reaching the plugs, by disconnecting each plug lead in turn at the spark plug end, and hold the end of the cable about $\frac{3}{16}$ in (5 mm) away from the cylinder block. Hold the lead with an insulated tool to avoid electric shocks. Spin the engine on the starter motor.
4 Sparking between the end of the cable and the block should be fairly strong with a regular blue spark. If current is reaching the plugs, then remove them and clean and regap them. The engine should now start.
5 If there is no spark at the plug leads take off the high tension (HT) lead from the centre of the distributor cap and hold it to the block as before. Spin the engine on the starter once more. A rapid succession of blue sparks between the end of the lead and the block indicates that the coil is in order and that the distributor cap is cracked, the rotor arm faulty, or the carbon brush in the top of the distributor cap is not making good contact with the rotor arm.

6 If there are no sparks from the end of the lead from the coil, check the connections at the coil end of the lead. If it is in order start checking the low tension (primary) circuit.
7 Use a 12V voltmeter, or a 12V bulb and two lengths of wire. With the ignition switch on, check that there is battery voltage between the coil primary winding positive (+) terminal and earth. If there is not, check the ignition switch (Section 13). Repeat the check between the negative (–) terminal and earth. If there is battery voltage on the positive terminal, but not on the negative one, the primary winding of the ignition coil may be defective. Check the ignition coil (Section 8), and the condenser (Section 7).
8 Check the igniter unit (Section 9).
9 On distributors with an external igniter, check the pulse generator (Section 10).

Engine misfires
10 If the engine misfires regularly run it at a fast idling speed. Pull off each of the plug caps in turn and listen to the note of the engine. Hold the plug cap in a dry cloth or with a rubber glove as additional protection against a shock from the HT (secondary) supply.
11 No difference in engine running will be noticed when the lead from the defective circuit is removed. Removing the lead from one of the good cylinders will accentuate the misfire.
12 Remove the plug lead from the end of the defective plug and hold it about $\frac{3}{16}$ in (5 mm) away from the block. Restart the engine. If the sparking is fairly strong and regular the fault must lie in the spark plug.
13 The plug may be loose, the insulation may be cracked, or the points may have burnt away giving too wide a gap for the spark to jump. Worse still, one of the points may have broken off. Either renew the plug, or clean it, reset the gap, and then test it.
14 If there is no spark at the end of the plug lead, or if it is weak and intermittent, check the ignition lead from the distributor to the plug. If the insulation is cracked or perished, renew the lead. Check the connections at the distributor cap.
15 If there is still no spark, examine the distributor cap carefully for tracking. This can be recognised by a very thin black line running between two or more contacts, or between a contact and some other part of the distributor. These lines are paths which now conduct electricity across the cap thus letting it run to earth. The only answer is a new distributor cap.
16 Apart from the ignition timing being incorrect, other causes of misfiring have already been dealt with under the section dealing with the failure of the engine to start. To recap – these are that:

> (a) The coil may be faulty giving an intermittent misfire
> (b) There may be a damaged wire or loose connection in the low tension circuit
> (c) The condenser may be short-circuiting
> (d) There may be a mechanical fault in the distributor

17 If the ignition timing is too far retarded, it should be noted that the engine will tend to overheat, and there will be a quite noticeable drop in power. If the engine is overheating and the power is down, and the ignition timing is correct, then the carburettor should be checked, as it is likely that this is where the fault lies.

4

Chapter 5 Clutch

Refer to Chapter 13 for specifications related to 1982 and 1983 US models

Contents

Specifications

General
Clutch type .... Single dry plate, diaphragm spring
Actuation .... Cable

Adjustment data
Free movement:
    At pedal .... $\frac{3}{8}$ to $1\frac{3}{16}$ in (10 to 30 mm)
    At release arm .... $\frac{1}{8}$ to $\frac{5}{32}$ in (3 to 4 mm)
Pedal disengagement height from floor .... $1\frac{3}{16}$ in (30 mm) minimum

Overhaul data

	Standard (new)	Service limit
Driven plate thickness	0.34 to 0.37 in (8.7 to 9.4 mm)	0.24 in (6.1 mm)
Rivet depth in driven plate	0.051 in (1.3 mm)	0.008 in (0.2 mm)
Driven plate run-out	0.032 in (0.8 mm) maximum	0.039 in (1.0 mm)
Pressure plate warpage	–	0.006 in (0.15 mm)

Torque wrench settings

	lbf ft	Nm
Pressure plate bolts	9	12
Clutch housing-to-engine bolts	33	45
Release fork shaft holder	17	24

1 Clutch mechanism – description

The clutch assembly is of single dry plate diaphragm spring type. The unit is conventional and operates as follows. When the clutch pedal is depressed, the clutch thrust bearing moves towards the centre of the clutch. The bearing acts on the inner fingers of the single piece diaphragm spring, thereby reducing the force exerted by the periphery of the spring on the pressure plate in the clutch. The pressure plate holds the clutch friction disc against the flywheel, and when the force exerted on the pressure plate and disc reduces to zero, the disc is free to move relative to the flywheel, and will not transmit engine power to the transmission.

Once the gearbox is not receiving power from the engine, gear selection can be made, followed by release of the clutch pedal. As the pedal is released, the thrust bearing moves away from the centre of the clutch. The diaphragm spring force on the pressure plate is restored and the disc is now held firmly against the flywheel so that engine power is transmitted via the flywheel and clutch disc to the transmission.

Detail features of the clutch include the fitting of four torsion springs in the friction disc, which smooth out any shock when the disc is brought onto contact with the flywheel. The disc periphery with the friction material is not connected directly to the splined hub, the torque is transmitted via the springs which are arranged circumferentially on the disc hub.

2 Clutch actuating system – description

A mechanically operated clutch actuating system is employed. It comprises an inner and outer cable assembly connecting the pendant type pedal to the clutch release lever (Fig. 5.2).

3 Clutch – adjustment

1 At the intervals specified in Routine Maintenance, check and adjust if necessary the free movement at the clutch pedal.
2 Place a ruler beside the clutch pedal pad and then move the pedal downward with the fingers until the clutch diaphragm spring resistance can be felt. The distance that the pedal pad has travelled should be as given in the Specifications.
3 If the pedal free movement requires adjustment, turn the adjusting nut at the release arm end of the cable (Fig. 5.2).

4 Clutch cable – renewal

1 Slacken the adjusting nut, unhook the cable from the upper end of the clutch pedal and then withdraw the cable assembly from the bulkhead into the engine compartment.
2 Pull the clutch release lever upwards so that the nipple on the end

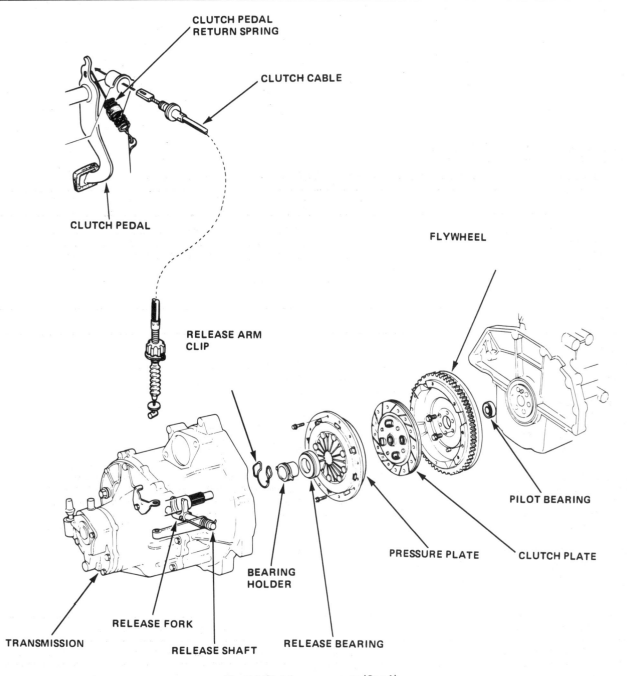

Fig. 5.1 Clutch components (Sec 1)

5

of the clutch cable can be detached from the eye on the end of the lever (photo).

3   Remove the cable from its support bracket on the transmission housing.

4   Installation of the new cable assembly is a reversal of removal. Adjust the free movement, as described in Section 3.

5 Clutch pedal – removal and refitting

1   Disconnect the clutch cable from the pedal, as described in the preceding Section.

2   Disconnect the pedal return spring.

3   Undo the nut from the end of the pedal pivot, remove the thrust washer and slide the pedal from the pivot.

4   Renew any pivot bushes as necessary. Reassembly is a reversal of removal but apply grease to the pivot.

5   Now adjust the pedal free movement, as described in Section 3.

6 Clutch – removal

1   Access to the clutch can be obtained in one of two ways. Either remove the engine/transmission complete and then separate the transmission as described in Chapter 1, or remove the transmission independently leaving the engine in position in the car, as described in Chapter 6.

2   The clutch assembly can now be unbolted and removed from the flywheel. Release the pressure plate bolts a turn at a time in diagonal sequence until the tension of the diaphragm spring has been relieved,

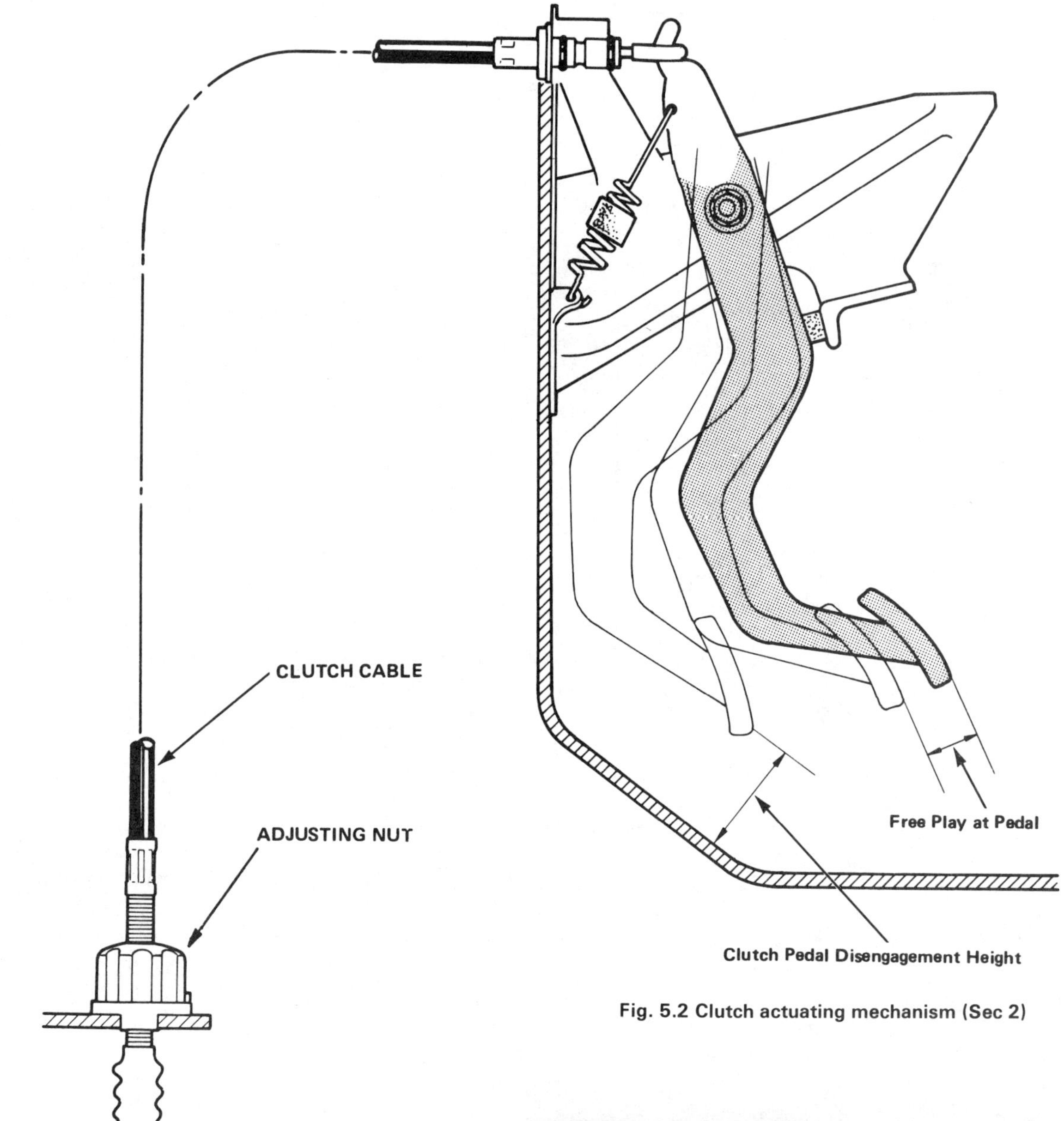

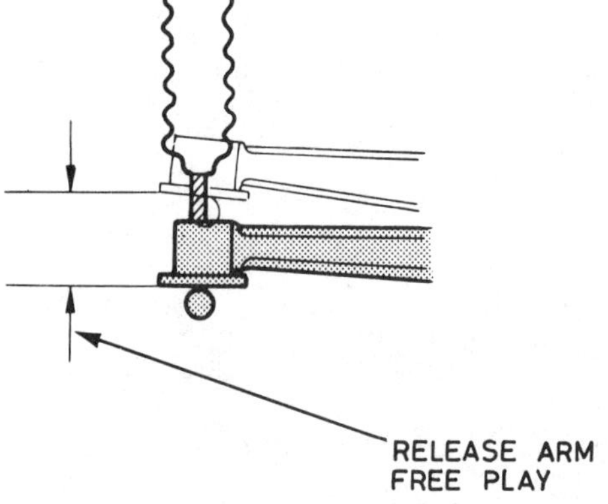

CLUTCH CABLE

ADJUSTING NUT

RELEASE ARM
FREE PLAY

Free Play at Pedal

Clutch Pedal Disengagement Height

Fig. 5.2 Clutch actuating mechanism (Sec 2)

4.2 Clutch cable attachment to clutch lever

then withdraw the bolts and lift the pressure plate and the driven plate from the flywheel. In order to hold the flywheel stationary while the pressure plate bolts are unscrewed, jam the starter ring gear with a large screwdriver or cold chisel.

7 Clutch – inspection and renovation

1 Unfortunately it is not possible to inspect the clutch without going to the considerable trouble of removing the assembly. Consequently, one waits for trouble to develop or makes a decision to check and overhaul it anyway, at a specific mileage. Wear of the clutch friction disc depends a great deal on how the car has been driven. Habitual clutch slipping will obviously cause rapid wear. If it is assumed that the friction disc will need replacement at 35 000 miles (56 000 km) and will be worth replacing at 25 000 miles (40 000 km) – there will be no significant waste of time and money if the work is done. Of course, a history of the car is very valuable for this decision. If, on the other hand, trouble is awaited, action must be taken immediately it occurs; otherwise further more costly wear could occur. Trouble usually comes in the form of slipping, when the engine speeds up and the car does not; or squealing, denoting that the friction material is worn to the rivets; or juddering denoting all sorts of trouble (see Section 10). Wear on the ball release bearing which presses onto the centre of the diaphragm every time the clutch is operated could also cause squealing if the wear was extreme. If the clutch is not examined when wear is apparent, the faces of the flywheel and pressure plate may be severely scored and call for costly replacement.

2 Having decided to dismantle the clutch, first examine the faces of the flywheel and the pressure plate. They should be smooth and shiny. If they are slightly ridged or scored, a new friction disc will be enough to regain satisfactory performance. If there is severe scoring, be prepared to buy a new pressure plate assembly and/or flywheel. If a new flywheel is installed, it will have to be balanced to match the original. If you put the badly scored surfaces back together with a new friction plate you will achieve short-lived results only. After a few thousand miles the same trouble will occur and judder will always be present.

3 The driven plate lining surfaces should be more than the specified minimum distance above the heads of the rivets, otherwise the disc is not really worth putting back. If the friction lining material shows signs of chipping or breaking up or has black areas caused by oil contamination it should also be renewed. The source of any oil contamination should be rectified before reassembly, otherwise the new disc will be similarly affected.

4 Unless the release bearing is known to be in perfect condition, it too should be renewed at time of clutch overhaul. It will be vexing to have to dismantle the clutch again if the release bearing fails at an early date!

5 The pressure plate friction surface should be checked for warping. If warping is outside the specified limits, or if cracks are visible, renew the pressure plate.

8 Clutch release bearing and mechanism – overhaul

1 Before reassembling the clutch and installing the transmission, examine the release components within the clutch bellhousing.

2 Any slackness or evidence of noise when the release bearing is spun with the fingers, or wear in the release lever shaft, will require renewal of the components.

3 Use a small screwdriver to prise the ends of the release arm bearing clip out of the holes in the fork, but take care not to bend the clip more than is necessary (photo).

4 Slide the bearing and holder off the shaft sleeve (photo).

5 If it is difficult to remove the bearing, unhook the release arm spring (photo). Bend up the locktab on the clutch fork bolt (photo) and remove the bolt.

6 Remove the clutch release shaft and then remove the release bearing and fork as an assembly.

9 Clutch – installation

1 Make sure that the friction surfaces of the pressure plate and the flywheel are quite clean and free from oil or grease.

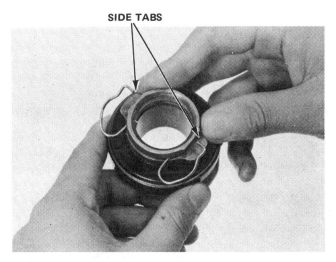

SIDE TABS

Fig. 5.3 Correct installation of release arm clip (Sec 8)

DOWEL PIN   HOLE

Align marks

Fig. 5.4 Clutch alignment marks (Sec 9)

ALIGNMENT TOOL

Fig. 5.5 Clutch plate alignment (Sec 9)

5

8.3 Clutch release arm bearing clip in hole in fork

8.4 Removing the clutch release bearing

8.5a Clutch release arm spring

8.5b Clutch fork bolt

9.2 Installing the clutch driven plate

2   Place the driven plate against the flywheel so that the projecting side faces away from the flywheel (photo).
3   Place the pressure plate assembly over the driven plate against the flywheel so that the pressure plate and flywheel marks are in alignment (Fig. 5.4). If a new pressure plate is being installed, it will not have any alignment marks and may be fitted in any position.
4   Insert the pressure plate bolts and tighten them finger tight only.
5   The driven plate must now be aligned, otherwise it will be impossible to mate the transmission to the engine as the gearbox input shaft will not pass through the splines of the driven plate and into engagement with the pilot bush in the centre of the flywheel. To do this, use a clutch aligning tool, an old input shaft or a suitable piece of dowelling which can be passed through the splined hub of the driven plate and engaged in the pilot bush of the flywheel. This action will have the effect of displacing the driven plate and so centralise it with the flywheel, the pressure plate bolts being only finger tight at this stage.
6   When the centralising tool is a sliding fit, withdraw it and tighten the pressure plate bolts in diametrically opposite sequence, a turn at a time to the specified torque.
7   Reconnect the transmission to the engine and install the complete unit to the car (Chapter 1) or refit the transmission to the engine if the latter is still in the car (Chapter 6) according to whichever method was used to gain access to the clutch.

10 Fault diagnosis – clutch

Symptom	Reason(s)
Judder when taking up drive	Loose engine or gearbox mountings Badly worn friction surfaces or contaminated with oil Worn splines on gearbox input shaft or driven plate hub Worn input shaft spigot bush in flywheel
Clutch spin (failure to disengage) so that gears cannot be meshed	Incorrect cable adjustment (too slack) Driven plate sticking on input shaft splines due to rust. May occur after vehicle standing idle for long period Damage or misaligned pressure plate assembly
Clutch slip (increase in engine speed does not result in increase in vehicle road speed – particularly on gradients)	Incorrect cable adjustment (too tight) Friction surfaces worn out or oil contaminated
Noise evident on depressing clutch pedal	Dry, worn or damaged release bearing Insufficient pedal free travel Weak or broken pedal return spring Weak or broken clutch release lever return spring Excessive play between driven plate hub splines and input shaft splines
Noise evident as clutch pedal released	Distorted driven plate Broken or weak driven plate torsion springs Insufficient pedal free travel Weak or broken clutch pedal return spring Weak or broken release lever return spring Distorted or worn input shaft Release bearing loose

5

Chapter 6 Manual transmission

Refer to Chapter 13 for specifications related to 1982 and 1983 US models

Contents

Specifications

General

Transmission type	Four or five forward speeds and reverse. Synchromesh on all forward gears
Gear ratios:	
1st	2.916 : 1
2nd	1.764 : 1
3rd	1.181 : 1
4th	0.846 : 1
5th (when fitted)	0.714 : 1
Reverse	2.916 : 1
Lubricant capacity:	
From dry	4.6 Imp pints (2.60 litres, 2.75 US quarts)
Drain and refill	4.4 Imp pints (2.50 litres, 2.60 US quarts)

Overhaul data – 4-speed

	Standard (new)	Service limit
Countershaft gear clearances:		
1st gear	0.001 to 0.003 in (0.03 to 0.08 mm)	0.007 in (0.18 mm)
2nd, 3rd and 4th gears	0.002 to 0.005 in (0.05 to 0.12 mm)	0.007 in (0.18 mm)
Replacement 1st gear thrust washers:		
A	0.077 to 0.078 in (1.95 to 1.98 mm)	
B	0.076 to 0.077 in (1.92 to 1.95 mm)	
C	0.074 to 0.076 in (1.89 to 1.92 mm)	
Replacement spacer collars	4 lengths available from 1.103 in (28.01 mm) to 1.107 in (28.13 mm)	
Shift forks:	**Standard (new)**	**Service limit**
Fork to synchroniser sleeve clearance	0.02 to 0.03 in (0.5 to 0.7 mm)	0.04 in (1.0 mm)
Fork finger thickness	0.25 to 0.26 in (6.4 to 6.5 mm)	0.23 in (6.0 mm)
Synchro ring to gear clearance	0.033 to 0.043 in (0.85 to 1.1 mm)	0.016 in (0.4 mm)
Mainshaft diameter	0.8656 to 0.8661 in (21.987 to 22.000 mm)	0.8634 in (21.930 mm)
Mainshaft run-out	0.0008 in (0.02 mm)	0.002 in (0.05 mm)
Countershaft diameter:		
Outboard of gear	1.1813 to 1.1818 in (30.004 to 30.017 mm)	1.1787 in (29.940 mm)
Inboard of gear	1.2592 to 1.2598 in (31.984 to 32.000 mm)	1.2571 in (31.930 mm)
Countershaft run-out	0.0008 in (0.02 mm)	0.002 in (0.05 mm)

Overhaul data – 5-speed

	Standard (new)	Service limit
Shift fork finger thickness – 5th gear	0.21 to 0.22 in (5.4 to 5.5 mm)	0.20 in (5.0 mm)

Mainshaft diameter:

Outboard of small gear	0.9837 to 0.9843 in (24.987 to 25.000 mm)	0.9815 in (24.930 mm)
Outboard of large gear	0.8653 to 0.8661 in (21.987 to 22.000 mm)	0.8634 in (21.930 mm)
5th gear clearance	0.002 to 0.015 in (0.05 to 0.38 mm)	–

All other overhaul data are as given for the 4-speed transmission

Torque wrench settings

	lbf ft	Nm
Countershaft locknut	65	90
Mainshaft locknut (4-speed)	33	45
Mainshaft locknut (5-speed)	43	60
Shift arm holder bolts	9	12
Shift fork-to-shaft bolts	12	17
Reverse shift fork nut	17	24
Transmission housing bolts	20	27
5th gear housing bolts	9	12
End cover bolts (early models)	9	12
Endplate bolts (later models)	7	10
Reversing light switch	9	12
Speedometer drive bolt	9	12
Transmission-to-engine bolts	33	45

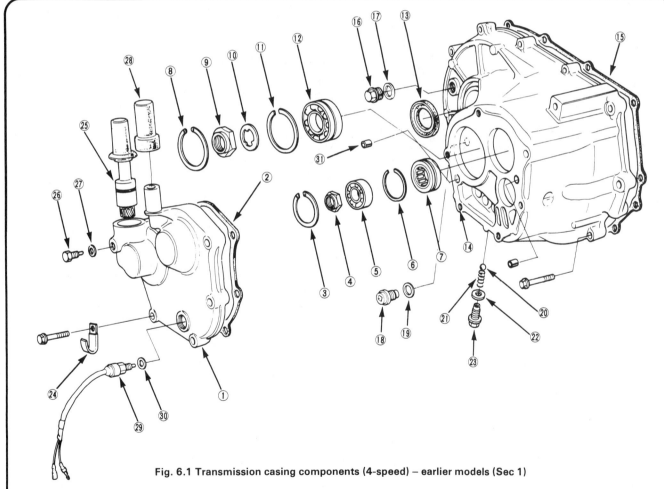

Fig. 6.1 Transmission casing components (4-speed) – earlier models (Sec 1)

1 End cover	9 Locknut	16 Oil filler plug	24 Wire clamp
2 Gasket	10 Spring washer	17 Washer	25 Speedometer drivegear
3 Snap-ring	11 Snap-ring	18 Drain plug	26 Special bolt
4 Locknut	12 Countershaft	19 Washer	27 Washer
5 Ball-bearing	ball-bearing	20 Detent ball	28 Breather cap
6 Snap-ring	13 Differential seal	21 Spring	29 Reversing light switch
7 Mainshaft bearing	14 Transmission housing	22 Washer	30 Washer
8 Snap-ring	15 Gasket	23 Retaining screw	31 Dowel pin

6

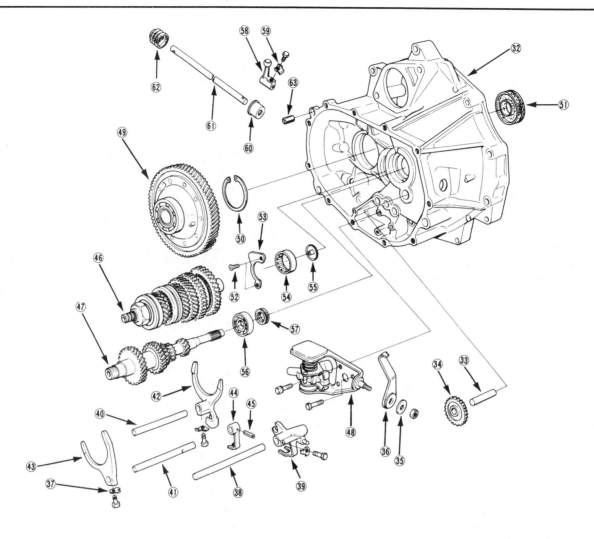

Fig. 6.2 Clutch housing components (4-speed) – earlier models (Sec 1)

32 *Clutch housing*	40 *1st/2nd gear shift shaft*	48 *Shift arm holder*	56 *Mainshaft ball-bearing*
33 *Reverse idler gear shaft*	41 *3rd/4th gear shift shaft*	49 *Differential assembly*	57 *Mainshaft seal*
34 *Reverse idler gear*	42 *1st/2nd gear shift fork*	50 *Snap-ring*	58 *Selector arm*
35 *Special washer*	43 *3rd/4th gear shift fork*	51 *Differential seal*	59 *Lockplate*
36 *Reverse gear shift fork*	44 *3rd/4th gear shift guide*	52 *Countersunk screw*	60 *Shift rod seal*
37 *Lockplate*	45 *Spring pin*	53 *Bearing retainer plate*	61 *Shift rod*
38 *Reverse gear shift shaft*	46 *Countershaft assembly*	54 *Countershaft bearing*	62 *Boot*
39 *Reverse shift guide*	47 *Mainshaft*	55 *Oil barrier plate*	63 *Dowel pin*

1 General description

The gearbox and final drive are mounted integrally with the engine to form a compact unit. The design of the gearbox is unusual in that the integral gears form part of the mainshaft rather than being on the countershaft (Figs. 6.1 and 6.2).

The gearbox is in line with the engine. Drive is taken from the flywheel and clutch through a mainshaft which carries the clutch driven plate.

There are two versions of the gearbox, one having four forward speeds and reverse and the other having a fifth speed gear mounted on an extension of the mainshaft. On both versions, gears are selected by a floor-mounted shift lever.

2 Gearbox – maintenance

1   At the intervals specified in Routine Maintenance, check the oil level with the vehicle standing on a level surface and with the oil at normal operating temperature.
2   Switch the ignition off and wipe clean the area round the oil filler bolt on the transmission.
3   Remove the bolt (Fig. 6.3) and insert a finger in the hole to check the oil level. If the oil is below the level of the hole, add oil of the specified grade until oil just starts to run out, then re-install and tighten the bolt.
4   Also at the mileage intervals specified in Routine Maintenance, drain the oil from the gearbox and then add fresh oil until the level is correct. The location of the drain plug is shown in Fig. 6.1.

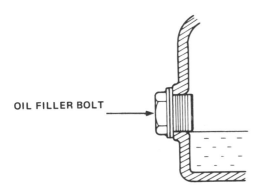

OIL FILLER BOLT →

Fig. 6.3 Oil filler bolt (Sec 2)

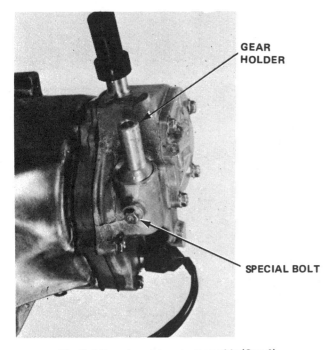

GEAR HOLDER

SPECIAL BOLT

Fig. 6.4 Speedometer gear assembly (Sec 4)

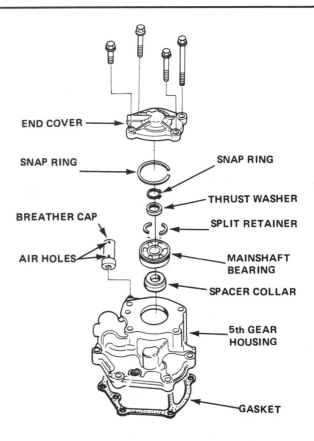

END COVER →

SNAP RING

SNAP RING

THRUST WASHER

BREATHER CAP

SPLIT RETAINER

AIR HOLES →

MAINSHAFT BEARING

SPACER COLLAR

5th GEAR HOUSING

GASKET

Fig. 6.5 End cover – earlier models (Sec 4)

3 Gearbox – removal and installation

1 The gearbox may be removed from the vehicle leaving the engine in position. Most of the operations necessary for removing the gearbox only are the same as those for removing the engine with gearbox and are illustrated in Chapter 1.

2 Disconnect the battery leads and also disconnect the earthing lead from the transmission.

3 Turn the ignition key so that the steering lock is released and put the gear lever to neutral.

4 In the engine compartment, disconnect the following wires:

(a) The battery positive cable to the starter motor
(b) The black/white wire from the starter solenoid
(c) The green/black and yellow wires from the reversing lamp switch
(d) The yellow/green wire from the temperature gauge sender unit (if fitted)
(e) The black/yellow and yellow wires from the ignition timing thermosensor (if fitted)

5 Remove the clip securing the speedometer cable to the transmission and withdraw the cable. Do not remove the speedometer gear holder.

6 Disconnect the clutch cable from the release arm.

7 Remove the transmission side mounting bolt from the starter motor, and the bolt from the engine top mounting.

8 Raise the front of the vehicle and support it on firmly based stands.

9 Drain the oil from the transmission and then reinstall the drain plug and washer.

10 Disconnect the left and right tie-rod end balljoints. Remove the bolt securing the brake hose to the suspension strut.

11 Remove the clamp bolt securing the steering knuckle to the suspension strut and tap the knuckle off the end of the strut (see Chapter 1, Section 4).

12 Turn the steering knuckle outwards as far as it will go and with a screwdriver against the inboard constant velocity joint, prise the driveshaft out of its housing about $\frac{1}{2}$ in (12 mm), to force the spring clip on the driveshaft out of its groove inside the differential, then pull the driveshaft out of the transmission.

13 Disconnect the shift lever torque rod from the transmission housing.

14 Slide back the spring clip on the shift rod. Drive out the spring pin using a pin punch and then disconnect the shift rod.

15 Place a jack beneath the engine and raise the engine just enough to take the weight off the engine mountings. **Caution:** *Use a block of wood between the head of the jack and the engine to prevent damage to the sump.* Alternatively, take the weight of the engine on a lifting sling and hoist.

16 Remove the front and rear torque rods and the brackets of the rear torque rod.

17 Remove the engine damper bracket from the transmission.

18 Remove the rear engine mounting and its bracket.

19 Place a piece of 1 in (25 mm) thick wood on the crossmember and then lower the engine so that its weight is taken by the crossmember.

20 Remove the remaining starter motor bolt and remove the starter motor.

21 Remove the two remaining transmission bolts and then support

6

the transmission on a jack or hoist, raising it just enough to take the weight off the engine.

22 Pull the transmission away from the engine until the gearbox mainshaft is clear of the clutch pressure plate, taking care to ensure that the weight of the transmission remains supported, then lower the transmission and remove it from beneath the vehicle.

23 Installation is the reverse of removal.

4 Gearbox (5-speed) – dismantling

1 With the transmission removed from the vehicle, clean the external surfaces thoroughly using paraffin, or a water-soluble proprietary degreasing agent.

2 Pull the breather cap from the breather pipe on the transmission cover.

3 Remove the bolt retaining the speedometer gear holder and pull out the speedometer gear assembly (Fig. 6.4).

4 The gearboxes of pre-1981 models have a 5th gear housing which differs from that of later models and the methods of removal are different.

Earlier models

5 Remove the four bolts from the end cover and remove the cover, snap-ring, thrust washer and split retainers (Fig. 6.5).

6 Pull 5th gear housing off the mainshaft and remove the mainshaft bearing from the housing.

7 Lift the spacer collar off the mainshaft.

Later models

8 Remove the two bolts from the end cover and remove the cover and oil barrier plate.

9 Using a hammer and pin punch, unstake the mainshaft locknut.

10 To remove the mainshaft nut requires some means of holding the mainshaft to prevent it from rotating. In the absence of the special tool (Fig. 6.6) which fits the mainshaft splines, an old clutch plate can be used, but directly clamping onto the splines is likely to damage them. Alternatively the nut can be released with an impact wrench, but a mainshaft holder will still be required for tightening it to the correct torque.

11 Having locked the mainshaft, use a 24 mm socket to remove the mainshaft nut, which has a *left-hand thread*.

12 Remove the six bolts from 5th gear housing and remove the housing.

13 Expand the snap ring which retains the mainshaft bearing in the housing and push the bearing out by hand.

14 Remove the gasket and dowel pins.

All models

15 Select reverse gear and then drive out the spring pin which secures 5th gear shift fork to its shaft.

MAINSHAFT HOLDER
Fig. 6.6 Special tool for preventing mainshaft from rotating (Secs 4 & 9)

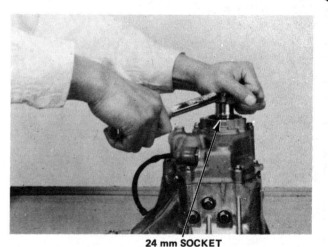

24 mm SOCKET
Fig. 6.7 Removing the mainshaft nut (Sec 4)

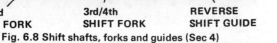

1st/2nd SHIFT SHAFT   3rd/4th SHIFT SHAFT   5th/REVERSE SHIFT SHAFT

1st/2nd SHIFT FORK   3rd/4th SHIFT FORK   REVERSE SHIFT GUIDE
Fig. 6.8 Shift shafts, forks and guides (Sec 4)

COUNTERSHAFT ASSY   MAINSHAFT ASSY

Fig. 6.9 Removing the gear assemblies (Sec 4)

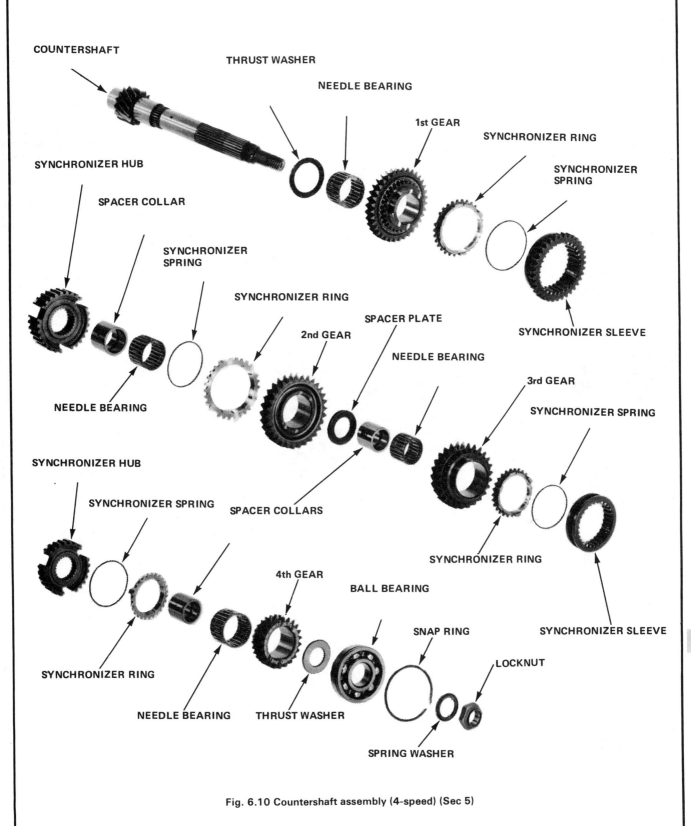

COUNTERSHAFT

THRUST WASHER

NEEDLE BEARING

1st GEAR

SYNCHRONIZER RING

SYNCHRONIZER SPRING

SYNCHRONIZER HUB

SPACER COLLAR

SYNCHRONIZER SPRING

SYNCHRONIZER RING

2nd GEAR

SPACER PLATE

NEEDLE BEARING

3rd GEAR

SYNCHRONIZER SPRING

SYNCHRONIZER SLEEVE

NEEDLE BEARING

SPACER COLLARS

SYNCHRONIZER RING

SYNCHRONIZER HUB

SYNCHRONIZER SPRING

4th GEAR

BALL BEARING

SNAP RING

LOCKNUT

SYNCHRONIZER SLEEVE

6

SYNCHRONIZER RING

NEEDLE BEARING

THRUST WASHER

SPRING WASHER

Fig. 6.10 Countershaft assembly (4-speed) (Sec 5)

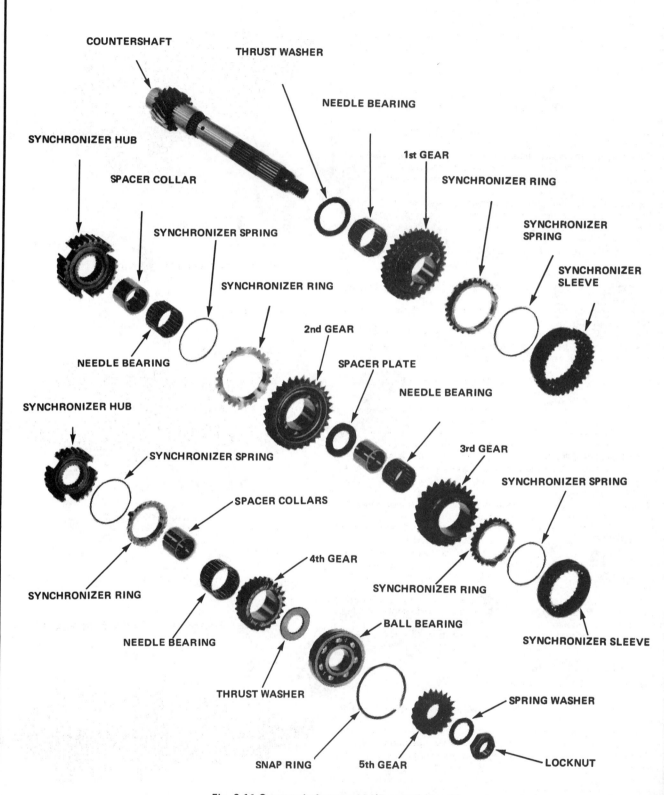

COUNTERSHAFT

THRUST WASHER

NEEDLE BEARING

1st GEAR

SYNCHRONIZER HUB

SYNCHRONIZER RING

SPACER COLLAR

SYNCHRONIZER SPRING

SYNCHRONIZER SPRING

SYNCHRONIZER RING

SYNCHRONIZER SLEEVE

2nd GEAR

NEEDLE BEARING

SPACER PLATE

NEEDLE BEARING

SYNCHRONIZER HUB

3rd GEAR

SYNCHRONIZER SPRING

SYNCHRONIZER SPRING

SPACER COLLARS

4th GEAR

SYNCHRONIZER RING

SYNCHRONIZER RING

NEEDLE BEARING

SYNCHRONIZER SLEEVE

BALL BEARING

THRUST WASHER

SPRING WASHER

SNAP RING

5th GEAR

LOCKNUT

Fig. 6.11 Countershaft assembly (5-speed) (Sec 5)

16 Remove 5th gear shift fork, synchronizer sleeve and hub as a unit. If the hub stays on the shaft, use a puller to remove it.

17 Remove the synchronizer ring with its spring, then remove 5th gear with its needle bearing and thrust washer.

18 On early models, remove the housing spacer, the snap-ring from the countershaft bearing and the snap-ring from the mainshaft bearing.

19 Remove the three detent ball retaining screws, their washers, springs and balls.

20 Remove the 11 bolts securing the housing and then loosen the housing from its gasket by tapping on the bosses around the edge with a soft hammer.

21 On later models expand the countershaft bearing snap-ring so that the transmission housing can be removed.

22 Remove the transmission housing, using a puller or slide hammer.

23 Pull out the reverse idler shaft and remove the reverse idler gear.

24 Remove the nut securing reverse gear shift fork and remove the shift fork.

25 Remove reverse gear shift fork, detent ball and spring. Keep the ball and spring separate from the other detent balls and springs.

26 Bend down the lockplate tabs of the shift fork bolts and remove the bolts and plates.

27 Remove 5th/reverse shift shaft and then withdraw the shift guide (Fig. 6.8).

28 Withdraw 1st/2nd gear shift shaft.

29 Withdraw 3rd/4th gear shift shaft and then remove 3rd/4th gear shift fork.

30 Push the synchronizer into position to engage 2nd gear and then remove 1st/2nd shift fork.

31 Remove the countershaft and mainshaft together (Fig. 6.9).

32 Remove the four bolts securing the shift arm holder, noting that the two end ones are standard bolts and that the two side ones are flange bolts.

33 Remove the shift arm holder and lift out the differential assembly.

5 Countershaft – dismantling and inspection

1 Before dismantling the countershaft assembly, inspect it for wear and damage and make the following measurements. If any of the measurements are outside the tolerances given in the Specifications, the spacer collar or thrust washer must be changed so that the correct dimension is achieved.

2 Measure the clearance between the thrust washer and 1st gear (Fig. 6.12), the spacer plate and 2nd gear (Fig. 6.13), the spacer plate and the shoulder of 3rd gear (Fig. 6.14) and the clearance between the thrust washer and the shoulder on 4th gear (Fig. 6.15).

3 If it is necessary to dismantle the countershaft, the mainshaft and countershaft will have to be temporarily refitted to the transmission and clutch housings. With the mainshaft holder installed (see Section 4), the countershaft locknut can be removed using a deep socket (32 mm diameter for 5-speed, 36 mm for 4-speed). If these tools are not available, it is advisable to take the gearbox to a Honda dealer or other automobile workshop to have the work done.

4 Assuming the tools to be available, unstake the countershaft locknut and remove it, then remove the geartrains from the housings.

5 On 5-speed models, remove the dished spring washer and 5th gear.

6 On all models, draw off the countershaft bearing and inspect it for wear and roughness of rotation.

7 Remove the splined washer and inspect it for damage to the splines.

8 Remove 4th gear, its needle bearing and spacer collar. Inspect the needle bearing for wear and smoothness of roller operation.

9 Withdraw the synchroniser ring, synchroniser hub and sleeve assembly.

10 Remove 3rd gear with its synchroniser ring, needle bearing, and sleeve. Inspect the needle bearing.

11 Remove the spacer plate, 2nd gear and its synchroniser ring, needle bearing and sleeve. Inspect the needle bearing.

12 Remove the 1st/2nd synchroniser hub and sleeve.

13 Remove 1st gear with its synchroniser ring, needle bearing and thrust washer. Inspect the needle bearing.

14 Inspect the inside surface of the synchroniser rings for wear, remove the springs from the outside of the rings and install new ones.

15 Inspect the synchroniser ring and matching teeth on the gears for

Fig. 6.12 Measuring 1st gear clearance (Sec 5)

Fig. 6.13 Measuring 2nd gear clearance (Sec 5)

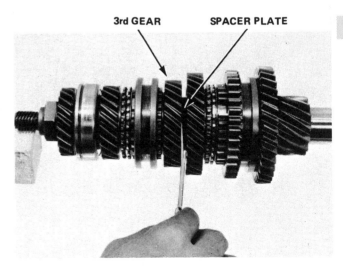

Fig. 6.14 Measuring 3rd gear clearance (Sec 5)

wear. The face of the teeth should be triangular and their points should not be rounded off.

16 Inspect the cone surfaces of 1st, 2nd, 3rd and 4th speed countershaft gears.

17 Place each synchroniser ring on its matching gear cone, spin the ring and allow it to stop. Measure the clearance between the ring and the gear (Fig. 6.16). If the clearance is less than the minimum specified, renew the synchroniser ring.

18 Inspect the teeth of all gears for uneven wear, chipping, cracking, scoring and scuffing.

19 Inspect the countershaft itself for wear, distortion and damage. Examine all oil passages and ensure that they are free from obstructions.

6 Mainshaft – inspection

1 Inspect the teeth of all gears for uneven wear, chipping, cracking, scoring and scuffing.

2 Inspect the mainshaft for wear, distortion and damage. Examine the oil passages and ensure that they are free from obstructions.

3 Check that the splines are not worn and are free from burrs.

4 On 5-speed boxes, measure the clearance between the shoulder of 5th gear and its thrust washer with the mainshaft and bearing assembled. The permissible clearance is listed in the Specifications. Also inspect the cone surface of the gear for wear.

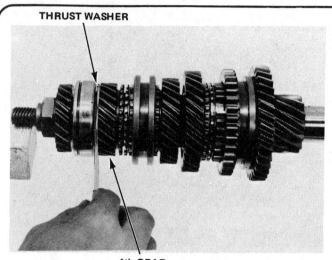

Fig. 6.15 Measuring 4th gear clearance (Sec 5)

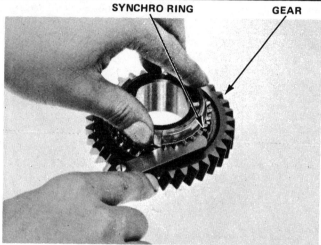

Fig. 6.16 Measuring synchroniser ring to gear clearance (Sec 5)

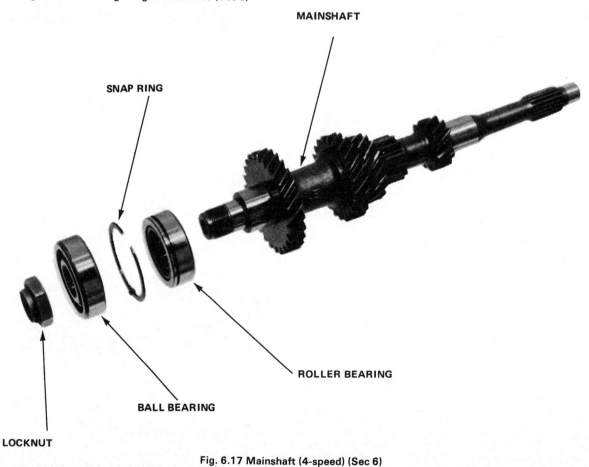

Fig. 6.17 Mainshaft (4-speed) (Sec 6)

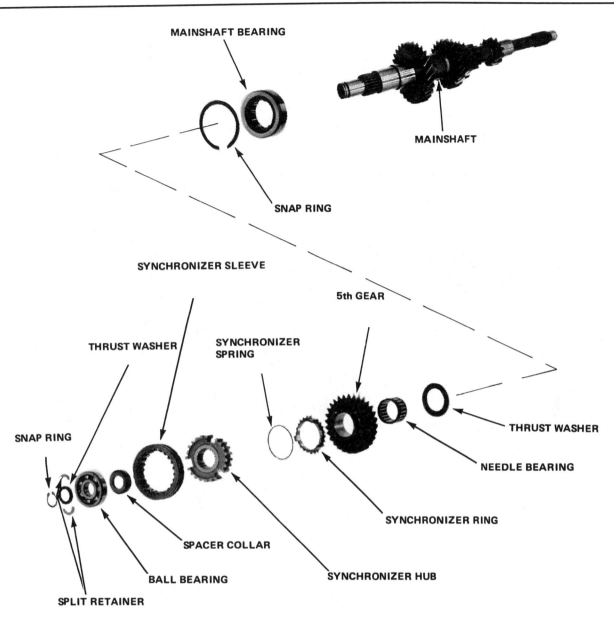

Fig. 6.18 Mainshaft (5-speed) earlier type (Sec 6)

7 Countershaft – reassembly

1 Ensure that all parts are scrupulously clean and that the assembly area is also clean. As each component is installed, lubricate it generously.
2 On to the countershaft install the thrust washer, 1st gear needle bearing and 1st gear (photos).
3 Install 1st gear synchroniser ring and spring, then the synchroniser hub and sleeve assembly (photos).
4 Install the spacer collar, 2nd gear needle roller bearing, 2nd gear synchroniser ring and spring and then 2nd gear (photos).
5 Install the spacer plate, 3rd gear sleeve and needle roller bearing, then 3rd gear and its synchroniser ring and spring (photos).
6 Install the synchroniser hub and sleeve of 3rd/4th gears as an assembly (photo).
7 Install the spacer collar, 4th gear needle roller bearing and 4th gear synchroniser ring and spring (photos).
8 Install 4th gear and the splined thrust washer (photos).
9 Install the countershaft bearing with the groove in the outer bearing race towards the threaded end of the countershaft.
10 On 5-speed boxes, install 5th gear, then the spring washer (dished

side towards the gear) and locknut (photos).
11 On 4-speed boxes, install the spring washer and locknut.
12 Reassemble the countershaft and mainshaft in the transmission housings, lock the mainshaft as described in Section 4 and tighten the countershaft locknut to the specified torque. Slacken the locknut and retighten it to settle the countershaft components.
13 Remove the geartrain again and recheck the gear clearances as described in Section 5. If all is well, stake the locknut into the groove on the countershaft.

8 Gearbox (5-speed) – reassembly

1 Ensure that all parts are scrupulously clean and that the assembly area is also clean. As each component is installed, lubricate it generously.
2 Install the snap-ring for the differential bearing in the clutch housing (Fig. 6.19), then install the differential assembly and tap it with a soft-headed hammer to seat the bearing on the snap-ring (photo).
3 Align the shift arm with the selector arm and install the shift arm holder. Install the two ordinary bolts at opposite ends of the holder and

7.2a Countershaft ready for assembly

7.2b Thrust washer ..

7.2c ... needle bearing ...

7.2d ... and 1st gear

7.3a 1st gear synchroniser ring and spring

7.3b Synchroniser hub and sleeve assembly

7.4a Spacer collar

7.4b 2nd gear needle roller bearing

7.4c 2nd gear synchroniser and spring

7.4d 2nd gear

7.5a Spacer plate

7.5b 3rd gear sleeve ...

7.5c .. and needle roller bearing

7.5d 3rd gear ...

7.5e ... and its synchroniser ring and spring

7.6 Synchroniser hub and sleeve of 3rd/4th gears

7.7a Spacer collar

7.7b 4th gear needle roller bearing

7.7c 4th gear synchroniser ring and spring

7.8a Install 4th gear ...

7.8b ... and the splined thrust washer

7.10a Countershaft bearing and 5th gear

7.10b Spring washer and locknut

8.2 Installing the differential assembly

6

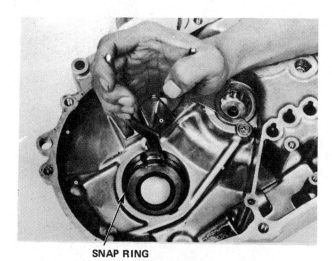

Fig. 6.19 Differential bearing snap-ring (Sec 8)

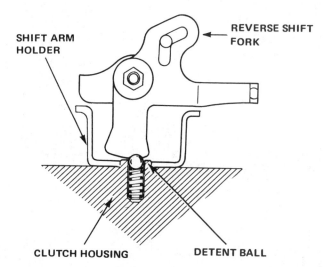

Fig. 6.20 Correct alignment of reverse shift fork and detent ball (Sec 8)

Fig. 6.21 Transmission housing bolts tightening sequence (Sec 8)

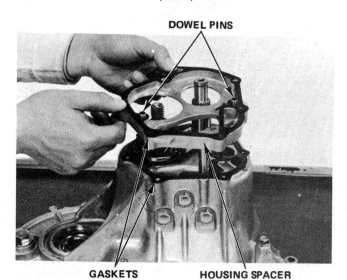

Fig. 6.22 Installing the transmission housing spacer (Sec 8)

the two flanged bolts in the other two holes and tighten the bolts (photos).
4   Hold the mainshaft and the assembled countershaft with their gears in mesh and install the two shafts into the casing (photo).
5   Lift the countershaft assembly enough to allow 1st/2nd gear shift fork to engage its groove in the synchroniser sleeve and then position the fork so that the lugs on the back of the fork fit over the shift arm (photo).
6   Insert 3rd/4th gear shift fork shaft into its fork and install the assembly with the shift guide hooked over the shift arm (photo).
7   Install 1st/2nd gear shift shaft (photo).
8   Hook 5th/reverse shift guide onto the shift arm and then install the shift shaft (photo).
9   Install the spring and detent ball for reverse gear shift fork into the hole in the clutch housing. Note that the detent ball is a different size from the detent balls of the three shift rods (photos).
10 Install reverse shift fork with its special washer and nut. Make certain that the fork is aligned with the detent ball (Fig. 6.20) and then tighten the nut (photos).
11 Install reverse idler gear and its shaft (photo).
12 Install the three special bolts and lockplates which secure the shift forks to the shift shafts, if not already installed. Tighten the bolts and bend the tab of the lockplates up against a flat on the bolt head.
13 Install the two dowel pins in the clutch housing and then put a new gasket in place.
14 Lightly oil the shift shafts, transmission shafts and differential

bearing to make it easier to install the transmission housing.
15 Lower the transmission housing onto the clutch housing being careful to ensure that the shift and transmission shafts enter their correct holes in the transmission housing (photo). Do not force on the housing. If it does not go into place easily, check for and correct any misalignment.
16 Expand the snap-ring of the countershaft bearing until the bearing can pass through and when the transmission housing is fully in place, prise up the countershaft so that the snap-ring engages in the groove in the outside of the bearing (photos).
17 Install the housing bolts and tighten them to the specified torque in the sequence shown in Fig. 6.21.
18 Install the three detent balls and springs, then install and tighten the retaining screws and washers (photo).
19 The final stages of reassembly differ for earlier and later models of gearbox.

Earlier models (pre-1981)

20 Install new gaskets on the transmission housing and housing spacer. Insert the dowels into the spacer and install the spacer on the housing (Fig. 6.22).
21 Install the thrust washer, needle bearing and 5th gear with its synchroniser ring and spring, then install the synchroniser hub, sleeve and shift fork as an assembly. Note that the shouldered face of the synchroniser hub should be nearest to 5th gear and the chamfered

8.3a Selector arm

8.3b Shift arm holder

8.4 Installing the gear assemblies

8.5 Position the shift fork lugs on the shift arm

8.6 Installing 3rd/4th gearshift fork and shaft

8.7 Installing 1st/2nd gearshift shaft

8.8 Reverse shift arm and shaft

8.9a Reverse gear spring ...

8.9b ... and detent ball

8.10a Reverse shift fork and special washer

8.10b Tighten the nut

8.11 Reverse idler gear and shaft

6

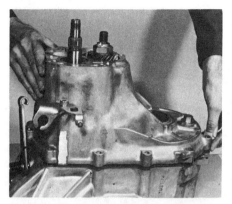
8.15 Lowering the transmission housing

8.16a Expand the snap-ring of the countershaft bearing

8.16b Snap-ring engaged in the groove in the bearing

8.18 Detent ball, spring, screw and washer

8.29a 5th gear thrust washer and needle bearing ...

8.29b ... and 5th gear ...

8.29c ... with its synchroniser ring and spring

8.29d Synchroniser hub, sleeve and shift fork

8.30 5th gear shift fork spring pin

8.33 Installing 5th gear cover

8.34 Install the mainshaft locknut

8.35 Tightening the mainshaft locknut

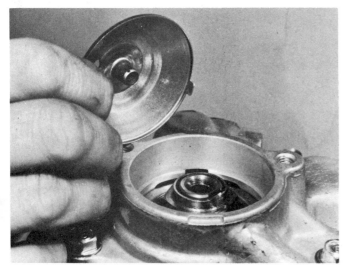

8.37 Oil barrier plate tang

8.38 Installing the end cover

8.39a Installing the reversing light switch ...

8.39b ... and the speedometer gear assembly

face of the synchroniser sleeve should be uppermost (Fig. 6.23).

22 Align the holes in 5th gear shift fork and shaft and drive in their spring pin.

23 Install the spacer collar with the larger diameter facing down.

24 Install the snap-ring in the groove of the countershaft bearing and install the bearing in the housing.

25 Install the housing. Insert and tighten the housing bolts and then install the split retainer onto the end of the shaft.

26 Install the thrust washer with its larger diameter facing the bearing and then install the snap-ring onto the shaft.

27 Install three new O-rings in the end cover and then install the oil barrier plate so that the tube on it aligns with the air passage in the end cover.

28 Install the end cover and insert and tighten its four retaining bolts. Install the breather pipe cap.

Later models

29 Install the thrust washer, needle bearing and 5th gear with its synchroniser ring and spring, then install the synchroniser hub, sleeve and shift fork as an assembly (photos). Note that the shouldered face of the synchroniser hub should be nearest to 5th gear and the chamfered face of the synchroniser sleeve should be uppermost (Fig. 6.23).

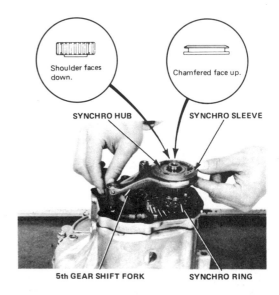

Shoulder faces down.

Chamfered face up.

SYNCHRO HUB   SYNCHRO SLEEVE

5th GEAR SHIFT FORK   SYNCHRO RING

Fig. 6.23 Installation of 5th gear synchroniser (Sec 8)

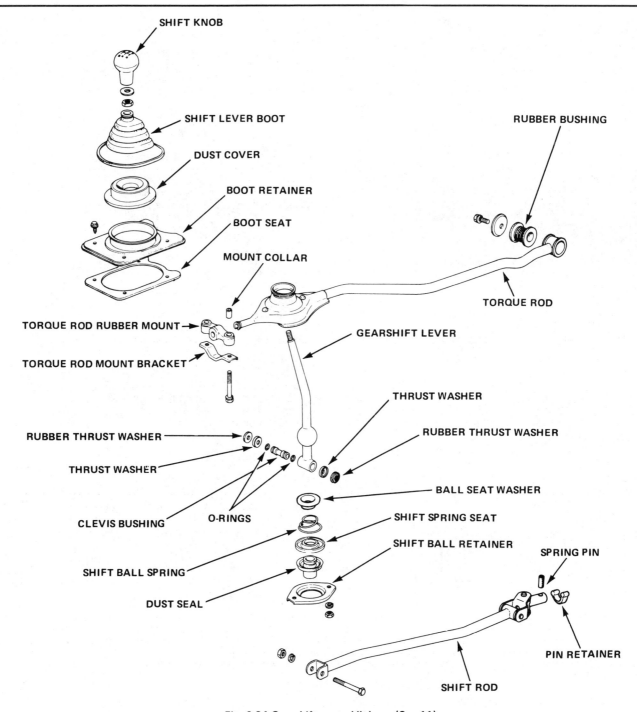

Fig. 6.24 Gearshift control linkage (Sec 11)

30 Align the holes in 5th gear shift fork and shift shaft and drive in the spring pin (photo).

31 Insert the two dowel pins and install a new gasket on the transmission housing.

32 Expand the snap-ring in the 5th gear housing and insert the mainshaft bearing with its part number downwards. Push the bearing down until the snap-ring is properly seated in the bearing and in the groove in the housing.

33 Install 5th gear cover, then insert and tighten its retaining bolts (photo).

34 Install a mainshaft holder, or devise some other means of preventing the splined end of the mainshaft from rotating. Shift the transmission into reverse gear and install the mainshaft locknut (photo) which has a *left-hand thread.*

35 Tighten the locknut to the specified torque (photo), then loosen it and retighten it to the same specified torque.

36 Stake the shoulder of the locknut into the groove in the mainshaft.

37 Align the oil barrier plate tang with the slot in the housing and install the oil barrier plate (photo).

38 Install the end cover (photo). Insert the two retaining bolts and tighten them.

39 Install the reversing lamp switch and the speedometer gear assembly (photos). Install the breather pipe cap.

---

9   Gearbox (4-speed) – dismantling

1   With the transmission removed from the vehicle, clean the external surfaces thoroughly using paraffin, or a water-soluble proprietary degreasing agent.

2   Pull the breather cap from the breather pipe on the transmission cover.
3   Remove the bolt retaining the speedometer gear holder and pull out the speedometer gear assembly.
4   The gearboxes of pre-1981 models have a different end cover from those of later models and their mainshafts are different.

Early models
5   Remove the six bolts from the end cover, remove the cover and remove the two snap-rings from the cover.
6   Using a hammer and a pin punch, unstake the mainshaft locknut.
7   To remove the mainshaft nut requires some means of holding the mainshaft to prevent it from rotating. In the absence of the special tool (Fig. 6.6) which fits the mainshaft splines, an old clutch plate can be used but directly clamping onto the splines is likely to damage them. Alternatively the nut can be released with an impact wrench, but a mainshaft holder will be required for tightening it to the correct torque.
8   Having locked the mainshaft, shift the transmission into gear and use a 30 mm socket to remove the mainshaft nut, which has a *left-hand thread*.
9   Lift off the ball-bearing and remove the snap-ring from the countershaft bearing.

Later models
10 Remove the two bolts from the end cover seal and remove the end cover seal and oil barrier plate.
11 Unstake the mainshaft nut and remove it as in paragraphs 6 to 8, except that the mainshaft nut requires a 24 mm socket.
12 Remove the six bolts from the housing cover, then remove the cover, gasket and dowel pins.

All models
13 Continue dismantling as described in Section 4, paragraphs 19 to 33, disregarding references to 5th gear compartments.

10 Gearbox (4-speed) – reassembly

1   The reassembly of the 4-speed gearbox is essentially the same as for the 5-speed box described in Section 8, paragraphs 1 to 18.
2   The final stages differ on the two models of gearbox and are the reverse of the dismantling instructions in the previous Section.

11 Gearshift control linkage – general

1   Any wear occurring in the linkage can only be corrected by renewal of the components concerned.
2   The most likely points of wear are at the shift lever ball seat, the bush at the base of the lever or the joints on the shift rod extension bar.
3   Dismantling is straightforward as shown in the accompanying illustration (Fig. 6.24).

12 Reversing light switch – testing, removal and installation

1   If the reversing lamps fail to illuminate, first check the bulbs and fuse. Next check the security of the connecting wires particularly at the switch.
2   If the foregoing are in order, the switch will have to be removed and a new one installed.
3   To remove the switch, disconnect the leads from its adjacent connector and then unscrew it from the transmission cover.
4   Before installing the new switch make sure that the sealing washer is in good condition.

13 Fault diagnosis – manual transmission

Symptom	Reason(s)
Ineffective synchromesh	Worn baulk rings or synchro hubs
Jumps out of one or more gears (on drive or overrun)	Weak detent springs, worn selector forks or worn gears
Noisy, rough, whining and vibration	Worn bearings and/or thrust washers (initially) resulting in extended wear generally due to play and backlash
Noisy and difficult engagement of gears	Clutch fault (see Chapter 5)

Note: *It is sometimes difficult to decide whether it is worthwhile removing and dismantling the gearbox for a fault which may be nothing more than a minor irritant. Gearboxes which howl, or where the synchromesh can be 'beaten' by a quick gearchange, may continue to perform for a long time in this state. A worn gearbox usually needs a complete rebuild to eliminate noise because the various gears, if re-aligned on new bearings, will continue to howl when different wearing surfaces are presented to each other.*

The decision to overhaul, therefore, must be considered with regard to time and money available, relative to the degree of noise or malfunction that the driver has to suffer.

6

Chapter 7 Automatic and Hondamatic transmission

Refer to Chapter 13 for specifications related to 1982 and 1983 US models

Contents

Specifications

Part A: Hondamatic transmission (2-speed)

Transmission type .... Semi-automatic with torque converter, two forward speeds and one reverse

Primary gear ratio .... 1 : 1 (direct)

Gear ratios
1st .... 1.565 : 1
2nd:
    Wagon .... 0.966 : 1
    Sedan and Hatchback .... 0.903 : 1
Reverse .... 2.045 : 1

Stall speed
1300 engine .... 2550 rpm
1500 engine .... 2800 rpm
Acceptable deviation from above .... $+400 \\ -300$ rpm

Oil pressure at test points
Standard .... 70 to 112 lbf/in^2 (5 to 8 kgf/cm^2)
Minimum .... 56 lbf/in^2 (4 kgf/cm^2)

Oil capacity
Drain and refill .... 4.5 Imp pints (2.5 litres/2.6 US quarts)
From dry .... 7.5 Imp pints (4.2 litres/4.4 US quarts)

Torque wrench settings – Hondamatic transmission

	lbf ft	Nm
Drain plug	30	41
Mainshaft locknut	36	50
Cooler hose unions	20	28
Valve body retainer bolt	9	12
Selector link arm lockbolt	9	12
Valve body securing bolts	9	12
Stator torque converter shaft sealing ring guide bolts	9	12
Servo body securing bolts	9	12
Reverse shift fork lockbolt	9	12
Transmission housing to torque converter housing:		
Small bolts	9	12
Large bolts	20	27

Transmission housing bearing retainer bolts	9	12
Reverse idler shaft holder bolts	9	12
Countershaft nut	70	97
Torque converter cover to pump	9	12
Transmission housing end cover	9	12
Torque converter housing to engine	33	45
Driveplate-to-torque converter bolts	9	12
Driveplate-to-crankshaft bolts	36	50

Part B: Automatic transmission (3-speed)

Transmission type .... Fully automatic with torque converter, three forward speeds and one reverse

Gear ratios
1st .... 2.380 : 1
2nd .... 1.500 : 1
3rd .... 0.969 : 1
Reverse .... 1.954 : 1

Stall speed
1500 .... 2550 rpm
1300 .... 2400 rpm
Acceptable deviation from above .... ± 300 rpm

Shift speeds*

Upshifts:	**1st to 2nd**	**2nd to 3rd**
Full throttle	28 to 33 mph (45 to 53 kph)	55 to 62 mph (89 to 100 khp)
Half throttle	17 to 22 mph (27 to 35 kph)	30 to 40 mph (48 to 64 kph)
No throttle (downhill)	10 to 15 mph (16 to 24 kph)	20 to 25 mph (32 to 40 kph)
Downshifts:	**3rd to 2nd**	**2nd to 1st**
Full throttle	50 to 60 mph (81 to 97 kph)	23 to 28 mph (37 to 45 kph)
No throttle	13 to 18 mph (21 to 29 kph)	5 to 10 mph (8 to 16 kph)

Transmission in 'D' and at operating temperature

Oil pressure at test points

	Standard	Minimum
Line	106.7 to 113.7 lbf/in² (7.5 to 8.0 kgf/cm²)	99.5 lbf/in² (7.0 kgf/cm²)
1st and 2nd clutches	99.5 to 113.7 lbf/in² (7.0 to 8.0 kgf/cm²)	92.4 lbf/in² (6.5 kgf/cm²)
Throttle	85.3 to 88.2 lbf/in² (6.0 to 6.2 kgf/cm²)	81.0 lbf/in² (5.7 kgf/cm²)
Governor	49.1 to 50.4 lbf/in² (3.45 to 3.55 kgf/cm²)	42.0 lbf/in² (3.3 kgf/cm²)
3rd clutch	106.7 to 113.7 lbf/in² (7.5 to 8.0 kgf/cm²)	99.5 lbf/in² (7.0 kgf/cm²)

Oil capacity
Drain and refill .... 2.6 US quarts (2.5 litres)
From dry .... 5.2 US quarts (4.9 litres)

Torque wrench settings – automatic transmission

	lbf ft	Nm
Speedometer gear holder	7	9
Valve and servo body securing bolts	9	12
Control shaft lever lockbolt	9	12
Accumulator cover	9	12
Governor valve and regulator valve	9	12
Reverse shift fork bolt	10	14
Throttle control shaft bolt	6	8
Parking lever bolt	10	14
Countershaft locknut	70	95
Mainshaft locknut	70	95
End cover bolts	9	12
Cooler pipe banjo	19	26
Cooler hose fitting	19	26
Torque converter cover	9	12
Rear torque rod bolts	54	75
Torque rod brackets	28	39
Front torque rod	54	75
Transmission housing-to-torque converter housing bolts	20	28

7

PART A: HONDAMATIC TRANSMISSION (2-SPEED)

1 Hondamatic transmission – general description

The main components of the semi-automatic transmission are the torque converter and a special gearbox enclosing two forward speeds and one reverse gear.

The torque converter is housed in an enlarged bellhousing between the engine and gearbox, and its appearance is that of a large almost hemispherical container with a ring gear for the starter motor attached to the face nearest the engine. The container encloses the torque converter system of vanes, and is kept full of oil under pressure by a pump mounted in the gearbox casing.

The transmission functions as follows. The engine delivers power to the torque converter which balances the speed and torque from the engine to the speed and torque 'required' by the gearbox. The converter has the characteristic that if the input speed from the engine is greater than the output speed to the gearbox, the output torque will be between 1 and 2 times greater than the input torque, depending on the difference of input and output speeds.

This torque characteristic is derived from the way the drive/impeller vanes in the converter are coupled to the output/turbine vanes. The impeller vanes are shaped so that as they rotate the oil in the impeller is flung radially outwards to the top tip of the vanes and forwards in the direction of the vanes rotation. The oil on leaving the impeller impinges onto the output turbine which is driven by the oil in the direction of rotation of the impeller. If the impeller is rotating faster than the turbine – typically when the engine is working to accelerate the car – the oil flung onto the turbine by the impeller creates a greater torque on the turbine than that exerted by the engine on the impeller. The stator in the converter serves to correct the direction of flow of oil from the turbine back to the impeller and improves the efficiency of the converter.

The power output from the converter is transmitted to the final drive via the two-speed gearbox. The gears are changed manually; number 1 (L) serves up to a speed of 50 mph (80 kph) and number 2 (* or D) is the cruising gear. Multiplate wet clutches attached to each gear train connect the selected train to the gearbox mainshaft and final drive via the fixed gears on the countershaft.

The Hondamatic is therefore a semi-automatic system, because the driver must still select the appropriate gear for the particular road conditions at the time. The torque converter adds a degree of flexibility to the gear selected, and does not take the need for thought, regarding choice of gear, from the driver.

2 Maintenance

1   At the intervals specified in Routine Maintenance, check the fluid level. To do this, run the car for a minimum of 5 miles (8 km) until the fluid is at normal operating temperature and then position the car on level ground and switch off the engine.
2   Unscrew and remove the dipstick, wipe it clean and re-insert it but do not screw it in. Withdraw the dipstick for the second time and read off the fluid level (Fig. 7.1).
3   Top up as necessary and install the dipstick, screwing it in finger tight only.
4   With a new vehicle, the transmission fluid should be renewed after the first 15 000 miles (24 000 km) and thereafter every 30 000 miles (48 000 km).

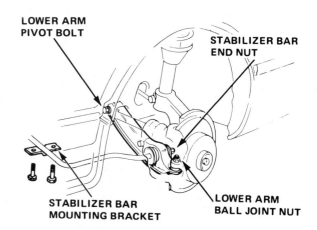

Fig. 7.2 Stabilizer bar to lower arm connection (Sec 3)

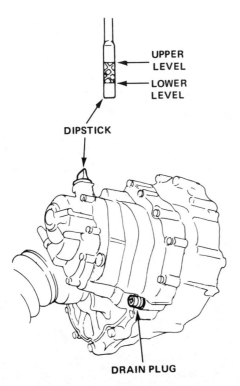

Fig. 7.1 Transmission dipstick and drain plug (Sec 2)

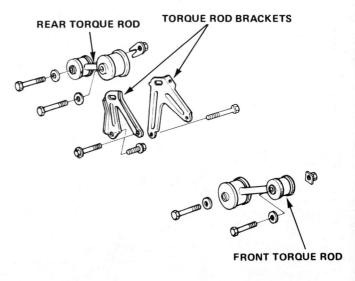

Fig. 7.3 Torque rods and brackets (Sec 3)

3   Hondamatic transmission – removal and installation

1   The Hondamatic transmission can be removed independently of
the engine leaving the latter in position in the car but obviously if any
major work is required to the engine at the same time, it will be easier
to remove the engine/transmission and then separate them, as
described in Chapter 1.
2   To remove the transmission on its own, first disconnect the
negative lead from the battery terminal and then disconnect the earth
strap from the transmission casing.
3   Place speed selector lever in 'N', and release the steering lock.
4   Disconnect the positive lead from the starter motor.
5   Disconnect the black/white lead from the starter solenoid.
6   Disconnect the lead from the water temperature sender unit.
7   On vehicles equipped with full emission control, disconnect the
leads from the ignition thermosensor.
8   Disconnect the oil cooler hoses from the transmission and plug the
hoses.
9   Unscrew and remove the starter motor securing bolt on the
transmission side.
10 Remove the top transmission mounting bolt.
11 Remove the front bolt from the rear torque rod bracket.
12 Remove the clip which secures the speedometer drive and
disconnect the cable.
13 Remove the console from around the selector lever. Refer to
Chapter 12 if necessary.
14 Disconnect the control cable from the selector lever. Refer to
Section 8 if necessary. Remove the cable retainer plate and extract the
cable.
15 Slacken the front roadwheel nuts, then jack up the front of the car
and support it securely. Remove the front wheels.
16 Drain the transmission fluid. Re-install the drain plug so that it
does not get lost.
17 Disconnect the lower arm balljoints from the steering knuckles,
referring to Chapter 11 if necessary. Similarly disconnect the steering
track rod balljoints.
18 Prise the inner constant velocity joints away from the transmission
to disconnect the driveshafts. Refer to Chapter 8 if necessary.
19 Remove the front stabiliser (anti-roll) bar from the vehicle.
20 Place a jack underneath the engine sump, with a block of wood
between the jack and the sump to spread the load. Jack up under the
engine just sufficiently to take the load off the engine/transmission
mountings.
21 Remove the front and rear torque rods, also the rear torque rod
brackets (Fig. 7.3).
22 Remove the rear engine mounting and bracket.
23 Place a block of wood approximately 1 x 2 x 4 in
(25 x 50 x 100 mm) between the engine sump and the front
crossmember. Lower the jack so that the engine rests on the block of
wood, then remove the jack.
24 Remove the engine damper bracket and the torque converter
cover plate.
25 Remove the 8 bolts which secure the torque converter to the
driveplate. It will be necessary to rotate the crankshaft, using a 19 mm
socket on the crankshaft pulley bolt, to gain access to the bolts. **Do
not** remove the 16 torque converter cover securing bolts.
26 Unscrew and remove the starter motor securing bolt on the engine
side. Remove the starter motor.
27 Remove the remaining torque converter housing to engine securing bolts.
28 Place a jack (preferably a trolley jack) under the transmission, and
raise it just enough to take the weight of the transmission.
29 Pull the transmission away from the engine far enough to clear the
locating dowel pins.
30 Lower the jack and withdraw the transmission from the car. Make
sure that the torque converter stays within its housing.
31 Installation is a reversal of the removal procedure, but note the
following points:

(a) *Tighten the torque converter securing bolts in criss-cross
sequence, first to half the specified torque, then to the final
torque*
(b) *When the transmission is installed, replenish the automatic
transmission fluid, then start the engine and shift through all
gear positions 3 times. Adjust the control cable if necessary
(Section 8)*

(c) *When the engine has reached operating temperature, switch
it off and check the fluid level in the transmission*

4   Hondamatic transmission – dismantling into major assemblies

1   Overhaul of the transmission will normally only be required after a
fault has been diagnosed after reference to Section 10.
2   Withdraw the torque converter from the converter housing.
3   Check that alignment marks are visible on the edges of the torque
converter pump and cover, if not, scribe marks to ensure refitting in
their original positions.
4   Unbolt the cover and separate the internal components, noting
carefully their sequence and orientation.
5   Unscrew and remove the fluid dipstick, unscrew the end cover
bolts and tap off the end cover using a soft-faced mallet.
6   Move the speed selector arm to the 'park' position.
7   Two special tools will now be required. One (07923 - 6890201)
to hold the splined end of the mainshaft still while the mainshaft
locknut is unscrewed with the other tool (07916 - 6390001) (Figs. 7.6
and 7.7).
8   Remove the low clutch, low gear, needle bearing and spacer as an
assembly then extract the thrust washer.
9   Relieve the staking on the countershaft nut, then unscrew and
remove it and lift off low gear (Fig. 7.8).
10 Remove the two bolts and three screws which secure the bearing
retainer. An impact screwdriver wiill probably be needed for the
screws since they have been staked in position.
11 Extract the bolts from the reverse idler shaft retainer.
12 Unscrew and remove the 14 bolts which hold the transmission
housing to the torque converter housing, then separate the housings.
Ideally, use Honda puller 07933 - 6890100; failing that, use a soft-
faced mallet on the housing bosses and carefully tap the housings
apart.
13 From the exposed geartrain lift off counter reverse gear and then
reverse shift fork/selector gear as an assembly having first withdrawn
the fork lockbolt.
14 Select 'neutral' and then lift the mainshaft and countershaft
geartrains away simultaneously with their gears meshed together.
15 Unbolt and remove the oil pump strainer and servo body and then
withdraw the lubrication pipe and sealing ring guide.
16 Remove the stop pin and then tap the stator torque converter
shaft out from the transmission housing side of the torque converter
housing.
17 Remove the valve body, pump gears and separator plate taking
care not to drop the check valve and spring. Remove the lockpin, valve
pin and spacers from the manual valve. Before removing the pump
driven gear, mark it so that it will be refitted with the same face
against the housing.
18 Remove the speed selector arm and parking pawl mechanism
after bending down the lockplate tabs and extracting the bolt.

5   Major assemblies – inspection and overhaul

Mainshaft
1   The mainshaft can be completely dismantled after extracting the
circlips. Check the bearings for wear, the teeth of the gears and the
splines of the shaft for wear or deformation. If the shaft is scored it
must be renewed together with any other faulty components.
2   Commence reassembly by installing the sealing ring, the two
circlips and the needle bearing, then the drive clutch (refer to
paragraph 5, this Section, for complete dismantling) and the clutch
thrust washer and thrust needle bearing. Follow with the collar, needle
bearing and drive gear. Rotate the drive gear until the splines engage
fully with the clutch discs. Install the thrust washers noting that the
thicker one must be fitted with the shouldered side against the drive
gear.

Countershaft
3   Inspect the countershaft components for wear and damage and
renew as necessary.
4   Reassemble by fitting the needle bearing, the circlip, the countershaft drive gear and reverse hub, the latter having its recessed side
towards the circlip.

7

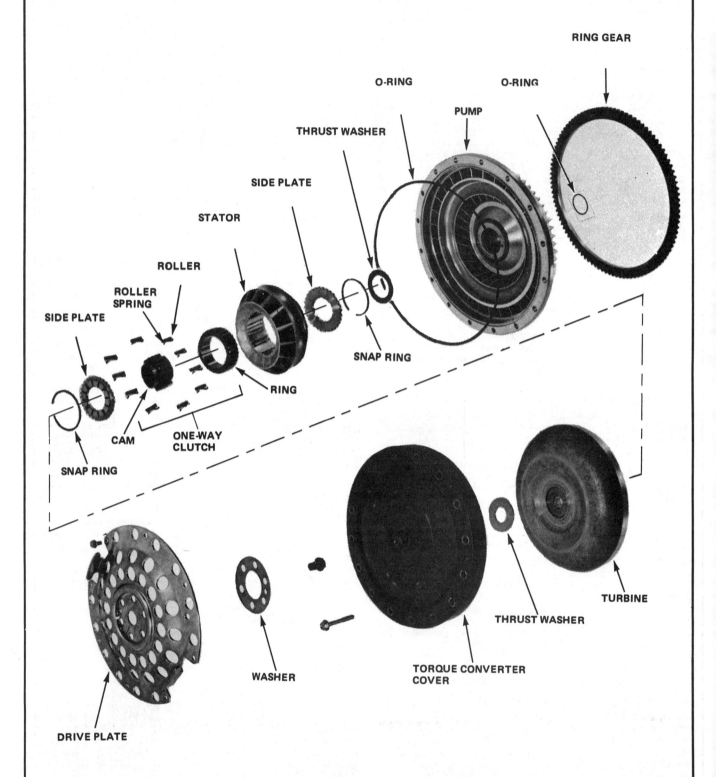

RING GEAR

O-RING

O-RING

PUMP

THRUST WASHER

SIDE PLATE

STATOR

ROLLER

ROLLER SPRING

SIDE PLATE

SNAP RING

RING

CAM

ONE-WAY CLUTCH

SNAP RING

TURBINE

THRUST WASHER

TORQUE CONVERTER COVER

WASHER

DRIVE PLATE

Fig. 7.4 Torque converter components (Sec 4)

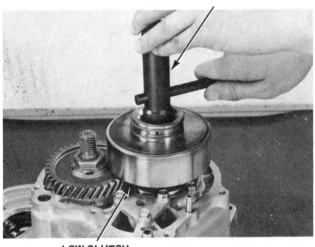

DIPSTICK

END COVER

Fig. 7.5 Remove the end cover (Sec 4)

MAINSHAFT

TORQUE CONVERTER HOUSING

MAINSHAFT HOLDER

Fig. 7.6 Mainshaft holder (Sec 4)

LOCKNUT WRENCH, 16 mm

LOW CLUTCH

Fig. 7.7 Special locknut wrench (Sec 4)

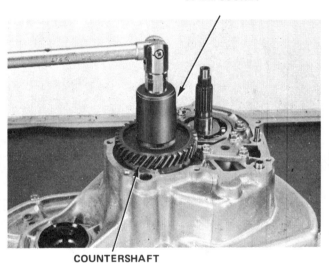

30 mm SOCKET

COUNTERSHAFT LOW GEAR

Fig. 7.8 Removing the countershaft locknut (Sec 4)

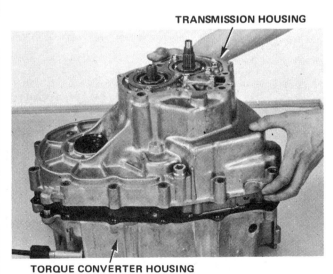

TRANSMISSION HOUSING

TORQUE CONVERTER HOUSING

Fig. 7.9 Separating the torque converter and transmission housings (Sec 4)

INNER RACE

NEEDLE BEARING

COUNTERSHAFT REVERSE GEAR

REVERSE SELECTOR SLEEVE

REVERSE SHIFT FORK

LOCK PLATE

Fig. 7.10 Removing the countershaft reverse gear (Sec 4)

7

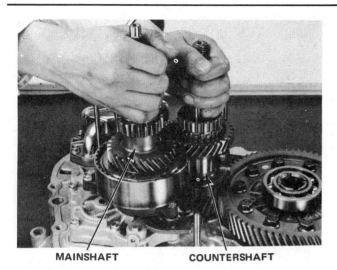

Fig. 7.11 Withdrawing the gear assemblies (Sec 4)

MAINSHAFT   COUNTERSHAFT

STATOR SHAFT

Fig. 7.12 Removing the torque converter shaft (Sec 4)

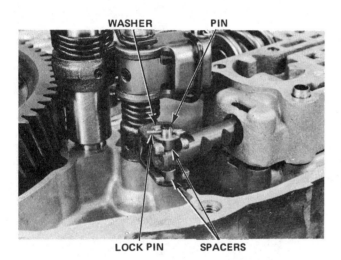

WASHER   PIN

LOCK PIN   SPACERS

Fig. 7.13 Valve lockpin and spacers (Sec 4)

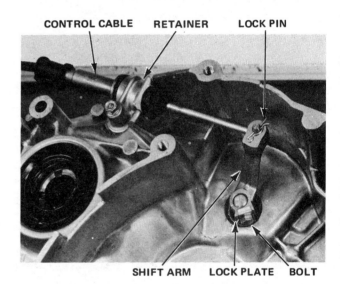

CONTROL CABLE   RETAINER   LOCK PIN

SHIFT ARM   LOCK PLATE   BOLT

Fig. 7.14 Shift arm bolt and lockplate (Sec 4)

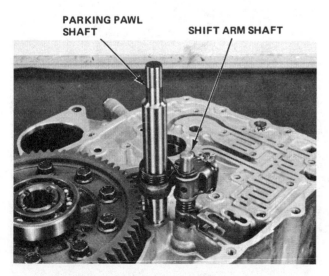

PARKING PAWL
SHAFT   SHIFT ARM SHAFT

Fig. 7.15 Shift arm and parking pawl shaft removal (Sec 4)

Low/Drive clutch

5   To dismantle the clutch, extract the circlip (snap ring) and lift away the end plate, discs and plates.

6   The clutch return coil spring must now be compressed with a suitable compressor (a long bolt with distance pieces will serve for this) so that the circlip, retainer and spring can be removed (Fig. 7.20).

7   Place the clutch drum on a soft surface and eject the clutch piston by applying air from a tyre pump at one oil hole while blocking the other with the finger.

8   Clean all components and renew any which are worn or damaged.

9   Apply clean transmission fluid to all parts and then commence reassembly by installing two oil seal rings to the clutch drum. Space the ring gaps 180° apart.

10 Install a new O-ring to the clutch piston and then fit the cushion spring as shown (Fig. 7.23).

11 Fit a new O-ring to the clutch drum hub.

12 Press the piston into the clutch drum squarely using firm finger pressure (Fig. 7.24).

13 Refit the clutch spring and retainer, compress the spring and fit the circlip.

14 Refit the clutch plates and discs alternately having liberally applied transmission fluid to them. Make sure that the clutch endplate has its flat side against the clutch disc. Install the large securing circlip.

15 Using a feeler blade, measure the clearance between the last clutch disc and the endplate. This should be between 0.020 and 0.032

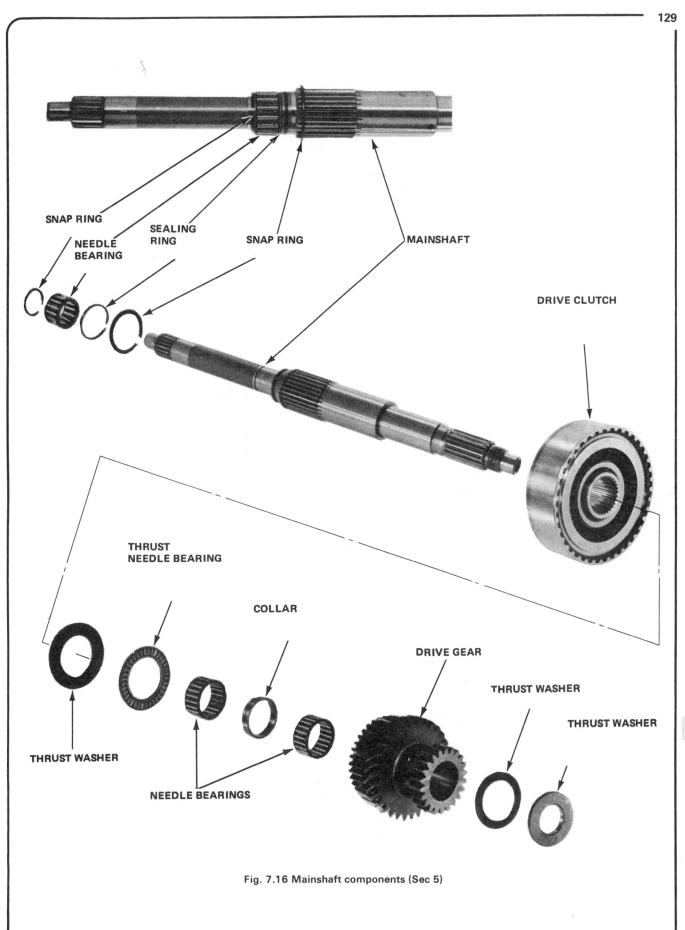

Fig. 7.16 Mainshaft components (Sec 5)

7

130

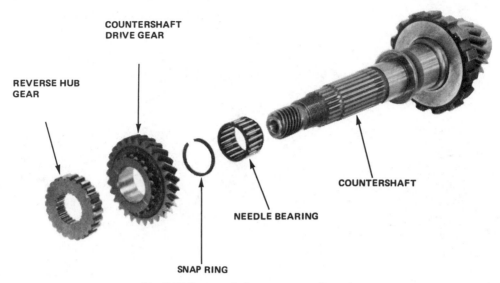

Fig. 7.17 Countershaft components (Sec 5)

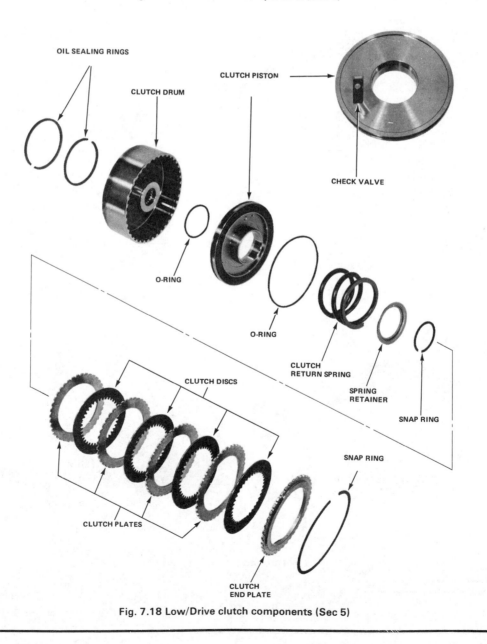

Fig. 7.18 Low/Drive clutch components (Sec 5)

SNAP RING

CLUTCH DRUM

Fig. 7.19 Removing the snap-ring (Sec 5)

CLUTCH SPRING COMPRESSOR

CLUTCH RETURN SPRING

Fig. 7.20 Compressing the clutch spring (Sec 5)

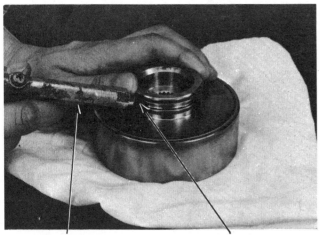

COMPRESSED AIR
HOSE NOZZLE   OIL PASSAGE HOLE

Fig. 7.21 Ejecting the clutch piston (Sec 5)

OIL SEAL RING

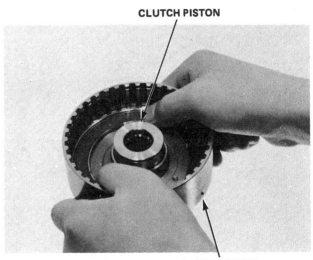

CLUTCH DRUM

Fig. 7.22 Install the oil seal rings (Sec 5)

CLUTCH PISTON

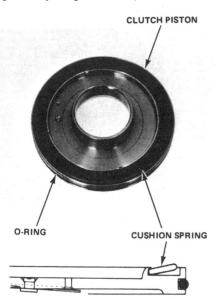

O-RING   CUSHION SPRING

Fig. 7.23 Installing the piston O-ring and cushion spring (Sec 5)

CLUTCH PISTON

CLUTCH DRUM

Fig. 7.24 Installing the clutch piston (Sec 5)

7

SNAP RING   SPRING RETAINER

RETURN SPRING

Fig. 7.25 Installing the clutch return spring, spring retainer and circlip (Sec 5)

in (0.5 and 0.8 mm). If the clearance is incorrect, change the endplate for one of different thickness, there are six different thicknesses available as spare parts.

Servo body

16 Clean and inspect the components of the servo body and blow out the passages with air from a tyre pump.
17 Renew the O-ring seal on the servo valve. Renew the valve and body if there is any sign of scoring.

Valve body

18 Dismantle, clean and inspect all components for wear or scoring. Renew as necessary.
19 Commence reassembly by installing the pressure regulator valve and inner and outer valve springs.
20 Install the retainer spring, spring seat and retainer. Align the hole in the retainer and tighten the bolt to the specified torque.
21 Install the manual valve, detent rollers and spring.
22 Install the pump gears and measure the clearance between the drive gear and the valve body using a feeler gauge. This should be between 0.002 and 0.006 in (0.05 and 0.15 mm).
23 Using a straight-edge and a feeler gauge, check the driven gear endfloat. This should be between 0.001 and 0.003 in (0.03 and 0.09 mm). Any deviation from these clearances will necessitate renewal of the components.

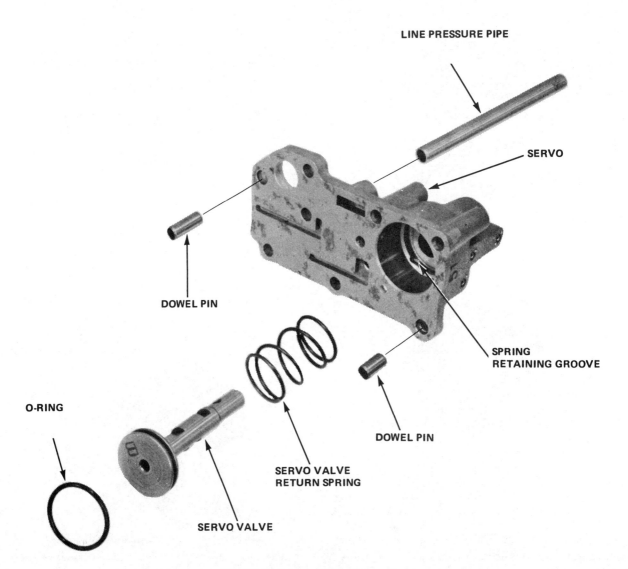

LINE PRESSURE PIPE

SERVO

DOWEL PIN

SPRING RETAINING GROOVE

DOWEL PIN

O-RING

SERVO VALVE RETURN SPRING

SERVO VALVE

Fig. 7.26 Servo components (Sec 5)

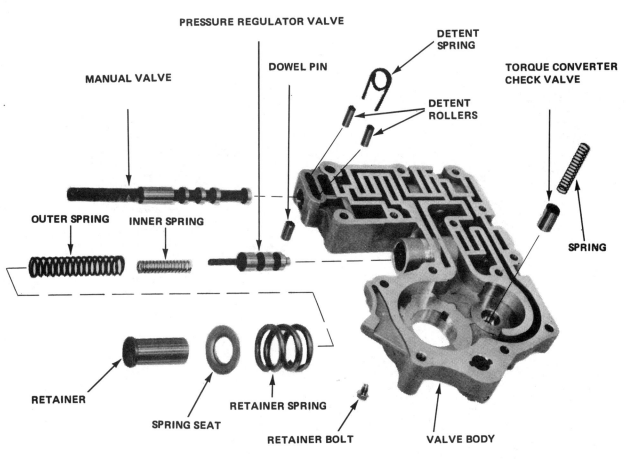

PRESSURE REGULATOR VALVE

MANUAL VALVE

DOWEL PIN

DETENT SPRING

TORQUE CONVERTER CHECK VALVE

DETENT ROLLERS

OUTER SPRING

INNER SPRING

SPRING

RETAINER

SPRING SEAT

RETAINER SPRING

RETAINER BOLT

VALVE BODY

Fig. 7.27 Servo valve components (Sec 5)

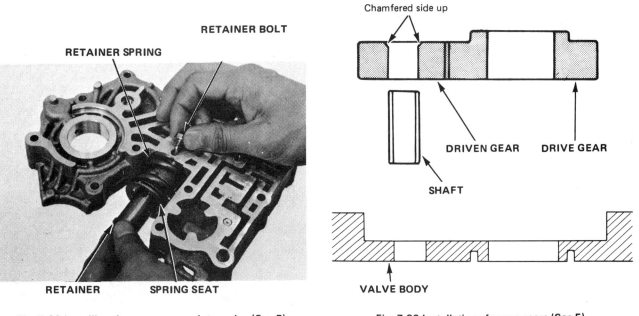

RETAINER BOLT

RETAINER SPRING

RETAINER

SPRING SEAT

Fig. 7.28 Installing the pressure regulator valve (Sec 5)

Chamfered side up

DRIVEN GEAR

DRIVE GEAR

SHAFT

VALVE BODY

Fig. 7.29 Installation of pump gears (Sec 5)

7

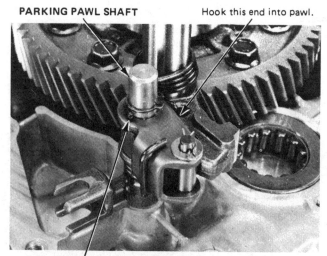

PARKING PAWL SHAFT — Hook this end into pawl.

Hook this end around shift arm shaft.

Fig. 7.30 Correct position of parking pawl spring (Sec 6)

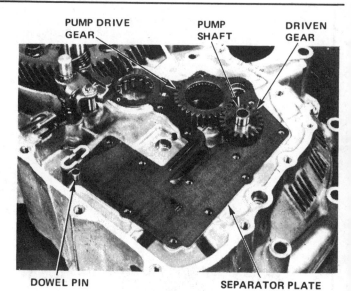

PUMP DRIVE GEAR — PUMP SHAFT — DRIVEN GEAR

DOWEL PIN — SEPARATOR PLATE

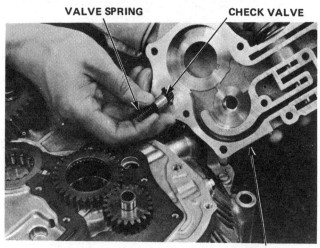

VALVE SPRING — CHECK VALVE

VALVE BODY

Fig. 7.32 Installation of check valve and spring (Sec 6)

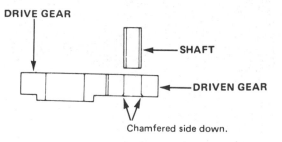

DRIVE GEAR — SHAFT — DRIVEN GEAR

Chamfered side down.

Fig. 7.31 Installation of pump gears (Sec 6)

Housing bearings and oil seals

24 The oil seals in the torque converter and transmission housing should be renewed as routine at the time of major overhaul.

25 The bearings, if worn, can be renewed by driving them out and the new ones in, using a piece of tubing as a drift. Always apply force to the bearing outer track which seats in the casing. The following points must be observed however. The differential must be removed before the countershaft bearing can be removed (refer to Chapter 8).

26 If the differential side bearings or the transmission or torque converter housings are renewed then the differential side clearance must be measured and if necessary adjusted as described in Chapter 8.

27 The reverse idler shaft and its bearings are removed from the outside of the transmission housing while the reverse idler gear is withdrawn into the interior. The sealing ring screws which are located in the end cover should be removed using an impact driver and re-staked when they are refitted.

6 Hondamatic transmission – reassembly

1 Assemble the parking pawl mechanism and speed shift lever and install in the torque converter housing.

2 Install the speed selector link arm, tighten the lockbolt to the specified torque and bend up the tab of the lockplate.

3 Install the separator plate, dowel pin, pump gears and shaft.

M6 x 1.0 x 80 — M6 x 1.0 x 18

M6 x 1.0 x 55 — M6 x 1.0 x 50

Fig. 7.33 Servo body bolt tightening sequence (Sec 6)

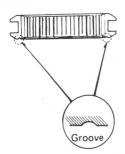

Groove

COUNTERSHAFT   REVERSE GEAR
                      SELECTOR SLEEVE

REVERSE SHIFT FORK
Un-marked side up.

Fig. 7.34 Installing reverse gear selector sleeve (Sec 6)

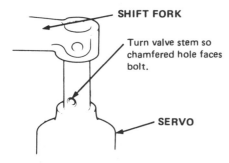

SHIFT FORK

Turn valve stem so
chamfered hole faces
bolt.

SERVO

Fig. 7.35 Installing the shift fork on the servo valve stem (Sec 6)

4   Fit the torque converter check valve and spring in the valve body and then install the valve body to the torque converter housing, tightening the securing bolts to the specified torque.
5   Attach the speed shift lever to the manual valve using the pin with a spacer in each side and finally securing it with the lockpin.
6   Insert the stator torque converter shaft.
7   Install the sealing ring guide and stop pin, tightening the guide bolts to the specified torque. Install the lubrication pipe.
8   Install the servo body gasket, dowel pins and body itself. Tighten the body securing bolts to the specified torque in the sequence shown. Make sure that the different length bolts are correctly positioned (Fig. 7.33).
9   Install the oil pump strainer using a new O-ring seal.
10 Mesh the mainshaft and countershaft gears together, and then install both assemblies simultaneously.
11 Assemble the reverse selector gear to the shift fork and install the

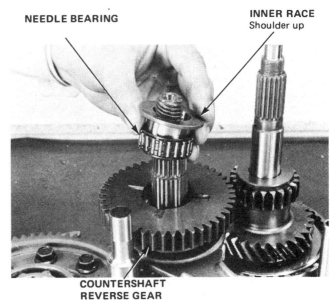

NEEDLE BEARING   INNER RACE
                        Shoulder up

COUNTERSHAFT
REVERSE GEAR

Fig. 7.36 Installing reverse gear needle bearing (Sec 6)

Raised shoulder side   COUNTERSHAFT
                              LOW GEAR

Fig. 7.37 Installing countershaft low gear (Sec 6)

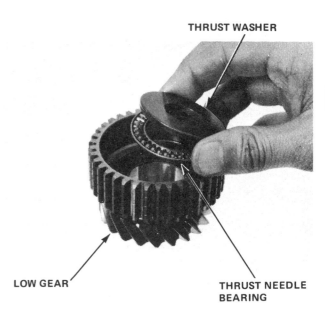

THRUST WASHER

LOW GEAR   THRUST NEEDLE
                  BEARING

Fig. 7.38 Low gear thrust bearing and thrust washer (Sec 6)

7

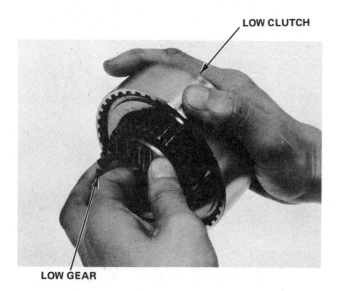

LOW CLUTCH

LOW GEAR

Fig. 7.39 Installing low gear and low clutch (Sec 6)

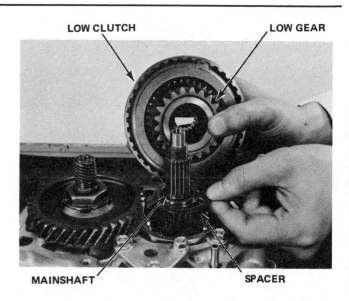

LOW CLUTCH   LOW GEAR

MAINSHAFT   SPACER

Fig. 7.40 Installing low gear and clutch assembly (Sec 6)

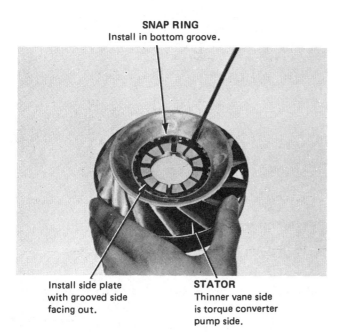

SNAP RING
Install in bottom groove.

Install side plate
with grooved side
facing out.

STATOR
Thinner vane side
is torque converter
pump side.

Fig. 7.41 Installing the stator and side plates (Sec 6)

assembly to the countershaft. Tighten the lockbolt to the specified torque and bend up the tab of a new lockplate.

12 Install the counter reverse gear, needle bearing and the inner collar into the countershaft.

13 Locate a new gasket and then install the transmission housing to the torque converter housing taking care not to bend the oil pipe. Install the connecting bolts, tightening them to the specified torque.

14 Install the bearing retainer to the transmission housing. Tighten the bolts to the specified torque and stake the screw heads.

15 Bolt on the reverse idler shaft retainer, tighten the bolts to the specified torque.

16 Fit the countershaft low gear so that the raised shoulder on the gear is towards the bearing retainer.

17 Install a new gasket and a new O-ring on the oil pipe and check that the locating dowels are in position.

18 Select 'park' and use the special tool to hold the mainshaft still. Screw on a new countershaft nut and tighten it to the specified torque, then stake the rim of the nut into the slot in the countershaft.

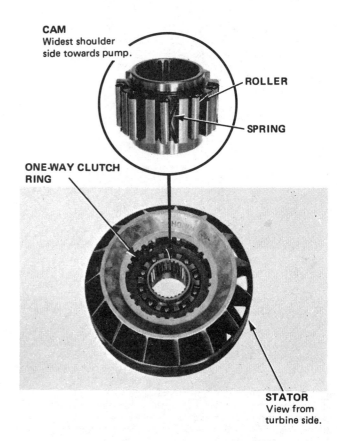

CAM
Widest shoulder
side towards pump.

ROLLER

SPRING

ONE-WAY CLUTCH
RING

STATOR
View from
turbine side.

Fig. 7.42 Installing the clutch rollers and springs (Sec 6)

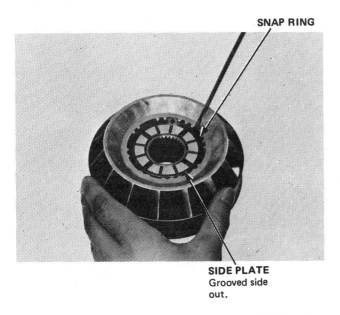

SNAP RING

SIDE PLATE
Grooved side
out.

Fig. 7.43 Installing the stator side plate and circlip (Sec 6)

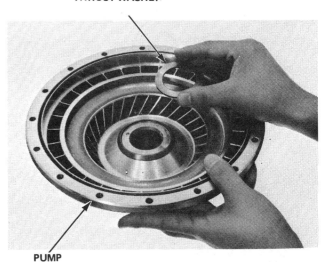

THRUST WASHER

PUMP

Fig. 7.44 Installing the thrust washer in the pump (Sec 6)

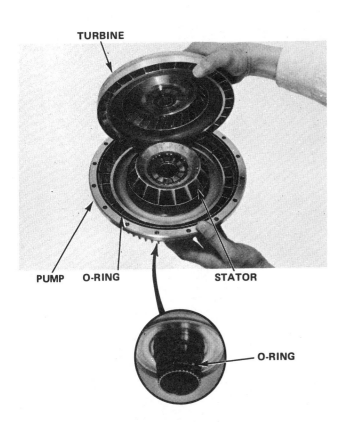

TURBINE

PUMP   O-RING   STATOR

O-RING

Fig. 7.45 Assembling the pump and turbine (Sec 6)

THRUST WASHER

Fig. 7.46 Installing the turbine thrust washer (Sec 6)

19 To the mainshaft install the thrust washer, spacer, inner collar and needle bearing.

20 Fit the thrust needle bearing and plain thrust washer into the recess in low gear.

21 Insert low gear into low clutch, rotating the gear until complete engagement is secured. Install the clutch and gear as an assembly to the mainshaft. Do not forget the spacer (Fig. 7.40).

22 Using the special tools, fit the lockwasher and screw the locknut onto the mainshaft. Tighten to the specified torque and bend up the tabs of the lockwasher.

23 Fit the end cover and dipstick to the transmission housing. Use a new cover gasket.

24 Install the torque converter into the torque converter housing. If the torque converter was dismantled, install the circlip and the stator side plate. Install the ring and cam in the stator followed by the rollers and springs.

25 Fit the second stator side plate and circlip and then insert the torque converter shaft into the stator from the pump side and check the operation of the one-way clutch.

26 Insert the thrust washer into the torque converter pump and then fit the stator into the pump followed by the serrated thrust washer.

27 Clean the grooves on the pump body thoroughly and then install new O-rings and fit the turbine to the pump.

28 Install the thrust washer to the turbine.

29 Fit the torque converter cover to the pump making sure to align the mating marks. Locate the starter ring gear so that the flat side is towards the cover and then tighten the securing bolts in the sequence shown (Fig. 7.48).

7

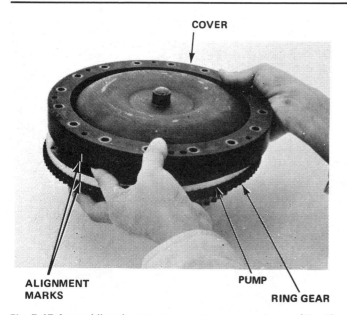

Fig. 7.47 Assembling the torque converter cover and pump (Sec 6)

COVER

ALIGNMENT MARKS

PUMP

RING GEAR

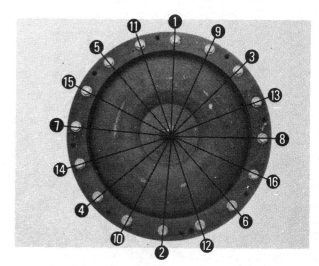

Fig. 7.48 Cover bolt tightening sequence (Sec 6)

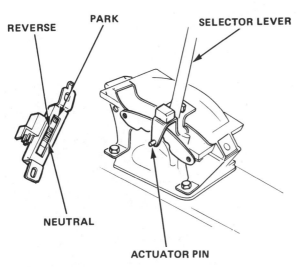

REVERSE

PARK

SELECTOR LEVER

NEUTRAL

ACTUATOR PIN

Fig. 7.49 Starter inhibitor switch installation (Sec 7)

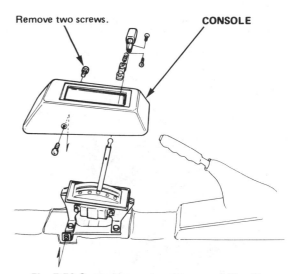

Remove two screws.

CONSOLE

Fig. 7.50 Control lever console removal (Sec 8)

7   Reversing lamp/starter inhibitor switch – removal and installation

1   Remove the centre console from inside the car.
2   Position the speed selector lever in 'neutral' and unbolt and remove the switch.
3   Installation is a reversal of removal, but make sure that the actuator rod engages fully in the slot in the switch slider.
4   The indicator lamp on the speed selector can be unclipped and the bulb renewed if required.

8   Speed selector cable – adjustment

1   Remove the centre console inside the car.
2   Move the speed selector lever to the reverse position.
3   Extract the clip and the clevis pin which secure the cable to the base of the speed selector lever.
4   The clevis pin should be a sliding fit when it is pushed into engagement through the holes in the cable end and the selector lever. If force is required, release the locknuts on the adjuster and rotate the

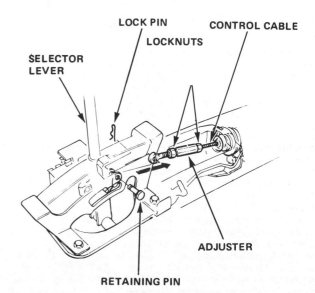

LOCK PIN

LOCKNUTS

CONTROL CABLE

SELECTOR LEVER

ADJUSTER

RETAINING PIN

Fig. 7.51 Control cable adjustment (Sec 8)

turnbuckle of the adjuster to shorten or lengthen the effective length of the cable as necessary.

9 Speed selector cable – renewal

1 Disconnect the cable at the selector lever as described in Section

8. Remove the two bolts from the cable retainer and extract the cable.
2 Similarly disconnect the cable at the transmission end, removing the torque converter cover plate for access. Remove the cable retainer.
3 Unhook the cable from any underbody brackets and remove it from the car.
4 Installation is a reversal of removal. Adjust the cable on completion as described in Section 8.

10 Fault diagnosis – Hondamatic transmission

Note: *It cannot be over-emphasised that before deciding that the transmission has developed a serious internal fault due to failure of a component, the fluid level should be checked and the adjustment of the speed selector cable inspected. Rupture of one of the oil cooler flexible hoses can cause immediate overheating and loss of drive and should these symptoms occur on the road, inspect these hoses first. For the stall test procedure, refer to Section 20.*

Symptom	Reason(s)
Erratic operation and excessive fuel consumption	Faulty one-way clutch in torque converter
Poor acceleration	Faulty oil feed - worn pump or clogged pick-up Faulty 'L' or 'D' clutches
No movement in 1 (low) but movement in 2 (normal) and R (reverse)	Faulty 'L' clutch
No movement in 2 or R but movement in 1	Faulty 'D' clutch
No movement in R but movement in 1 and 2	Incorrect selector cable adjustment Seized reverse gear selector
No movement in any speed selector position	Faulty servo valve Faulty oil pump Faulty pressure regulating valve Faulty selector mechanism

PART B: AUTOMATIC TRANSMISSION (3-SPEED)

11 Automatic transmission – general description

The main components of the automatic transmission are the torque converter and a special gearbox enclosing three forward speeds and one reverse gear.

The torque converter is housed in an enlarged bellhousing between the engine and gearbox and its appearance is that of a large, almost hemispherical container with a ring gear for the starter motor attached to the face nearest the engine. The container encloses the torque converter system of vanes and is kept full of oil under pressure by a pump mounted in the gearbox casing.

The transmission functions as follows. The engine delivers power to the torque converter which balances the speed and torque of the engine with the torque 'required' by the gearbox. The converter has the characteristic that if the input speed of the engine is greater than the output speed to the gearbox, the output torque will be between 1 and 2 times greater than the input torque, depending on the difference of the input and output speeds.

The torque characteristic is derived from the way the drive/impeller vanes in the converter are coupled to the output/turbine vanes. The impeller vanes are shaped so that as they rotate, the oil in the impeller is flung radially outwards to the top tip of the vanes and

forward in the direction of vane rotation. The oil on leaving the impeller impinges onto the output turbine which is driven in the direction of rotation of the impeller by the oil. If the impeller is rotating faster than the turbine, as when the engine is working to accelerate the car, the oil flung onto the turbine by the impeller creates a greater torque on the turbine than that exerted by the engine on the impeller. The stator in the converter serves to correct the direction of flow of oil from the turbine back to the impeller and improves the efficiency of the converter.

The power output from the converter is transmitted to the final drive via a transmission which has two parallel shafts on which are mounted the gears and three clutches. The clutches are operated by an hydraulic control system consisting of main, regulator and servo valves to give automatic changing of the gears.

The transmission has a selector lever having five positions giving the following selections.

P - Parking. The front wheels are locked by a parking pawl engaging with a parking gear on the countershaft.

R - Reverse. The reverse selector is engaged with the countershaft reverse gear and 2nd gear clutch is locked.

N - Neutral. All three clutches are released.

D - Drive. Starting from rest, 1st gear is selected and shifts to 2nd and 3rd automatically with increase in speed. On decelerating to stop,

7

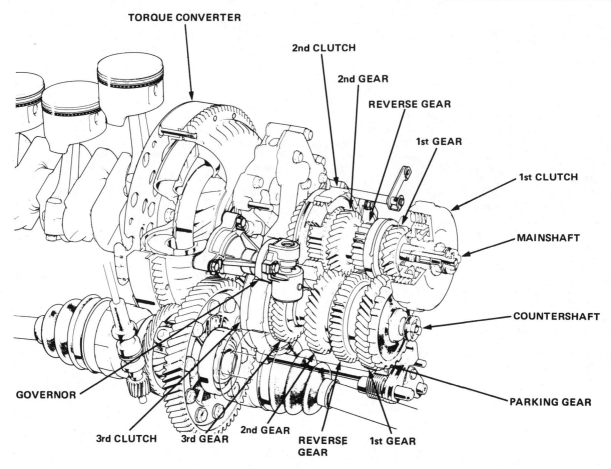

Fig. 7.52 Automatic transmission (phantom view) (Sec 11)

the shifts down through 2nd to 1st are automatic.

2 - Second. This is used for engine braking, or for starting off on slippery surfaces. The transmission stays in 2nd gear and does not shift up or down.

12 Maintenance

1   At the intervals specified in Routine Maintenance, check the level of the automatic transmission fluid. To do this, run the car for a minimum of 5 miles (8 km) until the fluid is at normal operating temperature and then position the car on level ground and switch the engine off.

2   Unscrew and remove the dipstick, wipe it with a piece of clean lint-free cloth and re-insert it, but do not screw it in. Withdraw the dipstick for the second time and read off the fluid level.

3   Top up as necessary and install the dipstick, screwing it finger tight only.

4   With a new vehicle the transmission should be drained and filled with fresh fluid at 15 000 miles (24 000 km), and thereafter at 45 000 miles (72 000 km) and every further interval of 30 000 miles (48 000 km).

13 Transmission – removal and installation

1   The automatic transmission can be removed independently of the engine, leaving the latter in position in the car, but if any major work is required on the engine at the same time, it is easier to remove the engine with the transmission attached and then separate them, as described in Chapter 1.

2   To remove the transmission on its own, first disconnect the negative lead from the battery terminal and the earth strap from the transmission casing.

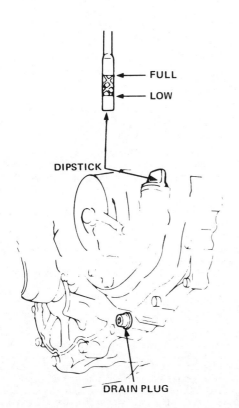

Fig. 7.53 Transmission dipstick and drain plug (Sec 12)

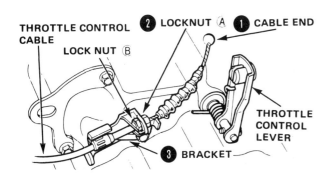

Fig. 7.54 Throttle cable attachment (Sec 13)

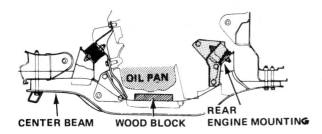

Fig. 7.55 Supporting the engine on the centre beam (Sec 13)

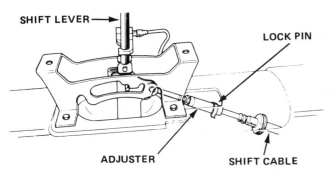

Fig. 7.56 Disconnecting the shift cable (Sec 13)

3   Release the steering lock and move the gear selector to N.
4   Disconnect the positive cable from the starter motor, the black/white wire from the starter solenoid, the yellow/green wire from the water temperature sender and the two wires from the ignition timing thermosensor.
5   Disconnect the hoses of the ATF cooler and tie them up by the radiator so that the fluid does not drain out.
6   Remove the starter mounting bolt on the transmission side and the top mounting bolt of the transmission.
7   Loosen the front wheel nuts. Apply the parking brake and chock the rear wheels, then raise the front of the car, support it on axle stands and remove the front wheels.
8   Drain the fluid from the transmission and re-install the drain plug and washer.
9   Unhook the throttle cable end from the throttle control lever (Fig. 7.54), slacken locknut 'A' and free the cable from the bracket.
10   Remove the clip from the speedometer cable and pull the cable out of its holder. Do not remove the holder because this may result in the speedometer gear falling into the transmission housing.
11   Remove the nuts and washers from the ends of the front stabiliser bar, remove the bolts from the mounting brackets and remove the brackets and the stabiliser bar.
12   Remove the pivot bolts from the lower control arms. Alternatively, use a balljoint separator to disconnect the two lower arm balljoints and those at the ends of the tie-rod, but this is more difficult.
13   Turn the right steering knuckle outwards as far as it will go and

then with a screwdriver against the inboard constant velocity joint, prise the right driveshaft about $\frac{1}{2}$ in (12 mm) out of the transmission housing. This will force the spring clip on the driveshaft out of its groove in the splines of the differential. Repeat the process on the other driveshaft, or leave doing this until the transmission has been separated from the engine.
14   Place a flat piece of wood on the head of a jack, place the jack beneath the transmission oil pan and raise the jack just enough to take the weight off the transmission mountings. **Do not** use a jack without a piece of wood between it and the transmission oil pan, or the pan may be damaged.
15   Remove the engine damper from the centre beam.
16   Remove the front and rear torque rods, and the brackets of the rear torque rod.
17   Remove the engine rear mounting and its bracket.
18   Place a block of wood 1 in (25 mm) thick on the centre beam beneath the engine oil pan and then lower the jack so that the engine rests on the centre beam (Fig. 7.55).
19   Remove the engine damper bracket and the torque converter cover plate from the transmission.
20   Remove the other mounting bolt from the starter motor and remove the starter motor.
21   Raise the jack under the transmission so that the transmission is supported.
22   Remove the centre console and the shift indicator.
23   Remove the lockpin from the adjuster and shift cable (Fig. 7.56).
24   Remove both bolts and pull the shift cable out of its housing.
25   Remove the eight bolts securing the torque converter to the driveplate, rotating the crankshaft to gain access to them. **Do not** remove the 16 bolts which hold the torque converter together.
26   Remove the two remaining transmission mounting bolts.
27   Pull the transmission away from the engine to free the two dowel pins.
28   Lower the jack and withdraw the transmission, taking care to retain the torque converter fully within its housing.
29   Installation is the reverse of removal. Refill the transmission with the correct grade and quantity of fluid and check the adjustment of the selector cable (Section 18).

14 Automatic transmission – dismantling into major assemblies

1   Overhaul of the transmission will normally only be required after a fault has been diagnosed after reference to Section 20 or 21.
2   Withdraw the torque converter from the converter housing.
3   Check that alignment marks are visible on the edges of the torque converter pump and cover. If not, scribe marks to ensure refitting in their original positions.
4   Unbolt the cover and separate the internal components, noting carefully their sequence and orientation (Fig. 7.57).
5   Unscrew and remove the dipstick, unscrew the end cover bolts and tap off the end cover using a soft-headed hammer.
6   Move the selector arm to the Park position.
7   A special tool will now be required to lock the mainshaft. The Honda tool numbers are either 07923-6890200 or 07923-6890201. Lock the mainshaft using the mainshaft holder (Fig. 7.58).
8   Remove the end cover, gasket, dowel pins and O-rings (Fig. 7.59).
9   Prise the staked edge of the locknut flange out of the notch in the 1st clutch, and then remove the mainshaft nut, which has a *left-hand thread*.
10   Lift off the 1st clutch and remove the thrust washer, needle bearing and 1st gear, then remove the needle bearing and thrust washer from the mainshaft.
11   Prise the staked edge of the locknut out of the notch in the parking gear. Remove the countershaft locknut and the pawl stop pin (Fig. 7.60).
12   Remove the parking pawl, shaft and spring (Fig. 7.61).
13   Remove the parking gear and countershaft 1st gear as an assembly (Fig. 7.62).
14   Remove the needle bearing and 1st gear collar from the counter-shaft. From the mainshaft remove the O-ring and 1st gear collar (Fig. 7.63).
15   Remove the reverse idler bearing holder.
16   Bend down the locking tab of the parking shift arm bolt and remove the bolt and the shift arm as an assembly. Remove the shift arm spring (Fig. 7.64).

7

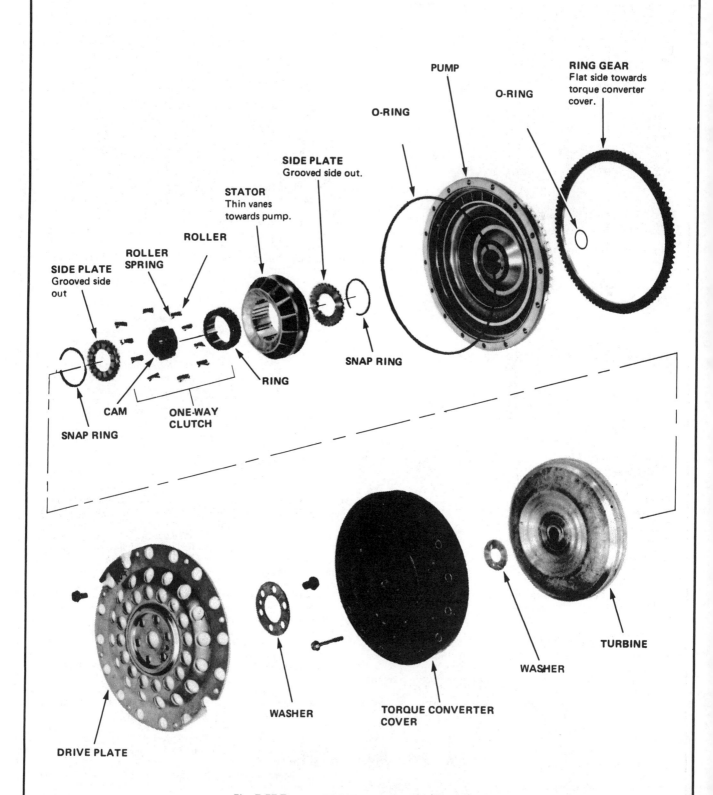

PUMP

O-RING

RING GEAR
Flat side towards
torque converter
cover.

O-RING

SIDE PLATE
Grooved side out.

STATOR
Thin vanes
towards pump.

ROLLER

SIDE PLATE
Grooved side
out

ROLLER
SPRING

SNAP RING

RING

SNAP RING

CAM

ONE-WAY
CLUTCH

SNAP RING

TURBINE

WASHER

DRIVE PLATE

WASHER

TORQUE CONVERTER
COVER

Fig. 7.57 Torque converter components (Sec 14)

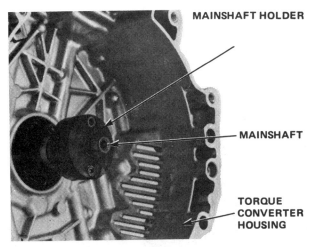

Fig. 7.58 Locking the mainshaft with the mainshaft holder (Sec 14)

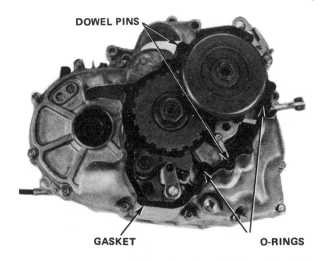

Fig. 7.59 The end cover gasket, dowels and O-rings (Sec 14)

Fig. 7.60 Countershaft locknut and pawl stop pin (Sec 14)

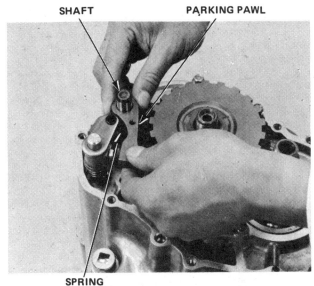

Fig. 7.61 Parking pawl, shaft and spring (Sec 14)

Fig. 7.62 Parking gear and countershaft 1st gear (Sec 14)

Fig. 7.63 Needle bearing, 1st gear collars and O-rings (Sec 14)

7

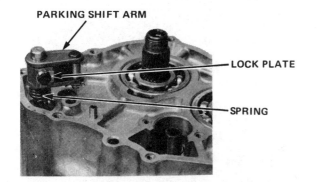

Fig. 7.64 Parking shift arm and spring (Sec 14)

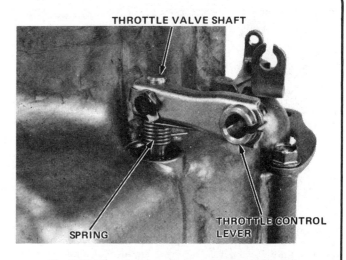

Fig. 7.65 Throttle control lever and spring (Sec 14)

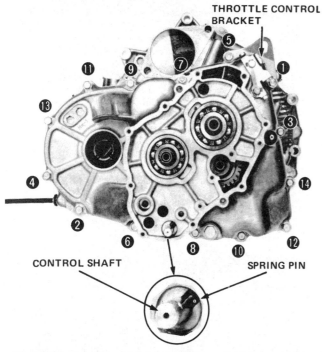

Fig. 7.66 Loosening and tightening sequence of transmission housing bolts (Sec 14)

Fig. 7.67 Loosening the housing joint with a puller (Sec 14)

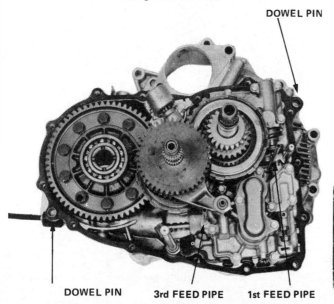

Fig. 7.68 Oil feed pipes and dowel pins (Sec 14)

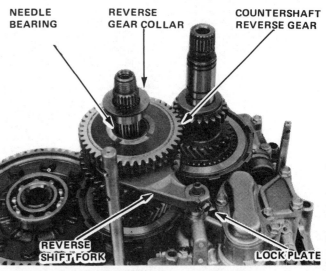

Fig. 7.69 Reverse gear and shift fork (Sec 14)

Fig. 7.70 Countershaft 2nd gear (Sec 14)

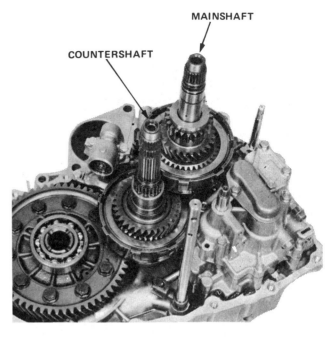

Fig. 7.71 Mainshaft and countershaft ready for removal (Sec 14)

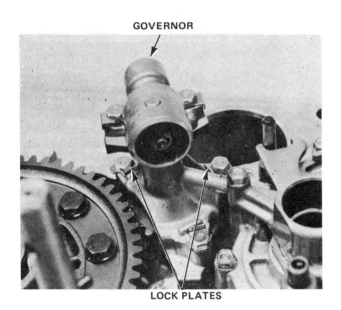

Fig. 7.72 Governor mounting details (Sec 14)

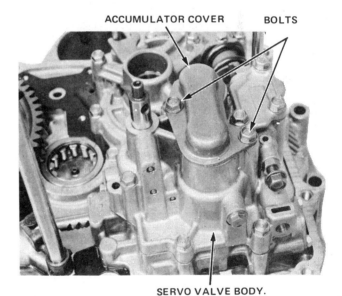

Fig. 7.73 Accumulator cover and servo valve body (Sec 14)

17 Bend down the locking tab of the throttle control lever bolt and remove the bolt, throttle control lever and spring (Fig. 7.65).
18 Unscrew the 14 bolts in the transmission housing in the sequence shown in Fig. 7.66 and remove all except No 1, which cannot be removed without removing the throttle control bracket. It is not necessary to remove this bracket to unscrew No 1 bolt fully. If the bracket is disturbed, the shift points will be altered.
19 Align the spring pin in the control shaft with the cut out in the transmission housing.
20 Using a universal plate puller, or special tool 07933-6890200 on the end of the countershaft, separate the two housings, then remove the puller and lift the transmission housing off the torque converter housing.

21 Remove the gasket, dowel pins and 1st and 3rd oil feed pipes (Fig. 7.68).
22 Remove reverse gear collar, needle bearing and countershaft reverse gear (Fig. 7.69).
23 Bend down the locktab on the bolt of the reverse shift fork. Remove the bolt, then remove the shift fork and selector sleeve as an assembly.
24 Remove countershaft second gear (Fig. 7.70) and then remove the mainshaft and countershaft together (Fig. 7.71). It is necessary to remove them at a slight angle to clear the governor.
25 Bend down the locking tabs of the three bolts securing the governor (Fig. 7.72). Remove the bolts and lift off the governor.
26 While pressing down on the accumulator cover to keep the springs

3rd ACCUMULATOR SPRING

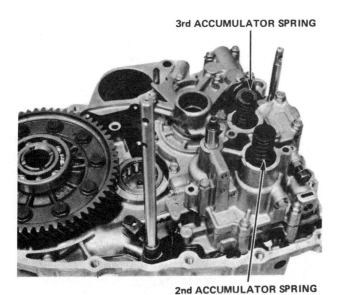

2nd ACCUMULATOR SPRING

Fig. 7.74 Accumulator springs (Sec 14)

THROTTLE CONTROL SHAFT   E-CLIP

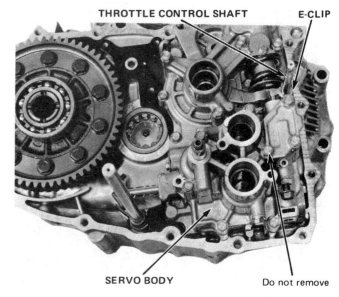

SERVO BODY   Do not remove

Fig. 7.75 Servo valve body bolts (Sec 14)

DOWEL PINS

SEPARATOR PLATE

Fig. 7.76 Separator plate and dowel pins (Sec 14)

STEEL BALL

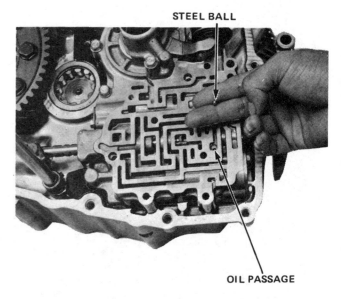

OIL PASSAGE

Fig. 7.77 Valve body oil passage and ball (Sec 14)

compressed, unscrew the cover bolts evenly and then remove the cover and accumulator springs.

27 Remove the E-clip from the throttle control shaft and remove the shaft.

28 Unscrew the seven bolts from the servo valve body and remove it. The inside bolt for the throttle control valve cover can stay in place.

29 Remove the separator plate and dowel pins (Fig. 7.76) and then remove the steel ball from the valve body oil passage (Fig.7.77). Do not use a magnet to remove the ball because the ball may then become magnetised.

30 Remove the six bolts and remove the regulator valve body (Fig. 7.78).

31 Remove the stator shaft arm, dowel pins, the stop pin and the four bolts holding the valve body to the torque converter housing (Fig. 7.79).

32 Remove the split pin, washer, rollers and clevis pin from the manual valve.

33 Remove the valve body, being careful not to lose the torque

converter check valve and spring (Fig. 7.80).

34 Remove the pump gears and shaft.

35 Remove the separator plate, dowel pins, check valve and spring.

36 Remove and discard the filter screen.

15 Major assemblies – inspection and overhaul

Mainshaft

1 The mainshaft can be dismantled completely after extracting the circlips (Fig.7.81). Check the bearings for wear, the teeth of the gears and the splines of the shaft for wear and deformation. Check the bearings for wear and damage by scuffing.

2 When reassembling, renew all O-rings and metal sealing rings, and lubricate all parts with clean transmission fluid. On all thrust needle bearings, the unrolled edge of the bearing cage faces the thrust washer.

3 Check the assembled mainshaft by measuring the clearance

Fig. 7.78 Regulator valve body bolts (arrowed) (Sec 14)

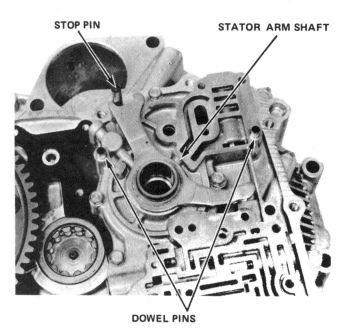

Fig. 7.79 Valve body bolts and dowels (Sec 14)

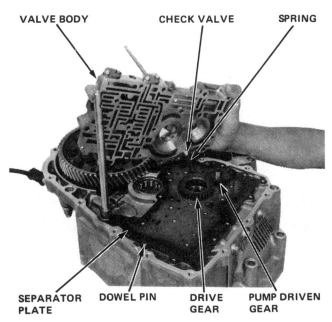

Fig. 7.80 Torque converter check valve and spring (Sec 14)

Clutches

7   The 1st, 2nd and 3rd clutches are identical and their dismantling and reassembly is the same as for the Hondamatic transmission (Section 5).

Regulator valve

8   Hold the retainer in place while removing the lock bolt (Fig. 7.88).
9   Clean all parts thoroughly in solvent and dry with blown air. Blow out all passages and inspect the pressure regulator valve for damage and wear. If any parts are worn or damaged, install a new regulator valve complete.
10   To assemble, install the pressure regulator valve and the inner and outer springs. Install the reaction spring, seat and retainer, lubricating all parts with ATF.
11   Align the hole in the retainer with the hole in the valve body, then press the retainer into the valve and tighten the lock bolt.

Servo

12   Clean all parts thoroughly in solvent and dry with blown air. Blow out all passages and inspect the ends of the oil passage pipe for damage and the modulator and servo valves for distortion, damage and wear. Do not adjust or remove the throttle pressure adjustment bolt (Fig. 7.89). Check the free lengths of the accumulator and servo valve return springs. The accumulator spring must not be less than 3.62 in (92 mm) long, nor the servo valve return spring less than 1.10 in (28 mm) long. Renew the springs if they are below this length, or if they are obviously distorted.
13   Lubricate all parts with ATF and assemble using new O-rings. If any parts of the assembly are worn or damaged, install a new servo valve complete.

Governor

14   Clean all parts thoroughly in solvent and dry with blown air. Blow out all passages and inspect the gear teeth and thrust washers for damage and wear. Check the holder for distortion and scoring, and the shaft for scoring.
15   Check the pipe for damage to its ends and examine all the internal parts of the governor housing for scoring and wear.
16   Lubricate all parts with ATF and then reassemble. If the governor does not work smoothly, or if any component is worn or damaged, install a new governor assembly.

Valve body

17   Clean all parts thoroughly in solvent and dry with blown air. Blow out all passages and inspect all parts for wear and scoring. If any

between the shoulder of the washer and the thrust needle bearing (Fig. 7.83). If the clearance exceeds 0.006 in (0.15 mm), measure the thickness of 2nd gear clutch splined thrust washer and select one from the eight different thicknesses available to give the correct clearance, which is between 0.003 and 0.006 in (0.07 and 0.15 mm).

Countershaft

4   Inspect the countershaft components for wear and damage, renewing as necessary.
5   Assemble the countershaft and measure the clearance between the shoulder of the selector hub and 2nd gear (Fig. 7.86). Seven different thicknesses of thrust washer are available to adjust this clearance. The correct clearance is 0.003 to 0.006 in (0.07 to 0.15 mm).
6   With the feeler gauge still in place for measuring 2nd gear clearance, measure the clearance between the thrust washer and the shoulder of 3rd gear, using another set of feeler gauges (Fig. 7.87). Seven different thicknesses of thrust washer are available to adjust this clearance. The correct clearance again is 0.003 to 0.006 in (0.07 to 0.15 mm). The thrust washer in this case is splined.

7

148

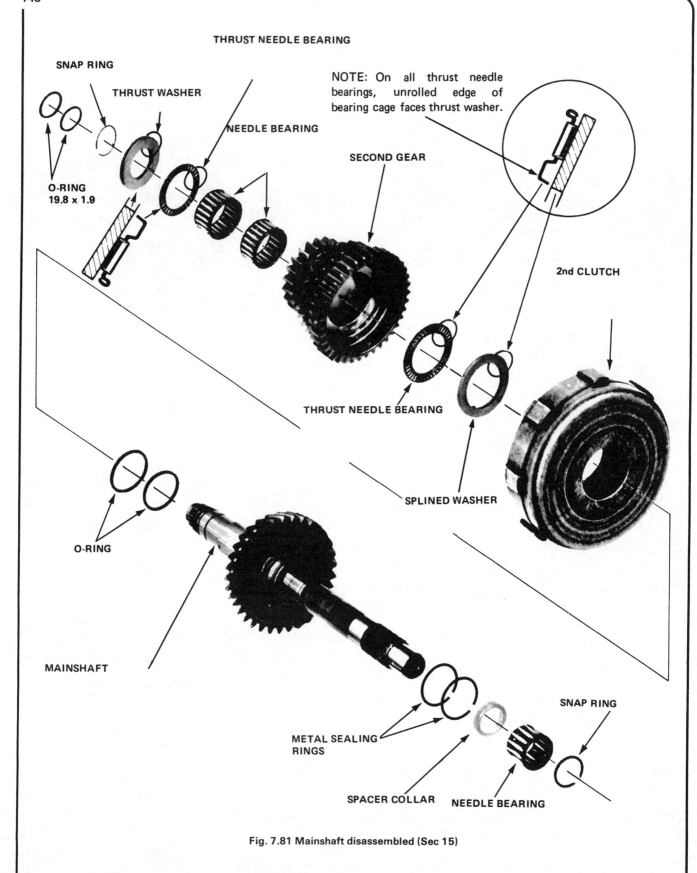

SNAP RING

THRUST WASHER

THRUST NEEDLE BEARING

NEEDLE BEARING

NOTE: On all thrust needle bearings, unrolled edge of bearing cage faces thrust washer.

SECOND GEAR

O-RING 19.8 x 1.9

2nd CLUTCH

THRUST NEEDLE BEARING

SPLINED WASHER

O-RING

MAINSHAFT

SNAP RING

METAL SEALING RINGS

SPACER COLLAR

NEEDLE BEARING

Fig. 7.81 Mainshaft disassembled (Sec 15)

Mainshaft Assembly

LOCK NUT

1st CLUTCH

MAINSHAFT

THRUST WASHER

THRUST NEEDLE BEARING

1st GEAR

NEEDLE BEARING

THRUST WASHER

SPACER COLLAR

BEARING

SNAP RING

WASHER

THRUST NEEDLE BEARING

2nd GEAR

NEEDLE BEARING

THRUST NEEDLE BEARING

SPLINED THRUST WASHER

SECOND CLUTCH

Assembled Mainshaft

Fig. 7.82 Mainshaft assembly (Sec 15)

Fig. 7.83 Measuring mainshaft 2nd gear clearance (Sec 15)

component is worn or damaged, install a new valve body assembly.
18 Start reassembling after coating all parts with ATF, first sliding the ball spring into the hole in the larger end of one of the shift valves. While holding the steel balls in place (Fig. 7.92) slide the sleeve over the valve. Install the shift spring and shift valve (Fig. 7.93) and secure them with the cover. Tighten the cover screws to a torque of 6 lbf ft (8 Nm). Repeat the process on the remaining shift valve.
19 Install the spring in the relief valve and install the valve into the body. Compress the spring with a screwdriver and then install the check valve cap by sliding its cut-out part over the screwdriver (Fig. 7.94).
20 Install the manual valve, detent rollers and spring.
21 Install the pump gears and shaft and with a straight-edge across the valve body face, use a feeler gauge to measure the endfloat of the gears. This should be between 0.001 and 0.003 in (0.03 and 0.08 mm).
22 Measure the clearance between the tips of the gear teeth and the valve body. For the drivegear this should be between 0.004 and 0.006 in (0.10 and 0.15 mm). The driven gear clearance should be between 0.002 and 0.006 in (0.05 and 0.15 mm). Excessive clearance will necessitate installing a new assembly.

Housing bearings and oil seals
23 The oil seals in the torque converter and transmission housings should be renewed if the transmission is dismantled.
24 The bearings, if worn, can be renewed by driving them out and the new ones in, using a piece of tubing as a drift. Always use a drift of a size which applies force only to the outer track of the bearing.
25 The mainshaft bearing of the converter housing must be driven in until it bottoms in the housing and the mainshaft seal must be flush with the housing.
26 When installing the countershaft bearing in the converter housing, first install the oil guide plate in the bearing hole and then drive the bearing in flush with the housing surface (Fig. 7.95). If the countershaft needle bearing is removed from the housing, a new needle bearing must be installed.
27 When removing the bearings from the transmission housing, expand the circlips with circlip pliers and push the bearings out by hand. Do not remove the circlips unless it is necessary to clean their grooves in the housing.
28 When installing the bearings, the part number on the bearing must face outwards. Expand the circlip with circlip pliers and push the bearing in part way. Release the circlip and push the bearing in until the circlip snaps into place round the bearing, also ensuring that the circlip is properly seated in the groove in the housing.

16 Automatic transmission – reassembly

Lubricate all parts with ATF before assembly.
1   Install the manual valve lever and control shaft into the torque converter housing and then install the control lever on the other end of the shaft. Insert the bolt, using a new locktab. Tighten the bolt to the specified torque and bend up the locktab.
2   Install a new filter screen with the supports facing inwards.
3   Install the separator plate, dowel pin, pump gears and shaft. The chamfered side of the driven gear should be towards the separator plate.
4   Install the check valve and spring, then install the valve body on the torque converter housing.
5   Tighten the 7 valve body bolts in the sequence shown in Fig. 7.96. Ensure that the pump drive gear rotates smoothly and that the pump shaft moves freely in both the axial and the normal operating directions. Tighten the bolts to the specified torque and recheck the free movement of the pump gears and shaft.
6   Install the stator shaft arm, stop pin and dowel pins.
7   Install the regulator valve and tighten its 6 bolts to the specified torque.
8   Insert the steel ball into the valve body oil passage and then install the separator plate, throttle control shaft and dowel pins..
9   Install the servo, taking care to use the correct length of bolt in each hole. Tighten the bolts to the specified torque in the sequence shown in Fig. 7.97.
10   Put a roller on each side of the manual valve stem, attach the valve

7

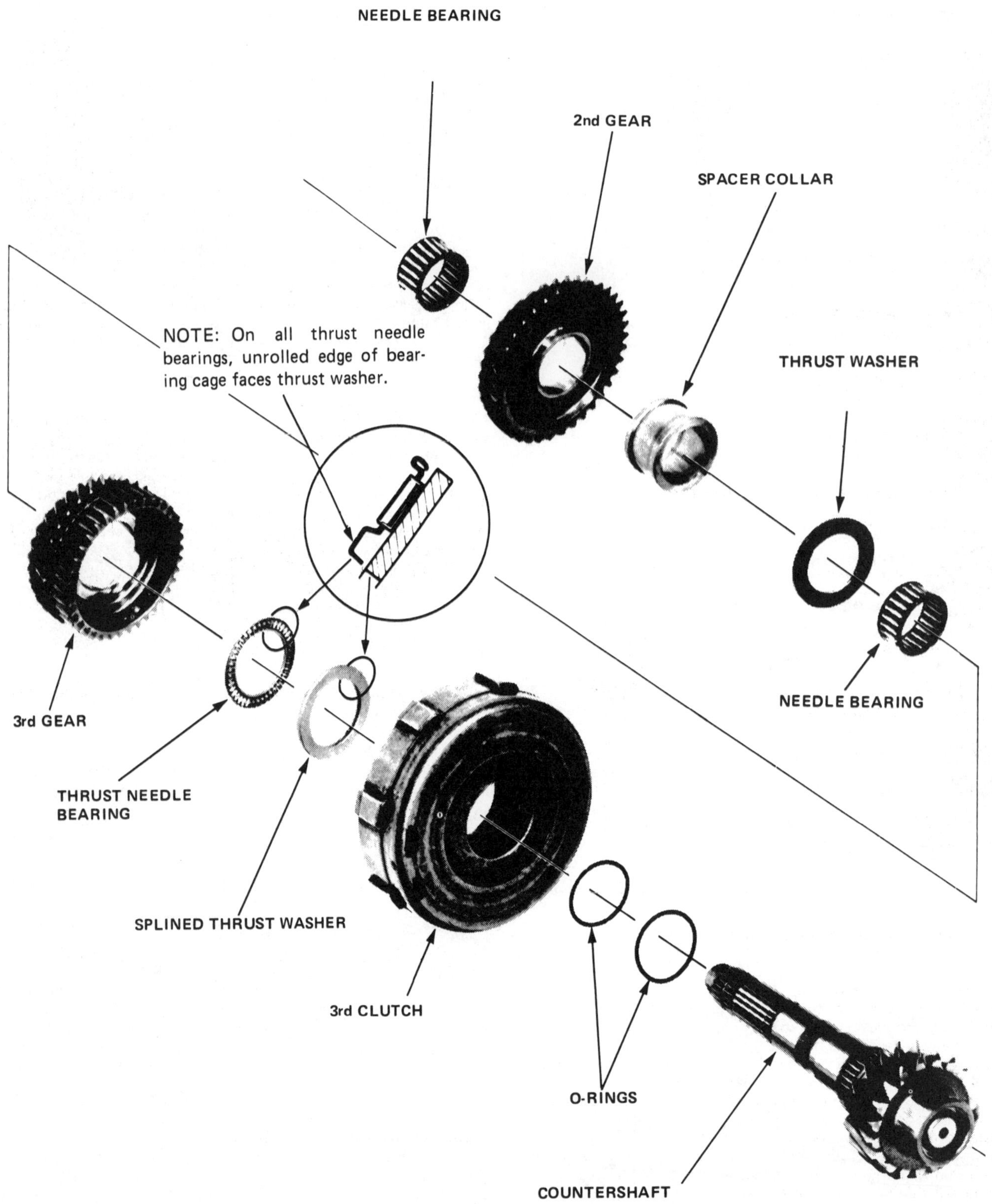

NEEDLE BEARING

2nd GEAR

SPACER COLLAR

THRUST WASHER

NOTE: On all thrust needle bearings, unrolled edge of bearing cage faces thrust washer.

3rd GEAR

NEEDLE BEARING

THRUST NEEDLE BEARING

SPLINED THRUST WASHER

3rd CLUTCH

O-RINGS

COUNTERSHAFT

Fig. 7.84 Countershaft disassembled (Sec 15)

Countershaft Assembly

LOCK NUT

PARKING GEAR

1st GEAR

NEEDLE BEARING

1st GEAR COLLAR

BEARING

REVERSE GEAR COLLAR

NEEDLE BEARING

REVERSE GEAR

REVERSE SELECTOR GEAR

SELECTER HUB

2nd GEAR

NEEDLE BEARING

SPACER COLLAR

THRUST WASHER

NEEDLE BEARING

3rd GEAR

THRUST NEEDLE BEARING

SPLINED THRUST WASHER

3rd CLUTCH

COUNTER SHAFT

Assembled Countershaft

Fig. 7.85 Countershaft assembly (Sec 15)

Fig. 7.86 Measuring countershaft 2nd gear clearance (Sec 15)

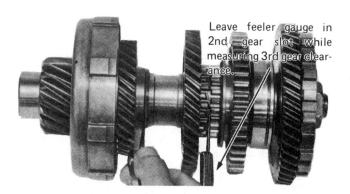

Leave feeler gauge in 2nd gear slot while measuring 3rd gear clearance.

Fig. 7.87 Measuring countershaft 3rd gear clearance (Sec 15)

to the lever with its pin and secure the pin with a split pin (Fig. 7.98).
11 Install the 2nd and 3rd accumulator springs, install the cover and tighten the bolts to the specified torque in a criss-cross pattern. Press down on the cover whilst tightening the bolts.
12 Install the governor and then its 3 bolts with new locktabs. Tighten the bolts to the specified torque and bend up the locktabs.
13 Insert the mainshaft and countershaft in place together. **Do not** force the shafts or attempt to drive them in.
14 Install countershaft 2nd gear.
15 Insert the reverse shift fork into its selector sleeve and install them as an assembly. The grooved side of the sleeve should be down and the unmarked side of the fork should be up.
16 Install the reverse shift fork over the servo valve stem with the valve stem turned so that the chamfered end of the hole through its stem aligns with the bolt hole in the shift fork. Insert the bolt with a new lockplate, tighten the bolt to the specified torque and bend up the locktab.
17 Install countershaft reverse gear, its needle bearing and reverse gear collar.
18 Install a new gasket, insert the two dowel pins into the converter housing and install the two oil feed pipes.
19 Install the transmission housing on the torque converter housing,

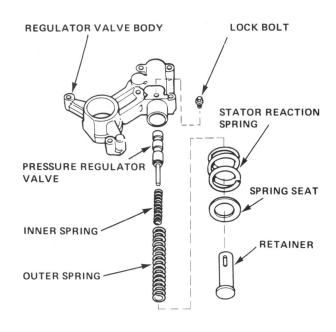

REGULATOR VALVE BODY

LOCK BOLT

STATOR REACTION SPRING

PRESSURE REGULATOR VALVE

SPRING SEAT

INNER SPRING

RETAINER

OUTER SPRING

Fig. 7.88 Regulator valve components (Sec 15)

7

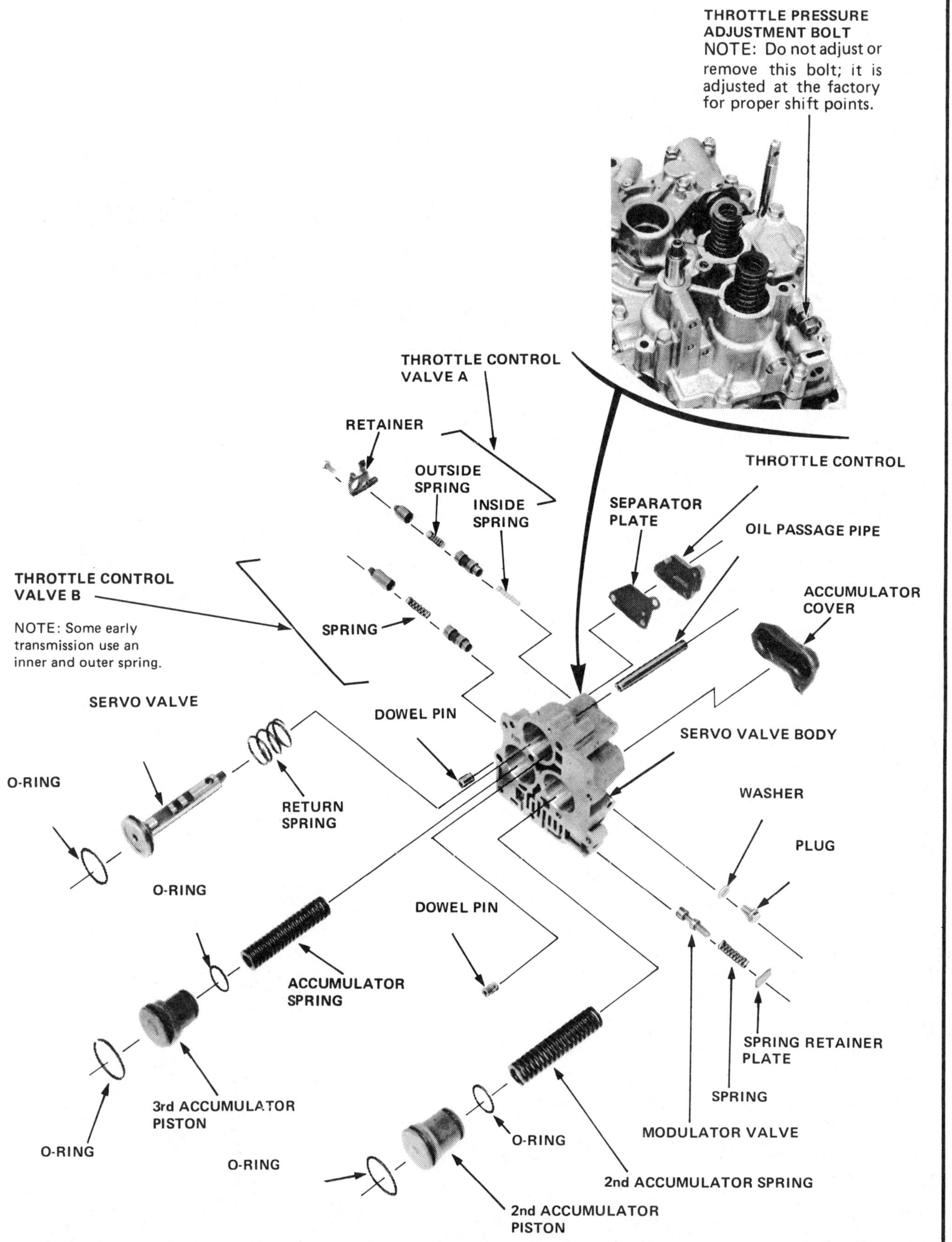

THROTTLE PRESSURE
ADJUSTMENT BOLT
NOTE: Do not adjust or
remove this bolt; it is
adjusted at the factory
for proper shift points.

THROTTLE CONTROL
VALVE A

RETAINER

OUTSIDE
SPRING

INSIDE
SPRING

THROTTLE CONTROL

SEPARATOR
PLATE

OIL PASSAGE PIPE

ACCUMULATOR
COVER

THROTTLE CONTROL
VALVE B

NOTE: Some early
transmission use an
inner and outer spring.

SPRING

SERVO VALVE

DOWEL PIN

SERVO VALVE BODY

O-RING

RETURN
SPRING

O-RING

WASHER

PLUG

O-RING

ACCUMULATOR
SPRING

DOWEL PIN

SPRING RETAINER
PLATE

3rd ACCUMULATOR
PISTON

SPRING

MODULATOR VALVE

O-RING

O-RING

O-RING

2nd ACCUMULATOR SPRING

2nd ACCUMULATOR
PISTON

Fig. 7.89 Servo valve assembly (Sec 15)

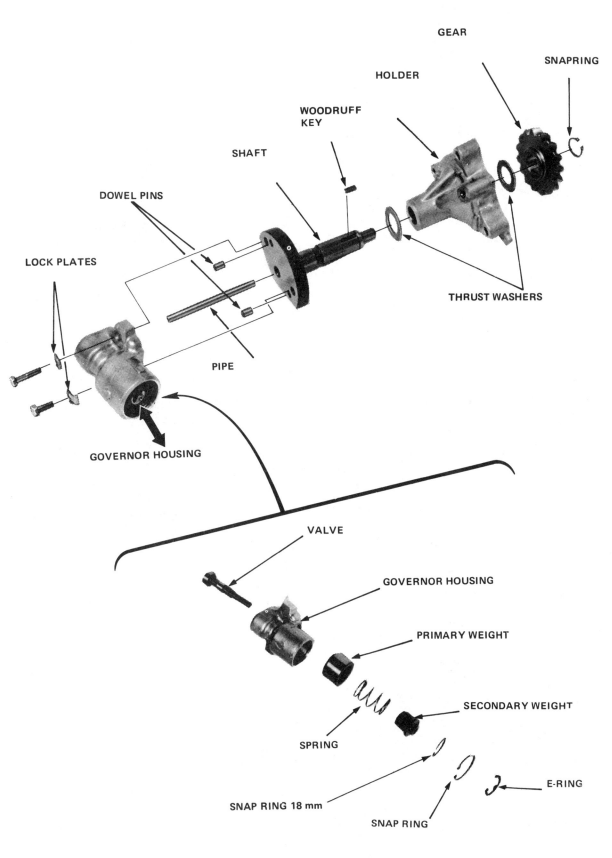

GEAR

SNAPRING

HOLDER

WOODRUFF KEY

SHAFT

DOWEL PINS

LOCK PLATES

THRUST WASHERS

PIPE

GOVERNOR HOUSING

VALVE

GOVERNOR HOUSING

PRIMARY WEIGHT

SECONDARY WEIGHT

SPRING

SNAP RING 18 mm

SNAP RING

E-RING

Fig. 7.90 Governor assembly (Sec 15)

7

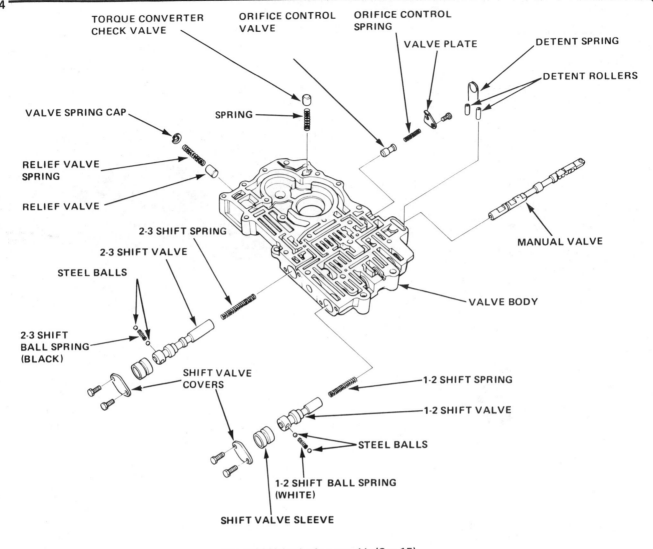

Fig. 7.91 Valve body assembly (Sec 15)

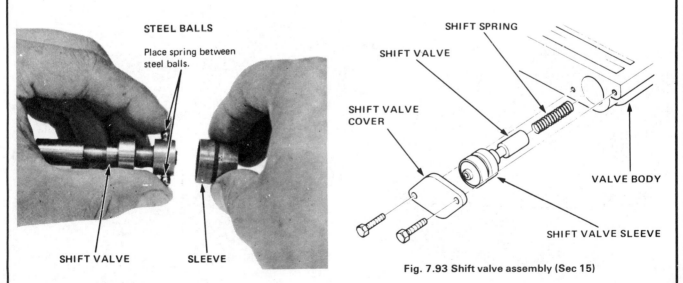

Fig. 7.92 Assembling the shift valve (Sec 15)

Fig. 7.93 Shift valve assembly (Sec 15)

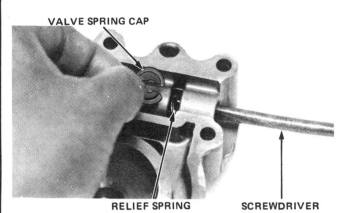

Fig. 7.94 Installing the relief valve (Sec 15)

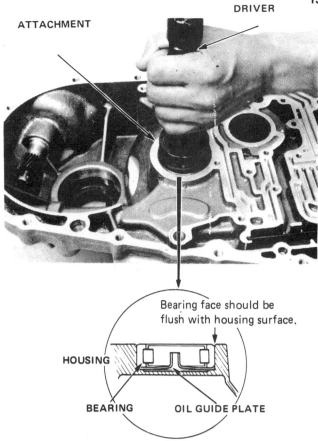

Fig. 7.95 Installing the torque converter housing countershaft bearing (Sec 15)

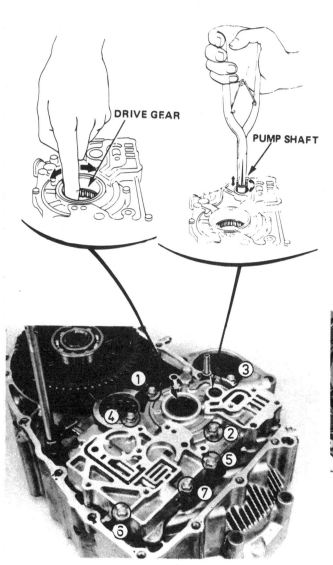

Fig. 7.96 Valve body bolt tightening sequence (Sec 16)

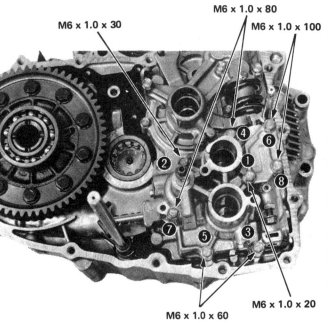

Fig. 7.97 Servo bolts tightening sequence (Sec 16)

7

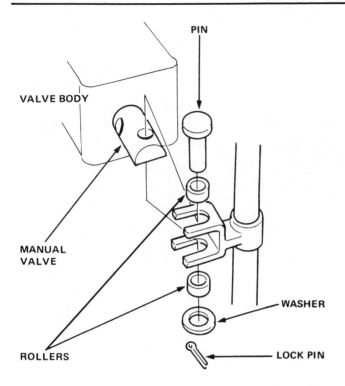

Fig. 7.98 Manual valve to valve lever attachment (Sec 16)

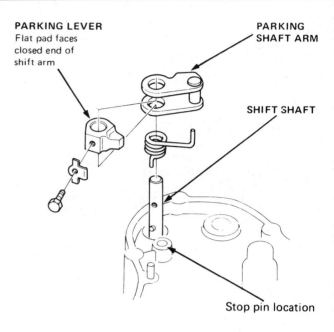

Fig. 7.99 Parking pawl and spring (Sec 16)

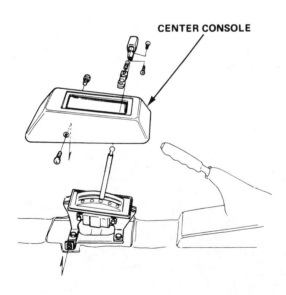

Fig. 7.100 Centre console removal (Sec 17)

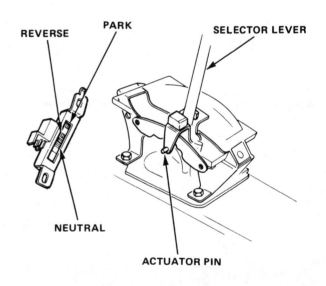

Fig. 7.101 Selector lever and switch (Sec 17)

taking care to ensure that the throttle control shaft lines up with its hole in the transmission housing. Insert the bolts and tighten them in three steps in the order shown in Fig. 7.66 to the specified torque. Take care not to bend the throttle housing bracket when tightening bolt No 1, because a damaged bracket will alter the transmission shift points.

20 Install the throttle control lever and its spring on the shaft. Insert the bolt with a new locktab. Tighten the bolt to the specified torque and bend up the locktab.

21 Install the parking shift arm and spring. The spring should put clockwise tension on the shift arm, forcing it against the stop pin (Fig. 7.99). Install the bolt with a new lockplate, tightening the bolt to the specified torque and bend up the locktab.

22 Install 1st gear collar and needle bearing on the countershaft, and the collar onto the mainshaft.

23 Install the reverse idler bearing holder, and install two new O-rings on the mainshaft.

24 Install countershaft 1st gear and the parking gear on the countershaft.

25 Install the stop pin, parking pawl shaft, parking pawl and pawl release spring. The end of the pawl release spring fits into the hole in the pawl and the spring should put clockwise tension on the pawl, forcing it away from the parking gear.

26 Move the shift lever to the Park position, install a new countershaft locknut and tighten it to the specified torque before staking it into the groove in the gear.

27 Install the needle bearing and thrust washer on the mainshaft, then 1st gear, thrust needle bearing and thrust washer. The unrolled edge of the thrust needle bearing should be towards the thrust washer.

28 Install 1st gear clutch onto the mainshaft.

29 Install a mainshaft holder to the splined end of the mainshaft, install a new mainshaft locknut on top of the 1st gear clutch and tighten the nut to the specified torque before staking the nut into the groove in the clutch. Note that the nut has a *left-hand thread*.

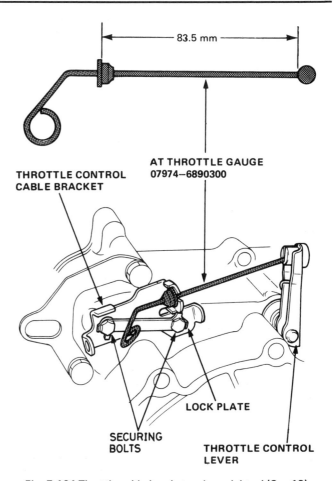

Fig. 7.104 Throttle cable bracket and special tool (Sec 19)

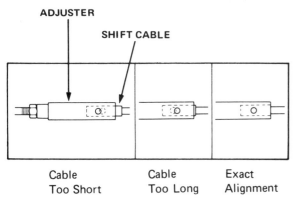

Fig. 7.102 Selector cable adjuster (Sec 18)

Fig. 7.103 Correct adjustment of cable (Sec 18)

30 Install the gasket, dowel pins and O-rings on the transmission cover and then install the end cover. Tighten the end cover bolts to the specified torque.

31 Install the dipstick and the transmission cooler banjo fitting, but do not tighten the banjo until after the transmission is installed and the cooler hoses are connected.

32 Install the transmission cooler hose fitting and tighten it to the specified torque.

17 Reversing lamp/starter inhibitor switch – removal and installation

1 Remove the two screws from the knob of the gear selector and remove the knob (Fig. 7.100). Remove the two screws from the shift indicator panel and lift away the panel.

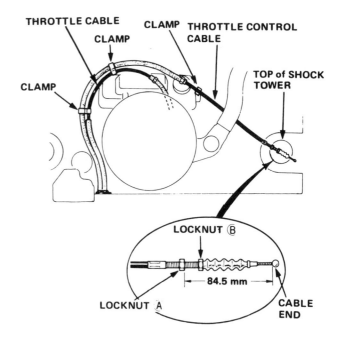

Fig. 7.105 Throttle control cable installation (Sec 19)

2   Position the selector lever in Neutral, detach the wiring harness plug from the switch and remove the two screws securing the switch.
3   Installation is the reverse of removal. Position the switch slider to neutral (Fig. 7.101), ensure that the selector lever is in Neutral, slip the switch over the actuator pin and secure it with its screws and lockwashers.
4   If the indicator lamp requires renewal, this may be done by pulling the lamp holder out of its housing.
5   When installing the selector panel, ensure that the green portion of the indicator aligns with the panel window.

18 Selector cable – adjustment

1   Start the engine, move the selector lever to Reverse and check that the gear engages.
2   With the engine switched off, remove the selector knob and centre console (see previous Section).
3   Move the selector lever to Drive and remove the lockpin from the cable adjuster (Fig. 7.102). Check that the hole in the adjuster is perfectly aligned with the hole in the selector cable (Fig. 7.103). If adjustment is required, slacken the locknut on the adjuster cable and turn the adjuster sleeve until the holes align properly. Note that the adjuster has two holes so that the cable can be adjusted in increments of 90°.
4   Tighten the locknut and install the lockpin on the adjuster. If the lockpin cannot be inserted without binding, the adjustment is still not correct.

19 Throttle cable – installation and adjustment

1   The throttle cable cannot be adjusted properly unless the adjustment of the throttle control bracket is correct. The setting of this requires a special tool (Fig. 7.104). If the bracket adjustment is known to be correct, proceed as follows.
2   Warm the engine up to normal operating temperature before attempting to adjust the throttle cable.
3   Clamp the throttle cable as shown in Fig. 7.105 and place the cable end on the shock tower.
4   Depress the accelerator pedal until there is no slack in the carburettor throttle cable and then adjust the distance between the throttle cable end and the nut 'A' to 84.5 mm. Take care not to turn nut 'A' after making this adjustment.
5   Insert the end of the throttle control cable in the groove of the throttle control lever and insert the cable adjuster in the throttle control cable bracket so that nut 'A' is against the face of the bracket.
6   Without moving nut 'A', tighten locknut 'B' until it is tight against the throttle control cable bracket.
7   Depress the accelerator pedal and check that the cable moves freely.

20 In-vehicle testing procedures

1   Road testing is an essential part of any fault diagnosis procedure for automatic or semi-automatic transmission. Before carrying out the procedure below, make sure that the transmission fluid level is correct and the cable(s) properly adjusted. If a stall test is to be carried out, the engine must be fully warmed up and in good condition.

Stall test

2   Apply the handbrake and chock the front wheels. Connect an independent tachometer to the engine where it can be viewed from the driving seat.
3   With the engine running and at normal operating temperature, engage D. Apply the brake pedal firmly, then depress the throttle pedal to the floor for six to eight seconds. Note the tachometer reading achieved.
4   *Wait two minutes to allow the transmission to cool,* then repeat the procedure in 1 or 2 and reverse. The stall speed should be equal in all ranges and within the specified limits.
5   If the stall speed is high in all ranges, suspect the fluid level, the oil pump output or the pressure regulator. The oil pick-up strainer could be clogged.
6   If the stall speed is low in all ranges, the engine may be in poor condition or the throttle cable maladjusted. Otherwise, suspect the one-way clutch in the torque converter.
7   If the stall speed is high in one particular gear, a defective clutch for that gear is suggested.
8   It is emphasised that the stall test is a demanding one for both engine and transmission, and should not be carried out over-frequently. *On no account test the stall speed for more than ten seconds at a time,* or serious damage due to overheating may result.

Road test

9   Make sure that nothing is restricting the full travel of the throttle pedal (eg mats or carpets). Warm up the engine.
10 With D engaged, the handbrake applied and the wheels chocked, depress the throttle pedal fully and release it. The engine should not stall.
11 Drive the vehicle with each range selected in turn and check for satisfactory operation under acceleration, when cruising and on the overrun.
12 Check the shift speeds against those given in the Specifications. Shift from D to 2 at 35 mph or so and check that an immediate downshift takes place. Accelerate from rest with 2 engaged and check that no upshift or downshift takes place.
13 Park the vehicle on a moderate slope, apply the handbrake and engage P. Release the handbrake and check that the vehicle remains stationary. Engage the handbrake again, or apply the footbrake, before releasing P.

21 Fault diagnosis – automatic transmission

Note: *It cannot be over-emphasised that before deciding that the transmission has developed a serious internal fault due to failure of a component, the fluid level should be checked and the adjustment of the speed selector cable inspected. Rupture of one of the oil cooler flexible hoses can cause immediate overheating and loss of drive and should these symptoms occur on the road, inspect these hoses first.*

Symptom	Reason(s)
Car does not move in any gear	Low fluid level
	Broken or maladjusted control cable
	Pump defective or sticking
	Pick-up strainer clogged
	Regulator valve or spring sticking or broken
	Servo defective
	Torque converter defective
Slip in all gears	Low fluid level
	Regulator valve defective
	Torque converter defective
	Pick-up strainer clogged

Symptom	Reason(s)
Car does not move in R but moves in forward gears	Sticking or defective servo Defective reverse gear or worn splines on selector
Poor acceleration in all gears	Low fluid level Clogged pick-up strainer Pump worn or regulator defective Throttle cable maladjusted Engine defective or brakes binding
No upshift from first (low) gear	Fault 1-2 shift valve Faulty second clutch
Upshift speeds too high	Carburettor cable maladjusted Governor faulty Throttle valve faulty
Upshift speeds too low	As above (speeds too high) Defective 1-2 shift valve Defective 2-3 shift valve
Kickdown point too low (upshifts satisfactory)	Defective 1-2 and/or 2-3 shift valve
Engine races during 2-3 shift (shift speed correct)	Defective throttle valve Defective accumulator Foreign material stuck in main orifice, or valve defective
Engine vibrates during 2-3 shift	Defective control valve Foreign material stuck in second orifice
Creep in N	Shift cable maladjusted First or second clutch faulty Throttle cable maladjusted Thrust bearing or thrust washer burnt or sticking
Difficulty in N-D shift	Shift cable maladjusted First clutch faulty Foreign material in low orifice
Difficulty in N-R shift	Servo shaft sticking Shift cable maladjusted Second clutch faulty

Malfunctions after rebuild

Symptom	Reason(s)
Loud noise whenever engine is running	Oil pump gear upside down
Car moves in L, but hesitates in D or OD	Low gear thrust washer incorrect Burrs on mainshaft Countershaft low gear incorrectly assembled
Car moves in D or OD, but hesitates in L	Drive gear thrust washer incorrect Burrs on mainshaft
Car will only move in R	Reverse gear selector sleeve upside-down
Car will not exceed 30 mph	Stator incorrectly assembled in torque converter
Vibration in all gears	Torque converter not fully seated

7

Chapter 8 Final drive and driveshafts

Refer to Chapter 13 for specifications related to 1982 and 1983 US models

Contents

Specifications

General

Final drive type	Mainshaft pinion gear and crownwheel
Driveshaft type	Open, unequal length, constant velocity joints at each end, driving front roadwheels

Final drive reduction ratio

Manual gearbox:

USA 1300 Hatchback (1980)	4.933 : 1
European Wagon	4.642 : 1
USA Hatchback (1981) and Wagon	4.428 : 1
European Hatchback	4.266 : 1
USA 1500 Hatchback (1980)	3.875 : 1

Automatic or Hondamatic transmission:

European and 1980 USA models	4.117 : 1
1981 USA models	3.875 : 1

Final drive lubrication

Common with gearbox oil or automatic transmission fluid

Torque wrench settings

	lbf ft	Nm
Driveshaft end nut (renew once removed)	108	150
Crownwheel bolts *(left-hand thread)*	72	100
Transmission casing-to-clutch bellhousing bolts	20	27
Transmission casing-to-torque converter housing bolts:		
Small	9	12
Large	20	27
Oil drain plug on transmission casing	30	41
Clutch or torque converter housing-to-engine bolts	33	45

1 General description

The final drive and differential assembly is located within the transmission casing and is of similar design in both manual and automatic transmission versions (Figs. 8.1 and 8.2).

The drive pinion is an integral part of the mainshaft. This meshes with the crownwheel which is bolted to the differential carrier. The differtial components are of conventional type and drive is transmitted to the front roadwheels.

2 Maintenance

1   Lubrication of the final drive is provided from the transmission oil. Topping up the oil in the gearbox or automatic transmission or draining and refilling these units at the specified intervals will automatically service the final drive as well.

2   Lubrication of the driveshaft inner joint is only required at time of dismantling. The joint cannot be repaired, but can be renewed separately.

3   The driveshaft outer joint cannot be dismantled and in the event of a fault or wear occurring, the driveshaft must be renewed complete.

4   The front hub bearings do not require lubrication except after dismantling and reassembly when they should be repacked with grease.

3 Final drive – removal, overhaul and refitting

1   Remove the manual gearbox or automatic transmission as described in Chapter 6 or 7 according to type.

2   Clean the external surfaces of the transmission unit using paraffin or water-soluble solvent and a stiff brush.

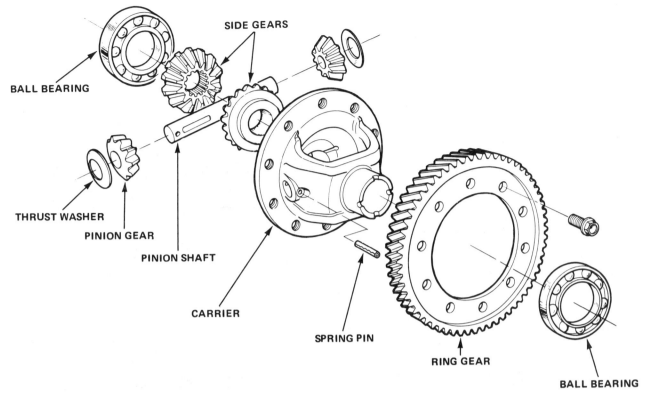

BALL BEARING

SIDE GEARS

THRUST WASHER

PINION GEAR

PINION SHAFT

CARRIER

SPRING PIN

RING GEAR

BALL BEARING

Fig. 8.1 Final drive components (manual transmission) (Sec 1)

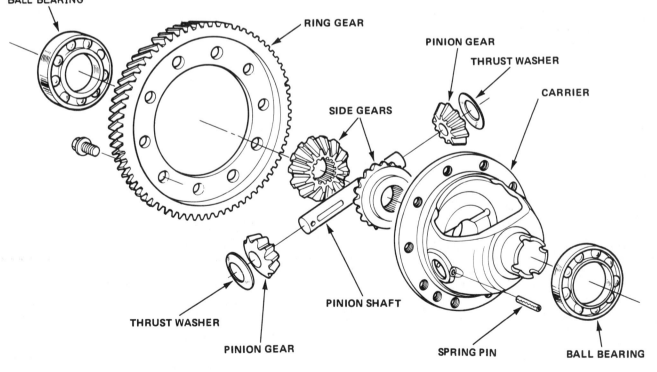

BALL BEARING

RING GEAR

PINION GEAR

THRUST WASHER

CARRIER

SIDE GEARS

THRUST WASHER

PINION GEAR

PINION SHAFT

SPRING PIN

BALL BEARING

Fig. 8.2 Final drive components (Hondamatic) (Sec 1)

8

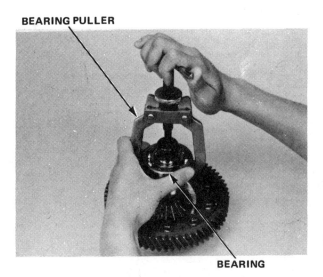

Fig. 8.3 Removing the differential carrier bearing (Sec 3)

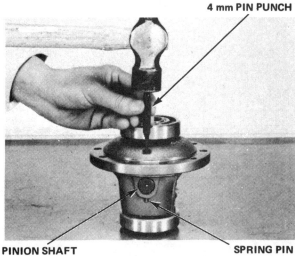

Fig. 8.4 Removing the differential shaft spring pin (Sec 3)

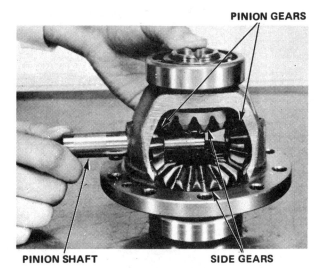

Fig. 8.5 Removing the pinion gears and shaft (Sec 3)

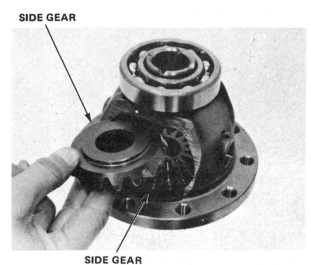

Fig. 8.6 Removing the side gears (Sec 3)

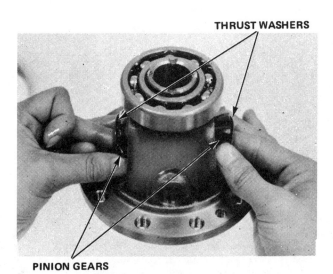

Fig. 8.7 Installing the pinion gears and thrust washers (Sec 3)

Fig. 8.8 Crownwheel installation (manual transmission) (Sec 3)

Chamfer on inside diameter of ring gear faces carrier.

Ring gear bolts to right-hand side of carrier.

Fig. 8.9 Crownwheel installation (Hondamatic) (Sec 3)

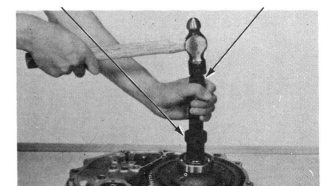

ATTACHMENT   DRIVER

DIFFERENTIAL ASSY   CLUTCH/TORQUE CONVERTER HOUSING

Fig. 8.10 Bottoming the differential assembly snap-ring (Sec 3)

Fig. 8.11 Manual transmission case bolt tightening sequence (Sec 3)

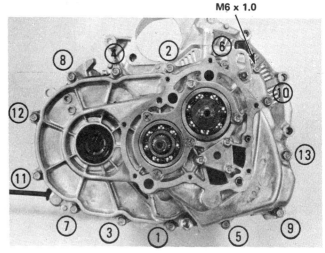

M6 x 1.0

Fig. 8.12 Hondamatic transmission case bolt tightening sequence (Sec 3)

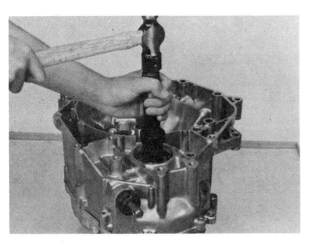

Fig. 8.13 Bottoming the differential assembly in the transmission housing (Sec 3)

CLUTCH/TORQUE CONVERTER HOUSING

FEELER GAUGE   SNAP RING

Fig. 8.14 Measuring snap-ring clearance (Sec 3)

8

3   Dismantle the gearbox by reference to the appropriate Section of Chapter 6 or 7.

4   The differential and crownwheel assembly should now be the only major item left in the transmission housing.

5   Using a tubular drift, applied the differential carrier bearing which is located in the transmission housing, release the bearing from its seat and then lift out the final drive assembly.

6   The bearings can be removed from both sides of the differential using a conventional puller (Fig. 8.3).

7   Secure the differential carrier in the jaws of a vice and then unscrew **(left-hand thread)** the bolts which secure the crownwheel to the differential carrier. Release the bolts half a turn at a time in diagonally opposite sequence.

8   After the crownwheel has been removed, drive out the spring pin which holds the pinion shaft in place in the differential (Fig. 8.4).

9   Drive the pin out by applying the drift to the side opposite to the differential carrier as shown. Extract the shaft and the pinion gears (Fig. 8.5).

10 Once the pinion gears and their shaft have been removed, the side gears can be extracted by moving them into the centre of the differential carrier and out of the aperture in the carrier (Fig. 8.6).

11 With the differential and final drive fully dismantled, thoroughly clean all components and examine for wear. Pay particular attention to the gear teeth. Check the ball bearings for wear; also check that they are an interference fit in their transmission casing seats.

12 When reassembling coat each component in Molykote or equivalent. Commence by installing the side gears into the differential carrier and then insert the pinion gears between the side gears. Rotate the side gears so aligning the pinion gear holes with the shaft holes.

13 Install the thrust washers (one behind each pinion gear) (Fig. 8.7) and insert the shaft. If the original components and thrust washers are being refitted insert the shaft tension pin. If new components have been fitted then before inserting the tension pin the backlash between the teeth of the side gears and the pinion gears must be checked. Move the gears carefully by finger pressure and check the backlash using a dial gauge or feeler blades. The backlash should be between 0.002 and 0.010 in (0.05 and 0.25 mm). If necessary, change the thrust washers for ones of different thickness (four sizes are available). The thrust washers on opposite sides must be of equal thickness. When adjustment is complete, drive in the shaft spring pin.

14 If the differential carrier bearings have been removed, install the new ones, driving them home with a tubular drift.

15 Install the crownwheel, tightening the securing bolts to the specified torque and remembering that they have left-hand threads. Note the difference in fitting of the crownwheel used with manual gearbox and Hondamatic transmission vehicles (Figs. 8.8 and 8.9).

16 Remove the oil seals from the clutch (or torque converter) housing and discard them and obtain new ones, but do not fit them at this stage.

17 Install the large circlip and then tap home the differential assembly into the clutch (or torque converter) housing (Fig. 8.10).

18 Locate a new gasket and fit the transmission housing, using a minimum of four bolts to secure it. Tighten the bolts to the specified torque, in the sequence shown in Figs. 8.11 or 8.12.

19 Use a drift and hammer to ensure that the differential assembly is bottomed in the transmission housing (Fig. 8.13).

20 Measure the clearance between the large circlip and the face of the outer track of the differential case bearing in the clutch (or torque converter) housing (Fig. 8.14). This side clearance should be between 0.004 and 0.006 in (0.10 and 0.15 mm). If it is outside this limit, extract the circlip and change it for one of the six alternative thicknesses which are available.

0.096 in (2.45 mm)   0.100 in (2.55 mm)
0.104 in (2.65 mm)   0.108 in (2.75 mm)
0.112 in (2.85 mm)   0.116 in (2.95 mm)

21 Apply oil to a new differential seat and install it in the clutch/torque converter housing.

22 Final reassembly and installation operations may now be carrried out by reversing the dismantling and removal procedure.

---

4   Driveshaft – removal and installation

1   The driveshafts are of unequal lengths with constant velocity joints incorporated at each end (photos). The inside end of the shaft is

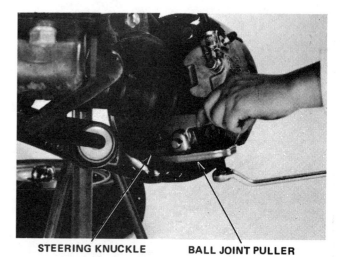

STEERING KNUCKLE   BALL JOINT PULLER

Fig. 8.15 Separating the balljoint from the lower control arm (Sec 4)

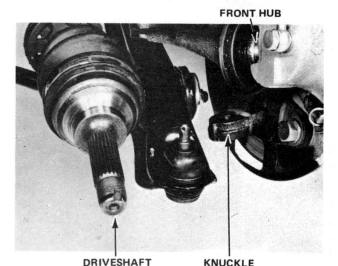

FRONT HUB

DRIVESHAFT   KNUCKLE

Fig. 8.16 Pull the hub off the driveshaft (Sec 4)

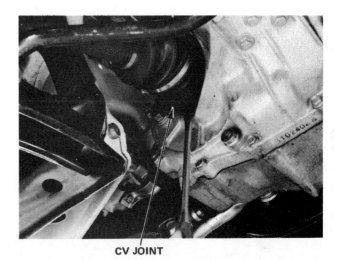

CV JOINT

Fig. 8.17 Prise the CV joint out of the transmission (Sec 4)

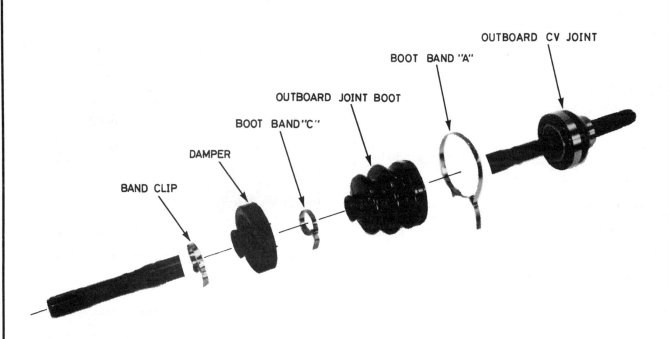

Fig. 8.18 Outboard CV joint components (Sec 5)

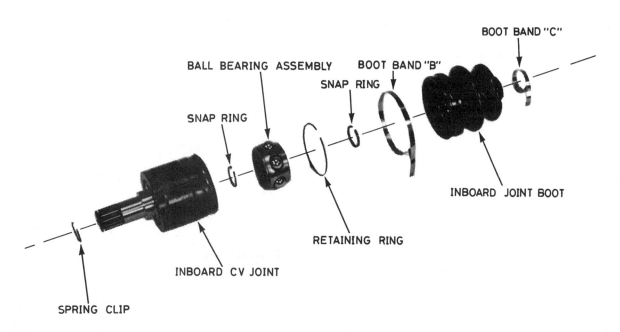

Fig. 8.19 Inboard CV joint components (Sec 6)

8

4.1a Inner constant velocity joint (transmission end)

4.1b Outer constant velocity joint (wheel hub end)

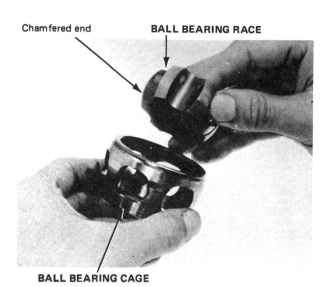

Fig. 8.20 Install chamfered end of race first (Sec 6)

Fig. 8.21 Press in balls until they are seated (Sec 6)

splined and fits into the centre of the output bevels of the differential; the outer end is splined as well, to accept the front wheel mounting flange. Each constant velocity joint comprises 6 steel balls caged between conformal joint halves.

2 As noted in Section 2, the constant velocity joints cannot be repaired, since components are not available. The inner joints can be renewed independently of the shaft; the outer joints cannot be dismantled or removed from the shaft, so if one is defective, the complete shaft must be renewed.

3 Commence removal by removing the centre cap from the wheel hub. Relieve the staking on the driveshaft spindle nut and slacken the hub. This nut is very tight; it must be renewed on reassembly.

4 Jack up the front of the car and support it securely. Remove the front roadwheel on the side being worked on.

5 Drain the transmission oil.

6 Disconnect the front suspension lower balljoint at the steering knuckle, using a balljoint separator or forked wedges (Fig. 8.15).

7 Pull the hub outwards until it is free of the driveshaft (Fig. 8.16).

8 Using a large screwdriver or a tyre lever, carefully prise the inboard CV joint outwards about $\frac{1}{2}$ in (12 mm) to force the spring clip past the groove in the splines of the differential gear (Fig. 8.17).

9 Pull the driveshaft out of the transmission case.

10 Installation is a reversal of removal. Use a new spring clip at the inboard end. Tighten all nuts and bolts to the specified torque. Finally

tighten the driveshaft spindle nut when the weight of the car is again on the wheels, and stake the nut into the groove on the spindle.

5 Driveshaft outer joint bellows – renewal

1 If when carrying out the visual inspection of the driveshaft dust excluding bellows recommended in 'Routine Maintenance', the bellows are found to be split or damaged, then they must be renewed.

2 Remove the driveshaft as described in the preceding Section.

3 Before the bellows on the outer joint can be removed, the inner joint must first be dismantled as described in the next Section.

4 With the inner joint removed, cut the securing bands from the bellows on the outer joint and slide the bellows from the driveshaft (Fig. 8.18).

5 Clean away any dirt and old grease from the joint and slide the new bellows up the driveshaft. Before locating the bellows over the outer joint pack it liberally with specified grease and then slide the bellows over the joint and fit two new securing clips. Note that the smaller clip must locate between the two humps on the driveshaft. Expand and compress the bellows when fitted to settle them.

6 The outer joint cannot be overhauled or dismantled and in the event of wear, the driveshaft must be renewed complete.

6 Driveshaft inner joint – dismantling, inspection and re-assembly

As mentioned elsewhere in this Chapter, the driveshaft inner joint can only be renewed as a complete assembly, since spare parts for overhaul are not available.

1 Remove the driveshaft, as described in Section 4.
2 Cut both securing clips from the inner joint bellows and slide the bellows off the joint down the driveshaft.
3 Extract the large ring on the inside of the joint housing and draw the housing from the joint.
4 Wipe away all grease to expose the circlip on the end of the driveshaft. Extract this circlip and withdraw the joint cage from the driveshaft.
5 To inspect the joint cage components, clean the cage and place it on the bench. Gently prise the balls out of the case, using a blunt screwdriver or similar.
6 Inspect the bearing race and cage for scoring or other evidence of wear. Inspect the race splines for wear or damage; if any is found, check the corresponding area on the driveshaft. Inspect the balls for pitting, chipping or other damage. Renew the joint complete if necessary; renew the rubber boot as a matter of course unless it is in perfect condition.
7 Reassemble the race and cage, noting that the chamfered end of the race goes into the cage first (Fig. 8.20). Press in the balls until they are seated, then grease the assembly thoroughly.
8 Refit the cage assembly to the housing, packing the housing cavity with the specified grease.
9 The remainder of reassembly is the reverse of the dismantling procedure. Use new clips to secure the rubber boot, making sure that the inner band locates between the humps in the driveshaft. Expand and compress the boot when fitted to settle it.

7 Fault diagnosis – final drive and driveshafts

Symptom	Reason(s)
Vibration	Roadwheels out of balance Worn driveshaft joints Bent driveshaft
Knock on taking up drive or on overrun	Worn driveshaft splines Loose roadwheel nuts Worn front suspension balljoints Worn driveshaft joints
Clicking noise on turns	Constant velocity joint(s) worn or damaged

8

Chapter 9 Braking system

Refer to Chapter 13 for specifications and information related to 1982 and 1983 US models

Contents

Specifications

System type

Footbrake	Hydraulic to all four wheels, with servo assistance. Discs front, self-adjusting drums rear. Dual hydraulic circuit
Handbrake	Mechanical to rear wheels only

Lining surface area

Front:

Hatchback	4.6 in² (29.5 cm²)
Sedan	5.5 in² (35.3 cm²)
Wagon	5.6 in² (36.1 cm²)

Rear:

Hatchback	6.2 in² (40 cm²)
Sedan	6.2 in² (40 cm²)
Wagon	7.4 in² (48 cm²)

Adjustment and repair data

Pedal height from floor (measured without floor mat)	7.25 in (184 mm)
Minimum friction material thickness:	
Disc pads	0.063 in (1.6 mm)
Shoes	0.079 in (2.0 mm)
Minimum brake disc thickness after regrinding:	
Hatchback	0.35 in (9 mm)*
Sedan and Wagon	0.39 in (10 mm)*
Disc run-out	0.006 in (0.15 mm) maximum
Maximum brake drum diameter after regrinding:	
Hatchback and Sedan	7.13 in (181 mm)*
Wagon	7.91 in (201 mm)*
*Or as marked on drum or disc	
Brake drum out-of-round	0.004 in (0.1 mm) maximum
Handlebar lever travel	4 to 8 clicks

Torque wrench settings

	lbf ft	Nm
Caliper mounting bolts	56	78
Caliper guide pin bolts:		
Hatchback	20	27
Sedan	13	18
Rear brake backplate-to-stub axle bolts	40	55
Bleed screws:		
Front	7	9
Rear	5	7

Pipe and hose unions:
   Front caliper   25   35
   Rear wheel cylinder   14   19
   Flexible hose to rigid pipeline   10   14
   Proportioning valve unions   14   19

1 General description

The braking system is of the four wheel, dual hydraulic circuit type with vacuum servo assistance. Disc brakes are installed on the front wheels and drum brakes on the rear (Fig. 9.1).

The disc brakes are inherently self-adjusting, and the rear drum brakes are self-adjusting due to the quadrant and ratchet mechanism which is actuated every time the brake pedal is depressed.

A dual proportioning valve is incorporated in the hydraulic circuit. This distributes the pressure diagonally between the front and rear brakes and also limits the pressure applied to the rear wheel cylinders to prevent the wheels from locking under heavy braking.

Switches are provided for fluid level warning, handbrake 'on' warning and brake light operation.

2 Maintenance

1 It cannot be emphasised too much that diligent inspection and maintenance of the braking system is essential to retain your safety in the car.

2 *Every week* remove the master cylinder hydraulic fluid cap and check the level of fluid which should be just up to the 'max' mark on the side of the reservoir. Check that the vent hole in the cap is clear. Any need for regular topping-up, regardless of quantity, should be viewed with suspicion, and the whole braking hydraulic system should be inspected for signs of leakage.

3 *Every 3000 miles (4800 km) or 3 months, whichever is the sooner,* closely examine all the flexible brake hoses, and hose connections. Use a mirror to inspect all parts of the hose, and remember to move the flexible hose so that cracks or other surface deterioration will be revealed. Renew any hoses which are not in anything but perfect condition, immediately. There is no way of knowing how dangerous a crack in a hose is.

Inspect all fixed metal brake pipes for corrosion and surface deterioration. These pipes are stressed by the fluid pressure in the braking system. Any corrosion on the outer surface can generate and propagate cracks in the metal which will lead ultimately to the sudden failure of the pipe.

4 *Every 6000 miles (9600 km) the thickness of friction material on both front and rear brake mechanisms should be checked.* The capability of the friction material to withstand heat is dependent on the thickness of the friction material on the brake pad or shoe. If the material has worn too thin, there is a risk that the material will

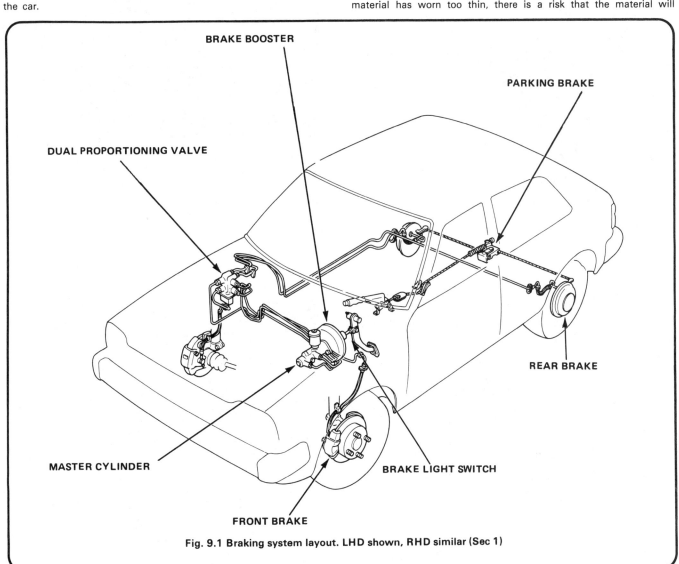

Fig. 9.1 Braking system layout. LHD shown, RHD similar (Sec 1)

9

disintegrate when hot with the consequent loss of braking.

5   *Every 18 months to 2 years (24 000 miles/38 000 km)* it is necessary to renew the hydraulic fluid in the braking system. The fluid should prevent corrosion within the braking system and withstand the high temperature experienced in the slave cylinders in the brake mechanism. The fluid in the brake pipes and slave cylinders deteriorates in time and old fluid is liable to boil when the brakes are in hard usage. The vapour in the brake lines will lead to inconsistency of braking effort.

6   It is good practice every 2 to 3 years to renew seals and hoses in the brake system as preventive maintenance.

7   If you have just acquired a secondhand car, it is strongly recommended that the whole brake system, drums, shoes, discs, pads, hoses, pipes, slave and master cylinders, are thoroughly examined. Even though the effectiveness of the braking system may be excellent, the friction material may be near the end of its useful life, and it will be as well to know this without delay.

3   Front brake pads – removal and installation

1   Raise the front of the vehicle, support it on firmly based stands and remove the front wheels.

Hatchback

2   Remove the lower guide pin bolt and swing the caliper upwards (photos).

3   Mark the pads so that the inner and outer pads can be identified and then remove the pads, shim and anti-rattle springs (Fig. 9.3) (photo).

4   Smear the backs of the pads and the two sides of the shim with silicone grease.

5   Install the anti-rattle springs, then insert the pads. If the old pads are being reinstalled, they must be on the same side of the brake disc as they were before removal.

6   Install the shim against the back of the outer pad (photo).

7   Open the bleed screws slightly and push the piston back so that the caliper will fit over the pads easily. Tighten the bleed screw.

8   Pivot the caliper down to its proper position. Install the guide bolt and tighten to the specified torque.

9   Depress the brake pedal several times to check that the caliper is working. Top up the master cylinder if necessary.

Sedan

10   The procedure for the Sedan is similar to that for the Hatchback except that the Sedan has a spring plate in addition to the pads, shim and anti-rattle springs.

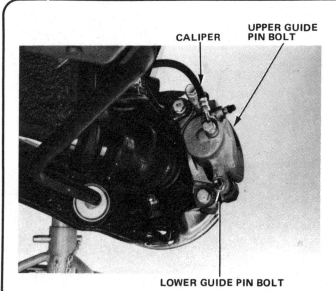

Fig. 9.2 Brake caliper bolts (Hatchback) (Sec 3)

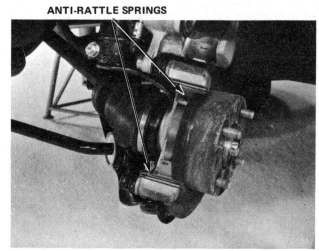

Fig. 9.3 Anti-rattle springs (Hatchback) (Sec 3)

Fig. 9.4 Removing the spring pins (Wagon) (Sec 3)

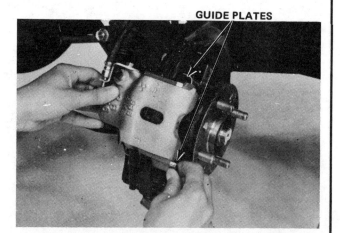

Fig. 9.5 Removing the guide plates (Wagon) (Sec 3)

3.2a Unscrewing the lower guide pin bolt

3.2b Caliper swung clear of brake disc

3.3 Removing an inner brake pad

3.6 Outer brake pad and shim

Fig. 9.6 Pulling the caliper free (Wagon) (Sec 3)

Fig. 9.7 Installing the brake pads and shim (Sec 3)

9

Wagon

11 Remove the spring pins from the guide plates (Fig. 9.4), pull out the guide plates (Fig. 9.5) and pull the caliper free (Fig. 9.6). Support the caliper by tying it to the suspension or bodywork so that the brake hose is not strained.

12 Remove the pads and the pad shim after having first marked the pads to show on which side of the disc they are installed.

13 Smear the backs of the pads and the two sides of the shim with silicone grease.

14 Install the pads. If the old pads are being reinstalled, make certain that they are reinstalled in their original positions.

15 Install the shim against the back of the outer pad (Fig. 9.7).

16 Open the bleed screw slightly and push the piston back so that the caliper will fit over the pads easily. Tighten the bleed screw.

17 Install the caliper on the mount.

18 Clean the sliding surfaces of the guide plates, lubricate them with silicone grease, install them and secure them with the spring clips.

19 Depress the brake pedal several times to check that the caliper is working.

4 Front brake pads – inspection

1 Remove the pads from the caliper and clean the pads and the shim with a wire brush.

2 Measure the thickness of pad material remaining. If this is below the minimum thickness given in the Specifications, discard the old pads.

3 If the lining thickness of the two pads of the same caliper differs by more than 0.08 in (2 mm), the pads should be discarded and new ones installed. Before installing the new pads, check that the caliper moves freely and has adequate lubricant. Pads should only be renewed in complete axle sets, even if not all are worn out.

4 Check that the pads are not contaminated by oil, hydraulic fluid or grease, and that their surface is not badly scored. If the pads have deep scoring, inspect the disc to see if it is still serviceable.

5 Brake calipers – removal and installation

1 With the vehicle firmly supported on stands, remove the front wheels.

2 Clamp the brake hose to limit the loss of fluid and then unscrew and remove the banjo bolt.

3 On the Hatchback, remove the guide pin bolts. On the Sedan remove the guide pins, and on the Wagon remove the spring pins and guide plates.

4 Remove the caliper assembly.

5 Installation is the reverse of removal. On completion bleed the hydraulic system as described in Section 17.

6 Brake calipers – dismantling and reassembly

1 On the Wagon only, remove the snap-ring from the piston boot.

2 Remove the boot.

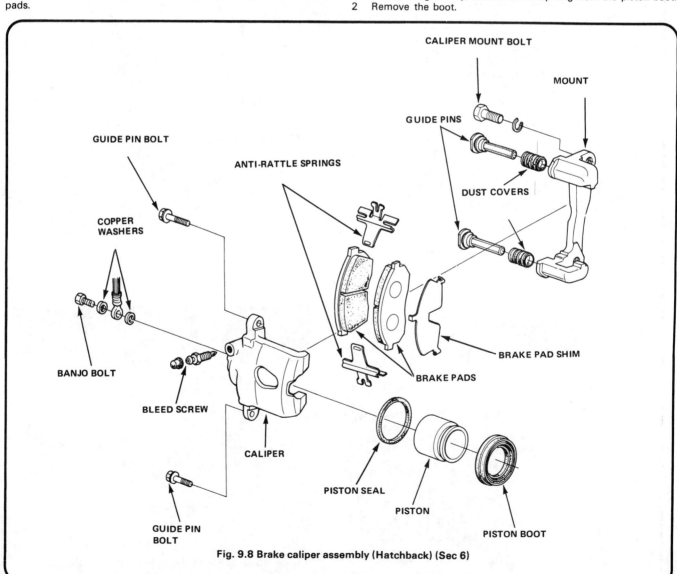

Fig. 9.8 Brake caliper assembly (Hatchback) (Sec 6)

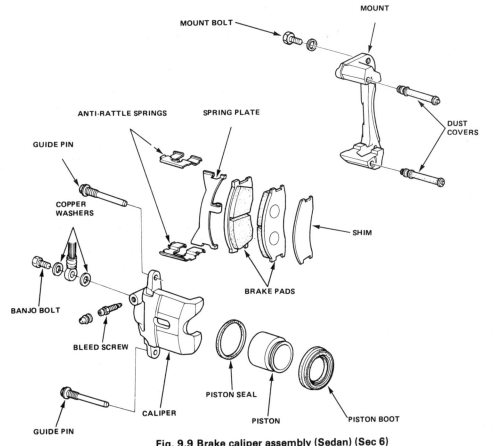

MOUNT BOLT

MOUNT

ANTI-RATTLE SPRINGS

SPRING PLATE

GUIDE PIN

DUST COVERS

COPPER WASHERS

SHIM

BANJO BOLT

BRAKE PADS

BLEED SCREW

PISTON SEAL

PISTON

PISTON BOOT

CALIPER

GUIDE PIN

Fig. 9.9 Brake caliper assembly (Sedan) (Sec 6)

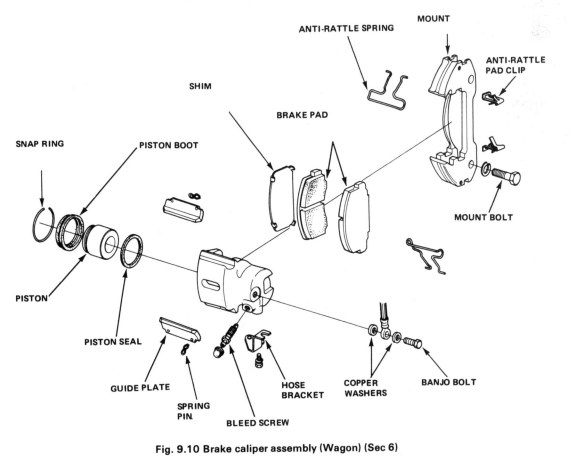

ANTI-RATTLE SPRING

MOUNT

ANTI-RATTLE PAD CLIP

SHIM

BRAKE PAD

SNAP RING

PISTON BOOT

MOUNT BOLT

PISTON

PISTON SEAL

GUIDE PLATE

SPRING PIN

BLEED SCREW

HOSE BRACKET

COPPER WASHERS

BANJO BOLT

Fig. 9.10 Brake caliper assembly (Wagon) (Sec 6)

9

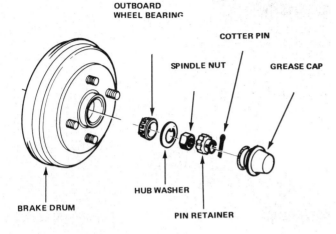

OUTBOARD WHEEL BEARING

COTTER PIN

SPINDLE NUT

GREASE CAP

HUB WASHER

PIN RETAINER

BRAKE DRUM

Fig. 9.11 Brake drum removal (Sec 8)

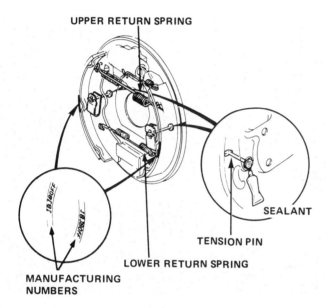

UPPER RETURN SPRING

SEALANT

TENSION PIN

LOWER RETURN SPRING

MANUFACTURING NUMBERS

Fig. 9.12 Installation of rear brake shoes (Sec 8)

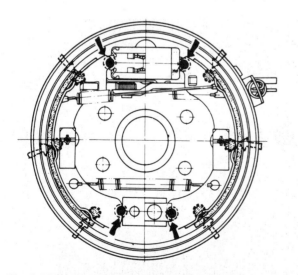

Fig. 9.13 Rear brake lubrication points (arrowed) (Sec 8)

3   Place a pad of rag in front of the piston, then use a tyre pump to blow in the brake hose hole to eject the piston.

4   Carefully remove the piston seal so that no damage is done to the cylinder bore.

5   Clean the piston and the cylinder bore with brake fluid and inspect them for damage and wear.

6   Lubricate a new piston seal with brake fluid and seat it carefully into the groove in the cylinder.

7   Install the boot onto the piston so that the lip of the boot seats in the piston groove.

8   Lubricate the piston with brake fluid and then press the piston into the caliper, taking care not to damage either the piston or the cylinder.

9   Seat the outer lip of the boot in the cylinder bore groove.

7   Brake discs – removal, inspection and installation

1   Unbolt the brake caliper and caliper mount assembly, as described in Section 5, and tie the caliper up out of the way. Avoid straining the hydraulic hose.

2   Pull the disc off the hub. If difficulty is experienced, screw two bolts into the tapped holes provided in the disc. Refer to Chapter 11, Section 3, for further details.

3   Use a wire brush to remove the rust and then inspect the disc for damage. Light scoring is normal and may be ignored. Heavy scoring or grooving may be removed by machining, provided that the thickness of the disc is not reduced below the specified minimum.

4   Thickness measurements should be made using a micrometer. Measure at eight equally spaced points, about $\frac{3}{4}$ in (20 mm) in from the edge.

5   Check the disc run-out as follows. Use two wheel nuts to hold the disc against the hub securely and then mount the dial gauge so that its measuring tip is against the front surface of the disc. Rotate the disc very slowly and note the variation in dial gauge reading. If the variation is more than the specified limit, remove the disc from the hub and re-install it on the hub 90° away from its former position. Recheck and repeat the process to find a satisfactory position.

6   If no satisfactory position can be found, it is likely that the disc is distorted and a new one must be installed.

8   Rear brake shoes – removal and installation

1   Raise the rear of the vehicle, support it on firmly based stands and remove the roadwheels. Chock the front wheels.

2   Prise the grease cap from the hub (photo) and withdraw the split pin (Fig. 9.11).

3   Remove the pin retainer (photo) and unscrew and remove the spindle nut.

8.2 Removing the hub grease cap

8.3 Removing the pin retainer

8.4 Removing the hub washer and outboard bearing race

8.6 Shoe retainer spring and pin

8.7 Brake shoe lower ends and lower return spring

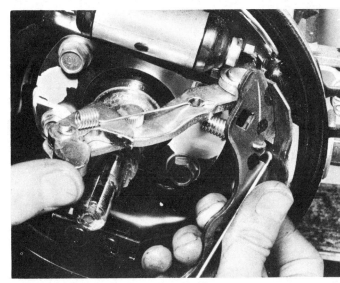

8.8 Disconnecting a shoe from the self-adjuster

8.11 Assembled rear brake ready for installation of the brake drum

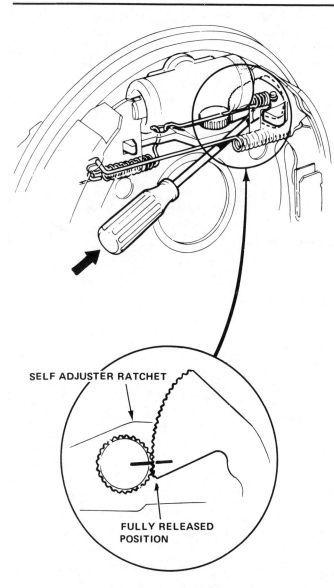

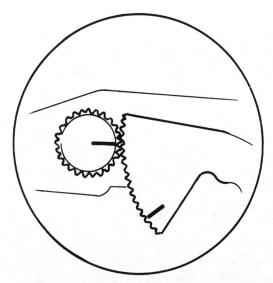

Fig. 9.14 Releasing the self-adjusting mechanism (Sec 9)

Fig. 9.15 Ratchet position when brakes have self-adjusted (Sec 9)

4   Remove the hub washer and the race of the outboard bearing (photo), then pull the brake drum off.
5   Mark the brake shoes so that if re-used they can be installed in the same position. Make a sketch of the way the brake springs are installed and the holes into which they are inserted.
6   Remove the shoe retainer springs and pins (photo).
7   Pull the lower ends of the shoes out of the slots in the brake backplate and remove the lower return spring (photo).
8   Unhook the upper return spring, disconnect the shoes from the self-adjuster (photo) and unhook the self-adjuster arm spring.
9   Set the self-adjuster ratchet to the fully released position and install the shoes by reversing the dismantling procedure. If new shoes are being installed, note that the manufacturing numbers marked on the edge of the shoes face towards the outside (Fig. 9.12).
10   Apply a small quantity of brake lubricant to the ends of the brake shoes and to the points where the shoes make contact with the brake backplate (Fig. 9.13). Take great care not to get grease on the surface of the linings, or on the inside of the drum.
11   Apply a small quantity of sealant to the head of the tension pin before installing it in the backplate and then install the retainer spring securely (photo).
12   After installing the brake drum, adjust the wheel bearing as described in Chapter 11. Operate the brakes several times to bring the self-adjusting mechanism into operation.

9   Rear brakes – inspection

1   Examine the inside of the drum for signs of excessive scoring and cracks. Scoring or grooving may be removed by machining, provided that the internal diameter remains within the limits given in the Specifications.
2   Measure the brake lining thickness. If it is below the limit given in the Specifications, discard the brake shoes and obtain new ones. Check that the linings have worn evenly. Unequal wear indicates that one of the wheel cylinder pistons is not moving freely. Check also that the linings are not damaged or contaminated. Linings should only be renewed in complete axle sets, even if not all are worn.
3   Examine the wheel cylinder for signs of leakage and check that the pistons move freely.
4   Check that the brake return and adjuster arm springs are not weak or damaged.
5   Check the operation of the self-adjuster mechanism by setting it to the fully released position using a screwdriver and then marking the engaged ratchet teeth (Fig. 9.14). Install the brake drum and spindle nut, then depress the brake pedal and remove the brake drum. Check that the ratchet has moved, showing that the brakes have self-adjusted (Fig. 9.15).

10   Rear wheel brake cylinder – removal, overhaul and installation

1   Remove the brake drum and brake shoes.
2   Clamp the brake hose as near as possible to the wheel cylinder, to minimise loss of brake fluid, and then disconnect the brake pipe from the cylinder. Plug the open end of the pipe.
3   Remove the two nuts and washers securing the cylinder to the brake backplate and remove the cylinder.
4   Remove the dust covers from the ends of the cylinder and extract the pistons and spring (Fig. 9.16).
5   Inspect the cylinder bore for scratching, scoring and corrosion and make a similar inspection of the pistons. If any metal part is no longer serviceable, install a new wheel cylinder complete.
6   If the metal parts are in satisfactory condition, remove the piston cups and install new ones. Install the cups without using any tool and position them on the pistons so that the flared end of the cup enters the cylinder first.
7   Lubricate the pistons, cups and cylinder bore with clean brake fluid. Install a piston in one end of the cylinder, then the spring and second piston into the other end.
8   Apply sealant to the surface of the cylinder which is in contact with the brake backplate, and install the cylinder by reversing the removal sequence.
9   After installation of the cylinder and the reassembly of the brakes, bleed the hydraulic system (Section 17).

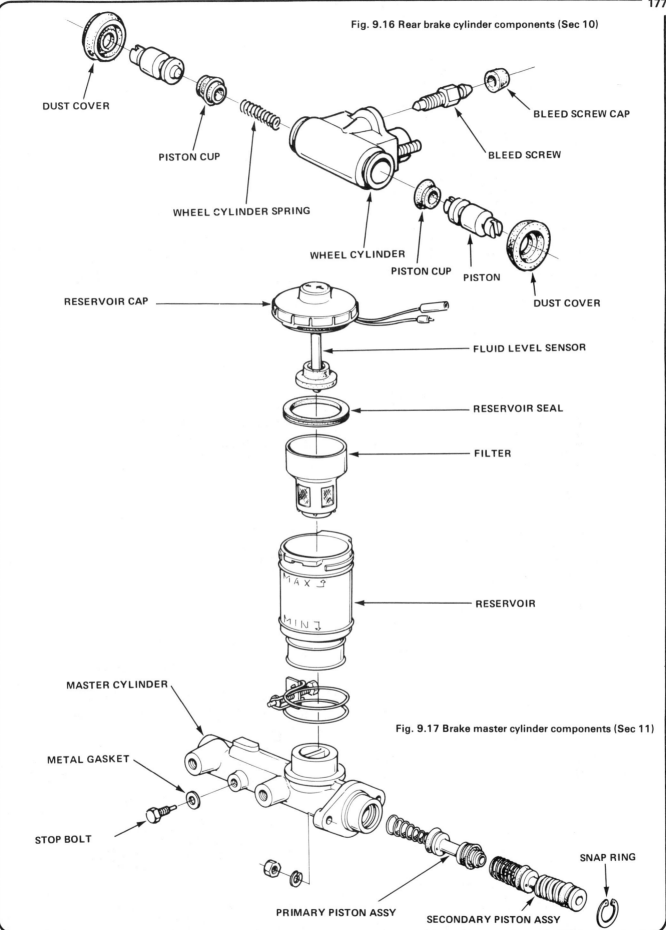

Fig. 9.16 Rear brake cylinder components (Sec 10)

DUST COVER

PISTON CUP

WHEEL CYLINDER SPRING

BLEED SCREW CAP

BLEED SCREW

WHEEL CYLINDER

PISTON CUP

PISTON

DUST COVER

RESERVOIR CAP

FLUID LEVEL SENSOR

RESERVOIR SEAL

FILTER

RESERVOIR

MASTER CYLINDER

Fig. 9.17 Brake master cylinder components (Sec 11)

METAL GASKET

STOP BOLT

SNAP RING

PRIMARY PISTON ASSY

SECONDARY PISTON ASSY

MAX

MIN

9

11 Master cylinder – removal, overhaul and installation

1   Disconnect the fluid level switch leads at the master cylinder reservoir cap.

2   Disconnect the fluid lines from the master cylinder, catching the fluid which runs out, and then plug or cap the lines to prevent dirt from entering. Take care not to spill hydraulic fluid on the vehicle's paintwork.

3   Unbolt and remove the master cylinder from the front face of the vacuum servo.

4   Unscrew the reservoir cap and tip out the fluid.

5   Remove the filter from the reservoir and clean out the sediment (Fig. 9.17).

6   Remove the circlip from the mouth of the cylinder and unscrew and remove the stop bolt from the side of the cylinder.

7   With a wad of rag held over the mouth of the cylinder and with the secondary port of the cylinder plugged or covered with a finger, apply air pressure from a tyre pump to the primary port to eject the pistons.

8   Clean all parts thoroughly using brake fluid.

9   Check the cylinder bore for wear and damage. If it is not satisfactory, obtain a new master cylinder complete.

10 New piston cups are not obtainable separately, so new piston assemblies are required when the cylinder is dismantled.

11 Lubricate all parts with brake fluid and install the piston assemblies. To ease assembly, rotate the pistons while inserting them.

12 Press the pistons into the cylinder until the primary piston spring is compressed, then insert and tighten the stop bolt, using a new metal gasket. Install the circlip in the mouth of the cylinder.

13 Before re-installing the master cylinder, check the clearance between the piston and the pushrod of the servo (Section 12).

14 Installation is a reversal of the removal procedure. After installation, bleed the hydraulic system (Section 17).

12 Brake servo – removal and installation

1   Remove the brake master cylinder as described in the previous Section.

2   Slacken the hose clip and disconnect the vacuum hose from the servo.

3   Remove the split pin and then the clevis pin connecting the brake pedal to the pushrod yoke.

4   Remove the four nuts on the pedal side of the front bulkhead which secure the servo. Remove the servo.

5   Before installing the servo, check the clearance between the end of the servo pushrod and the master cylinder piston. This cannot be measured directly with the master cylinder in place and must be measured indirectly using some form of depth gauge. Measure the depth of the secondary piston from the mounting flange of the master

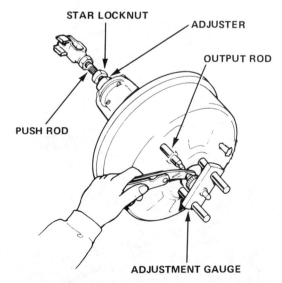

Fig. 9.18 Adjusting the pushrod to piston clearance (Sec 12)

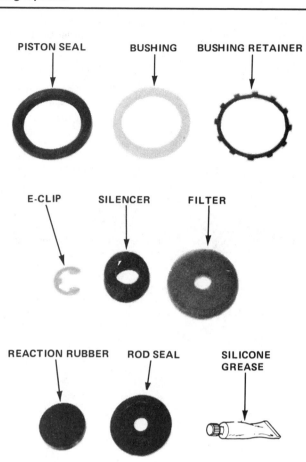

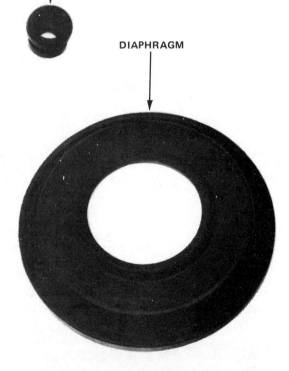

Fig. 9.19 Rebuild kit for 5 in brake servo (Sec 14)

cylinder and the projection of the pushrod from the front face of the servo. The projection from the servo should be smaller by 0.008 to 0.016 in (0.2 to 0.4 mm). To adjust the clearance, loosen the star locknut on the servo pushrod and turn the adjuster in or out to obtain the correct clearance (Fig. 9.18). Tighten the locknut and recheck.

13 Brake servo – testing

1 Check the functioning of the servo as follows. With the engine stopped, depress the brake pedal several times to release any vacuum, then depress the pedal hard and hold it depressed for 15 seconds. If the pedal sinks, there is a fault in the hydraulic system and the brake master and wheel cylinders should be inspected.

2 With the pedal depressed, start the engine. If the pedal sinks slightly when vacuum is established, the servo is working. If there is no effect on the pedal, the servo is not functioning.

3 Check for leaks by depressing the brake pedal with the engine running and then stopping the engine, holding the pedal depressed. If the pedal height remains constant for 30 seconds, the servo is satisfactory. If the pedal rises, indicating loss of vacuum, the servo is defective.

4 With the engine stopped, depress the brake pedal several times using normal pressure. If the amount which the pedal can be depressed decreases successively, the servo is satisfactory. If the pedal travel remains constant, inspect the servo check valve, which is installed in the vacuum hose to the servo.

5 To test the operation of the check valve, mark the hose to show which end is connected to the servo and then disconnect it from the servo and from the manifold. (If the hose is not marked and is then installed the wrong way round, the servo will not work.)

6 Blow through one end of the hose and then through the other. If the check valve is satisfactory, air will pass through from the booster end, but not from the manifold end.

14 Brake servo – dismantling and reassembly

1 Ascertain whether the servo is of 5 in or 6.5 in diameter and obtain the appropriate rebuild kit (Fig. 9.19 or 9.20) before starting the dismantling.

2 Drill a piece of plate or metal section which can be bolted to the master cylinder fixing studs on the servo, so that it can then be held in a vice. Alternatively screw two nuts onto each of the master cylinder mounting studs, lock the nuts and grip the nuts in the vice jaws.

3 Drill two pieces of bar or tubing to use as torque arms for removing the rear housing (Fig. 9.21).

4 Scribe a mark across the front and rear housings to ensure the same positioning of the parts on reassembly. On the 6.5 in type, remove the lock spring and lockplate (Fig. 9.22).

5 With the servo mounted in a vice, press down on the torque arms, because the housing is spring-loaded, and turn the arms anti-clockwise until the locking tabs are free of the slots in the housing. Remove the front housing.

5 in type (Fig. 9.23)

6 Remove the yoke and then push the piston/diaphragm assembly out of the rear housing.

7 Using a screwdriver, prise the bushing retainer, bushing and piston seal out of the housing.

8 Remove the locknut, adjuster and filter from the piston rod, then remove the circlip and pull out the valve assembly.

9 Remove the E-clip from the valve assembly and dismantle the assembly.

10 Remove the diaphragm from the piston and remove the reaction plate and rubber.

11 Remove the rod seal from the front housing.

12 During assembly, use only silicone grease and proceed as follows. Use new parts where supplied in the overhaul kit.

13 Seat the valve in the groove in the valve holder. Thread the valve and holder onto the pushrod.

14 Install the inner spring, outer spring and spring seat into the valve holder and secure them with the E-clip.

15 Apply silicone grease to the inner and outer surfaces of the piston tube, press the valve assembly into the booster piston tube, then install the circlip.

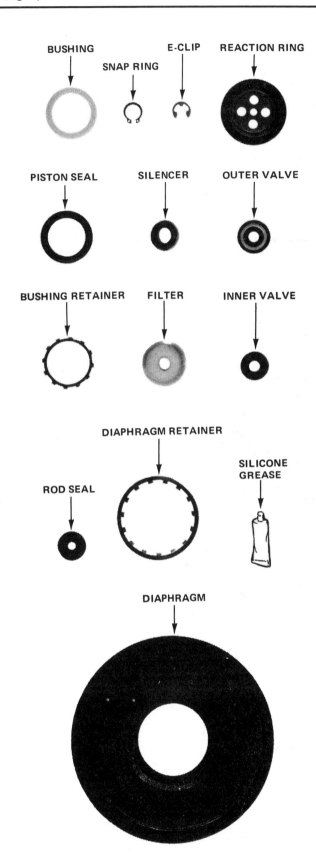

Fig. 9.20 Rebuild kit for 6.5 in brake servo (Sec 14)

9

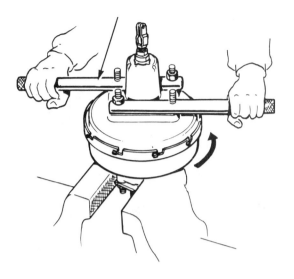

Fig. 9.21 Torque arms for removing the servo cover (Sec 14)

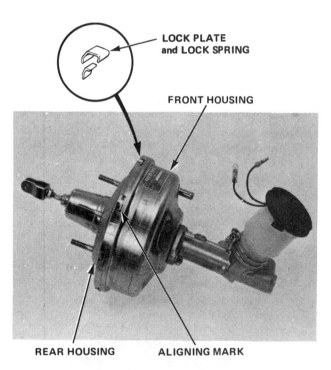

LOCK PLATE
and LOCK SPRING

FRONT HOUSING

REAR HOUSING   ALIGNING MARK

Fig. 9.22 Lockplate and spring (6.5 in servo) (Sec 14)

16 Install the diaphragm, reaction rubber and reaction plate.
17 Apply silicone grease to the piston seal, install the seal and retainer in the rear housing and drive the retainer in until the seal bottoms.
18 Apply silicone grease to the rod seal and install the rod seal, with its grooved side up, into the front housing.
19 Install the output rod, collar and spring and mount the front housing in the jaws of the vice.
20 With the torque arms attached to the rear housing, align the scribe marks of the two housings, press the rear housing into the front one and turn it clockwise to lock.
21 Check to ensure that when the two parts are assembled, the end of the pushrod protrudes through the bore in the front housing.
22 Before installing the servo and master cylinder, check the master cylinder pushrod to piston clearance (Section 12).

6.5 in type (Fig. 9.24)

23 After separating the two housings, remove the reaction cover, reaction ring and reaction plates from the rear housing.
24 Using a screwdriver, prise the bushing retainer, bushing and piston seal out of the housing.
25 Remove the snap-ring from the pushrod and remove the valve holder assembly.
26 Remove the E-clip from the valve holder assembly and dismantle the valves.
27 Using a screwdriver, prise off the diaphragm retainer and then remove the diaphragm from the piston.
28 Remove the rod seal from the front housing.
29 During assembly use silicone grease only and proceed as follows. Use new parts where supplied in the overhaul kit.
30 Seat the inner valve into the groove in the pushrod, with the recessed end of the valve towards the threaded end of the rod.
31 Install the outer valve onto the valve holder.
32 Install the pushrod through the valve holder and seat the metal end of the outer valve in the groove in the inner valve.
33 Install the inner and outer valve springs, spring seat and felt silencer, and secure them with the E-clip.
34 Thread the foam filter on to the pushrod. Screw on the adjuster and locknut, but do not tighten them.
35 Install a new diaphragm on the piston and then press on the retaining ring.
36 Apply silicone grease to the inner and outer surfaces of the piston tube and then press the valve assembly into the piston tube.
37 Apply silicone grease to the piston seal, install the seal and retainer in the rear housing and drive the retainer in until the seal bottoms. The open face of the piston seal should be away from the piston seal bushing.
38 Install the diaphragm and piston assembly into the rear housing and install the snap-ring in the groove of the pushrod.
39 Apply silicone grease to the rubber parts and then install the reaction plates with their rounded parts towards the reaction ring, and the reaction ring with its rubber end facing towards the reaction plates. Install the reaction cover.
40 Complete the assembly as described in paragraphs 18 to 22. After reassembling the two parts of the housing, install the lock spring and lock plate.

15 Proportioning valve – description

1   The proportioning valve assembly incorporates two valves to provide the following functions. It distributes brake fluid to the right front and rear left wheel cylinders, and to the left front and right rear cylinders, to prevent loss of pressure to both wheels on one side in the event of failure in one circuit.
2   The proportioning valve assembly also limits the pressure to the rear wheel cylinders under heavy braking conditions, to prevent the rear wheels from locking.
3   The proportioning valve cannot be repaired and if it is suspect, a new valve should be installed. If one wheel locks during normal braking, this suggests that the valve is defective.

16 Hydraulic pipes – inspection and renewal

1   Inspect the brake lines, as suggested in Section 2.
2   Examine first all the unions for signs of leaks. Then look at the flexible hoses for signs of fraying and chafing (as well as for leaks). This is only a preliminary inspection of the flexible hoses, as exterior condition does not necessarily indicate interior condition which will be considered later.
3   The steel pipes must be examined equally carefully. They must be thoroughly cleaned and examined for signs of dents or other percussive damage, rust and corrosion. Rust and corrosion should be scraped off, and, if the depth of pitting in the pipes is significant, they will need renewal. This is most likely in those areas underneath the chassis and along the rear suspension arms where the pipes are exposed to the full force of road and weather conditions.
4   Rigid pipe removal is usually quite straightforward. The unions at each end are undone and the pipe drawn out of the connection. The clips which may hold it to the car body are bent back and it is then

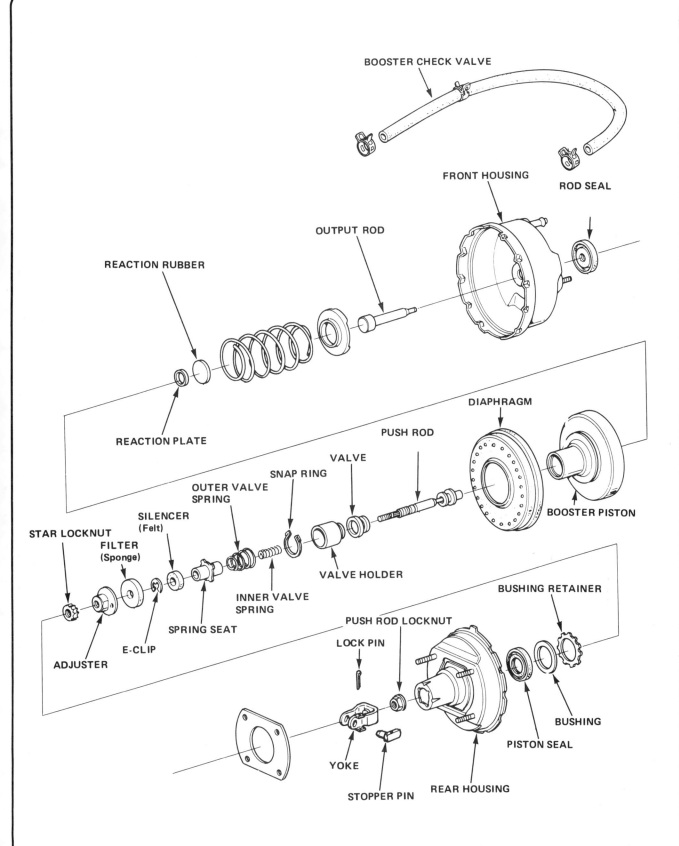

Fig. 9.23 5 in brake servo components (Sec 14)

9

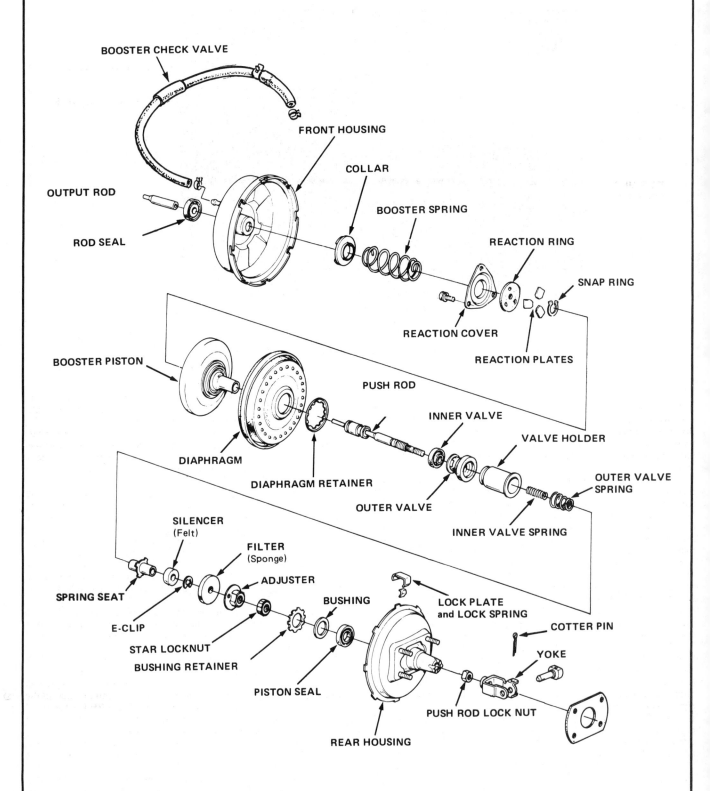

Fig. 9.24 6.5 in brake servo components (Sec 14)

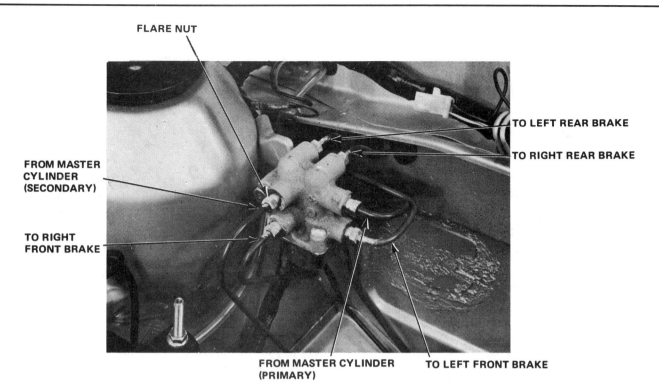

FLARE NUT

FROM MASTER
CYLINDER
(SECONDARY)

TO RIGHT
FRONT BRAKE

TO LEFT REAR BRAKE

TO RIGHT REAR BRAKE

FROM MASTER CYLINDER
(PRIMARY)

TO LEFT FRONT BRAKE

Fig. 9.25 Proportioning valve (Sec 15)

removed. Underneath the car the exposed unions can be particularly stubborn, defying all efforts of an open ended spanner. As few people will have the special split ring spanner required, a self-grip wrench is the only answer. If the pipe is being renewed, new unions will be provided. If not, then one will have to put up with the possibility of burring over the flats on the union and of using a self-grip wrench for installation also.

5   Flexible hoses are always fitted to a rigid support bracket where they join a rigid pipe, the bracket being fixed to the chassis or rear suspension arm. The rigid pipe unions must first be removed from the flexible union. Then the locknut securing the flexible pipe to the bracket must be unscrewed, releasing the end of the pipe from the bracket. As these connections are usually exposed they are, more often than not, rusted up and a penetrating fluid is virtually essential to aid removal. When undoing them, both halves must be supported as the bracket is not strong enough to support the torque required to undo the nut and can be snapped off easily.

6   Once the flexible hose is removed, examine the internal bore. If clear of fluid it should be possible to see through it. Any specks of rubber which come out or signs of restriction in the bore, mean that the inner lining is breaking up and the pipe must be renewed.

7   Rigid pipes which need renewal can usually be purchased at your local garage where they have the pipe, unions and special tools to make them up. All that they need to know is the pipe length required and the type of flare used at the ends of the pipe. These may be different at each end of the same pipe. It is a good idea to take the old pipe along as a pattern.

8   Refitting of pipes is a straightforward reversal of the removal procedure. Also any acute bends should be put in by the garage on a bending machine, otherwise there is the possibility of kinking the pipe and restricting the bore area and fluid flow.

9   With the pipes refitted, bleed the system as described in Section 17.

17 Hydraulic system – bleeding

1   If any of the hydraulic components in the braking system have been removed or disconnected, or if the fluid level in the master cylinder has been allowed to fall appreciably, it is inevitable that air will have been introduced into the system. The removal of all this air from the hydraulic system is essential if the brakes are to function correctly, and the process of removing it is known as bleeding.

2   There are a number of one-man, do-it-yourself, brake bleeding kits currently available from motor accessory shops. It is recommended that one of these kits should be used wherever possible as they greatly simplify the bleeding operation and also reduce the risk of expelled air and fluid being drawn back into the system (photo).

3   If one of these kits is not available then it will be necessary to gather together a clean jar and a suitable length of clear plastic tubing which is a tight fit over the bleed screw, and also to engage the help of an assistant.

4   Before commencing the bleeding operation, check that all rigid pipes and flexible hoses are in good condition and that all hydraulic unions are tight. Take great care not to allow hydraulic fluid to come into contact with the vehicle paintwork, otherwise the finish will be seriously damaged. Wash off any spilled fluid immediately with cold water.

5   If hydraulic fluid has been lost from the master cylinder, due to a leak in the system, ensure that the cause is traced and rectified before proceeding further or a serious malfunction of the braking system may occur.

6   To bleed the system, clean the area around the bleed screw at the wheel cylinder to be bled. If the hydraulic system has only been partially disconnected and suitable precautions were taken to prevent further loss of fluid, it should only be necessary to bleed that part of the system. The braking circuits are linked diagonally, ie RH front with LH rear and vice versa. However, if the entire system is to be bled, start at the wheel furthest away from the master cylinder.

7   Remove the master cylinder filler cap and top up the reservoir. Periodically check the fluid level during the bleeding operation and top up as necessary.

8   If a one-man brake bleeding kit is being used, connect the outlet tube to the bleed screw and then open the screw half a turn. If possible position the unit so that it can be viewed from the car, then depress the brake pedal to the floor and slowly release it. The one-way valve in the kit will prevent dispelled air from returning to the system at the end of each stroke. Repeat this operation until clean hydraulic fluid, free from air bubbles, can be seen coming through the tube. Now tighten the bleed screw and remove the outlet tube.

9

17.2 Brake bleeding equipment

18.4 Brake equalizer and adjuster

19.5 Handbrake cable connection to brake lever

9   If a one-man brake bleeding kit is not available, connect one end of the plastic tubing to the bleed screw and immerse the other end in the jar containing sufficient clean hydraulic fluid to keep the end of the tube submerged. Open the bleed screw half a turn and have your assistant depress the brake pedal to the floor and then slowly release it. Tighten the bleed screw at the end of each downstroke to prevent expelled air and fluid from being drawn back into the system. Repeat this operation until clean hydraulic fluid, free from air bubbles, can be seen coming through the tube. Now tighten the bleed screw and remove the plastic tube.

10 If the entire system is being bled the procedures described above should now be repeated at each wheel, finishing at the wheel nearest to the master cylinder. Do not forget to recheck the fluid level in the master cylinder at regular intervals and top up as necessary.

11 When completed, recheck the fluid level in the master cylinder, top up if necessary and refit the cap. Check the 'feel' of the brake pedal

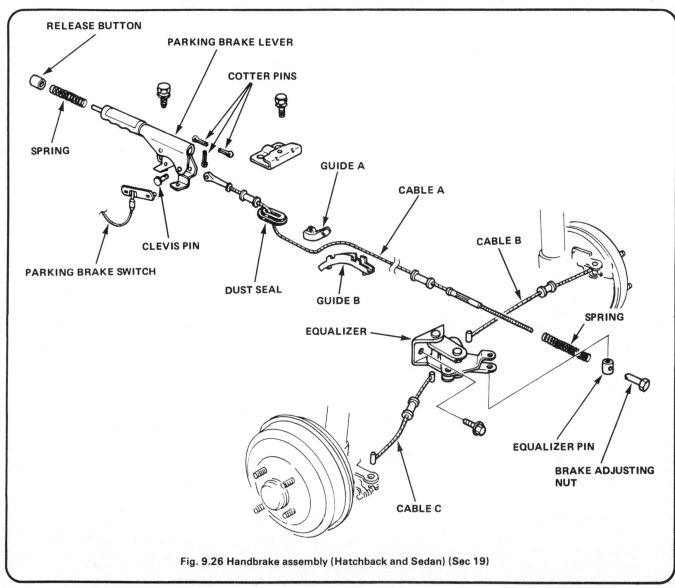

Fig. 9.26 Handbrake assembly (Hatchback and Sedan) (Sec 19)

which should be firm and free from any 'sponginess' which would indicate air still present in the system.

12 Discard any expelled hydraulic fluid as it is likely to be contaminated with moisture, air and dirt which makes it unsuitable for further use.

18 Handbrake – adjustment

1 The rear brakes are self-adjusting, so before making any adjustment to the handbrake, depress the brake pedal several times to ensure that the self-adjusting mechanism is set.

2 The handbrake should not need more than eight clicks on the ratchet for it to be fully engaged. If it requires adjustment, proceed as follows.

3 Raise the rear wheels off the ground and support the vehicle on firmly based stands.

4 Slacken the adjusting nut of the brake equalizer (photo) and pull the brake lever up to the first click.

5 Tighten the equalizer nut until the rear wheels just drag when turned.

6 Release the handbrake fully and check that the wheels turn without any drag. If necessary slacken the equalizer nut to achieve this.

7 Check that the handbrake lever moves between four and eight clicks to apply the brake fully. If it does not, check all the cables and linkages.

19 Handbrake cable – renewal

1 The handbrake system comprises a lever assembly inside the car, a single cable which connects the lever assembly to the equaliser lever mounted underneath the car between the rear wheels, and finally two further cables which run across between each rear brake and through the equaliser (Figs. 9.26 and 9.27).

2 The single cable is retained to the handbrake lever by a single pin, and to the equaliser by the special adjusting nut. The whole removal and refitting task is accomplished from beneath the car.

3 The cables which run between the equaliser and the rear brakes are the ones most likely to stretch and wear.

4 The equaliser is bolted to the rear suspension crossmember (Sedan and Hatchback) or to the rear axle beam (Wagon).

5 To renew a rear cable, slacken off the adjusting nut at the equaliser to give enough slack in the system, then disconnect the cable at the brake backplate (photo). The split pin which secures the clevis pin may be difficult to remove if it has been in position for some years. If penetrating oil does not free it, break off one end and drive the remains out using a pin punch or similar. Use new split pins on reassembly.

6 Once the cable has been disconnected at the backplate, it can be manoeuvred out of its slot in the equaliser.

7 When any cable has been renewed, adjust the linkage as described in Section 18.

8 Grease the cables liberally to reduce corrosion and promote smooth operation.

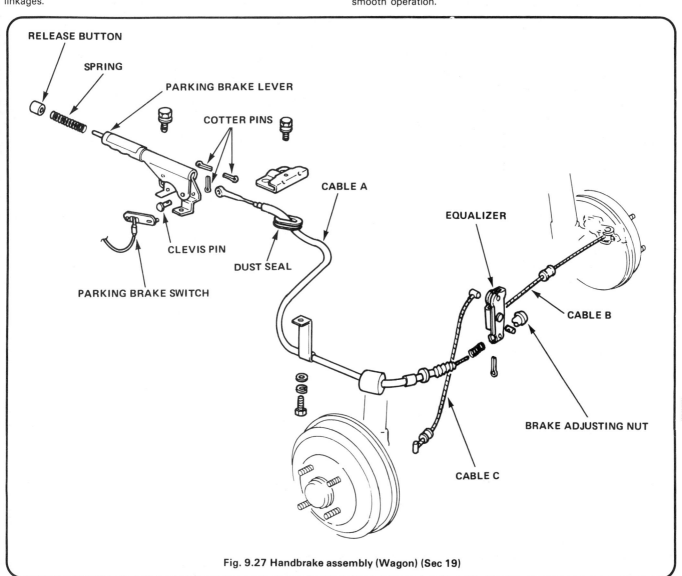

Fig. 9.27 Handbrake assembly (Wagon) (Sec 19)

9

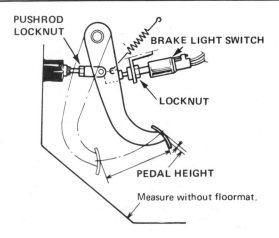

Fig. 9.28 Brake pedal height measurement (Sec 20)

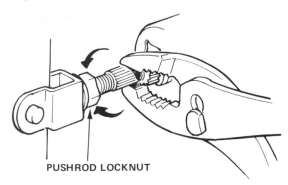

Fig. 9.29 Brake pedal height adjustment (Sec 20)

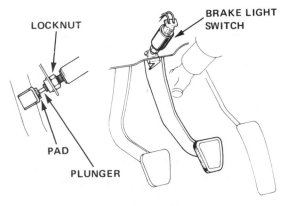

Fig. 9.30 Brake light switch adjustment (Sec 31)

21.1 Brake light switch (arrowed)

20 Brake pedal – height adjustment

1   The height of the brake pedal from the floor is governed by the length of the brake servo pushrod.
2   With the floor mats removed, measure the height from the floor of the highest point of the pedal rubber. The correct height is given in the Specifications.
3   To adjust pedal height, slacken the locknut on the pushrod yoke, where it is connected to the pedal lever, and screw the pushrod in or out until the correct dimension is achieved (Fig. 9.29). If the pedal height does not increase when the rod is screwed out, loosen the brake light switch locknut and back the switch off until it is no longer in contact with the pedal arm.
4   After adjusting the height of the brake pedal, adjust the brake light switch.

21 Brake light switch – adjustment

1   Slacken the locknuts of the brake light switch (photo) and screw the switch in until its plunger is fully depressed with the threaded part of the switch bearing on the pad on the pedal arm (Fig. 9.30). Disconnect the wires if necessary to stop them getting twisted.
2   Back the switch off half a turn and tighten the locknuts fully.
3   Check that the brake lights go on when the pedal is depressed and that they go off when the pedal is released.

22 Fault diagnosis – braking system

Symptom	Reason(s)
Brake grab	Out of round drums Excessive run-out of discs Rust on drum or disc Oil stained linings or pads
Brake drag	Faulty master cylinder Foot pedal return impeded Reservoir breather blocked Seized caliper or wheel cylinder piston Incorrect adjustment of handbrake Weak or broken shoe return springs
Excessive pedal effort required	Linings or pads not yet bedded-in, or incorrect grade Drum, disc or linings contaminated with oil or grease Scored drums or discs Faulty vacuum servo unit
Brake pedal feels hard	Glazed surfaces of friction material Rust on disc surfaces Seized caliper or wheel cylinder piston
Excessive pedal travel	Low reservoir fluid level Disc run-out excessive Worn front wheel bearings Air in system Worn pads or linings Self-adjusters faulty (rear brakes)
Pedal creep during sustained application	Fluid leak Internal fault in master cylinder Faulty servo unit non-return valve
Pedal 'spongy'	Air in system Perished flexible hose Loose master cylinder mounting nuts Faulty master cylinder Reservoir breather blocked
Fall in reservoir fluid level	Normal due to pad or lining wear (very slow fall) Leak in hydraulic system

9

Chapter 10 Electrical system

Refer to Chapter 13 for specifications and information related to 1982 and 1983 US models

Contents

Specifications

System type .... Alternator and battery, 12V negative earth

Battery
Type .... Lead acid
Capacity .... 40, 45 or 47 Ah

Alternator
Output .... 35 or 45 A
Minimum brush length .... 0.22 in (5.5 mm)

Starter motor
Type .... Pre-engaged, series wound
Rating .... 0.8 or 0.9 kW
Minimum brush length:
    Nippondenso 0.9 kW .... 0.33 in (8.5 mm)
    Nippondenso 0.8 kW .... 0.39 in (10 mm)
    Hitachi 0.8 kW .... 0.47 in (12 mm)

Voltage regulator
Control voltage .... 13.5 to 14.5
Armature gap .... Not less than 0.02 in (0.5 mm)
Point gap .... 0.016 to 0.047 in (0.4 to 1.2 mm)

Fuses
Main fuse 55A
Fuses in box (left to right):
  1 Wiper/washer 15A
  2 Turn signals, reversing lights, fuel gauge, temperature gauge, warning lights and clock 10A
  3 Fuel pump, voltage regulator, emission control equipment (if fitted) 10A
  4 Cooling fan 15A
  5 Blower motor 15A
  6 Heated rear window and radio (some models) 15A
  7 Brake lights, hazard lights, horn 15A
  8 Interior light, lighter, door buzzer, clock (some models) 10A
  9 Side, tail, number plate and panel lights 15A

10 Left headlight – high beam	10A
11 Right headlight – high beam	10A
12 Left headlight – low beam	10A
13 Left headlight – low beam	10A
Fuse in clip (when fitted) – Radio	10A

Bulbs (typical)

	Wattage
Headlights:	
Halogen	60/50
Tungsten	45/40
Front turn signal/position lights	21/5
Side marker lights	5
Rear turn signal lights	21
Brake/tail lights	21/5
Reversing lights	21
Number plate lights	5
Interior lights	5
Tailgate light	3.4
Panel and warning lights	1.2

Torque wrench settings

	lbf ft	Nm
Alternator mounting bolts:		
M8	18	26
M10	33	46
Alternator adjuster link bolt	18	26
Alternator pulley nut	42	58
Starter motor securing bolts	32	45
Wiper arm securing nuts:		
Windscreen	10	14
Tailgate	6	8

1 General description

The electrical system is a 12 volt negative earth type. The major components comprise a lead acid type battery; an alternator, belt-driven from the crankshaft pulley; and a pre-engaged starter motor.

The battery supplies a steady current to the ignition system and for all the electrical accessories. The alternator maintains the charge in the battery and the voltage regulator adjusts the charging according to the battery's demands.

2 Battery – maintenance and inspection

1 Check the battery electrolyte level weekly by lifting off the cover or removing the individual cell plugs. The tops of the plates should be just covered with the liquid. If not, add distilled water so that they are just covered. Do not add extra water with the idea of reducing the intervals of topping-up. This will merely dilute the electrolyte and reduce charging and current retention efficiency. On batteries fitted with patent covers, troughs, glass balls and so on, follow the instructions marked on the cover of the battery to ensure correct addition of water.

2 Keep the battery clean and dry all over by wiping it with a dry cloth. A damp top surface could cause tracking between the two terminal posts with consequent draining of power.

3 Every three months remove the battery and check the support tray clamp and battery terminal connections for signs of corrosion – usually indicated by a whitish green crystalline deposit. Wash this off with clean water to which a little ammonia or washing soda has been added. Then treat the terminals with petroleum jelly and the battery mounting with suitable protective paint to prevent the metal being eaten away. Clean the battery thoroughly and repair any cracks with a proprietary sealer. If there has been any excessive leakage the appropriate cell may need an addition of electrolyte rather than just distilled water.

4 If the electrolyte level needs an excessive amount of replenishment but no leaks are apparent, it could be due to overcharging as a result of the battery having been run down and then left on recharge from the vehicle rather than outside source. If the battery has been heavily discharged for one reason or another, it is best to have it continuously charged at a low amperage for a period of many hours. If it is charged from the car's system under such conditions the charging will be intermittent and greatly varied in intensity. This does not do the battery any good at all. If the battery needs topping-up frequently, even when it is known to be in good condition and not too old, then the voltage regulator should be checked to ensure that the charging output is being correctly controlled. An elderly battery, however, may need topping-up more than a new one because it needs to take in more charging current. Do not worry about this provided it gives satisfactory service.

5 When checking a battery's condition a hydrometer should be used. On some batteries where the terminals of each of the six cells are exposed, a discharge tester can be used to check the condition of any one cell also. On modern batteries the use of a discharge tester is no longer regarded as useful as the replacement or repair of cells is not an economic proposition. The table in Section 3 gives the hydrometer readings for various states of charge. A further check can be made when the battery is undergoing a charge. If, towards the end of the charge, when the cells are meant to be 'gassing' (bubbling), one cell appears not to be, then it indicates that the cell or cells in question are probably breaking down and the life of the battery is limited.

3 Battery – charging and electrolyte replenishment

1 It is possible that in winter, when the load on the battery cannot be recuperated quickly during normal driving time, external charging is desirable. This is best done overnight at a 'trickle' rate of 1 to 1.5 amps. Alternatively a 3 to 4 amp rate can be used over a period of four hours or so. Check the specific gravity in the latter case and stop the charge when the reading is correct. Most modern charging sets reduce the rate automatically when the fully charged state is neared. Rapid boost charges of 30 to 60 amps or more may get you out of trouble or can be used on a battery that has seen better days. They are not advisable for a good battery that may have run flat for some reason.

2 Electrolyte replenishment should not normally be necessary unless an accident or some other cause such as contamination arises. If it is necessary then it is best first to discharge the battery completely and then tip out all the remaining liquid from all cells. Then acquire a quantity of mixed electrolyte from a battery shop or garage according to the specifications in the table given. The quantity required will depend on the type of battery but 3 to 4 Imp pints (1.7 to 2.3 litres) should be more than enough for most. When the electrolyte has been put into the battery a slow charge, not exceeding one amp, should be

10

given for as long as is necessary to fully charge the battery. This could be up to 48 hours.

3   The specific gravity of the battery electrolyte at various states of charge is given in the table below:

	Climate below 80°F (26.7°C)	Climate above 80°F (26.7°C)
Fully charged	1.270 to 1.290	1.210 to 1.230
Half charged	1.190 to 1.210	1.120 to 1.150
Discharged completely	1.110 to 1.130	1.050 to 1.070

Note: If the electrolyte temperature is significantly different from 60°F (15.6°C) then the specific gravity reading will be affected. For every 5°F (2.8°C) it will increase or decrease inversely with the temperature by 0.002.

4   Battery – removal and installation

1   The battery is located within the engine compartment on the right-hand side. It is held in place by two tie-rods and pressed steel angle strip.
2   To remove the battery, begin by disconnecting the negative (earth) lead from the battery and bodyshell. Then disconnect the positive lead from the battery.
3   Once the leads have been removed, undo and remove the two nuts which tension the tie-rods onto the angle strip which secures the battery. Lift the angle strip aside once the rod nuts have been undone.
4   Lift the battery from its seating in the bodyshell, taking great care not to spill any of the highly corrosive electrolyte.
5   Installation follows the reversal of the removal procedure. Reconnect the positive lead first and smear the clean terminal posts and lead clamp assembly beforehand with petroleum jelly in order to prevent corrosion. **Do not use ordinary grease,** it does not prevent corrosion of the terminal and does not conduct electricity.

5   Alternator – general description

The main advantage of the alternator lies in its ability to provide a relatively high power output at low revolutions. Driving slowly in traffic with a dynamo means a very small charge or even no charge at all, reaching the battery.

The alternator is of the rotating field, ventilated design and comprises principally a laminated stator on which is wound a 3 phase output winding, and a twelve pole rotor carrying the field windings.

Each end of the rotor shaft runs in ball race bearings which are lubricated for life. Aluminium end brackets hold the bearings and incorporate the alternator mounting lugs. The rear bracket supports the silicone diode rectifier pack which converts the ac output of the machine to a dc output, for battery charging and output to the voltage regulator.

The rotor is belt-driven from the engine crankshaft pulley through a pulley keyed to the rotor shaft. A special centrifugal action fan adjacent to the pulley, draws cool air through the machine. This fan forms an integral part of the alternator specification. It has been designed to provide adequate airflow with the minimum of noise at all speeds of rotation of the machine.

The rectifier pack of silicon diodes is mounted on the inside of the rear end casing, the same mounting is used by the brushes which contact slip rings on the rotor to supply the field current. The slip rings are carried on a small diameter moulded drum attached to the rotor. By keeping the circumference of the slip rings to a minimum, the contact speed and therefore the brush wear is minimised.

6   Alternator – maintenance and precautions

1   Maintenance consists of occasionally wiping the outside of the alternator free from dirt and grease and checking the security of the electrical connections.
2   Correct tensioning of the drivebelt is essential to maintain the proper power output from the alternator. A deflection of $\frac{1}{2}$ in (12.7 mm) under firm thumb pressure must be provided at the centre point of the longest run of the belt.

3   To adjust the tension, release the alternator mounting bolts and the adjuster link bolt and pivot the alternator either towards or away from the engine as necessary. Retighten the bolts on completion of adjustment. Do not lever against the alternator body, it is fragile.
4   Take extreme care when making circuit connections to a vehicle fitted with an alternator and observe the following. When making connections to the alternator from a battery always match correct polarity. Before using electric arc welding equipment to repair any part of the vehicle, disconnect the connector from the alternator and disconnect the battery positive terminal. Never start the car with a battery charger connected. Always disconnect both battery leads before using a mains charger. If boosting from another battery, always connect in parallel using heavy cable.

7   Alternator – testing, removal and installation

1   Check the ignition warning light circuit by turning the ignition switch on. If the warning light does not come on, unplug the voltage regulator connector and connect pin L to earth. If the light now comes on, the voltage regulator warning light contacts are defective and a new voltage regulator is required.
2   If the warning light does not light when performing the foregoing test, check the bulb, fuses and associated wiring.
3   When the light is operating with the ignition on, start the engine and let it idle. The light should go out. If the light stays on regardless of engine speed, or only goes out at high engine speeds, the alternator or voltage regulator is suspect. (It is assumed that the drivebelt is intact and correctly tensioned). Proceed as follows.
4   With the engine idling and all connections made, insert voltmeter probes into the back of the voltage regulator connector (Fig. 10.1). Connect the positive probe to terminal N (black/white wire) and the negative probe to terminal E (black wire). The voltage reading should be within 1 volt of half the alternator output voltage, ie 7 ± 1V.
5   If the correct voltage reading is obtained but the ignition warning light does not go out, the alternator is functioning correctly and the voltage regulator must be defective. Renew the regulator (Section 9).
6   If the voltage reading in paragraph 4 is zero, the alternator itself or the wiring from the alternator to the regulator is suspect.
7   If the ignition warning light functions normally, but the battery does not appear to be receiving a charge, connect a voltmeter across the battery terminals. With the engine stopped, the reading should be 12 to 13 V. Start the engine and run it at 2000 to 4000 rpm; the reading should rise to between 13.5 and 14.5 V. Switch on all the car's electrical equipment: with the engine running at more than idle speed, no significant voltage drop should occur.
8   Further testing of the alternator and regulator should be left to an

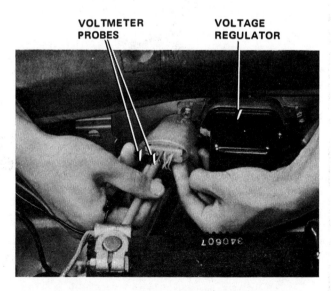

VOLTMETER PROBES   VOLTAGE REGULATOR

Fig. 10.1 Testing the voltage regulator (Sec 7)

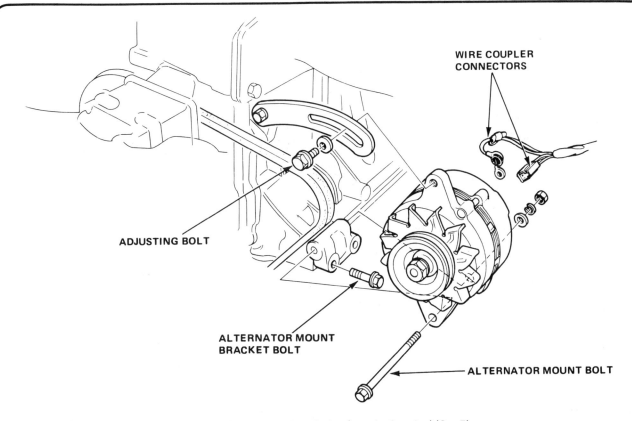

Fig. 10.2 Alternator installation (standard engine) (Sec 7)

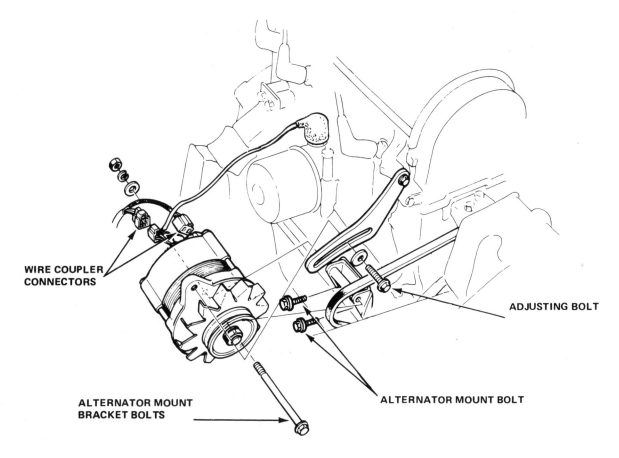

Fig. 10.3 Alternator installation (CVCC engine) (Sec 7)

10

7.10a Alternator mounting bracket bolts

7.10b Alternator adjuster bolt

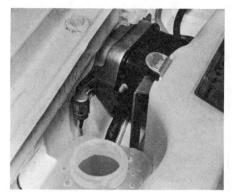

9.1 Voltage regulator

auto electrician, due to the risk of further damage being caused if incorrect procedures are followed.

9   To remove the alternator, first disconnect the battery, then disconnect the alternator wiring harness connectors.

10 Remove the two bolts securing the alternator mounting bracket to the engine block and the alternator belt adjusting bolt and remove the alternator (photos).

11 Installation is the reverse of removal. Make certain that the connections are clean and secure and adjust the tension of the belt as described in Section 6.

8   Alternator – dismantling and reassembly

1   This task should only be attempted if specialist equipment and expertise is available.

2   Remove the end pulley by undoing the retaining nut whilst holding the shaft with a 6 mm Allen key.

3   Make alignment marks on the end members and centre part of the alternator with a centre punch, to ensure correct alignment on assembly.

4   Undo and remove the three long bolts which hold the alternator together. Separate the two ends and stator assembly gently, only use gentle taps with a light mallet to loosen the ends.

5   Watch the position of the washers and spacers, and insulators. It is essential to fit them back correctly.

6   Unsolder the brush holder lead and separate the brush holder from the stator. Label the leads with tags to ensure correct reassembly.

7   Unsolder the stator leads from the rectifier diodes; be careful not to overheat the diodes. Hold their terminals with long nose pliers to absorb the soldering iron heat.

8   Check the continuity of the rotor field windings and check for shorting to the rotor core and shaft.

9   Measure the length of the brushes, they should not be less than the minimum specified. New brushes may be fitted by unsoldering the worn ones, inserting the new brushes and soldering the wires to the new brushes.

10 Check the functioning of each diode. If any diodes show high resistance in both directions or low resistance in both directions they are defective.

11 When resoldering leads to diodes, be as quick as possible, and sink the terminal heat into long nose pliers. Diodes on the plate have a red stripe and those on the negative earthed plate have a black stripe.

12 When installing the rotor into the rear casing, raise the brushes in the holders and hold raised by pushing a pin through the rear casing and brushes. The pin will hold the brushes so that there is little likelihood of them getting damaged as the rotor and slip rings pass into the rear casing. After installation, remove the pin to allow the brushes to rest on the slip rings.

13 Once assembled, tighten the pulley nut to its specified torque and check the rotor for easy rotation.

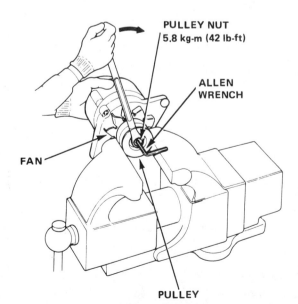

PULLEY NUT
5.8 kg-m (42 lb-ft)

ALLEN WRENCH

FAN

PULLEY

Fig. 10.4 Tightening the alternator pulley (Sec 8)

9   Voltage regulator – description, removal and installation

1   The voltage regulator unit (photo) comprises two main parts, the voltage regulator and the ignition/battery discharge warning light relay.

2   The voltage regulator governs the current that is fed into the alternator field coils. When the alternator is not developing more than 12 volts, the regulator relay coil remains weak and the field coils receive a full field current.

3   Once the alternator voltage reaches 14 volts, the regulator relay switches off the direct supply of field current to the alternator, and switches the supply through a series resistor. This limits the field current, and hence the voltage developed by the alternator.

4   The battery charging lamp relay operates off the full return current to the alternator. It is connected directly to the centre point of the star wound output windings of the three-phase alternator. The relay coil is therefore a low resistance device and functions to switch the ignition warning light return.

5   Although it is possible to adjust the operation of both regulator relay and warning light relay, it is not a task that can be recommended without specialist knowledge and equipment.

6   If the regulator has been found faulty, the unit should be removed and a new one put in its place.

7   To do this, disconnect the wiring harness plug from the regulator and remove the screws securing the regulator to the bodyshell.

8   Installation is the reverse of removal.

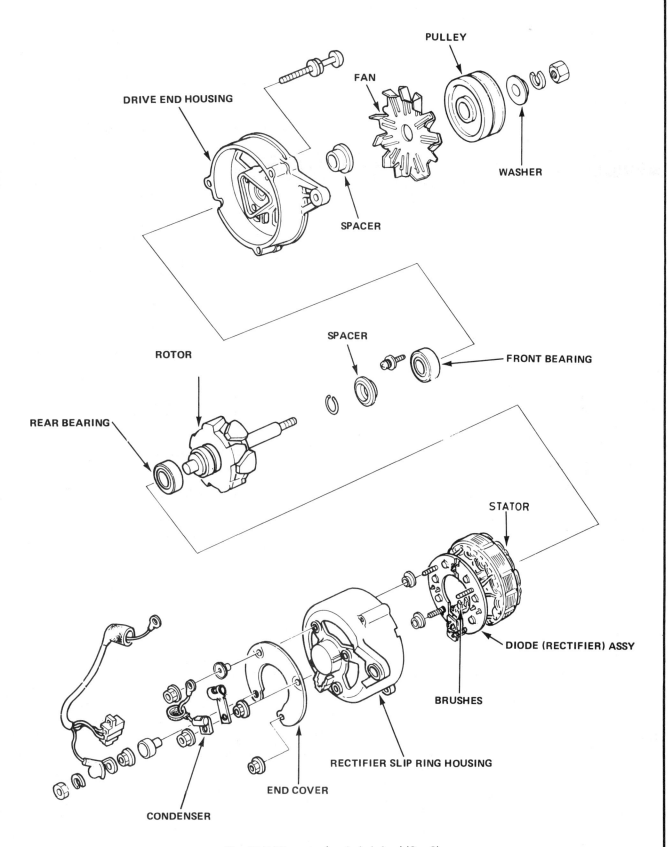

DRIVE END HOUSING

FAN

PULLEY

WASHER

SPACER

ROTOR

SPACER

FRONT BEARING

REAR BEARING

STATOR

DIODE (RECTIFIER) ASSY

BRUSHES

RECTIFIER SLIP RING HOUSING

END COVER

CONDENSER

Fig. 10.5 Alternator (exploded view) (Sec 8)

10

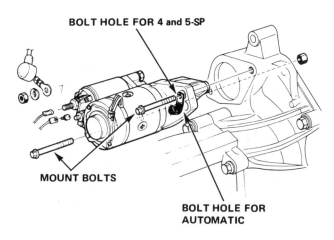

BOLT HOLE FOR 4 and 5-SP

MOUNT BOLTS

BOLT HOLE FOR
AUTOMATIC

Fig. 10.6 Starter motor removal (standard engine) (Sec 12)

ENGINE-SIDE
MOUNT BOLT

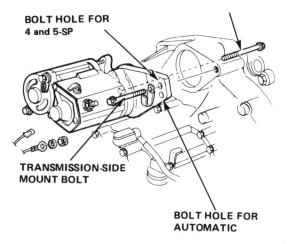

BOLT HOLE FOR
4 and 5-SP

TRANSMISSION-SIDE
MOUNT BOLT

BOLT HOLE FOR
AUTOMATIC

Fig. 10.7 Starter motor removal (CVCC engine) (Sec 12)

10 Starter motor – general description

Three different types of starter motor are used on the models covered by this manual, but the operating principle is the same in all cases. A series-wound dc motor drives a pinion which engages with the ring gear of the flywheel or driveplate when a solenoid is energised. When the pinion engages the solenoid closes the starter motor switch causing the motor to rotate. The drive includes an overrunning clutch which prevents damage to the motor by overspeeding. When the solenoid is de-energised, the drivegear retracts and the motor is switched off.

11 Starter motor – testing in car

1   If the starter motor fails to turn the engine when the switch is operated, there are four possible reasons why:

(a)   The battery is flat
(b)   The electrical connections between the switch, solenoid, battery and starter motor are failing somewhere to pass the

necessary current from the battery through to the starter motor and earth
(c)   The solenoid switch is defective
(d)   The starter motor is either jammed or electrically defective

2   The test procedure for the starter system is as follows.
3   Remove the battery connections, starter/solenoid power connections and the engine earth strap, and thoroughly clean them and refit them. Smear petroleum jelly around the battery connections to prevent corrosion. Corroded connections are the most frequent cause of electrical system malfunctions.
4   If the starter still doesn't work check the battery as follows. Switch on the headlights, if they go dim after a few seconds, the battery is definitely at fault. If the lights shine brightly, operate the starter switch and watch what happens to the lights. If they go dim, then you know that power is reaching the starter motor but failing to turn it. In this event check that the motor is not jammed. Place the car in gear and rock the car to-and-fro. If the starter system still does not operate properly, proceed to the next test.
5   Note whether a clicking noise is heard each time the starter switch is operated. This is the solenoid operating, but it doesn't necessarily follow that the main contacts are closing properly. If a click is not heard from the solenoid, it will most probably be defective. The solenoid contact can be checked by putting a voltmeter or bulb across the main cable connection on the starter side of the solenoid and earth. When the switch is operated there should be a reading of 12 volts or the bulb should light up. If there is no reading or lighted bulb, the solenoid unit is faulty and should be renewed. Finally, if it is established that the solenoid is not faulty, and 12 volts are getting to the starter, then the motor should be removed for inspection.

12 Starter motor – removal and installation

1   The starter motor is accessible with the engine in the car. It is at the transmission end of the engine, above the gearbox, and is held by two bolts.
2   Disconnect both battery leads.
3   Disconnect the starter motor and solenoid cables from the starter motor.
4   On standard engines, remove the lower bolt of the starter motor. The bolt passes through the transmission casing and has a nut on its end. Remove the other mounting bolt which screws into the transmission casing (Fig. 10.6).
5   On CVCC engines, the starter motor is also held by two bolts. One of these passes through the transmission housing and screws into the starter motor mounting flange and the other passes through the starter motor and screws into the transmission casing (Fig. 10.7).
6   After removing the bolts, lift the motor clear.
7   Installation is the reverse of removal, but ensure that the mounting flanges of the motor and transmission casing are clean and that the electrical connections are clean and tight. Tighten the bolts to the specified torque.

13 Starter motor solenoid (non-reduction type) – removal and installation

1   The solenoid is retained to the starter block by two bolts or two nuts. Undo the electrical connection between the starter and solenoid switch from the solenoid. Then undo and remove the two solenoid retaining bolts or nuts and lift the solenoid away. Take care to unhook the solenoid plunger from the pinion carriage lever. On Hitachi motors recover the return spring retainer plate.
2   The solenoid is not repairable, and no attempt should be made to dismantle it; if it has been proven faulty, it should be renewed. If the solenoid only is suspected, the resistance may be checked by connecting a multimeter across the 'S' and 'M' terminals on the solenoid. If an open-circuit is found (infinite resistance) the solenoid is definitely faulty.
3   To refit the solenoid, ensure that the plunger is properly hooked onto the pinion carriage lever, and that the plate which retains the plunger and lever return spring is in position (Hitachi).
4   Make sure that the electrical connections are clean and properly made.

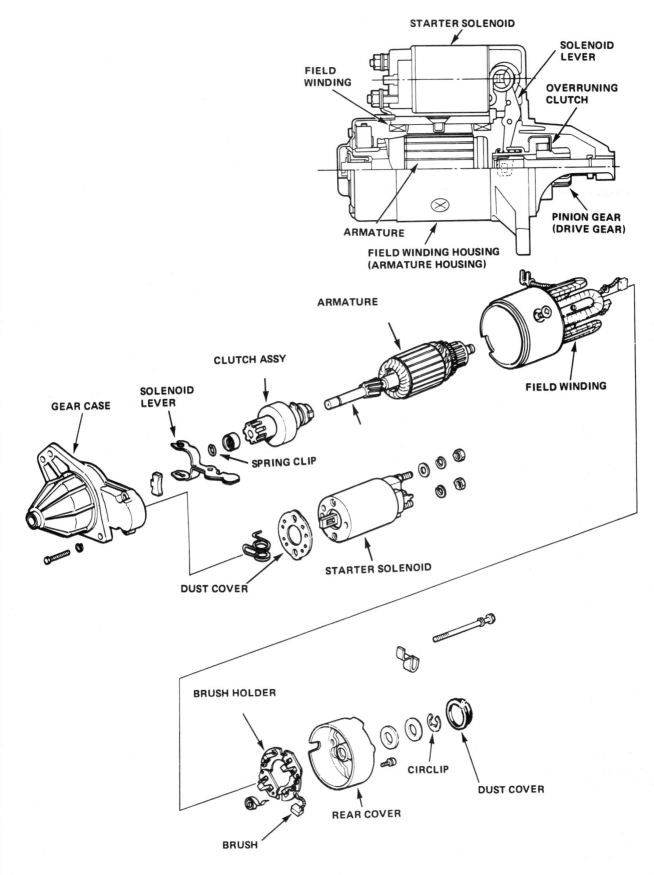

STARTER SOLENOID

SOLENOID LEVER

FIELD WINDING

OVERRUNING CLUTCH

ARMATURE

FIELD WINDING HOUSING (ARMATURE HOUSING)

PINION GEAR (DRIVE GEAR)

ARMATURE

CLUTCH ASSY

FIELD WINDING

GEAR CASE

SOLENOID LEVER

SPRING CLIP

DUST COVER

STARTER SOLENOID

BRUSH HOLDER

CIRCLIP

DUST COVER

BRUSH

REAR COVER

Fig. 10.8 Hitachi starter motor (standard engine) (Sec 14)

10

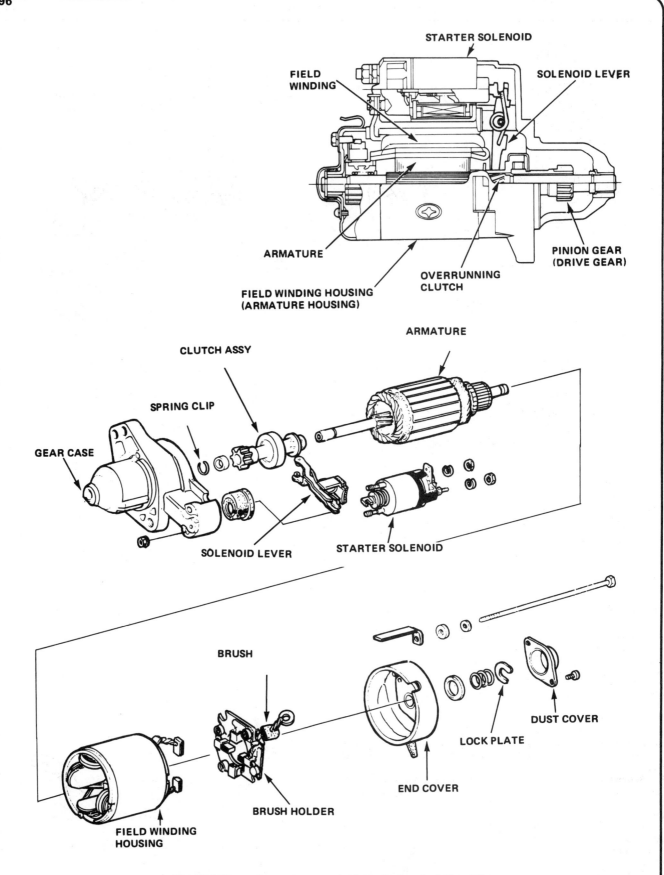

STARTER SOLENOID

FIELD WINDING

SOLENOID LEVER

ARMATURE

PINION GEAR (DRIVE GEAR)

FIELD WINDING HOUSING (ARMATURE HOUSING)

OVERRUNNING CLUTCH

CLUTCH ASSY

ARMATURE

SPRING CLIP

GEAR CASE

SOLENOID LEVER

STARTER SOLENOID

BRUSH

DUST COVER

LOCK PLATE

END COVER

BRUSH HOLDER

FIELD WINDING HOUSING

Fig. 10.9 Nippondenso starter motor (standard engine) (Sec 14)

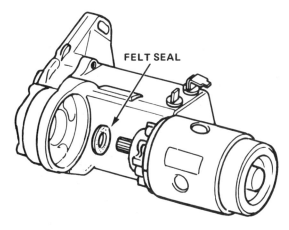

Fig. 10.10 Armature shaft felt seal (Sec 14)

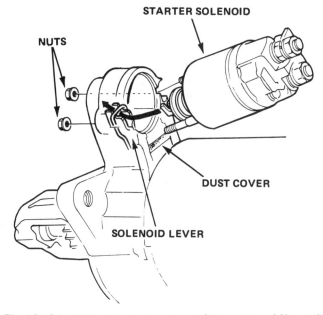

Fig. 10.12 Installing the starter solenoid (Nippondenso) (Sec 14)

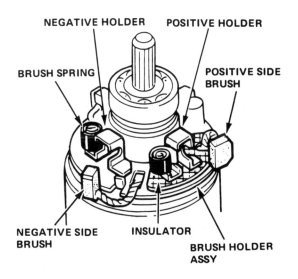

Fig. 10.11 Identification of positive and negative brushes (Sec 14)

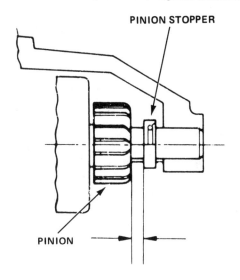

Fig. 10.13 Pinion to pinion stopper clearance (Sec 14)

14 Starter motor (non-reduction gear type) – dismantling and reassembly

1   Although there are minor constructional differences between the Hitachi and Nippondenso starter motors, their general construction is similar (Figs. 10.8 and 10.9).

2   Remove the solenoid as described in the previous Section.

3   Remove the dust cover from the shaft end bearing. Lever off the circlip from the end of the motor shaft and remove the thrust washers.

4   Remove from the end cover the screws which secure the brush holder.

5   Remove the two through bolts and tap off the motor end cover, leaving the brush holder in position round the commutator.

6   Separate the field winding housing and the gear case and remove the armature.

7   To remove the pinion gear from the armature, hold the armature, pinion upwards, in a soft-jawed vice. Push back the sleeve over the pinion stop ring to expose the spring clip. Extract the clip and then lift off the pinion assembly. Use a new clip on reassembly.

8   Extract the brushes from their holders and measure the length of the brushes. If they are less than the specified service limit, install a new field winding housing and brush holder assembly. To seat new brushes after installing them in their holders, slip a strip of fine sandpaper, grit side up, over the commutator and rotate the armature smoothly to sand the brushes to the same contour as the commutator.

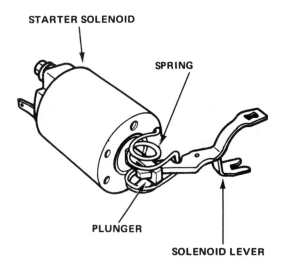

Fig. 10.14 Installing the solenoid (Hitachi) (Sec 14)

10

9 Clean the commutator with solvent and a lint-free rag and examine it for damage and excessive wear. Check the insulation resistance between each commutator segment and the shaft. If there is any continuity, install a new armature. Check that there is continuity between every segment of the armature. If there is an open-circuit between any segments, install a new armature.

10 Examine the teeth of the pinion gear. If the teeth are damaged, install a new overrunning clutch assembly.

11 Check the free movement of the overrunning clutch along the shaft. If the movement is not free, or if the clutch slips when the armature is rotated while the drivegear is held stationary, install a new clutch assembly. It is unlikely that any problem of clutch binding will be due to the spiral spline on the shaft.

12 Check that the pinion can be rotated in one direction relative to the armature shaft, but not in the opposite direction.

13 Reassembly is the reverse of dismantling, but the following points should be noted.

14 When installing the armature and field winding assemblies of the starter motors of standard engines into the gear case, install the felt seal on the armature shaft (Fig. 10.10).

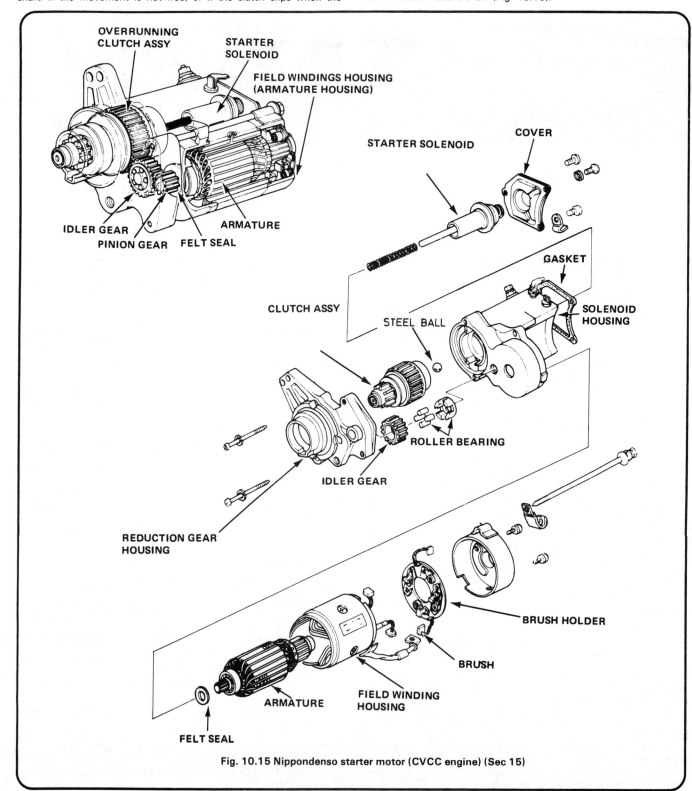

Fig. 10.15 Nippondenso starter motor (CVCC engine) (Sec 15)

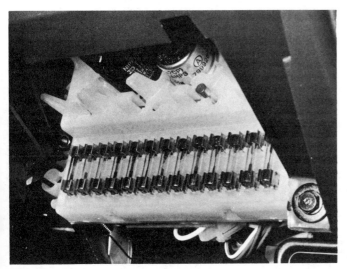

16.1a Fuse block

16.1b Fuse block cover

15 Do not interchange the brushes between positive and negative holders. Positive holders are separated from the metal plate by insulators (Fig. 10.11).
16 On the Nippondenso starter, ensure that the hook on the end of the solenoid plunger engages in the slot in the solenoid lever (Fig. 10.12). After assembling, measure the clearance between the pinion stopper and the pinion with the clutch pushed out by the starter solenoid (Fig. 10.13). The specified clearance is 0.004 to 0.157 in (0.1 to 4.0 mm).
17 On the Hitachi starter, the solenoid lever and spring must be assembled as shown in Fig. 10.14. After assembling, measure the clearance between the pinion stopper and the pinion with the clutch pushed out by the starter solenoid. The specified clearance is 0.012 to 0.098 in (0.3 to 2.5 mm).
18 Adjustment of the clearance is made by changing the washer thickness at the commutator end of the shaft.

15 Starter motor – (reduction gear type) – dismantling and reassembly

1 The reduction gear type starter motor can be dismantled as shown in Fig. 10.15 after removing the two bolts from the reduction gear housing and the two from the armature housing.
2 The solenoid may be inspected after removing the three bolts from the solenoid cover, but solenoid parts are not available separately.
3 No adjustments are required, but check that all worn components are renewed to prevent excessive endfloat, or radial clearance of internal gears.
4 Renew the armature housing and brush holder assembly if the length of the brushes is less than the specified minimum.

16 Fuses – general

1 The fuse block is located under the instrument panel on the right-hand side (photos). The ratings of the fuses and the circuits protected are given in the Specifications.
2 Always renew a blown fuse with one of the same rating and if it blows twice in quick succession, find the reason (usually faulty insulation in the wiring) before renewing the fuse again.
3 A heavy capacity fusible link is incorporated in the lead from the positive terminal of the battery and in the event of this blowing and the complete electrical system becoming dead, your Honda dealer should be consulted before any attempt to repair the circuit (photo).

17 Relays – general

1 The turn signal relay, hazard relay, and any other relays which are used for the additional facilities available on some models, are incorporated as plug-in units on the fuse panel (photo).
2 In the event of a fault occurring in the operation of the flasher lamps, first check the bulbs, particularly if the flash rate of the signals on one side is much faster than on the other.
3 Check the security of the electrical leads, particularly the effectiveness of any earth leads from the lamps.
4 If the fault is found to lie in the relay, unplug the relay and install a new one. The pins of the relays are offset to prevent incorrect installation.

18 Bulbs – renewal

Headlamps (bulb type)
1 To renew a bulb in this type of headlamp, peel back the dust excluding boot from the rear of the lamp and pull off the connector plug (photo).
2 Twist the bulb holder from its recess and extract the bulb from the holder (photos).

Headlamp (sealed beam)
3 Remove the headlamp trim (photos), depress the lamp unit and twist it clockwise to release it from its spring-loaded screws.
4 On some lamps a parking lamp window is incorporated on the headlamp reflector, in which case, disconnect the parking lamp bulb.
5 Disconnect the headlamp unit plug.
6 Refit the new lamp unit by reversing the removal and disconnection operations.
7 Provided the adjustment screws have not been disturbed, beam adjustment will not be required.

Front flasher/parking lamps
8 The front lens can be removed after the two retaining screws have been undone (photo).
9 The bulb may be removed and replaced once the lens is off (photo).
10 If it is necessary to remove the light housing, the two retaining nuts accessed through the inspection holes beneath the bumper, need to be removed.

10

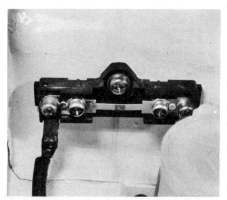
16.3 Fusible link

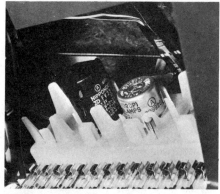
17.1 Turn signal and hazard relays

18.1 Headlamp protective rubber boot

18.2a Removing the bulb holder

18.2b Removing the bulb

18.3a Removing the headlamp trim screw

18.3b Removing the headlamp trim

18.8 Front flasher/parking lamp lens screws

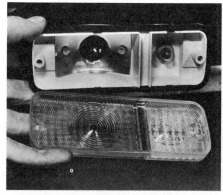
18.9 Front flasher/parking lamp bulb

18.13 Side marker lamp

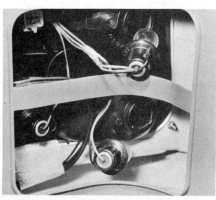
18.14 Rear combination lamp bulbs

18.17 Rear number plate light and bulb

18.20 Reversing light bulb renewal

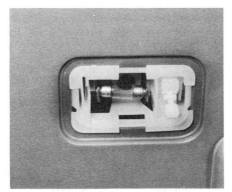
18.21a Luggage compartment light

18.21b Roof light with cover removed

18.22 Renewing a warning light bulb

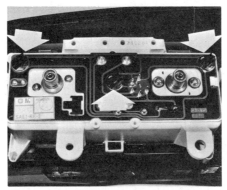
18.23a Instrument panel bulb holders (arrowed) accessible with instrument panel removed

18.23b Renewing an instrument panel bulb

11 Lift the light unit from the bumper and separate the electrical connector which serves the light.
12 Installation follows the reversal of removal, but as always, ensure that the electrical connections are clean and secure. Also ensure that the water seals are in good order and properly positioned.

Side marker lamps (N America) – direction indicator repeater lamps (Europe)
13 Access to the bulbs is obtained by unscrewing the two lens retaining screws and lifting the lens from the lamp body (photo).

Rear combination lamps
14 The bulbs in these lamp clusters are accessible through plugs or small covers within the luggage compartment (photo).
15 Pull the bulb holder free, withdraw it and extract the bulb.
16 Fitting the new bulb is a reversal of removal.

Rear number plate lamp
17 To gain access to the bulb, unscrew the two securing screws from the lens and remove the lens (photo).
18 To remove the lamp unit, remove the tailgate trim and extract the two securing screws.
19 Refit by reversing the removal operation.

Reversing lamps
20 Access to the bulbs is obtained by extracting the two lens securing screws and lifting off the lens (photo).

Interior lamps
21 To gain access to the bulbs, prise the lens carefully from the lamp base (photos).

Warning and indicator lamps
22 Warning light bulbs can be renewed by removing the access panel on the top of the dash and withdrawing the bulb holder (photo).

23 In order to renew the instrument panel bulbs, it is necessary to remove the instrument panel (see Chapter 12) (photos).

19 Headlamps – alignment

1 For accurate alignment of the headlamps, optical beam setting equipment is required.
2 In an emergency and as a temporary measure, adjustment can be made by inserting a screwdriver through the headlight trim and turning the appropriate screw (Figs. 10.16 and 10.17).

HORIZONTAL ADJUSTMENT SCREW

VERTICAL ADJUSTMENT SCREW

Fig. 10.16 Headlamp adjustment screws (Hatchback and Wagon) (Sec 19)

10

20 Ignition switch – testing, removal and installation

1   The ignition switch can be tested without removing the steering column lock/switch assembly. The continuity of the switch in its various positions is shown in Figs. 10.18 and 10.19.
2   Removal and installation of the lock/switch is described in Chapter 11.

21 Combination switch – removal and installation

1   The combined lighting, turn signal and windscreen wiper switch assembly which is fitted to the upper end of the steering column, can be removed in the following way. First disconnect the battery earth lead.

2   Remove the steering wheel as described in Chapter 11 (photo).
3   Unscrew and remove the screw which secures the two sections of the steering column shroud and remove them.
4   Pull the turn signal cancelling sleeve off the top of the steering column (Fig. 10.20).
5   Disconnect the switch wires from the loom by pulling apart the multi connector plugs.
6   Remove the two screws securing the switch assembly and remove the switch assembly (Fig. 10.21).
7   Installation is the reverse of removal.

22 Horns and horn switch – general

1   The horns are not built to enable adjustments or repairs to be made to them. In the event of a fault developing, remove the horn and check its operation by connecting it across the battery.

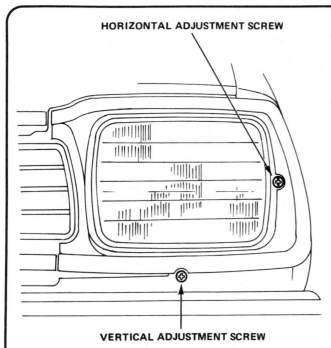

Fig. 10.17 Headlamp adjustment screws (Saloon) (Sec 19)

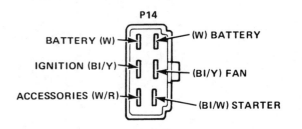

	TERMINAL				
POSITION	ACC	BAT	IG	ST	FAN
O (LOCK)					
I (ACC)	o———o				
II (ON)	o———o———o				o
III (START)		o———o———o———o			o
COLOR	W/R	W	Bl/Y	Bl/W	Bl Y

Fig. 10.18 Ignition switch continuity (1980) (Sec 20)

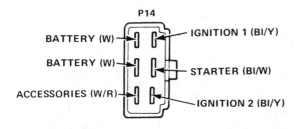

	ACC	BAT	IG₁	ST	IG₂
O (LOCK)					
I (ACC)	o———o				
II (ON)	o———o———o			o
III (START)		o———o———o		o
	W/R	W	Bl/Y	Bl/W	Bl Y

Fig. 10.19 Ignition switch continuity (1981) (Sec 20)

TURN SIGNAL CANCELLING SLEEVE

Fig. 10. 20 Removing the turn signal cancelling sleeve (Sec 21)

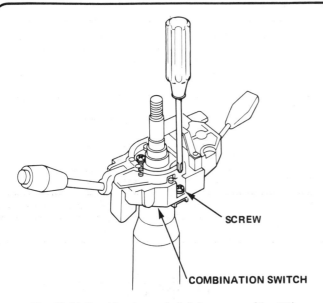

SCREW

COMBINATION SWITCH

Fig. 10.21 Combination switch fixing screws (Sec 21)

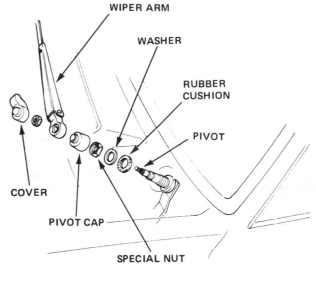

WIPER ARM

WASHER

RUBBER CUSHION

PIVOT

COVER

PIVOT CAP

SPECIAL NUT

Fig. 10.22 Windscreen wiper arm and linkage detail (Sec 23)

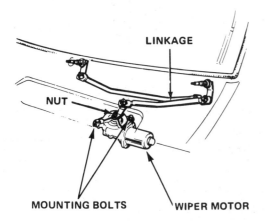

LINKAGE

NUT

MOUNTING BOLTS

WIPER MOTOR

Fig. 10.23 Windscreen wiper motor and linkage (Sec 24)

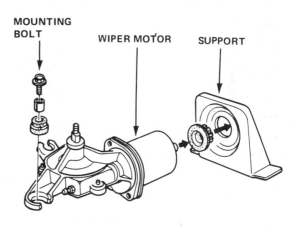

MOUNTING BOLT

WIPER MOTOR

SUPPORT

Fig. 10.24 Windscreen wiper motor and support (Sec 24)

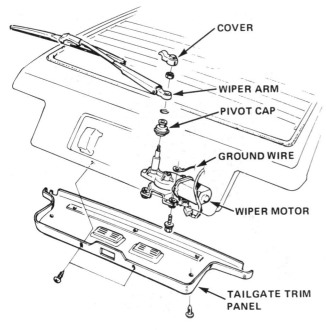

COVER

WIPER ARM

PIVOT CAP

GROUND WIRE

WIPER MOTOR

TAILGATE TRIM PANEL

Fig. 10.25 Rear window wiper assembly (Sec 25)

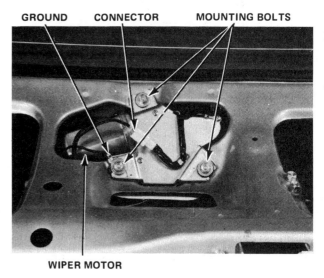

GROUND   CONNECTOR   MOUNTING BOLTS

WIPER MOTOR

Fig. 10.26 Rear window wiper motor fixing bolts (Sec 25)

203

10

21.2 Steering wheel removed, to expose combination switch and turn signal cancelling sleeve

23.2 Disengaging the wiper blade from the wiper arm

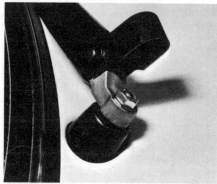

23.3 Wiper arm spindle nut and cover

2   If the horn is satisfactory, check the connecting leads and the fuse in the fuse block.

3   A horn contact spring is incorporated in the steering wheel of models with standard steering wheels. On models with sport steering wheels there are four horn buttons incorporated in the steering wheel.

4   For access to the horn contacts, remove the steering wheel and dismantle it as described in Chapter 11.

23 Windscreen wiper blades and arms – removal and installation

1   The wiper blades should be renewed whenever they cease to wipe the screen effectively.

2   To remove a wiper blade, pull the arm away from the windscreen, lift the small spring clip and pull the wiper blade off the wiper arm (photo).

3   To remove a wiper arm, pull off the cover from the spindle nut (photo) and remove the nut, then pull the arm off its spindle (Fig. 10.22).

4   When installing the arm, make sure that the wiper motor is in the parked position by turning the ignition on, operating the wiper switch momentarily and allowing the motor to stop before switching the ignition off. Position the arm so that the blade is $\frac{3}{8}$ to $\frac{3}{4}$ in (10 to 20 mm) above the rubber at the lower edge of the glass.

24 Windscreen wiper motor and linkage – removal and installation

1   Remove the windscreen wiper blades and arms.
2   Remove the pivot cap, unscrew the special nut beneath it and remove the washer and rubber cushion.
3   Remove the air scoop and bonnet seal.
4   Put mating marks on the wiper motor spindle and the link connected to it, then remove the motor spindle nut and disconnect the link. If the motor is not to be dismantled, the motor and linkage can be removed without separating them (Fig. 10.23).
5   Remove the wiper motor mounting bolts and disconnect the wiring connector, then remove the motor.
6   Remove the linkage.
7   Installation is the reverse of removal. Before tightening the motor mounting bolts, push the motor firmly against the support (Fig. 10.24).

25 Rear wiper motor – removal and installation

1   Remove the tailgate trim.
2   Remove the wiper arm as in Section 23.
3   Disconnect the wiring connector.
4   Remove the three mounting bolts and remove the motor (Fig. 10.25).
5   When installing, ensure that the earth (ground) wire is clamped under the left-hand mounting bolt (Fig. 10.26).

26 Fault diagnosis – electrical system

Symptom	Reason(s)
Starter motor fails to turn	
No electricity at starter motor	Battery discharged
	Battery defective internally
	Battery terminal leads loose or earth lead not securely attached to body
	Loose or broken connections in starter motor circuit
	Starter motor switch or solenoid faulty
Electricity at starter motor: faulty motor	Starter brushes badly worn, sticking, or brush wires loose
	Commutator dirty, worn or burnt
	Starter motor armature faulty
	Field coils earthed
Starter motor turns engine very slowly	
Electrical defects	Battery in discharged condition
	Starter brushes badly worn, sticking, or brush wires loose
	Loose wires in starter motor circuit
Starter motor operates without turning engine	
Mechanical damage	Pinion or flywheel gear teeth broken or worn

Starter motor noisy or excessively rough engagement
Lack of attention or mechanical damage   Pinion or flywheel gear teeth broken or worn
                                                          Starter motor retaining bolts loose

Battery will not hold charge for more than a few days
Wear or damage   Battery defective internally
                                                          Electrolyte level too low or electrolyte too weak due to leakage
                                                          Plate separators no longer fully effective
                                                          Battery plates severely sulphated

Insufficient current flow to keep battery charged   Battery plates severely sulphated
                                                          Drivebelt slipping
                                                          Battery terminal connections loose or corroded
                                                          Alternator not charging
                                                          Short in lighting circuit causing continual battery drain
                                                          Regulator unit not working correctly

Ignition light fails to go out, battery runs flat in a few days
Alternator not charging   Drivebelt loose and slipping or broken
                                                          Brushes worn, sticking, broken or dirty
                                                          Brush springs weak or broken
                                                          Commutator dirty, greasy, worn or burnt
                                                          Alternator field coils burnt, open, or shorted
                                                          Commutator worn

Regulator or cut-out fails to work correctly   Regulator incorrectly set
                                                          Cut-out incorrectly set
                                                          Open-circuit in wiring of cut-out and regulator unit

Horn
Horn operates all the time   Horn push either earthed or stuck down
                                                          Horn cable to horn push earthed

Horn fails to operate   Blown fuse
                                                          Cable or cable connection loose, broken or disconnected
                                                          Horn has an internal fault

Horn emits intermittent or unsatisfactory noise   Cable connections loose
                                                          Horn defective

Lights
Lights do not come on   If engine not running, battery discharged
                                                          Sealed beam filament burnt out or bulbs broken
                                                          Wire connections loose, disconnected or broken
                                                          Light switch shorting or otherwise faulty

Lights come on but fade out   If engine not running, battery discharged
                                                          Wire connections loose, disconnected or broken
                                                          Light switch shorting or otherwise faulty

Lights give very poor illumination   Lamp glasses dirty
                                                          Lamp badly out of adjustment
                                                          Dirty or corroded connections

Lights work erratically – flashing on and off, especially over bumps   Battery terminals or earth connection loose
                                                          Lights not earthing properly
                                                          Contacts in light switch faulty

Wipers
Wiper motor fails to work   Blown fuse
                                                          Wire connection loose, disconnected, or broken
                                                          Brushes badly worn
                                                          Armature worn or faulty
                                                          Field coils faulty

Wiper motor works very slowly and takes excessive current   Commutator dirty, greasy or burnt
                                                          Armature bearings dirty or unaligned
                                                          Armature badly worn or faulty
                                                          Gearbox lacks lubricant

Wiper motor works slowly and takes little current   Brushes badly worn
                                                          Commutator dirty, greasy or burnt
                                                          Armature badly worn or faulty

Wiper motor works but wiper blades remain static   Wiper motor gearbox parts badly worn

Wipers do not stop when switched off or stop in wrong place   Auto-stop device faulty

10

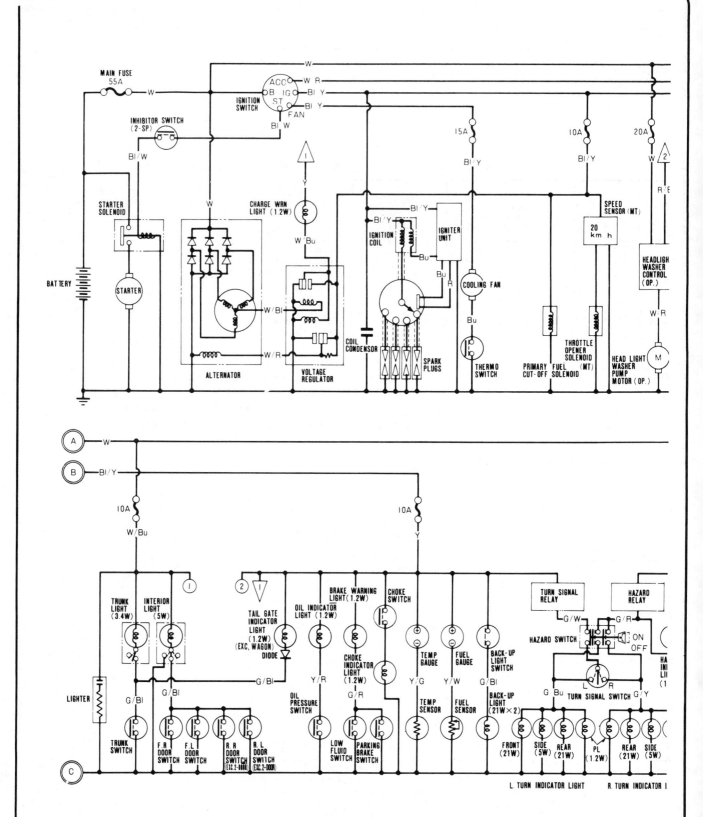

Fig. 10.27 Wiring diagram – models for Germany and Belgium

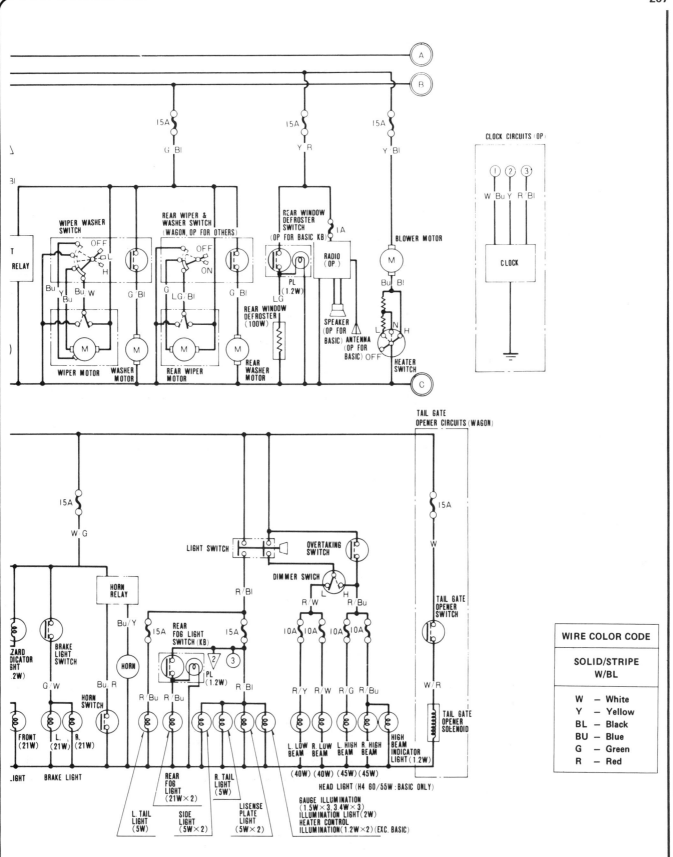

Fig. 10.27 (continued) Wiring diagram – models for Germany and Belgium

WIRE COLOR CODE
SOLID/STRIPE W/BL
W – White
Y – Yellow
BL – Black
BU – Blue
G – Green
R – Red

10

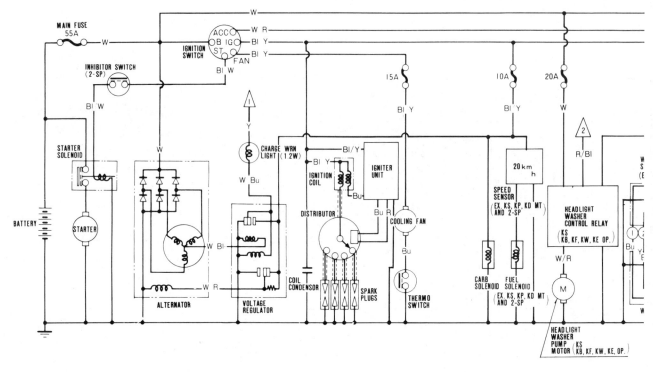

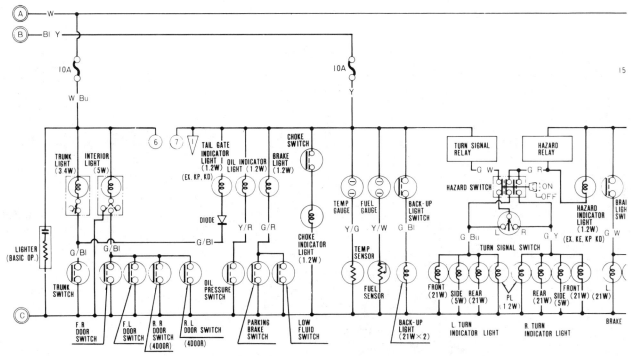

Fig. 10.28 Wiring diagram – models for UK and remainder of Europe

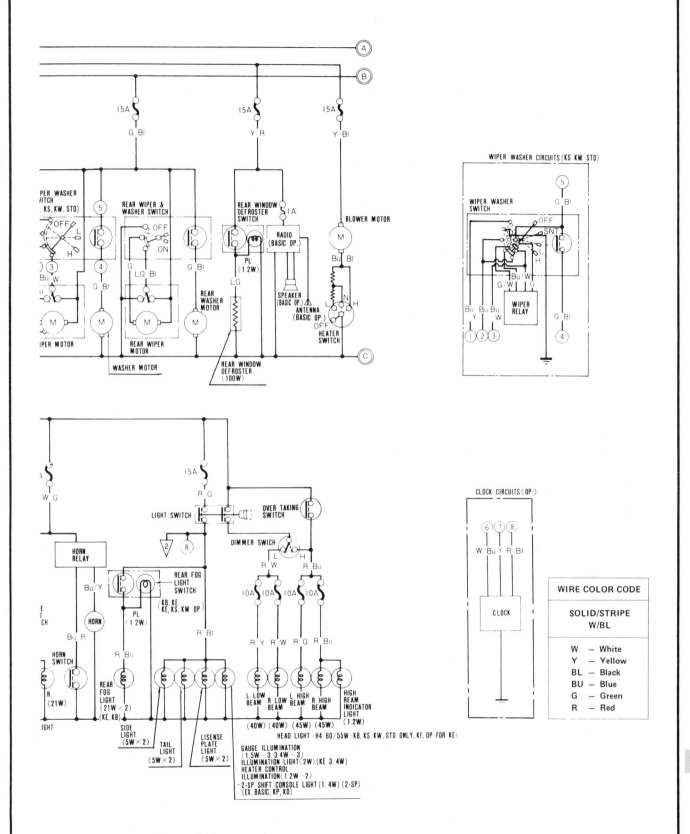

Fig. 10.28 (continued) Wiring diagram – models for UK and remainder of Europe

10

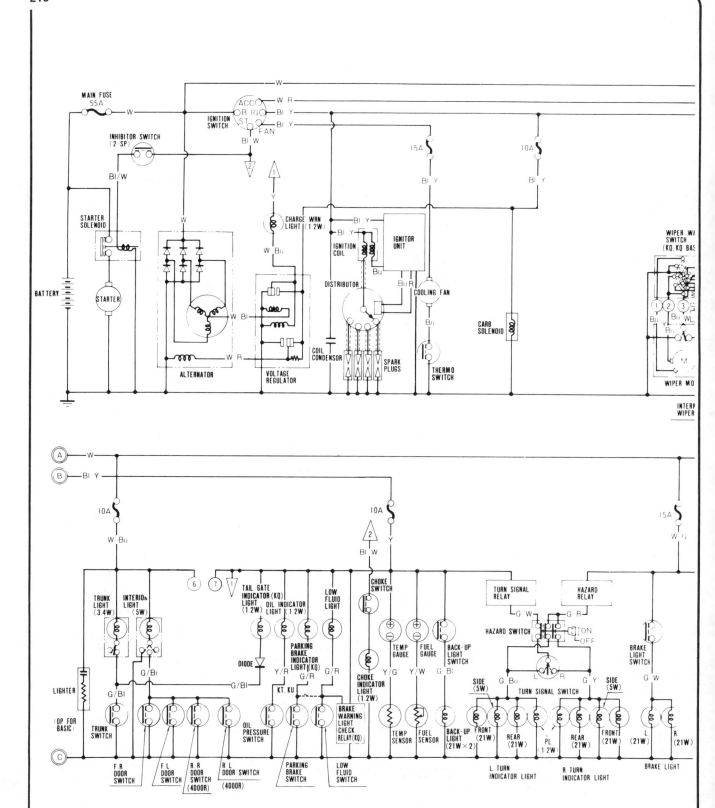

Fig. 10.29 Wiring diagram – models for Australia

211

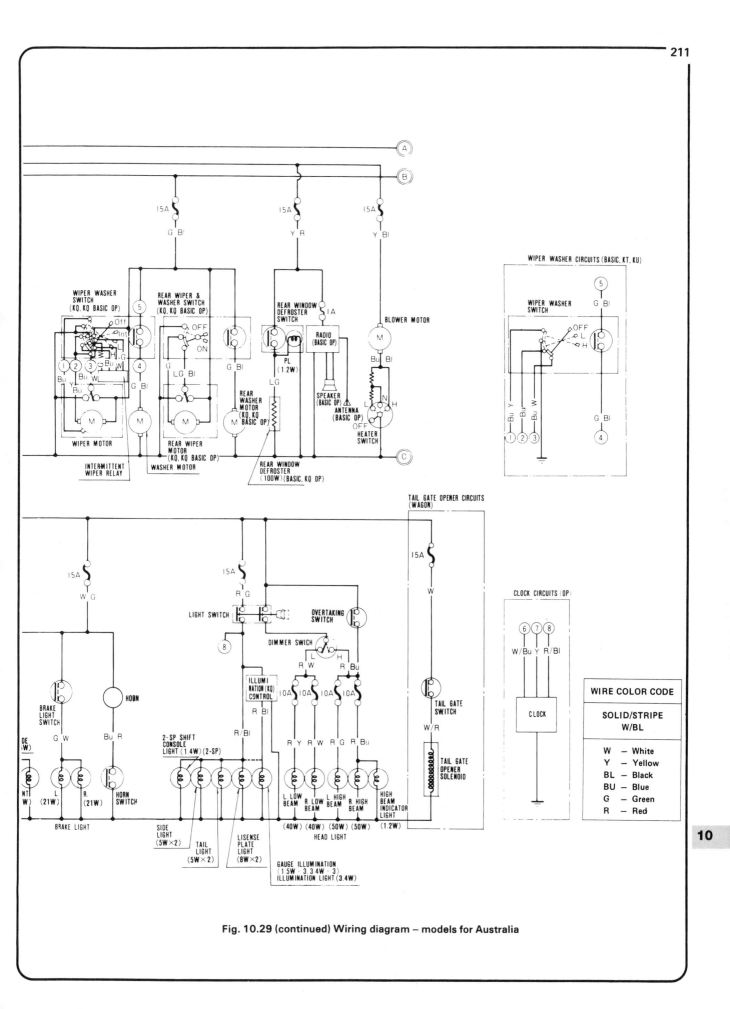

Fig. 10.29 (continued) Wiring diagram – models for Australia

10

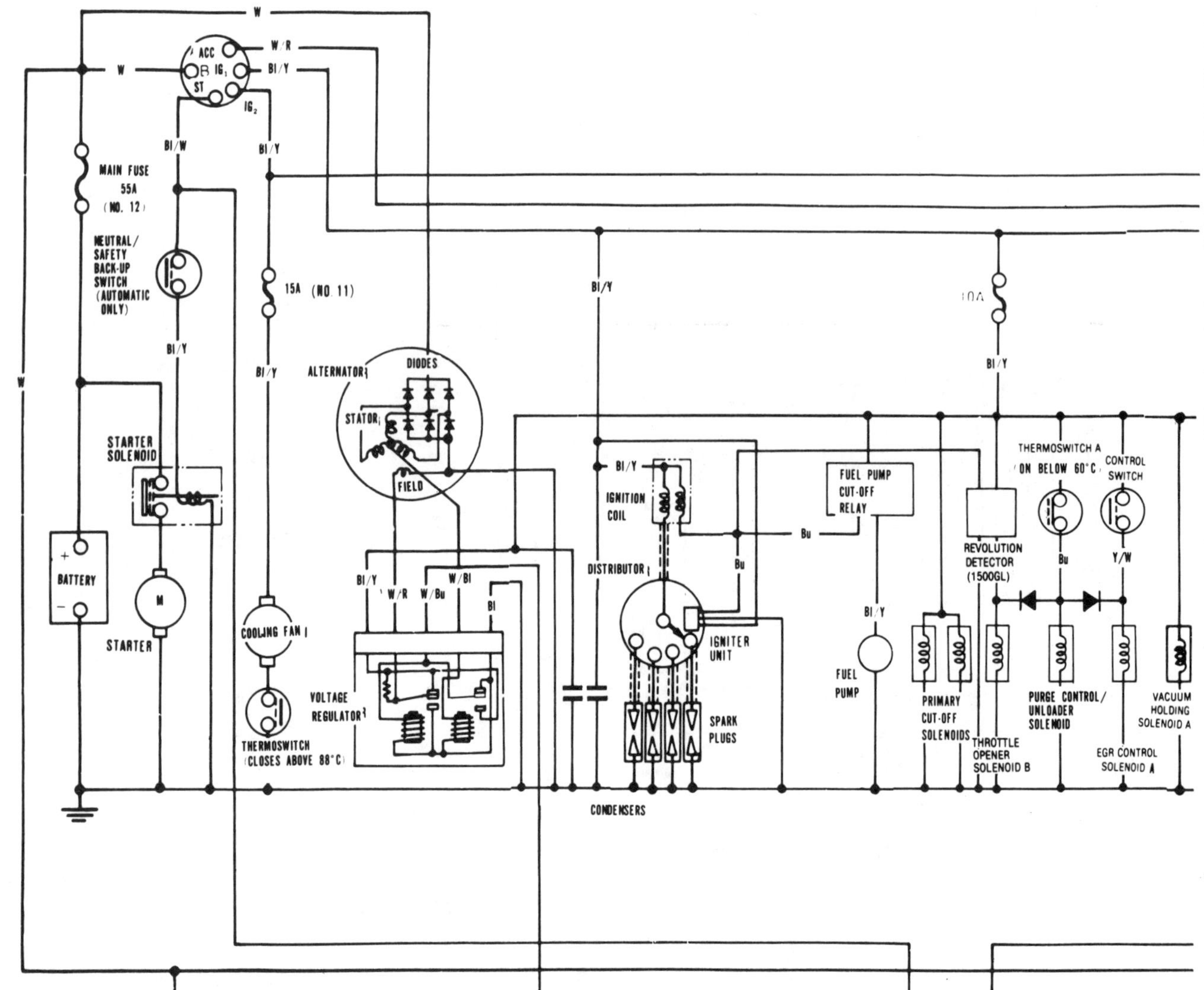

ACC
B IG₁
ST
IG₂

W
W/R
Bl/Y

W
W

MAIN FUSE
55A
(NO. 12)

Bl/W

NEUTRAL/
SAFETY
BACK-UP
SWITCH
(AUTOMATIC
ONLY)

15A (NO. 11)

Bl/Y

Bl/Y

Bl/Y

STARTER
SOLENOID

Bl/Y

Bl/Y

10A

Bl/Y

ALTERNATOR
DIODES

STATOR

FIELD

+ BATTERY −

M
STARTER

COOLING FAN

THERMOSWITCH
(CLOSES ABOVE 88°C)

Bl/Y
W/R
W/Bu
Bl

VOLTAGE
REGULATOR

Bl/Y
IGNITION
COIL

DISTRIBUTOR

CONDENSERS

IGNITER
UNIT

SPARK
PLUGS

Bu

Bu

FUEL PUMP
CUT-OFF
RELAY

Bl/Y

FUEL
PUMP

PRIMARY
CUT-OFF
SOLENOIDS

THROTTLE
OPENER
SOLENOID B

REVOLUTION
DETECTOR
(1500GL)

THERMOSWITCH A
(ON BELOW 60°C)
Bu

PURGE CONTROL/
UNLOADER
SOLENOID

CONTROL
SWITCH
Y/W

EGR CONTROL
SOLENOID A

VACUUM
HOLDING
SOLENOID A

10A (NO. 7)

W/Bu

TAIL GATE
INDICATOR
LIGHT (1.2W)

DIODE

LIGHTER

TRUNK
LIGHT
(3.4W)

INTERIOR
LIGHT
(5W)

G/Bl

TRUNK
SWITCH

DOOR
BUZZER

W/Bu R/Bl Y

G/Bl

IGNITION
SWITCH

F.R.
DOOR
SWITCH

F.L.
DOOR
SWITCH

R.R.
DOOR
SWITCH
WAGON

CLOCK

INTAKE
THERMO-
SWITCH
(ON ABOVE 14°C)

R.L.
DOOR SWITCH
WAGON

W/Bu

CHG WRN
LIGHT (1.2W)

AUTO
CHOKE
HEATER

RESISTOR

SEAT BELT
BUZZER TIMER

RETRACTOR
SWITCH

OIL
PRESSURE
SWITCH

SEAT BELT
INDICATOR
LIGHT
(1.2W)

Bu Y

R/Bu

Y R

PARKING
BRAKE
SWITCH

Bl/W

OIL INDICATOR
LIGHT (1.2W)

BRAKE WARNING
LIGHT 1.2W

G R

TEMP
SENSOR

BRAKE
WARNING
LIGHT CHECK
RELAY

LOW
FLUID
SWITCH

10A (NO. 13)

Y

TEMP
GAUGE
Y/G

FUEL
GAUGE
Y/W

FUEL
SENDER

BACK-UP
LIGHT
SWITCH
(G/Bl)

BACK-UP
LIGHT
(32CP × 2)

Fig. 10.30 Wiring diagram – USA Hatchback and Wagon (except California). For colour code see European wiring diagrams

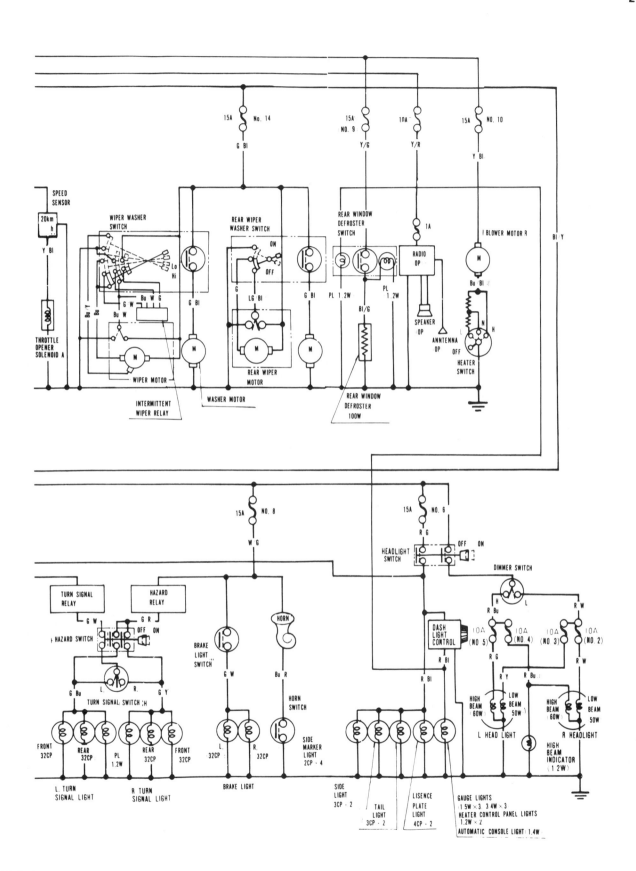

Fig. 10.30 (continued) Wiring diagram – USA Hatchback and Wagon (except California). For colour code see European wiring diagrams

10

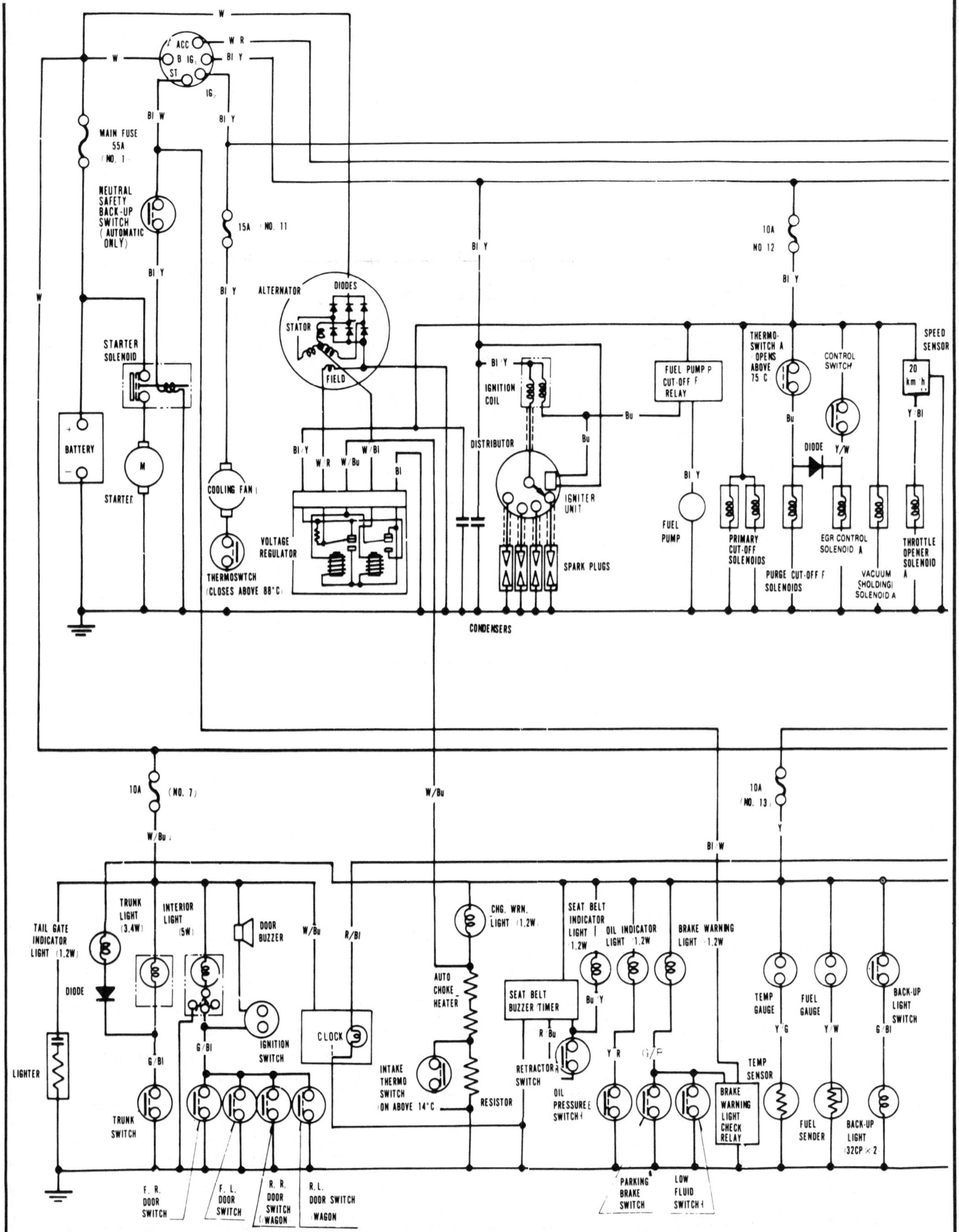

Fig. 10.31 Wiring diagram – USA Sedan (except California). For colour code see European wiring diagrams

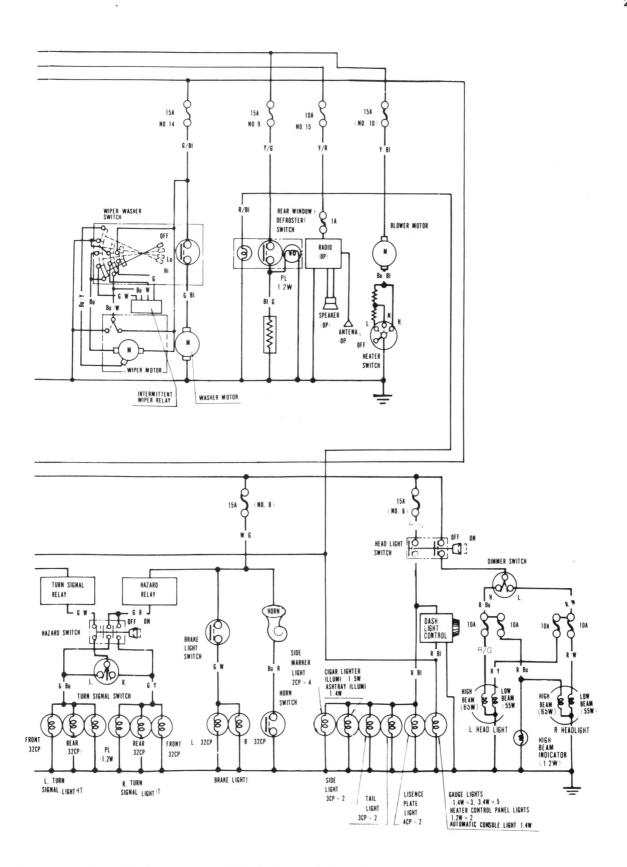

Fig. 10.31 (continued) Wiring diagram – USA Sedan (except California). For colour code see European wiring diagrams

10

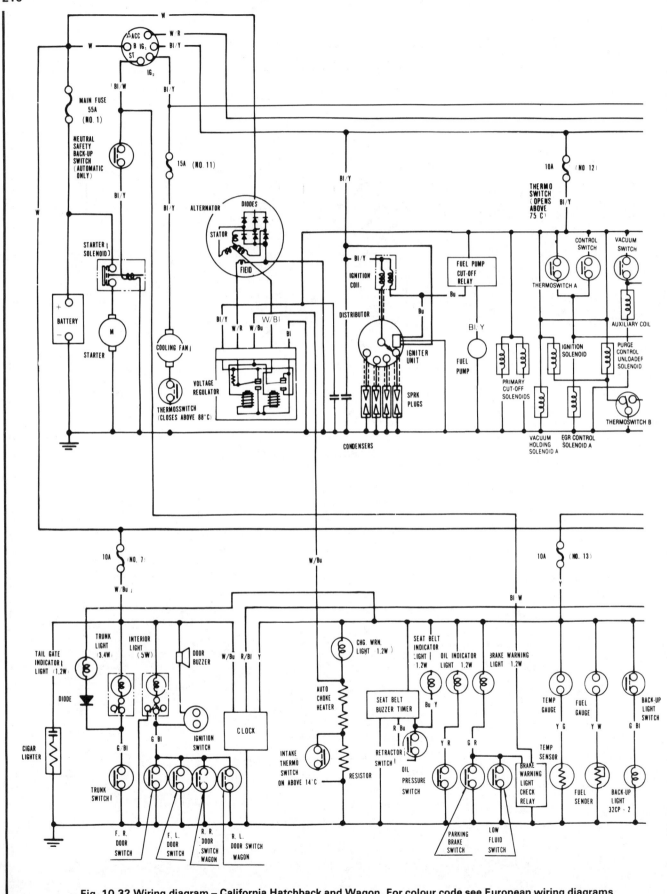

Fig. 10.32 Wiring diagram – California Hatchback and Wagon. For colour code see European wiring diagrams

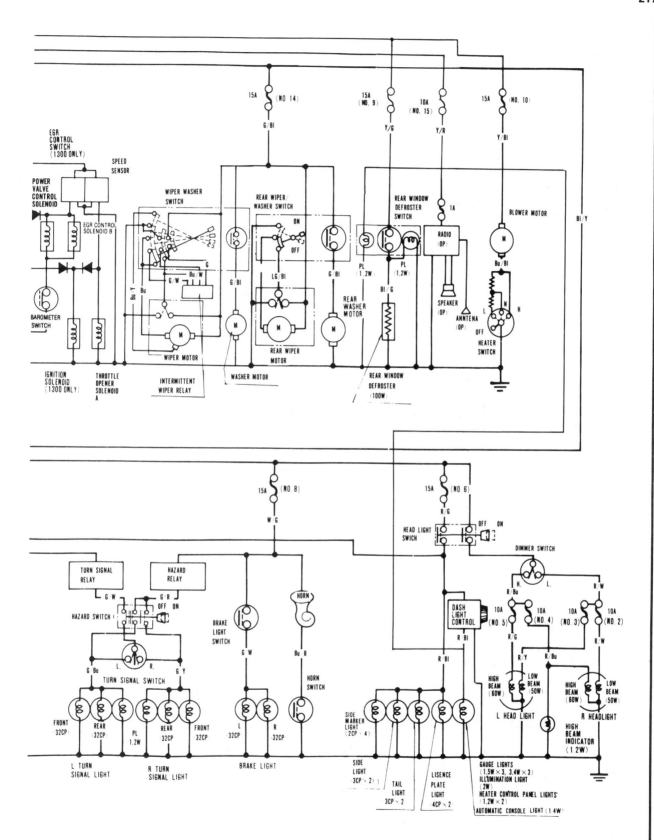

Fig. 10.32 (continued) Wiring diagram – California Hatchback and Wagon. For colour code see European wiring diagrams

10

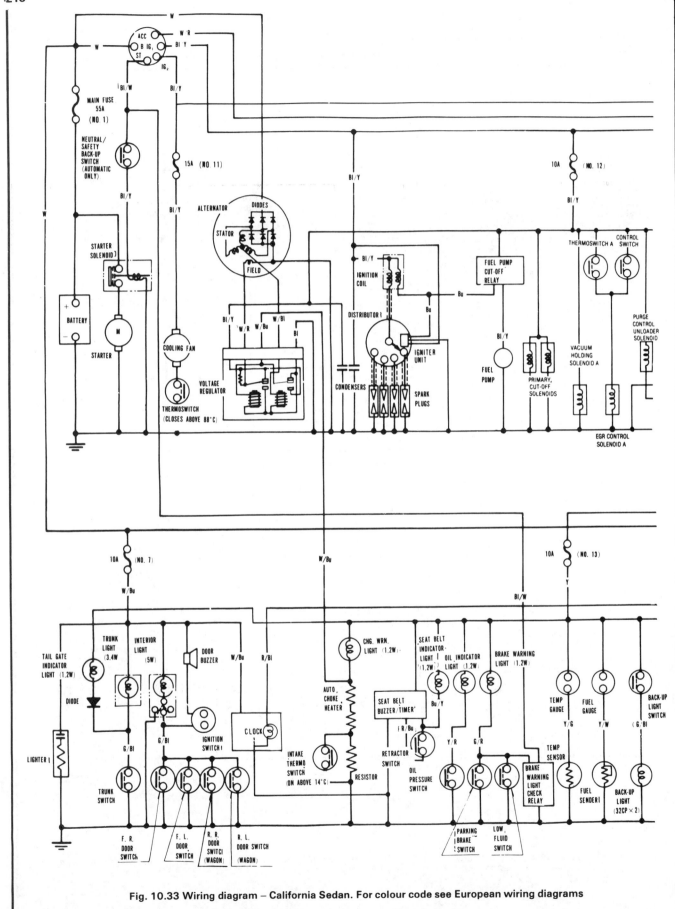

Fig. 10.33 Wiring diagram – California Sedan. For colour code see European wiring diagrams

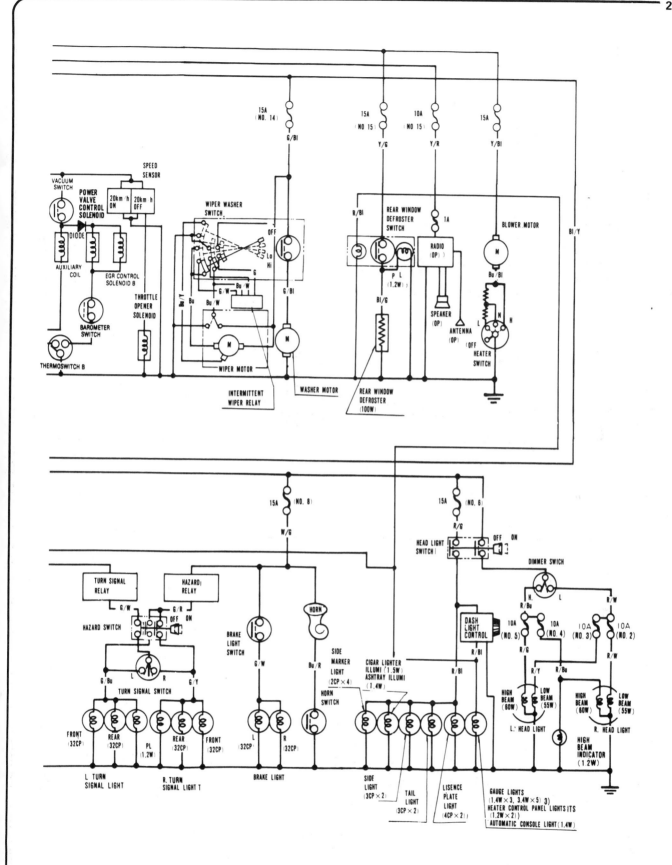

Fig. 10.33 (continued) Wiring diagram – California Sedan. For colour code see European wiring diagrams

10

Chapter 11 Suspension and steering

Refer to Chapter 13 for specifications and information related to 1982 and 1983 US models

Contents

Specifications

Front suspension .... Independent, MacPherson strut with stabiliser (anti-roll) bar

Rear suspension
    Hatchback and Sedan .... Independent, MacPherson strut
    Wagon .... Leaf springs, tubular axle, double-acting telescopic shock absorbers

Steering .... Rack and pinion, collapsible steering column and shaft

Front wheel alignment
Camber (non-adjustable) .... $0° \pm 1°$
Caster (non-adjustable):
    Hatchback and Sedan .... $1° \ 45' \pm 1°$
    Wagon .... $1° \pm 1°$
Toe-out .... $0 \pm \frac{1}{8}$ in (0 ± 3 mm)
Kingpin inclination .... $12° \ 20' \pm 1° \ 30'$

Rear wheel alignment (Hatchback and Sedan)
Camber .... $-0° \ 30'$
Toe-in .... $5/64 \pm 5/64$ in (2 ± 2 mm)

Front coil and spring free length
    1500:
        New .... 12.35 in (313.7 mm)
        Service limit .... 11.80 in (299.7 mm)
    1300:
        New .... 12.28 in (312.0 mm)
        Service limit .... 11.73 in (298.0 mm)

Rear coil spring (Hatchback and Sedan) free length
    1300 and 1500:
        New .... 11.77 in (299.0 mm)
        Service limit .... 11.22 in (285.0 mm)
    1500 GL:
        New .... 12.24 in (311.0 mm)
        Service limit .... 11.69 in (297.0 mm)

Roadwheels and tyres

Roadwheels	$4\frac{1}{2}$J
Tyres:	
UK	6.15-13, 155-13 or 155 SR-13
US-standard:	
HB	6.00 S12
GL	145 SR-12
US – optional	145 SR-13, 155 SR-12
Tyre pressures:	
1300	24 lbf/in² (1.68 kgf/cm²)
1500	26 lbf/in² (1.82 kgf/cm²)

Torque wrench settings

	lbf ft	Nm
Front suspension		
Axleshaft nut*	108	150
Track control arm balljoint nut	25	35
Strut spring seat nut	16	23
Strut upper mounting nut*	33	45
Strut-to-knuckle pinch-bolt	36	50
Stabiliser bar bracket bolts	28	39
Stabiliser bar end nuts*	32	44
Track control arm pivot bolt	28	39
Rear suspension (Sedan and Hatchback)		
Stub axle nut	See text (Section 9)	
Brake backing plate bolts	40	55
Suspension lower arm to stub axle carrier	40	55
Suspension lower arm inner pivot bolt	40	55
Strut to stub axle carrier pinch-bolt	36	50
Radius arm-to-body bolt	61	85
Radius arm-to-stub axle carrier nuts*	72	100
Strut piston nut and locknut	24	33
Strut upper mounting nuts	17	24
Rear suspension (Wagon)		
Shock absorber upper mounting	32	44
Shock absorber lower mounting	32	44
Rear axle nut	See text (Section 9)	
Spring shackle nuts	32	44
Spring pin nut	32	44
Spring pin mountings	16	22
Spring U-bolts	33	46
Steering		
Rack adjuster locknut	18	25
Steering column lower mounting	16	22
Steering column upper mounting nuts	9	13
Rack and pinion mounting bolts	10	14
Steering shaft joint pinch-bolts	22	30
Steering wheel nut	29	40
Track rod end locknuts	32	44
Track rod end balljoint pin nuts	32	44
Track rod to rack	54	75
Wheels		
Roadwheel nuts	58	80

Must be renewed once removed

---

1 General description

The front suspension is of independent MacPherson strut type. The strut is secured at its upper end to the inner wing and it is retained at its lower end by a track control arm. A stabiliser bar is fitted.

The rear suspension on all models except the Wagon is very similar to that of the front. The rear suspension on the Wagon comprises a tubular axle attached to semi-elliptic leaf springs and double acting telescopic shock absorbers.

The steering system is of rack and pinion type having a universally jointed steering shaft which is compressible and a collapsible steering column.

2 Maintenance and inspection

It is essential to maintain the suspension and steering systems in good order if the safety of your car is to be preserved. Even small amounts of wear in the suspension joints and steering system will affect the handling of the car to a dangerous extent. It is for that reason that the law requires checks to be made on the condition and serviceability of the suspension particularly, as well as the more obvious components such as lights, tyres and chassis.

The components that demand particular attention are as follows:

(a) *Lower knuckle balljoint*
(b) *Steering tie-rod balljoints*
(c) *Top anchorage for the MacPherson struts*

11

(d) Anchorages and bushes for anti-roll bar
(e) The shock absorbers
(f) Lower control arm pivot bushes

All of these points should be tested with a stout lever or screwdriver to see whether there is any movement between them and the fixed components. Checks on the suspension should always be made with the car jacked up and supported on chassis stands. It will be easier to detect small amounts of wear and movement when normal imposed loads are not acting on the suspension members. Together with the mechanical tests on the suspension and steering joints, the components themselves should be checked for seviceability, particularly:

(a) Steering rack mounting bolts, tightness
(b) Steering column shaft couplings
(c) Steering column retention bolts
(d) Steering wheel retention
(e) Front and rear wheel hub bearings

There should be no play – or failure – in any single part of any of the aforementioned components. It is dangerous to use a vehicle in a doubtful condition of this kind.

Finally, all parts should be kept clean and rust free. If rust is found, use rust proof paint to restore the part's condition. Rust left can cause cracks and possibly failure of that suspension member.

3 Front knuckle and hub – removal and installation

1 Prise the locknut tab away from the spindle and then loosen the hub nut using a socket spanner and a long bar. This nut is very tight.
2 Loosen the wheel nuts slightly.
3 Raise the front of the car and support it on axle stands placed under the strengthened parts of the body.
4 Remove the wheel nuts, the wheel and the spindle nut.
5 Remove the brake caliper mounting bolts and hang the caliper on a piece of wire so that the brake hose is not strained.
6 Screw two M8 x 1.25 x 12 bolts into the disc and turn them alternately two turns at a time to push the disc away from the hub.
7 Remove the split pin from the tie-rod end and remove the castellated nut, then use a balljoint separator to remove the tie-rod from the knuckle.
8 Remove the lower control arm balljoint in a similar manner.
9 Remove the shock absorber pinch-bolt, then tap the knuckle until it is free of the shock absorber.
10 Pull the knuckle assembly off the axle.
11 Press the hub from the knuckle, taking care not to damage the splash guard.
12 Installation is the reverse of removal. Use a new spindle nut and stake it after tightening to the specified torque.

4 Front wheel bearings – removal and installation

1 With the knuckle removed, remove the splash guard and snap-ring, then remove the outboard bearing (Fig. 11.1).
2 Turn the knuckle over and remove the inboard bearing and inner race.
3 The removal of the outer race requires special tools as it has to be pressed out. The inner race of the outboard bearing requires a special puller.
4 When the races have been removed, remove the outer dust seal from the hub.
5 Wash all parts in solvent before reassembly. Pack both bearings with grease and apply grease to the outer race and both inner races. Pack grease into the groove and around the sealing lip of the dust seals.
6 Installation is the reverse of removal.

5 Front shock absorbers – removal and installation

1 Slacken the nuts of the front wheels, raise the front of the car and support it on axle stands placed under the strengthened parts of the body.

2 Remove the front wheels.
3 Remove the brake hose bracket and the caliper mounting bolts, then support the caliper by a wire hook attached to the body (Fig. 11.2). Take care not to strain the brake hose.
4 Remove the pinch-bolt from the shock absorber attachment to the knuckle, and tap the knuckle off the shock absorber.
5 Remove the rubber cap from the top of the shock absorber, remove the nut and washer and lower the shock absorber.
6 Installation is the reverse of removal, but take care to turn the shock absorber so that the brake hose bracket is turned outwards before clamping the knuckle to the shock absorber.

6 Front shock absorbers – dismantling, inspection and re-assembly

1 **Do not** attempt to dismantle the shock absorbers without using a proper spring compressor and take care to use it in accordance with its manufacturer's instructions.
2 Compress the spring just enough to enable the seat nut to be undone. Remove the nut and carefully release the spring compressor. (If the same spring is to be refitted, it may be left in the compressor).
3 Remove the mount base, dust seal, bearing spacer, needle roller bearing, thrust race, bushing, upper spring seat and boot (Fig. 11.3).
4 Remove the spring and bump stop.
5 Check the damper, dust seal and needle roller bearing for damage and deterioration and renew if necessary.
6 Examine the shock absorber for leaks. Extend and compress the piston several times over its entire stroke, checking that it moves smoothly and with uniform resistance. Renew the shock absorber if defects are apparent.
7 Reassemble in the reverse order, noting the following points. Coat both sides of the needle roller bearing with grease, and position the ends of the spring against the steps in the shock absorber and the upper spring seat (Fig. 11.4).
8 Insert a hexagon wrench in the top of the shock absorber to prevent it from turning and tighten the spring seat nut to the specified torque.

7 Front suspension stabiliser (anti-roll) bar – removal and installation

1 Place the car on level ground and apply the handbrake.
2 Loosen the nuts of the front roadwheels, raise the front of the car, support it on stands placed beneath the suspension subframes and remove the front wheels.
3 Support the front wheel hub while removing the control arm balljoint from the base of the knuckle member.
4 Extract the split pin which locks the balljoint nut, then unscrew and remove the nut.
5 Use a separator to disconnect the balljoint and remove the pin from the knuckle (Fig. 11.5).
6 Remove the two bolts from each of the two brackets which clamp the stabiliser bar to the subframe (photo).
7 Remove the pivot bolts from the lower arms and detach the lower arms from the suspension.
8 Remove the nuts and washers from the ends of the stabiliser bar (photo) and disconnect the bar from the lower arms.
9 Start reassembly by installing the lower control arms loosely.
10 Install the threaded ends of the stabiliser bar into the control arms, with the painted stripe on the bar to the left of the car.
11 Align the inside edge of the paint stripe with the stabiliser bar bushing and install the brackets.
12 Connect the balljoints and tighten them. Tighten the lower arm pivot bolts. Fit new nuts on the ends of the stabiliser bar and tighten to the specified torque.
13 Refit the roadwheels and lower the car to the ground.

8 Rear wheel bearings – removal and installation

1 Chock the front wheels of the car securely with the vehicle on level ground.

223

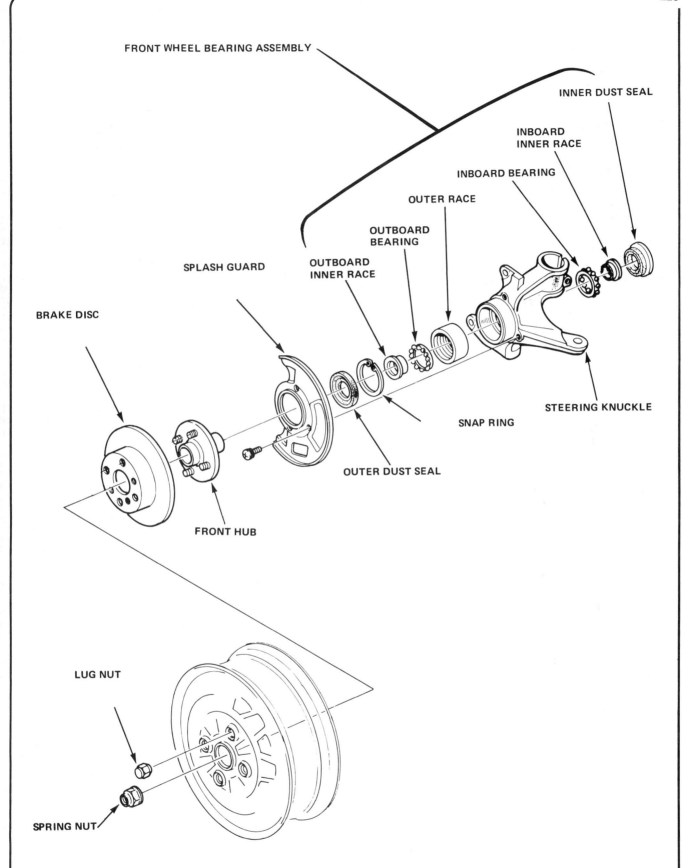

Fig. 11.1 Front wheel and hub assembly (Sec 4)

11

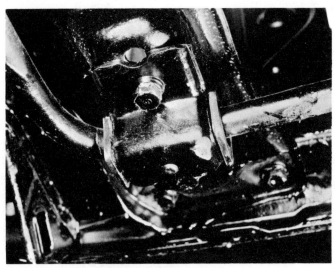

7.5 Front suspension stabiliser bar bracket

7.8 Front suspension stabiliser bar end nut and washer

2   Loosen the rear wheel nuts, raise the rear of the car and support it on stands placed beneath the strengthened parts of the chassis.
3   Remove the rear wheels.
4   Remove the grease cap from the hub. Withdraw the split pin and remove the pin retainer (Fig. 11.6).
5   Unscrew and remove the spindle nut and then remove the hub washer and the outer bearing.
6   Pull the brake drum off.
7   Prise out the grease seal and remove the inner bearing.

8   Drive the inboard and outboard bearing races out of the drum with a hammer and punch, tapping two diagonally opposite points of the race alternately so that the race remains square to the bore.
9   Clean the bearing seats thoroughly. Clean the bearings thoroughly and examine them for roughness, damage and wear.
10 Drive in the inboard race, using a tubular drift, and then turn the drum over and drive in the outboard bearing race.
11 Check that both races are fully seated and then grease both the bearings and their races. Pack grease into the space between the races.
12 Install the inner bearing into the brake drum.
13 Pack the groove of a new seal with grease and grease the lip, then install the seal using a hammer and a block of wood. Take care to ensure that the seal enters the drum squarely and then tap it home fully.
14 Install the drum on the spindle, then install the outer bearing, hub washer and spindle nut.
15 Tighten the spindle nut as described in the following Section and then install the pin retainer, split pin and grease cap after partially filling the cap with fresh grease.

9 Rear wheel bearings – adjustment

1   Proceed as described in Section 8, paragraphs 1 to 4.
2   Tighten the spindle nut to 14 to 22 lbf ft (20 to 30 Nm) and rotate the brake drum by hand to seat the bearings.
3   Slacken the spindle nut about two turns and then tighten it to 3 lbf ft (5 Nm).
4   Install the pin holder so that its slots align as nearly as possible with the hole in the spindle. If necessary, tighten the nut just sufficiently to allow the holes in the pin holder and spindle to be aligned.
5   Install a new split pin and lock it.
6   Refit the grease cap and roadwheel, then lower the car to the ground.

10 Rear suspension components (Hatchback and Saloon) – removal and installation

1   Place the car on level ground and chock the front wheels.
2   Loosen the rear wheel nuts, jack up the rear of the car and support it on stands placed under the strengthened parts of the chassis.
3   Remove the rear wheels.
4   Disconnect the parking brake cable. Disconnect the brake hose and plug it or clamp it to prevent loss of fluid. Remove the brake backplate complete with shoes.
5   Remove the inner bolt from the lower control arm and remove the radius arm pivot bolt (Fig. 11.7).

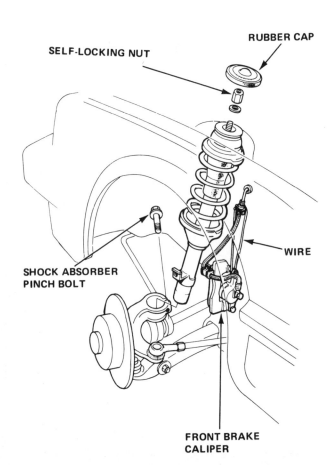

SELF-LOCKING NUT

RUBBER CAP

SHOCK ABSORBER PINCH BOLT

WIRE

FRONT BRAKE CALIPER

Fig. 11.2 Front shock absorber removal (Sec 5)

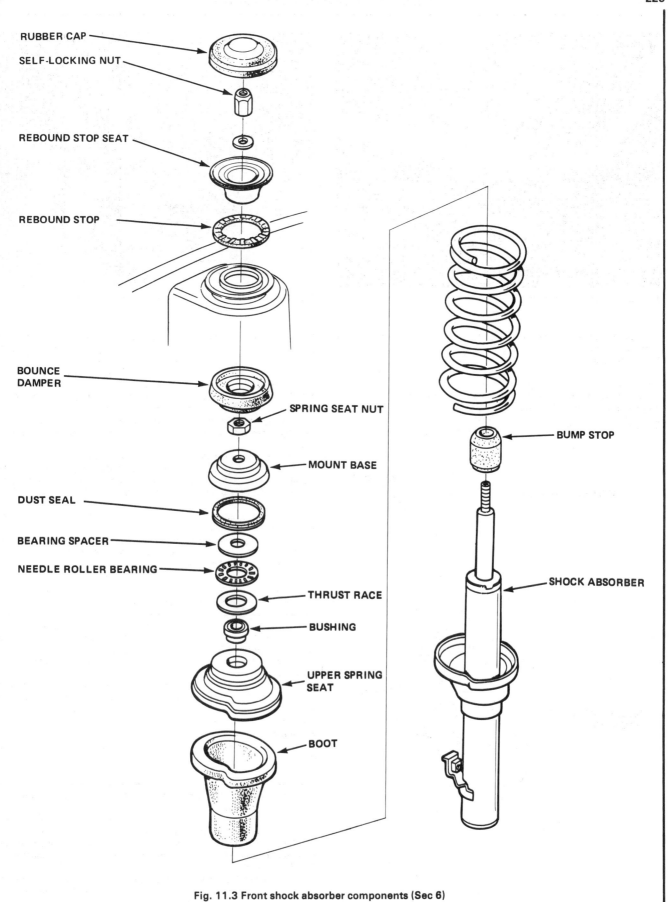

RUBBER CAP

SELF-LOCKING NUT

REBOUND STOP SEAT

REBOUND STOP

BOUNCE DAMPER

SPRING SEAT NUT

MOUNT BASE

DUST SEAL

BEARING SPACER

NEEDLE ROLLER BEARING

THRUST RACE

BUSHING

UPPER SPRING SEAT

BOOT

BUMP STOP

SHOCK ABSORBER

Fig. 11.3 Front shock absorber components (Sec 6)

11

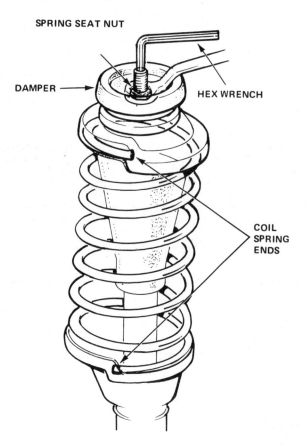

Fig. 11.4 Installationn of front suspension spring (Sec 6)

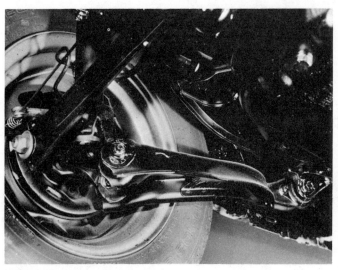

10.12 Control arm and radius pivot bolts

6   Remove the clamp bolt securing the shock absorber to the hub carrier and tap the hub carrier assembly off the bottom of the shock absorber.

7   Remove the two nuts and washers from the top of the shock absorber and remove the shock absorber.

8   Installation is the reverse of removal, but the following points should be noted.

9   Align the tab on the shock absorber with the slot in the hub carrier, then install the shock absorber and tighten the clamp bolt.

10 Install the lower control arm and radius arm loosely in the frame.

11 Use a new lockplate when refitting the brake backplate.

12 Place a jack under the rear hub carrier and raise the jack until the

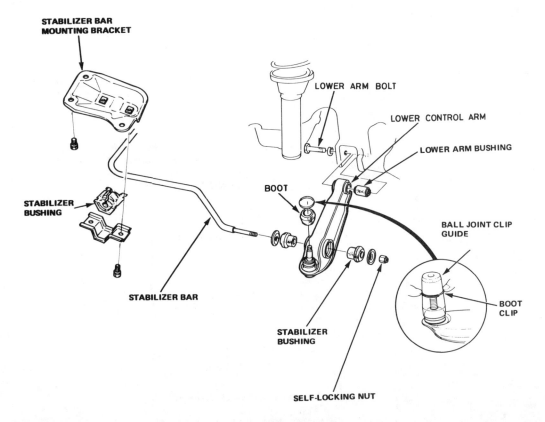

Fig. 11.5 Front stabiliser bar removal (Sec 7)

car just lifts off the axle stand, then tighten the control arm and radius arm pivot bolts (photo).

13 Bleed the brake hydraulic system on completion (Chapter 9).

11 Rear shock absorbers (Hatchback and Saloon) – dismantling, inspection and reassembly

1 The components of the shock absorber are shown in Fig. 11.8.

2 Dismantling, inspection and reassembly is similar to the procedure for the front shock absorbers described in Section 6.

12 Rear suspension components (Wagon) – removal and installation

1 Place the car on level ground and chock the front wheels.

2 Loosen the rear wheel nuts, jack up the rear of the car and support it on stands placed under the strengthened parts of the chassis.

3 Remove the rear wheels.

4 Disconnect and plug the brake pipes form the rear axle, and disconnect the parking brake cables from the equalizer.

5 Support the centre of the rear axle with a jack and remove the lower mounting bolts of the shock absorbers.

6 Remove the nut from the spring front mounting. Remove the bolts securing the spring pin to the chassis and remove the pin.

7 Remove the nuts securing the rear spring shackles to the body and lower the jack to free the suspension from the body.

8 The suspension may be dismantled completely as shown in Fig. 11.9.

9 Check the spring and shackle bushings for deterioration. Check the springs and spring clamp bracket for cracks and damage. Check the shock absorber bushings and bump stop for deterioration and damage.

10 Examine the shock absorber for leaks, damage and smooth operation with uniform resistance over its whole range of movement. If one shock absorber is found to be defective, it is advisable to fit new ones to both sides of the vehicle.

11 Reassembly and installation are the reverse of removal, but note that the arrow marked on the leaf spring must face forward (Fig. 11.10).

12 Install the bolts loosely initially and do not do the final tightening until all parts have been installed and the vehicle is resting with its full weight on the rear suspension.

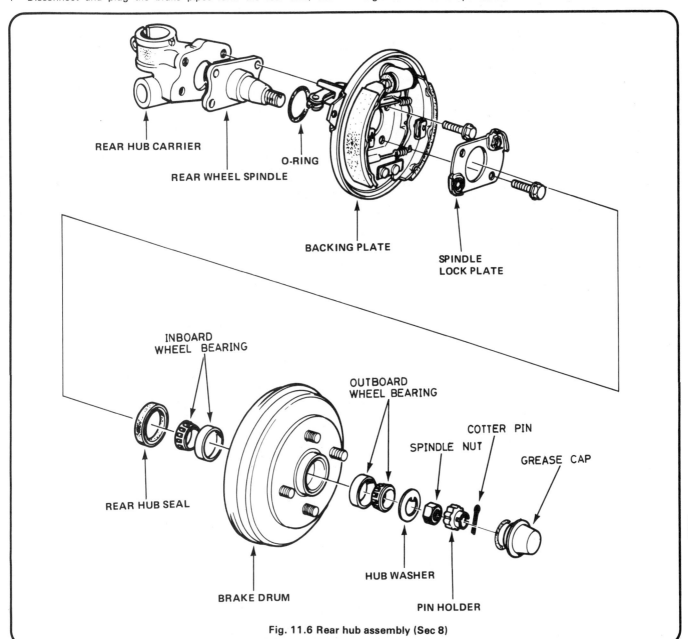

Fig. 11.6 Rear hub assembly (Sec 8)

11

13.8 Steering arm balljoint nut and split pin

13 Track rod end ball joints – removal and installation

1   Set the steering wheel and the front roadwheels in the straight-ahead position.

2   Using two spanners, hold the track rod end quite still while the locknut is released. Do not unscrew the locknut more than a $\frac{1}{4}$ of a turn.

3   Withdraw the split pin from the balljoint taper pin and unscrew and remove the castellated nut.

4   Using a balljoint separator or forked wedges, separate the track rod end balljoint from the steering arm.

5   Grip the track rod to prevent it turning and unscrew and remove the track rod end from it.

6   If the balljoint taper pins can be easily moved or there is any endfloat when the taper pin is pushed or pulled, then the track rod end must be renewed. If the bellows are split or damaged, release their clips and renew them.

7   Again gripping the track rod to prevent it turning, screw on the new track rod end. When it is correctly aligned so that it can be re-inserted into the eye of the steering arm, tighten the locknut by the same amount through which it was unscrewed. If this is carried out correctly, the front wheel toe-in will not have been altered too much but even so the front wheel alignment must be checked, as described in Section 21.

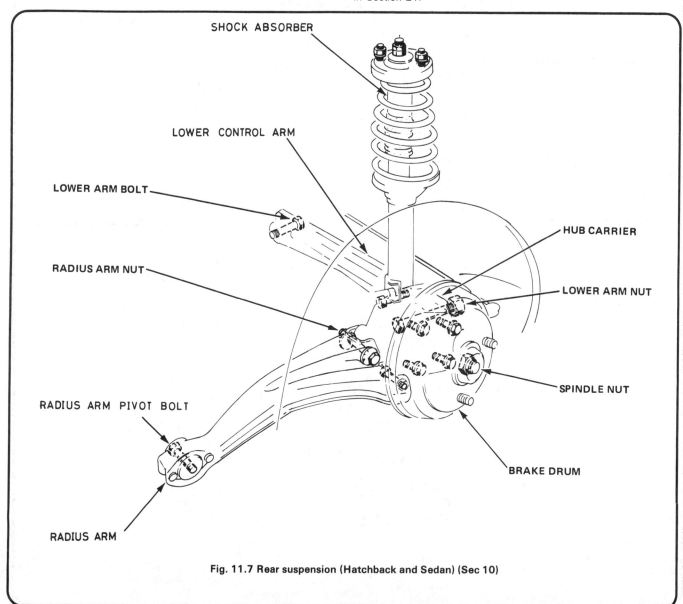

Fig. 11.7 Rear suspension (Hatchback and Sedan) (Sec 10)

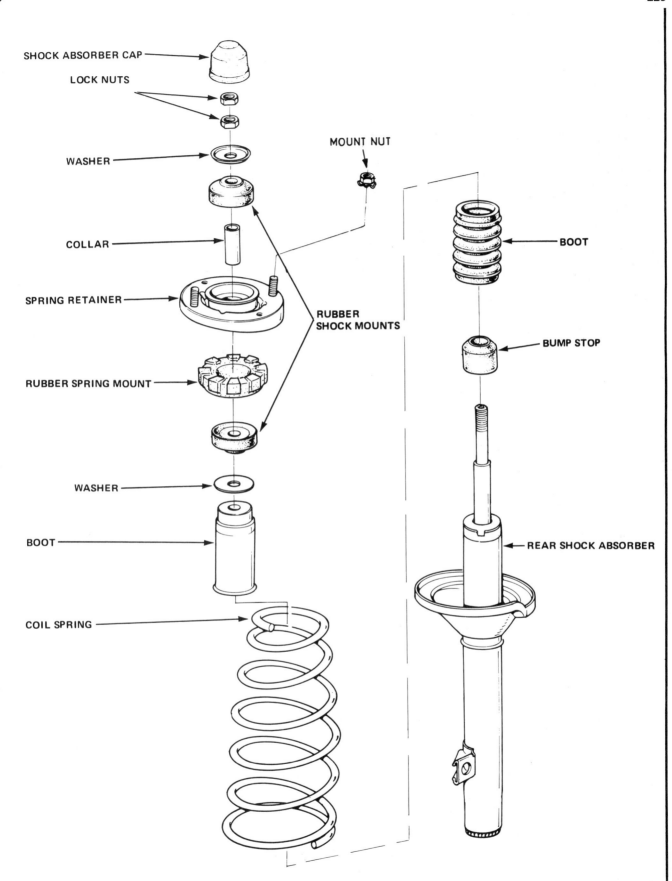

Fig. 11.8 Rear shock absorber components (Sec 11)

11

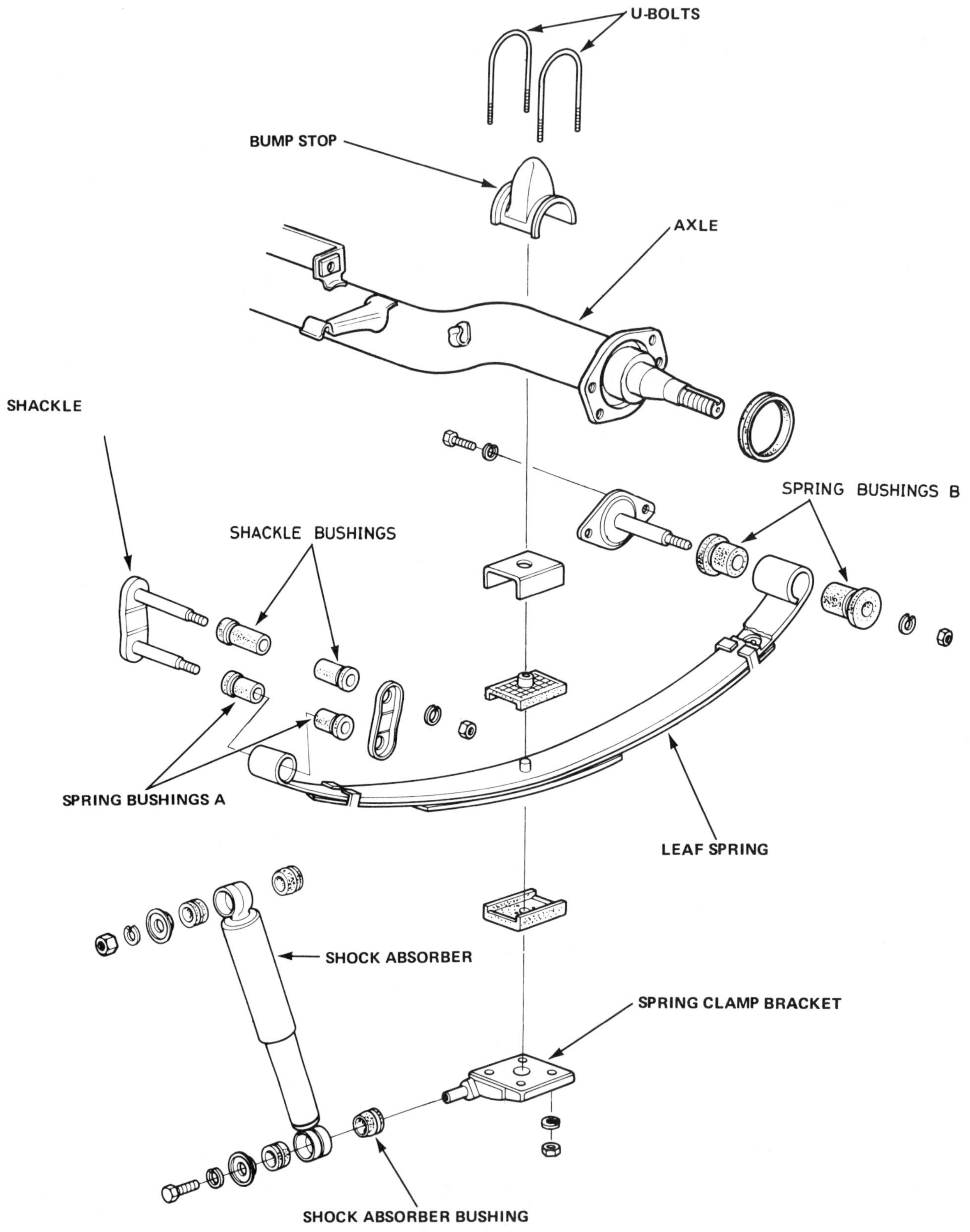

U-BOLTS

BUMP STOP

AXLE

SHACKLE

SPRING BUSHINGS B

SHACKLE BUSHINGS

SPRING BUSHINGS A

LEAF SPRING

SHOCK ABSORBER

SPRING CLAMP BRACKET

SHOCK ABSORBER BUSHING

Fig. 11.9 Rear suspension (Wagon) (Sec 12)

8   Connect the balljoint taper pin to the steering arm, screw on and tighten the castellated nut to the specified torque and insert a new split pin (photo).
9   Check that the steering rack flexible bellows have not twisted; if they have, straighten them.

14 Steering – adjustment and checking for wear

1   Apart from visual detection of wear in the steering linkage and joints, time for overhaul can be assumed if the steering wheel can be moved more than 0.39 in (10.0 mm) without transmitting any movement to the front roadwheels.
2   A further test can be carried out by raising the front roadwheels and attaching a spring balance to one of the spokes of the steering

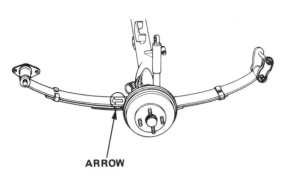

ARROW

Fig. 11.10 Arrow on leaf spring points to front (Sec 12)

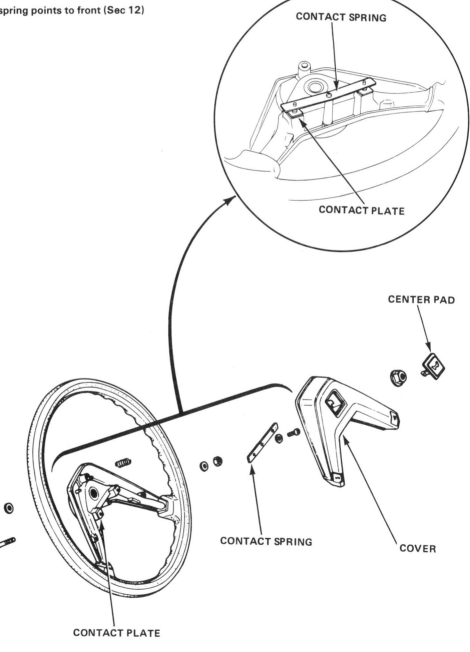

CONTACT SPRING

CONTACT PLATE

CENTER PAD

CONTACT SPRING

COVER

SLIP RING

CONTACT PLATE

Fig. 11.11 Steering wheel assembly (Tokyo Seat) (Sec 15)

11

wheel. The force required to turn the wheel should not exceed 3.3 lb (1.5 kg), otherwise check the adjustment of the rack guide screw in the following way.

3   Release the rack guide adjusting screw locknut.

4   Tighten the adjusting screw until it just seats.

5   Now unscrew the adjusting screw $\frac{1}{8}$th of a turn (45°) and retighten the locknut.

6   Recheck the turning force of the gear again using the spring balance attached to the steering wheel.

15 Steering wheel – removal, dismantling and installation

1   Two makes of steering wheel are used, and although the removal and installation of the steering wheel is the same for both, subsequent dismantling is slightly different.

2   Set the roadwheels in the straight-ahead position.

3   Disconnect the battery negative lead.

4   Prise the centre pad out of the steering wheel (photo) and remove the steering wheel nut.

5   Mark the steering wheel hub and also the steering shaft so that the marks can be aligned when the wheel is installed.

6   Rock the steering wheel from side to side gently and at the same time pull it steadily with both hands. **Do not** jar or tap the wheel off the shaft because this may damage the collapsible steering column.

7   To dismantle the Tokyo Seat type of wheel (Fig. 11.11), remove the screws securing the slip ring to the steering wheel, remove the screws from the underside of the wheel and remove the cover.

8   To dismantle the Nippon Purasuto type (Fig. 11.12), remove the screws securing the slip ring to the lower cover. Remove the screws from the lower cover, then remove the upper cover, contact spring and lower cover.

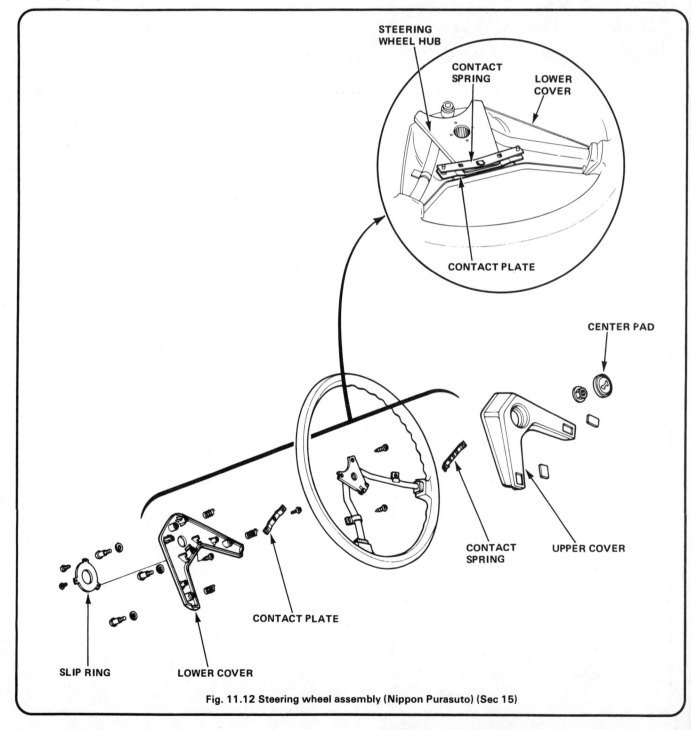

Fig. 11.12 Steering wheel assembly (Nippon Purasuto) (Sec 15)

15.4 Steering wheel pad removed to expose the steering wheel nut

9 Before reassembling, clean the horn electrical contacts. After reassembly check that the contact spring to contact plate clearance is 0.04 in (1 mm) at both ends.

10 Installation of the steering wheel is the reverse of removal. After reconnecting the battery, check that the horn works.

16 Steering column lock – removal and installation

1 Disconnect the lead from the battery negative terminal.

2 Jack up the front roadwheels and turn the steering until the column locks.

3 Remove the lower section of the steering column shroud (four screws).

4 Disconnect the ignition switch wiring connector (photo).

5 The lock/switch assembly is secured to the column by shear bolts and the ends of the bolts will have to be centre-punched and drilled out using a $\frac{1}{4}$ in. (6.35 mm) drill. Alternatively, use a stud extractor.

6 Install the new lock/switch assembly and screw in the new shear bolts only finger-tight, then test the lock for smooth operation by inserting the ignition key and withdrawing it, at the same time turning the steering wheel.

7 If the tongue of the lock is engaging positively in the cut-out in the

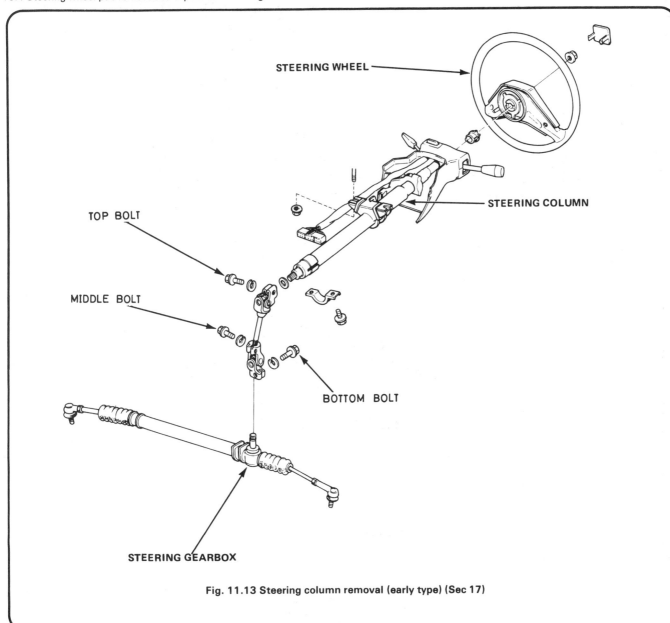

Fig. 11.13 Steering column removal (early type) (Sec 17)

STEERING WHEEL

STEERING COLUMN

TOP BOLT

MIDDLE BOLT

BOTTOM BOLT

STEERING GEARBOX

11

16.4 Steering column lock and ignition switch wiring connector

column, fully tighten the shear bolts evenly until their heads break off.
8   Reconnect the ignition switch plug and refit the column lower shroud. Lower the jack.

17 Steering column – removal and installation

1   Remove the steering wheel as described in Section 15.
2   Disconnect the wiring plugs at the side of the column for the ignition switch, the hazard warning switch and the direction indicator, lighting and wiper switches.
3   Set the front roadwheels in the straight-ahead position and then mark the relative alignment of the steering shaft lower universal joint to the pinion shaft.
4   Unscrew and remove the pinch-bolt from the lower joint.
5   Unscrew and remove the nuts from the column upper mounting bracket.
6   Unscrew and remove the two bolts from the column lower mounting bracket.
7   Withdraw the steering column assembly into the vehicle interior.
8   Installation is the reverse of removal. Slip the splined shaft into the top joint of the connector so that the bolt will be installed across the flat part of the shaft and ensure that the shaft is pushed down to the bottom of the connector. Do not forget to refit the bushing (early type column only).

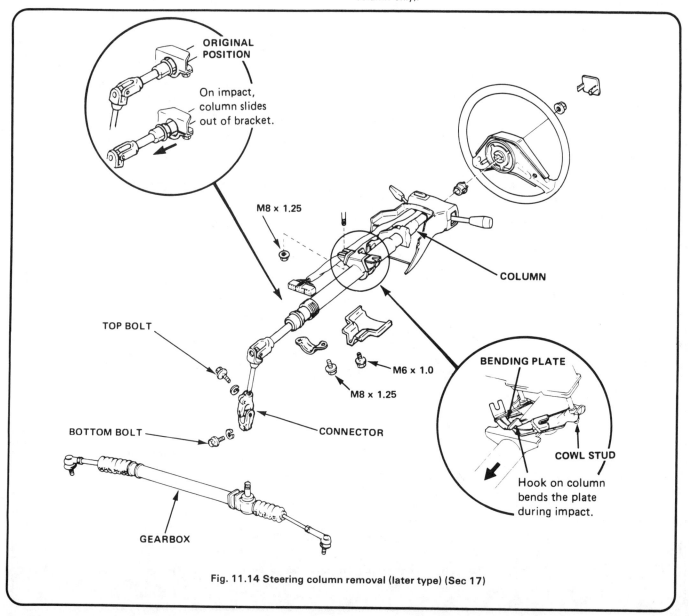

Fig. 11.14 Steering column removal (later type) (Sec 17)

9   Install all bolts loosely and ensure that the bending plate is seated firmly and under the hook on the column, then tighten the bolts and nuts to the specified torques.

18 Steering column – dismantling, inspection and reassembly

Early type (without shear pins)
1   If not already done, remove the upper and lower covers.
2   Remove the turn signal cancelling sleeve.
3   Remove the screws securing the combination switch, then remove the switch.
4   Take off the rubber bands holding the bending plate and upper bracket together. Remove the bending plate and bracket.
5   Remove the snap-ring and washer from the top of the shaft.
6   Insert the ignition key and turn it to position I.
7   From the bottom of the shaft, remove the plastic collar, shaft bushing and hanger bushing.
8   Withdraw the steering shaft from the bottom of the column.
9   Remove the thrust ring, bushing and horn ground ring from the top of the column. Dismantling is now complete.
10 Check the steering shaft for straightness and examine the hanger bushing for wear or damage.

11 Check the plastic collar and the bending plate for cracks, distortion or other damage. Such damage may mean that the vehicle has been in an accident.
12 Check the upper bushing and the thrust ring for wear or damage.
13 Renew worn or damaged parts as necessary, then commence reassembly as follows.
14 Install the horn ground ring and the column bushing to the top of the column.
15 Place the thrust ring in position and carefully tap it home, using a plastic mallet.
16 Grease the upper bushing, and coat the shaft with rust-inhibiting oil.
17 Insert the shaft into the column from the bottom, taking care not to bend the horn ground ring.
18 Pack grease into the bottom end of the steering column, then install the hanger bushing. Apply light hammer blows, via a suitable drift, to make sure the hanger bushing is seated.
19 Install the plastic collar at the bottom of the column, aligning the projection on the collar with the hole in the column.
20 Install the washer and snap-ring to the top of the shaft.
21 The remainder of the reassembly follows the reverse of the dismantling procedure. Note the correct fitting of the bending plate (Fig. 11.18).

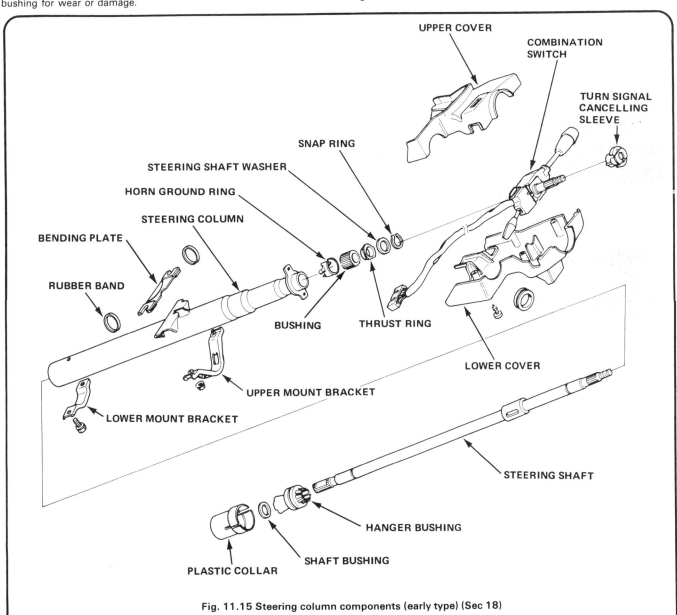

Fig. 11.15 Steering column components (early type) (Sec 18)

11

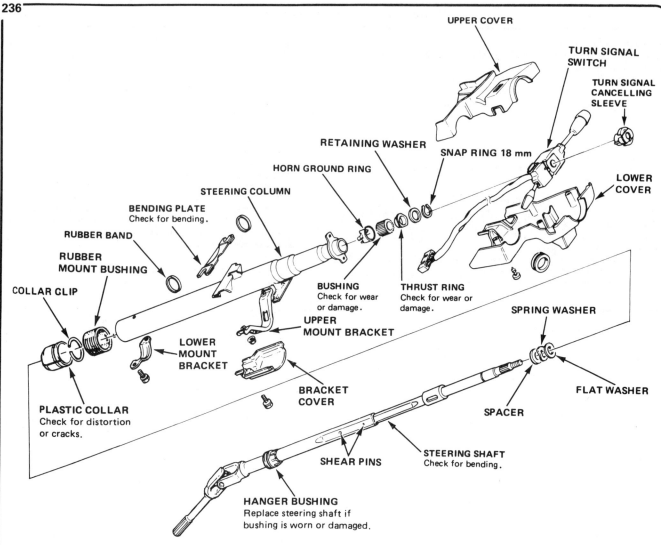

UPPER COVER

TURN SIGNAL SWITCH

TURN SIGNAL CANCELLING SLEEVE

RETAINING WASHER

HORN GROUND RING

SNAP RING 18 mm

STEERING COLUMN

LOWER COVER

BENDING PLATE
Check for bending.

RUBBER BAND

RUBBER MOUNT BUSHING

COLLAR CLIP

BUSHING
Check for wear or damage.

THRUST RING
Check for wear or damage.

SPRING WASHER

UPPER MOUNT BRACKET

LOWER MOUNT BRACKET

FLAT WASHER

PLASTIC COLLAR
Check for distortion or cracks.

BRACKET COVER

SPACER

STEERING SHAFT
Check for bending.

SHEAR PINS

HANGER BUSHING
Replace steering shaft if bushing is worn or damaged.

Fig. 11.16 Steering column components (later type) (Sec 18)

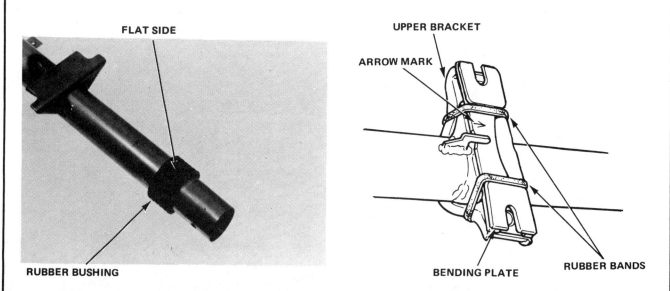

FLAT SIDE

UPPER BRACKET

ARROW MARK

RUBBER BUSHING

BENDING PLATE

RUBBER BANDS

Fig. 11.17 Installing the rubber mount bushing (later type column) (Sec 18)   Fig. 11.18 Installing the bending plate and rubber bands (Sec 18)

Later type (with shear pins)

22 Take care not to drop the shaft, as the impact could break the shear pins in the shaft.

23 Dismantling is essentially as described above, paragraphs 1 to 10. Note however the following differences, referring to Fig. 11.16:

    (a)   *A cover is fitted to the upper mounting bracket*
    (b)   *The hanger bushing is integral with the bottom of the shaft, as is the top universal joint.*
    (c)   *A clip secures the plastic collar, with a rubber bushing immediately above it*
    (d)   *A spring washer, flat washer and spacer are fitted at the top of the shaft*

24 Inspection is as described in paragraphs 10 to 12. If the hanger bushing is worn or damaged, the complete shaft must be renewed.

25 Reassemble the steering column as follows.

26 Install the horn earthing ring, insert the column bushing and set the steering thrust ring in position.

27 Tap the steering thrust ring in, using a plastic mallet, and then grease the thrust ring and column bushing.

28 Slide the rubber mount bushing on to the column, with the flat side of the bush uppermost (Fig. 11.17).

29 Install the spacer, spring washer and flat washer on the top of the column. The concave side of the spring washer should be towards the top of the shaft.

30 Install the plastic collar and clip on the lower end of the steering shaft and then coat the shaft with a rust inhibitor.

31 Insert the steering shaft into the bottom of the steering column, taking care not to damage the horn earthing ring.

32 Grease the lower end of the steering shaft and the inside of the bottom of the column and then push the hanger bushing as far as it will go into the bottom of the column.

33 Install the plastic collar on the bottom of the steering column so that the projection inside the collar locates in the hole in the column and then install the collar clip in the groove round the collar.

34 Install the retaining washer and snap-ring on the top of the column, then install the turn signal switch and cancelling sleeve.

35 Use rubber bands to assemble the upper bracket and bending plate to the column. The plate should be under the hook on the column and the arrow on the plate should be on the upper side of the plate and point downwards (Fig. 11.18).

36 Install the upper and lower column covers and the upper bracket cover.

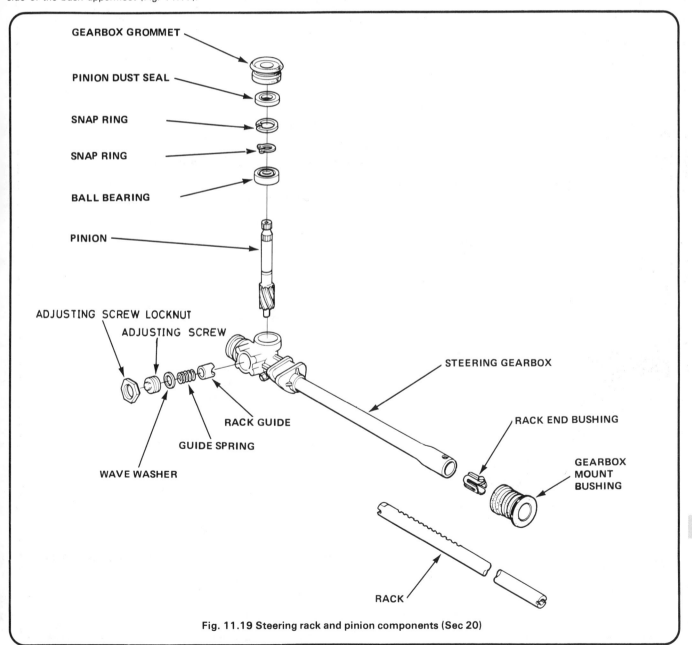

Fig. 11.19 Steering rack and pinion components (Sec 20)

19.4 Steering rack mounting bracket

Fig. 11.20 Rear wheel camber adjuster (Hatchback and Sedan)
(Sec 22)

19 Steering rack and pinion assembly – removal and installation

1 Loosen the nuts of the front roadwheels, jack up the car and support it on stands, then remove the wheels.
2 Remove the split pins from the nuts of the track rod ends and unscrew the nuts halfway.
3 Break the joints, using a balljoint separator, then remove the nuts and disconnect the joints.
4 Remove the bolt which clamps the steering shaft connector to the pinion shaft and then remove the bolts from the two steering rack mounting brackets (photo). Remove the brackets.
5 Rotate the steering rack 180°, so that the pinion shaft is downwards, and then remove the assembly through the opening on the left side (LHD) or right side (RHD) of the vehicle.
6 Installation is the reverse of removal. Fill the track rod boots with grease.

20 Steering rack and pinion assembly – dismantling, inspection and reassembly

1 Carefully clamp the gearbox in a soft-jawed vice.
2 Loosen the clamp bands on the gaiters, pull the gaiters back and bend back the tabs of the track rod lockwashers.
3 Using two spanners, unscrew the track rods and then remove them.
4 Remove the adjuster screw locknut and adjusting screw, then remove the wave washer, guide spring and rack guide (Fig. 11.19).
5 Remove the pinion boot, pinion dust seal and snap-ring, then pull the pinion out of the steering gearbox.
6 Slide the rack out of the steering gearbox.
7 Clean all parts thoroughly. Examine the pinion and rack for damage and wear. Measure the free length of the guide spring. If it is less than 1.04 in (26.3 mm), renew the spring.
8 Start installation by applying a light smear of grease to the rack end bushing. Insert the bushing until its projection locates in the round hole in the gearbox. It is important that the slots in the bushing are kept free from grease, otherwise their function as air passages will be impaired.
9 Slide the mount bushing on to the gearbox so that the end of the bushing is in line with the end of the gearbox.
10 Reassemble the gearbox in the reverse order to disassembly, using new stop washers and lockwashers on the track rod ends. Fill the pinion housing with grease.
11 Screw the track rods in while holding the lockwashers so that their tabs locate in the slots in the end of the rack. After tightening the track rods to the specified torque, bend up the lockwasher tabs. Install the boots and secure them with bands.

12 Adjust the rack guide after reinstalling the gearbox on the vehicle (Section 14).

21 Steering angles and front wheel alignment

1 Accurate front wheel alignment is essential for good steering and slow tyre wear. Before considering steering angles, check that the tyres are correctly inflated, that the wheels are not buckled, the hub bearings are not worn and that the steering linkage is in good order without slackness or wear in the joints.
2 Wheel alignment consists of four factors:
Camber, which is the angle at which the wheels are set from vertical when viewed from the front of the vehicle. The camber angle is regarded as positive when the wheels are tilted outwards at the top.
Castor, which is the angle between the steering axis and a vertical line when viewed from the side of the vehicle. The castor angle is regarded as positive when the steering axis is inclined rearward at the top.
Steering axis (kingpin) inclination, which is the angle, when viewed from the front of the vehicle between the vertical and an imaginary line drawn between the upper and lower suspension leg pivots.
Toe-in or toe out is the amount by which the wheels deviate from parallel lines drawn through the centre points of the wheel rims.
3 All angles except toe-out are set in production and are non-adjustable.
4 It is recommended that front wheel alignment is set by your Honda dealer who will have the necessary setting equipment. However, a reasonably accurate alternative can be carried out in the following way.
5 Place the vehicle on level ground with the wheels in the straight-ahead position.
6 Obtain or make a tracking gauge from metal tubing or angle having one fixed and one adjustable pointer which will contact the roadwheel outer rims at hub height.
7 Measure the distance between the rim edges at the front of the wheels, withdraw the gauge without altering its setting and push or pull the vehicle until the roadwheel has turned through 180°. Now use the gauge to measure the distance between the rim edges at the rear of the wheels. This dimension should be the same as the one previously taken at the front of the wheels (ie zero toe-out). A small difference is permitted – see Specifications
8 Where the toe-out is found to be incorrect, slacken the locknuts on each track rod and rotate each track rod an exactly equal amount. Turn each track rod clockwise (when viewed from the centre of the car) to reduce the toe-out or anti-clockwise to increase the toe-out.
9 Re-check the alignment using the gauge and then retighten the track rod end locknuts, making sure that the balljoints are in the centre of their arcs of travel and that the rack bellows are not twisted.

22 Rear wheel alignment

1 Adjustment of the rear wheel toe-in is provided on a cam plate on the trailing arms of the Hatchback and Sedan (Fig. 11.20).
2 It is recommended that adjustment is made only if adequate measuring equipment is available.
3 Ensure that the parking brake is released and then while preventing the adjusting bolt from rotating, loosen the locknut.
4 The required setting is achieved by turning the adjusting bolt. Each notch on the cam plate changes the toe-in by 0.630 in (16 mm), but these notches are for reference only and should not be used for adjustment, or for comparing the settings on the two sides of the vehicle.
5 Tighten the locknut after making the adjustment

23 Roadwheels and tyres – general

1 Whenever the roadwheels are removed it is a good idea to clean the insides of the wheels to remove accumulations of mud and in the case of the front one, disc pad dust.
2 Check the condition of the wheel for rust and repaint if necessary.

3 Examine the wheel stud holes. If these are tending to become elongated or the dished recesses in which the nuts seat have worn or become overcompressed, then the wheel will have to be renewed.
4 With a roadwheel removed, pick out any embedded flints from the tread and check for splits in the sidewalls or damage to the tyre carcass generally.
5 Where the depth of tread pattern is 1 mm or less, (or as laid down by local legislation), the tyre must be renewed.
6 Rotation of the roadwheels to even out wear may be a worthwhile idea if the wheels have been balanced off the car. Include the spare wheel in the rotational pattern. With radial tyres, it is recommended that the tyres are moved between front and rear on the same side and not from side to side of the vehicle.
7 If the wheels have been balanced on the car then they cannot be moved round the car as the balance of wheel, tyre and hub will be upset.
8 It is recommended that wheels are re-balanced halfway through the life of the tyres to compensate for the loss of tread rubber due to wear.
9 Finally, always keep the tyres (including the spare) inflated to the recommended pressures and always refit the dust caps on the tyre valves. Tyre pressures are best checked first thing in the morning when the tyres are cold.

24 Fault diagnosis – suspension and steering

Symptom	Reason(s)
Steering feels vague, car wanders and floats at speed	Tyre pressures uneven Shock absorbers worn Spring broken Steering gear balljoints badly worn Suspension geometry incorrect Steering mechanism free play excessive Front suspension and rear axle pick-up points out of alignment (Wagon)
Stiff and heavy steering	Tyre pressures too low Corroded swivel joints Corroded steering and suspension balljoints Front wheel toe-out incorrect Suspension geometry incorrect Steering gear incorrectly adjusted too tightly Steering column badly misaligned
Wheel wobble and vibration	Wheel nuts loose Wheels and tyres out of balance Steering balljoints badly worn Hub bearings badly worn Steering gear free play excessive Front springs weak or broken

11

Chapter 12 Bodywork and fittings

Contents

1 General description

The bodyshell and underframe is of welded all-steel unitary construction.

The front wings are attached with bolts and screws and can be removed and replaced economically in the event of damage due to a collision.

Two and four door Sedan body styles are available, also three and five door Hatchbacks and a wagon (Estate) but not all body versions are available in all territories. A heater is fitted as standard and a full air-conditioning system is available as an option where climate conditions warrant it.

2 Maintenance – bodywork and underframe

1 The general condition of a car's bodywork is the thing that significantly affects its value. Maintenance is easy but needs to be regular. Neglect, particularly after minor damage, can lead quickly to further deterioration and costly repair bills. It is important also to keep watch on those parts of the car not immediately visible, for instance the underside, inside all the wheel arches and the lower part of the engine compartment.

2 The basic maintenance routine for the bodywork is washing – preferably with a lot of water, from a hose. This will remove all the loose solids which may have stuck to the car. It is important to flush these off in such a way as to prevent grit from scratching the finish. The wheel arches and underframe need washing in the same way to remove any accumulated mud which will retain moisture and tend to encourage rust. Paradoxically enough, the best time to clean the underframe and wheel arches is in wet weather when the mud is thoroughly wet and soft. In very wet weather the underframe is usually cleaned of large accumulations automatically and this is a good time for inspection.

3 Periodically, it is a good idea to have the whole of the underframe of the car steam cleaned, engine compartment included, so that a thorough inspection can be carried out to see what minor repairs and renovations are necessary. Steam cleaning is available at many garages and is necessary for removal of the accumulation of oily grime which sometimes is allowed to become thick in certain areas. If steam cleaning facilities are not available, there are one or two excellent grease solvents available which can be brush applied. The dirt can then be simply hosed off.

4 After washing paintwork, wipe off with a chamois leather to give an unspotted clear finish. A coat of clear protective wax polish will give added protection against chemical pollutants in the air. If the paintwork sheen has dulled or oxidised, use a cleaner/polisher combination to restore the brilliance of the shine. This requires a little effort, but such dulling is usually caused because regular washing has been neglected. Always check that the door and ventilator opening drain holes and pipes are completely clear so that water can be drained out. Bright work should be treated in the same way as paintwork. Windscreens and windows can be kept clear of the smeary film which often appears, by adding a little ammonia to the water. If they are scratched, a good rub with a proprietary metal polish will often clear them. Never use any form of wax or other body or chromium polish on glass.

3 Maintenance – upholstery and carpets

1 Mats and carpets should be brushed or vacuum cleaned regularly to keep them free of grit. If they are badly stained remove them from the car for scrubbing or sponging and make quite sure they are dry before refitting. Seats and interior trim panels can be kept clean by a wipe over with a damp cloth. If they do become stained (which can be more apparent on light coloured upholstery) use a little liquid detergent and a soft nail brush to scour the grime out of the grain of the material. Do not forget to keep the head lining clean in the same way as the upholstery. When using liquid cleaners inside the car do not over-wet the surfaces being cleaned. Excessive damp could get into the seams and padded interior causing stains, offensive odours or even rot. If the inside of the car gets wet accidentally it is worthwhile taking some trouble to dry it out properly, particularly where carpets are involved. *Do not leave oil or electric heaters inside the car for this purpose.*

4 Minor body damage – repair

The photographic sequences on pages 246 and 247 illustrate the operations detailed in the following sub-sections.

Repair of minor scratches in the car's bodywork

If the scratch is very superficial, and does not penetrate to the metal of the bodywork, repair is very simple. Lightly rub the area of the scratch with a paintwork renovator, or a very fine cutting paste, to remove loose paint from the scratch and to clear the surrounding bodywork of wax polish. Rinse the area with clean water.

Chapter 12 Bodywork and fittings

Apply touch-up paint to the scratch using a thin paint brush; continue to apply thin layers of paint until the surface of the paint in the scratch is level with the surrounding paintwork. Allow the new paint at least two weeks to harden: then blend it into the surrounding paintwork by rubbing the paintwork, in the scratch area, with a paintwork renovator or a very fine cutting paste. Finally, apply wax polish.

Where the scratch has penetrated right through to the metal of the bodywork, causing the metal to rust, a different repair technique is required. Remove any loose rust from the bottom of the scratch with a penknife, then apply rust inhibiting paint to prevent the formation of rust in the future. Using a rubber or nylon applicator fill the scratch with bodystopper paste. If required, this paste can be mixed with cellulose thinners to provide a very thin paste which is ideal for filling narrow scratches. Before the stopper-paste in the scratch hardens, wrap a piece of smooth cotton rag around the top of a finger. Dip the finger in cellulose thinners and then quickly sweep it across the surface of the stopper-paste in the scratch; this will ensure that the surface of the stopper-paste is slightly hollowed. The scratch can now be painted over as described earlier in this Section.

Repair of dents in the car's bodywork

When deep denting of the car's bodywork has taken place, the first task is to pull the dent out, until the affected bodywork almost attains its original shape. There is little point in trying to restore the original shape completely, as the metal in the damaged area will have stretched on impact and cannot be reshaped fully to its original contour. It is better to bring the level of the dent up to a point which is about $\frac{1}{8}$ in (3 mm) below the level of the surrounding bodywork. In cases where the dent is very shallow anyway, it is not worth trying to pull it out at all. If the underside of the dent is accessible, it can be hammered out gently from behind, using a mallet with a wooden or plastic head. Whilst doing this, hold a suitable block of wood firmly against the outside of the panel to absorb the impact from the hammer blows and thus prevent a large area of the bodywork from being 'belled-out'.

Should the dent be in a section of the bodywork which has double skin or some other factor making it inaccessible from behind, a different technique is called for. Drill several small holes through the metal inside the area – particularly in the deeper section. Then screw long self-tapping screws into the holes just sufficiently for them to gain a good purchase in the metal. Now the dent can be pulled out by pulling on the protruding heads of the screws with a pair of pliers.

The next stage of the repair is the removal of the paint from the damaged area, and from an inch or so of the surrounding 'sound' bodywork. This is accomplished most easily by using a wire brush or abrasive pad on a power drill, although it can be done just as effectively by hand using sheets of abrasive paper. To complete the preparation for filling, score the surface of the bare metal with a screwdriver or the tang of a file, or alternatively, drill small holes in the affected area. This will provide a really good 'key' for the filler paste.

To complete the repair see the Section on filling and re-spraying.

Repair of rust holes or gashes in the car's bodywork

Remove all paint from the affected area and from an inch or so of the surrounding 'sound' bodywork, using an abrasive pad or a wire brush on a power drill. If these are not available a few sheets of abrasive paper will do the job just as effectively. With the paint removed you will be able to gauge the severity of the corrosion and therefore decide whether to renew the whole panel (if this is possible) or to repair the affected area. New body panels are not as expensive as most people think and it is often quicker and more satisfactory to fit a new panel than to attempt to repair large areas of corrosion.

Remove all fittings from the affected area except those which will act as a guide to the original shape of the damaged bodywork (eg headlamp shells etc). Then, using tin snips or a hacksaw blade, remove all loose metal and any other metal badly affected by corrosion. Hammer the edges of the hole inwards in order to create a slight depression for the filler paste.

Wire brush the affected area to remove the powdery rust from the surface of the remaining metal. Paint the affected area with rust inhibiting paint; if the back of the rusted area is accessible treat this also.

Before filling can take place it will be necessary to block the hole in some way. This can be achieved by the use of zinc gauze or aluminium tape.

Zinc gauze is probably the best material to use for a large hole. Cut a piece to the approximate size and shape of the hole to be filled, then position it in the hole so that its edges are below the level of the surrounding bodywork. It can be retained in position by several blobs of filler paste around its periphery.

Aluminium tape should be used for small or very narrow holes. Pull a piece off the roll and trim it to the approximate size and shape required, then pull off the backing paper (if used) and stick the tape over the hole; it can be overlapped if the thickness of one piece is insufficient. Burnish down the edges of the tape with the handle of a screwdriver or similar, to ensure that the tape is securely attached to the metal underneath.

Bodywork repairs – filling and re-spraying

Before using this Section, see the Sections on dent, deep scratch, rust holes and gash repairs.

Many types of bodyfiller are available, but generally speaking those proprietary kits which contain a tin of filler paste and a tube of resin hardener are best for this type of repair. A wide, flexible plastic or nylon applicator will be found invaluable for imparting a smooth and well contoured finish to the surface of the filler.

Mix up a little filler on a clean piece of card or board – measure the hardener carefully (follow the maker's instructions on the pack) otherwise the filler will set too rapidly or too slowly.

Using the applicator apply the filler paste to the prepared area; draw the applicator across the surface of the filler to achieve the correct contour and to level the filler surface. As soon as a contour that approximates the correct one is achieved, stop working the paste – if you carry on too long the paste will become sticky and begin to 'pick up' on the applicator. Continue to add thin layers of filler paste at twenty-minute intervals until the level of the filler is just proud of the surrounding bodywork.

Once the filler has hardened, excess can be removed using a metal plane or file. From then on, progressively finer grades of sandpaper should be used, starting with a 40 grade production paper and finishing with 400 grade wet-and-dry paper. Always wrap the abrasive paper around a flat rubber, cork, or wooden block – otherwise the surface of the filler will not be completely flat. During the smoothing of the filler surface the wet-and-dry paper should be periodically rinsed in water. This will ensure that a very smooth finish is imparted to the filler at the final stage.

At this stage the dent should be surrounded by a ring of bare metal, which in turn should be encircled by the finely 'feathered' edge of the good paintwork. Rinse the repair area with clean water, until all of the dust produced by the rubbing-down operation has gone.

Spray the whole repair area with a light coat of primer – this will show up any imperfections in the surface of the filler. Repair these imperfections with fresh filler paste or bodystopper, and once more smooth the surface with abrasive paper. If bodystopper is used, it can be mixed with cellulose thinners to form a really thin paste which is ideal for filling small holes. Repeat this spray and repair procedure until you are satisfied that the surface of the filler, and the feathered edge of the paintwork are perfect. Clean the repair area with clean water and allow to dry fully.

The repair area is now ready for final spraying. Paint spraying must be carried out in warm, dry, windless and dust free atmosphere. This condition can be created artificially if you have access to a large indoor working area, but if you are forced to work in the open, you will have to pick your day very carefully. If you are working indoors, dousing the floor in the work area with water will help to settle the dust which would otherwise be in the atmosphere. If the repair area is confined to one body panel, mask off the surrounding panels; this will help to minimise the effects of a slight mis-match in paint colours. Bodywork fittings (eg chrome strips, door handles etc) will also need to be masked off. Use genuine masking tape and several thicknesses of newspaper for the masking operations.

Before commencing to spray, agitate the aerosol can thoroughly, then spray a test area (an old tin, or similar) until the technique is mastered. Cover the repair area with a thick coat of primer; the thickness should be built up using several thin layers of paint rather than one thick one. Using 400 grade wet-and-dry paper, rub down the surface of the primer until it is really smooth. While doing this, the work area should be thoroughly doused with water, and the wet-and-dry paper periodically rinsed in water. Allow to dry before spraying on more paint.

Spray on the top coat, again building up the thickness by using several thin layers of paint. Start spraying in the centre of the repair area and then, using a circular motion, work outwards until the whole repair area and about 2 inches of the surrounding original paintwork is covered. Remove all masking material 10 to 15 minutes after spraying on the final coat of paint.

Allow the new paint at least two weeks to harden, then, using a paintwork renovator or a very fine cutting paste, blend the edges of the paint into the existing paintwork. Finally, apply wax polish.

5   Major body damage – repair

1   Because the body is built on the unitary principle, major damage must be repaired by a competent body repairer with the necessary jigs and equipment.
2   In the event of a crash that resulted in buckling of body panels, or damage to the roadwheels, the car must be taken to a Honda dealer or body repairer where the bodyshell and suspension alignment may be checked.
3   Bodyshell and/or suspension misalignment will cause excessive wear of the tyres, steering system and possibly transmission. The handling of the car also will be affected adversely.

6   Doors – tracing and silencing rattles

1   The most common cause of door rattles is a misaligned loose or worn striker, but other causes may be:

(a) Loose door handles, window winder handles and door hinges
(b) Loose, worn or misaligned door lock components
(c) Loose or worn remote control mechanism

2   It is quite possible for door rattles to be the result of a combination of these faults, so careful examination must be made to determine the cause of the noise.
3   If the leading edge from the striker loop is worn, and as a result the door rattles, renew it and adjust the position.
4   If the leading edge of the lock pawl is worn, and as a result the door rattles, fit a new door latch assembly.
5   Examine the hinge; it is quite possible that it has worn and caused rattles. Renew the hinge if necessary.

7   Radiator grille and bonnet – removal and installation

1   The bonnet hinges are bolted to the frame across the front of the

7.1 Bonnet hinge bolts

7.2a Removing a lower grille screw (Hatchback)

7.2b Removing an upper grille screw (Hatchback)

7.2c Removing a bumper apron screw

engine compartment (photo) and it is necessary to remove the grille to gain access to the hinge bolts.

2   Remove the headlight trims (4 screws) and the grille (3 screws on Saloon) (Fig. 12.1). On the Hatchback and Wagon, remove the 5 screws from the grille (photos) and 2 screws from the bumper apron (Fig. 12.2) (photo).

3   Undo and remove the hinge bolts (Fig. 12.3) and lift off the bonnet, preferably with the aid of an assistant.

4   The latch is secured to the engine compartment rear bulkhead by three screws. A cable assembly connects the release lever in the car. Grease should be smeared into the latch periodically.

5   Installation of the bonnet is the reverse of removal. Vertical movement of the hinges is provided for by slotted holes. Fore and aft adjustment is achieved by placing shims beneath the hinges.

6   The striker is welded to the bonnet. Adjustment of the latch engagement is achieved by slackening the latch screws and moving the latch.

8   Front wing – removal and installation

1   Remove the bonnet, as described in the preceding Section, together with the radiator grille.

2   Detach the mudflap from the rear of the wing.

3   Disconnect the leads from the side marker lamp.

4   Using a wire brush, clean away as much mud and underseal as possible from the threads of the upper securing bolts.

5   Clean the dirt from the heads of the bolts and self-tapping screws at the forward end of the wing.

6   Apply penetrating fluid to all the wing securing bolts and screws and then unscrew and remove them.

7   Cut round the seam of the wing to release the adhesion of the mastic and lift the wing from the body.

8   Clean away all old mastic and paint any rusty or corroded metal work with protective paint.

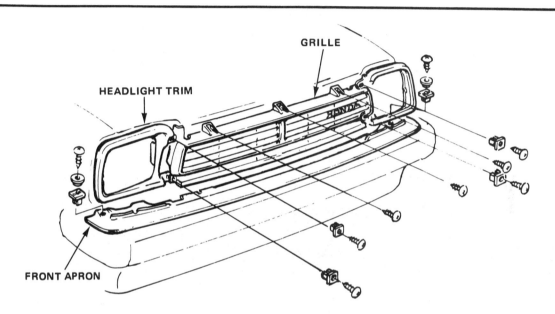

Fig. 12.1 Headlight trim and grille attachments (Saloon) (Sec 7)

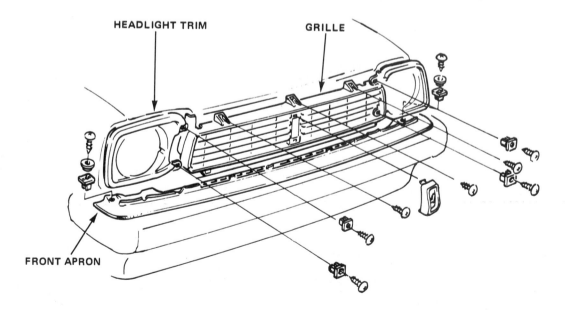

Fig. 12.2 Headlight trim and grille attachments (Hatchback and Wagon) (Sec 7)

12

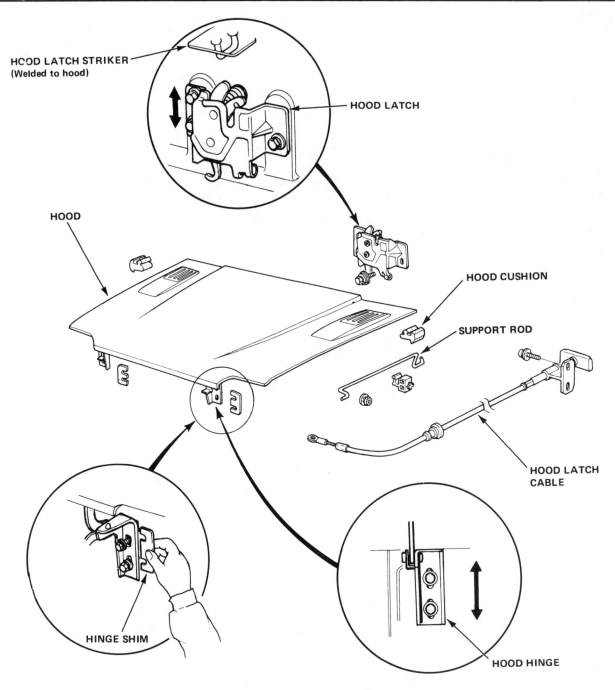

Fig. 12.3 Bonnet (hood) components (Sec 7)

9   The new wing will be supplied in primer.
10   Locate a thick bead of mastic on the mating flange of the body. Install the wing and insert and tighten the securing bolts and screws.
11   Refit the sealing strip, the radiator grille and the bonnet.
12   Reconnect the side marker lamp.
13   If required the motif can be unclipped from the side of the original wing and refitted to the new one.
14   Apply underseal coating to the underside of the wing and then refinish the outside to match the rest of the body paintwork.

9   Bumpers – removal and installation

1   The bumper may be of differing types depending upon whether the vehicle operates in territories where impact absorbing mountings are insisted upon.

2   With either type, removal and dismantling is simply a matter of unbolting the overriders and the bumper blades from their brackets or special reinforced truss (Figs. 12.4 and 12.5).

10   Boot lid – removal and installation

1   Open the lid, disconnect the number plate lights at their connectors and disconnect the switch wire.
2   Push the retainer sleeve of the latch cable out of its slot and disconnect the cable end from the latch.
3   Mark round the hinges with a soft pencil, then remove the hinge bolts and lift off the lid.
4   Installation is the reverse of removal. Equalise the gap between the body and the lid by adjusting the hinge positions. Use shims if necessary to make the boot lid flush with the wings.

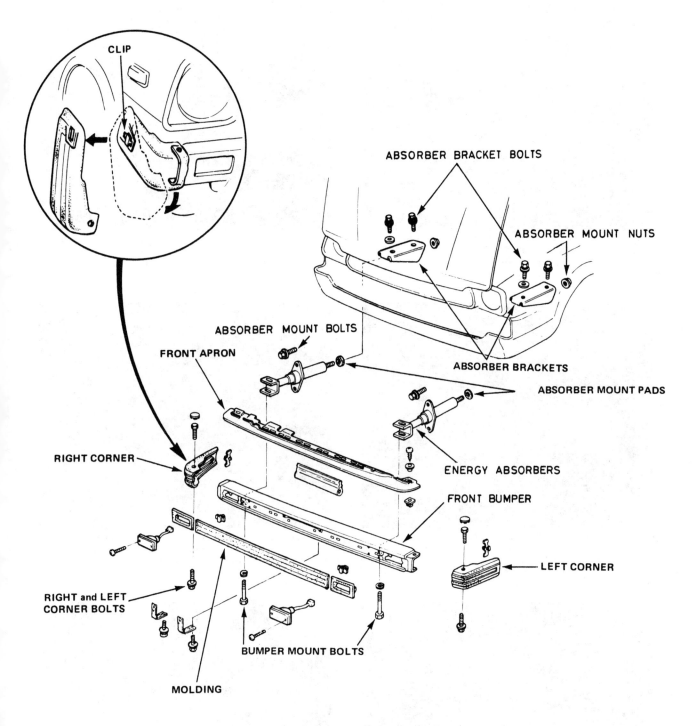

Fig. 12.4 Front bumper components (Sec 9)

5   After installation check the closure of the lid and if necessary adjust the latch by moving the striker.

---

11 Tailgate – removal and installation

1   Remove the screws and clips from the tailgate trim panel and remove the panel.
2   Remove the plastic shield, disconnect the wiring harness plugs and disconnect the washer hose from the nozzle.
3   Remove the tailgate cover, attach a piece of cord to the tailgate wiring harness and pull the harness out of the tailgate, leaving the cord in place to assist in threading the harness back through the tailgate.
4   Support the tailgate and remove the nut from both ends of the support strut.
5   Prise the headliner off the tailgate opening flange to give access to the hinge bolts and then with the help of an assistant remove the hinge bolts and lift away the tailgate.
6   Installation is the reverse of removal.
7   After installation, check the closure of the lid. If necessary, move the lock striker or place a packing shim under it to provide firm and smooth engagement of the latch.

12

This photo sequence illustrates the repair of a dent and damaged paintwork. The procedure for the repair of a hole is similar. Refer to the text for more complete instructions

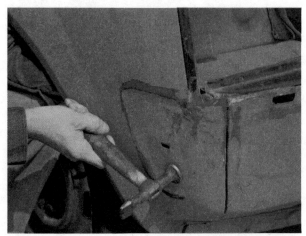

After removing any adjacent body trim, hammer the dent out. The damaged area should then be made slightly concave

Use coarse sandpaper or a sanding disc on a drill motor to remove all paint from the damaged area. Feather the sanded area into the edges of the surrounding paint, using progressively finer grades of sandpaper

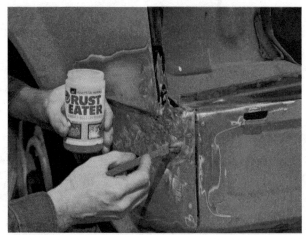

The damaged area should be treated with rust remover prior to application of the body filler. In the case of a rust hole, all rusted sheet metal should be cut away

Carefully follow manufacturer's instructions when mixing the body filler so as to have the longest possible working time during application. Rust holes should be covered with fiberglass screen held in place with dabs of body filler prior to repair

Apply the filler with a flexible applicator in thin layers at 20 minute intervals. Use an applicator such as a wood spatula for confined areas. The filler should protrude slightly above the surrounding area

Shape the filler with a surform-type plane. Then, use water and progressively finer grades of sandpaper and a sanding block to wet-sand the area until it is smooth. Feather the edges of the repair area into the surrounding paint.

Use spray or brush applied primer to cover the entire repair area so that slight imperfections in the surface will be filled in. Prime at least one inch into the area surrounding the repair. Be careful of over-spray when using spray-type primer

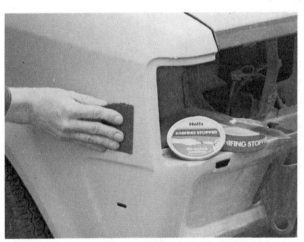

Wet-sand the primer with fine (approximately 400 grade) sandpaper until the area is smooth to the touch and blended into the surrounding paint. Use filler paste on minor imperfections

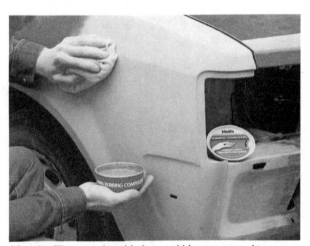

After the filler paste has dried, use rubbing compound to ensure that the surface of the primer is smooth. Prior to painting, the surface should be wiped down with a tack rag or lint-free cloth soaked in lacquer thinner

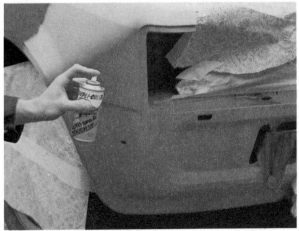

Choose a dry, warm, breeze-free area in which to paint and make sure that adjacent areas are protected from over-spray. Shake the spray paint can thoroughly and apply the top coat to the repair area, building it up by applying several coats, working from the center

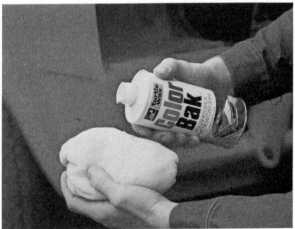

After allowing at least two weeks for the paint to harden, use fine rubbing compound to blend the area into the original paint. Wax can now be applied

248

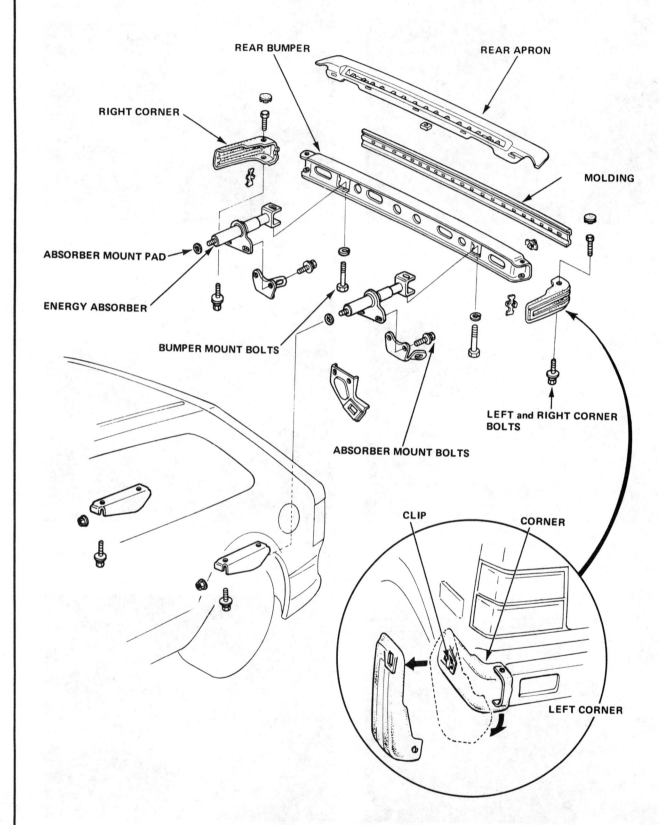

RIGHT CORNER

REAR BUMPER

REAR APRON

MOLDING

ABSORBER MOUNT PAD

ENERGY ABSORBER

BUMPER MOUNT BOLTS

ABSORBER MOUNT BOLTS

LEFT and RIGHT CORNER BOLTS

CLIP

CORNER

LEFT CORNER

Fig. 12.5 Rear bumper components (Sec 9)

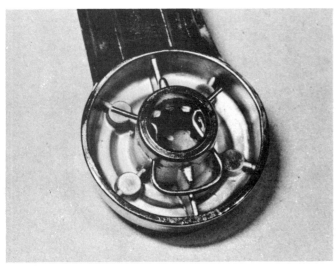

12.1 Window regulator handle and clip

12.2 Withdrawing the regulator handle

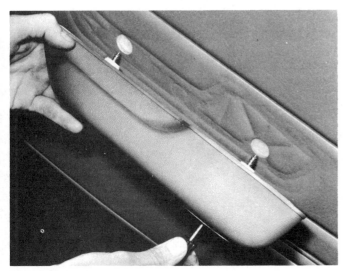

12.3 Removing the armrest

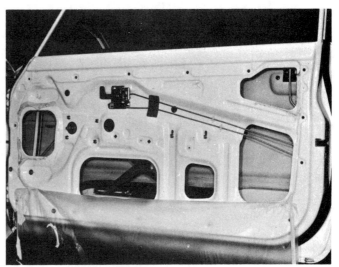

12.7 Door waterproof sheet peeled back

12 Door interior trim panel – removal and installation

1   Press the bezel which surrounds the window regulator handle inwards and extract the securing clip (photo) using a piece of hooked wire or a thin screwdriver.
2   Withdraw the window regulator handle from its splines (photo).
3   Remove the armrest (two screws) (photo).
4   Extract the single screw and withdraw the dished plate from behind the door remote control lever.
5   The door lock inner knob is removed by turning it in an anticlockwise direction.
6   Insert a flat blade at the bottom edge of the door and prise the trim panel from the door. Now insert the fingers and working round the edge of the door release all the panel clips and lift the panel away.
7   Carefully peel off the waterproof sheet from the door (photos).
8   Installation is a reversal of removal, but use new trim panel clips where required and install the regulator handle so that when the glass is fully raised, the handle points forwards and upwards at an angle of 45°.

13 Front door lock and glass – removal and installation

1   Remove the interior trim panel as described in the preceding Section.
2   Disconnect the latch and lock rods from the outside door handle (Fig. 12.6).
3   Remove the two nuts from the outside handle (photo) and remove the handle.
4   Remove the clip, lock arm and spring from the lock, then pull off the retainer and remove the lock (photo).
5   Remove the three door edge screws securing the door latch (photo). Remove the screws from the inside handle (photo) and remove the complete latch assembly, unsnapping the control rods if necessary.
6   Temporarily install the regulator handle and lower the window until the two window fixing bolts are accessible (photo). Remove the bolts and then remove the glass by tilting the front edge down and lifting the glass out through the window opening (Fig. 12.7).
7   Installation is the reverse of removal. Grease the sliding surfaces

12

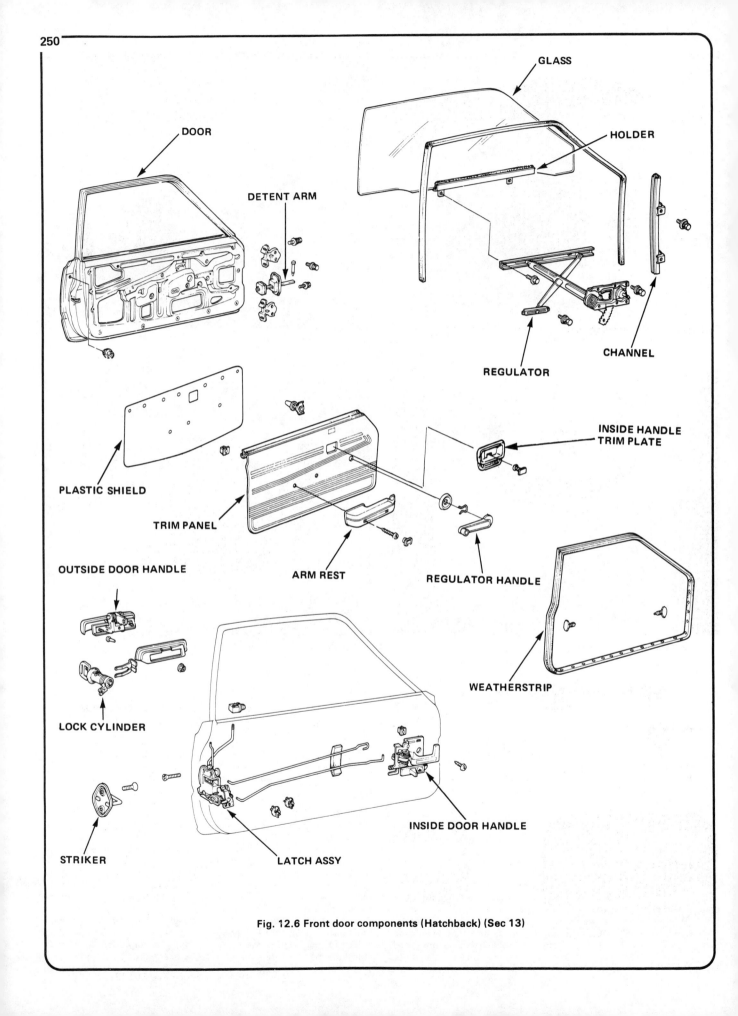

DOOR

DETENT ARM

GLASS

HOLDER

CHANNEL

REGULATOR

PLASTIC SHIELD

TRIM PANEL

INSIDE HANDLE
TRIM PLATE

OUTSIDE DOOR HANDLE

ARM REST

REGULATOR HANDLE

LOCK CYLINDER

WEATHERSTRIP

STRIKER

LATCH ASSY

INSIDE DOOR HANDLE

Fig. 12.6 Front door components (Hatchback) (Sec 13)

13.3 Outside door handle showing latch rod and fixing nuts

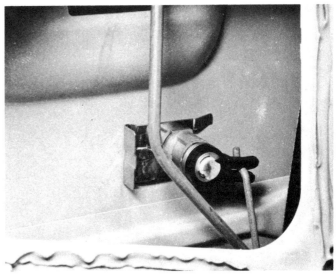

13.4 Lock assembly and retainer

13.5a Door latch screws

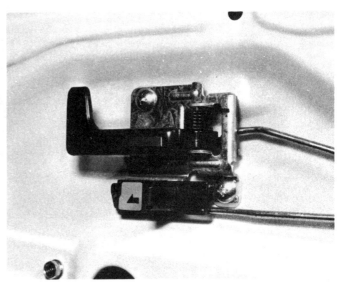

13.5b Inside handle screws

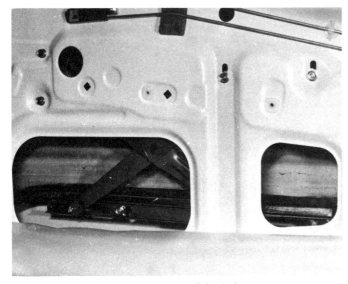

13.6 Window lowered to give access to fixing bolts

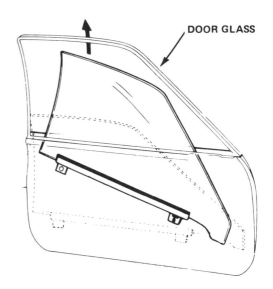

DOOR GLASS

Fig. 12.7 Door glass removal (Sec 13)

12

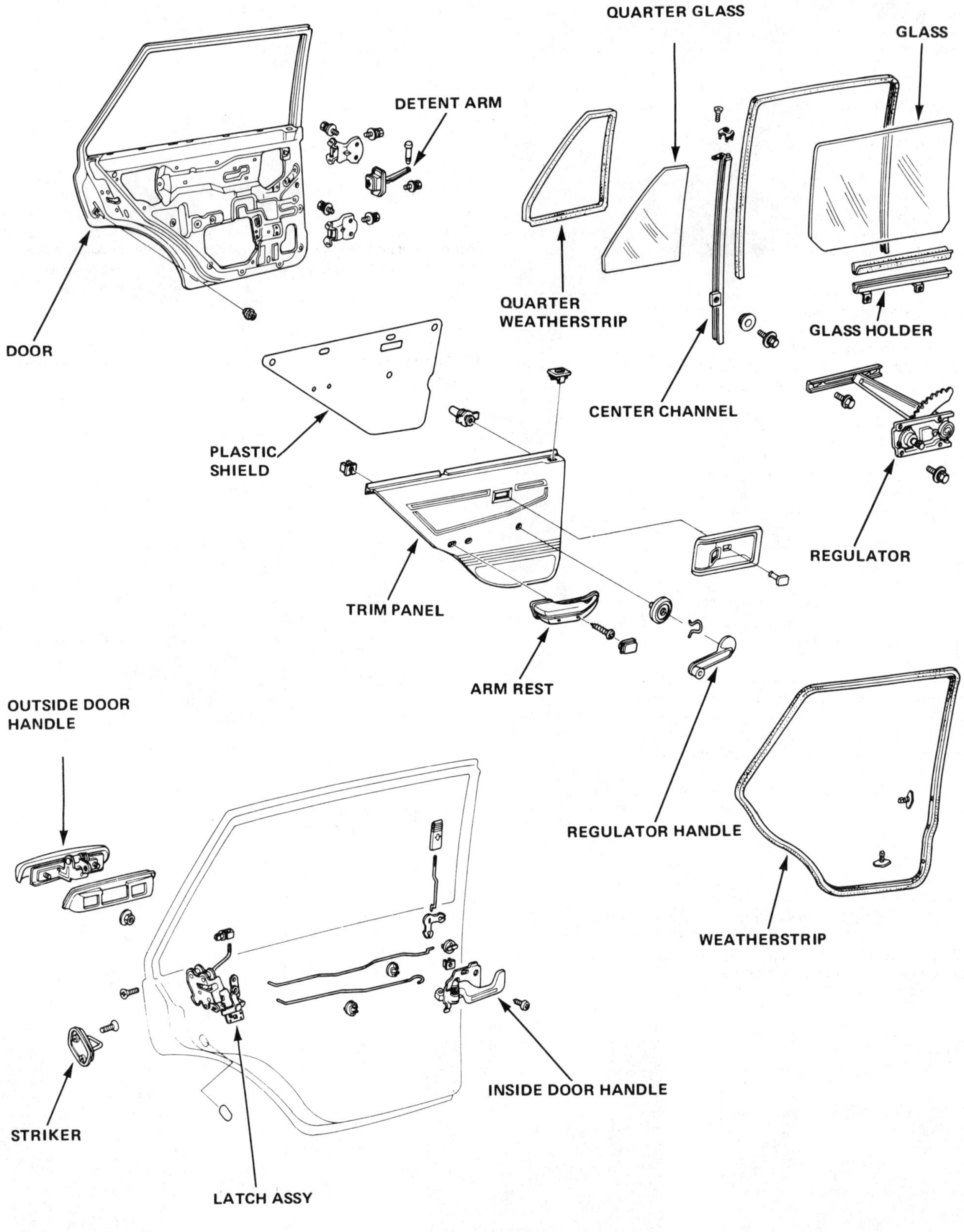

QUARTER GLASS

GLASS

DETENT ARM

QUARTER
WEATHERSTRIP

CENTER CHANNEL

GLASS HOLDER

DOOR

PLASTIC
SHIELD

REGULATOR

TRIM PANEL

ARM REST

OUTSIDE DOOR
HANDLE

REGULATOR HANDLE

WEATHERSTRIP

STRIKER

INSIDE DOOR HANDLE

LATCH ASSY

Fig. 12.8 Rear door components (Wagon) (Sec 14)

of the window regulator and before finally tightening the window glass securing bolts, check that the window can be moved up and down freely and smoothly.

8   Install the regulator handle so that it points forward and upwards at 45° when the window is closed.

14 Rear door lock and glass – removal and installation

1   The removal is similar to that of the front door described previously (Fig. 12.8).

2   When removing the door inside handle it is necessary to unsnap the control rods from their guides (photo).

3   Before removing the window glass, remove the quarter glass after removing the two centre channel screws from the top edge of the door and the bolt from the bottom end of the channel.

15 Doors – removal, installation and adjustment

1   The door hinge plates are bolted to the body pillars.

2   To remove a door, open it wide and support it on a jack placed under its bottom edge. Use a rag or a piece of rubber to protect the door edge.

3   Mark the position of the hinge plates on the body pillars to facilitate refitting. Drive out the pin of the door check (photo).

4   Unscrew and remove the bolts from the body pillars and lift the door from the body. Retain any shims which may be located under the hinge plates.

5   Refitting is a reversal of removal.

6   Any adjustment required to set the door evenly within the door frame can be carried out by releasing the hinge bolts. If the door is not flush with the adjacent body panels, loosen the hinge plate bolts on the door itself and move the door as necessary.

7   Smooth and positive closure of the door can be arranged by releasing the screws on the lock striker (photo) and moving it in whichever direction is required.

16 Windscreen glass – removal and installation

1   The windscreens are held in rubber mouldings which are 'locked' by the trim moulding in the outer side of the rubber surround.

2   Removal of the windscreen proceeds as follows; begin by carefully extracting the bright trim moulding from the windscreen seal. The ends of the trim can be exposed by moving the moulding joint covers to one side.

3   Once the trim has been removed, enlist the help of at least one person, then with one person inside the car and one outside, very carefully push the windscreen outwards from its aperture beginning at either top corner of the screen.

4   The rubber moulding around the screen should deform to allow the screen to move outwards once the trim has been removed.

5   Check that the rubber moulding is in good condition, and that no cracks or surface deterioration can be found.

6   Fit the rubber moulding around the screen, and then insert a

length of string or cord into the major slot on the periphery of the seal. Pass it totally around the seal, and let it emerge with about 5 inches (127 mm) of overlap and 8 inches (203 mm) hanging near one of the bottom corners.

7   Position the glass and seal into the window aperture from the outside with the string hanging into the car interior. Again enlist the help of at least one person and press the screen into the aperture.

8   Press the screen at the point where the strings emerge from the rubber moulding, then pull the strings to bring the lip of the moulding around the edge of the window aperture. Continue to apply pressure to the screen near to the moving parts of the string which are being pulled slowly and smoothly from the seal.

9   Once the strong has been pulled out of the seal, check that the seal is properly fitted on both sides of the window aperture.

10   Now that the rubber seal and screen glass are in place, 'lock' the seal by pressing the bright trim moulding into the outside of the seal. Lubricate the seal with soap solution to ease the insertion of the trim. A special tool, which can be improvised, is necessary to lift the seal rubber lips over each side of the bright trim.

17 Centre console (automatic transmission) – removal and installation

1   Remove the speed selector knob.

2   Remove the two securing screws from the sides of the console and lift it away (Fig. 12.9).

3   Installation is the reverse of removal.

4   Reference should also be made to Chapter 7, for further details of the speed selector lever.

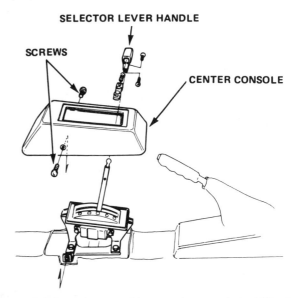

Fig. 12.9 Console removal (automatic transmission) (Sec 17)

14.2 Door latch control rods and guides

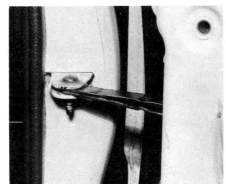

15.3 Door check and pin

15.7 Door striker screws

12

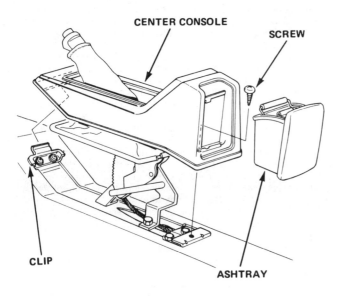

Fig. 12.10 Console removal (manual transmission) (Sec 18)

18 Centre console (manual transmission) – removal and installation

1   Remove the ashtray and then remove the two screws beneath it (Fig. 12.10).
2   Push the console forward to disengage it from its clip and then lift it clear.
3   Installation is the reverse of removal.

19 Instrument panel – removal and installation

Hatchback and Wagon
1   Remove the steering wheel as described in Chapter 11. Disconnect the battery earth lead.
2   Remove the bulb access panel (photo), then remove the two screws thus made visible (Fig. 12.11) (photo).
3   Remove the two lower mounting screws (photo) and pull the panel forward (photo) to give access to its rear.
4   Disconnect the speedometer cable (photo) and the tachometer cable (if applicable).
5   Disconnect the wiring connectors and remove the instrument panel.

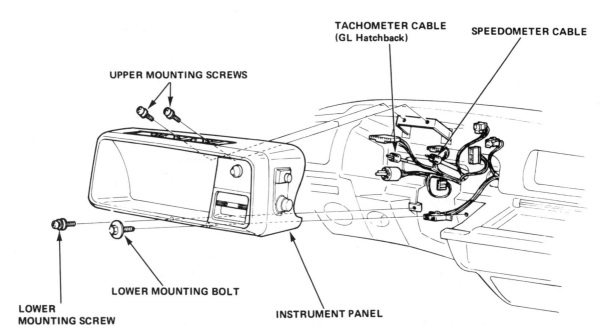

Fig. 12.11 Instrument panel removal (Hatchback and Wagon) (Sec 19)

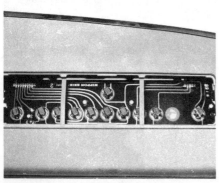

19.2a Bulb access panel removed

19.2b Removing an instrument panel upper screw

19.3a Removing an instrument panel lower screw

19.3b Pulling the instrument panel forward

19.4 Disconnecting the speedometer cable

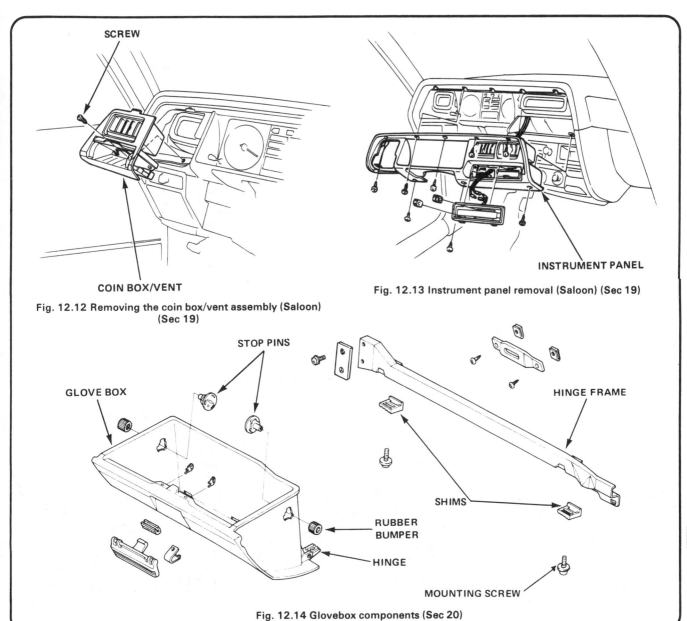

SCREW

COIN BOX/VENT

Fig. 12.12 Removing the coin box/vent assembly (Saloon) (Sec 19)

INSTRUMENT PANEL

Fig. 12.13 Instrument panel removal (Saloon) (Sec 19)

STOP PINS

GLOVE BOX

HINGE FRAME

SHIMS

RUBBER BUMPER

HINGE

MOUNTING SCREW

Fig. 12.14 Glovebox components (Sec 20)

12

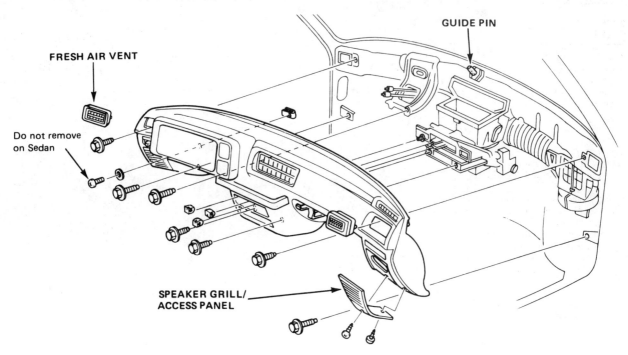

Fig. 12.15 Dashboard removal (Sec 21)

LOWER MOUNT NUT

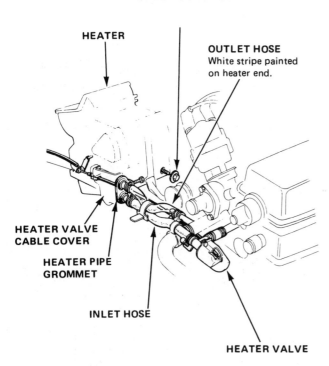

Fig. 12.16 Heater pipe connections (Sec 22)

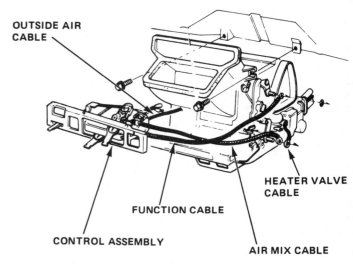

Fig. 12.17 Heater control cables (Sec 22)

11 To remove the gauge assembly, remove the four gauge mounting screws, disconnect the speedometer and tachometer cables (as applicable). Disconnect the wiring harness and remove the instrument panel.

All models
12 Installation is the reverse of removal. When installing the instrument panel, take care that the speedometer and tachometer cables are not kinked or strained.

20 Glovebox – removal and installation

1   Remove the two hinge mounting screws.
2   Turn the stop pins 90° amd remove them, then lift the glovebox out (Fig. 12.14).
3   Installation is the reverse of removal. To make the glovebox fit flush with the dash and latch properly, move each pair of hinge shims closer together, or further apart.

Sedan
6   Remove the cover and the two nuts from the upper bracket of the steering column. Disconnect the battery earth lead.
7   Remove the screw from the coin box/vent assembly (Fig. 12.12).
8   Pull the knob off the control levers. Insert a screwdriver into the slot at one end of the heater control panel and pull the panel out.
9   Remove the three screws from the control bracket mounting.
10   Remove the eight screws from the instrument panel and remove the panel (Fig. 12.13).

21 Dashboard – removal and installation

1   Remove the bolts from the lower bracket of the steering column, then remove the cover and nuts from the upper bracket and lower the column to the floor.
2   Disconnect the battery earth lead. Remove the nuts and bolts from the fuse box and turn the fuse box over and disconnect the wiring harnesses.
3   Remove the heater control panel and the heater control bracket mounting screws.
4   Remove the instrument panel from the Hatchback and Wagon, and the panel and gauge assembly from the Sedan (Section 19).
5   Pull out the ashtray and the right and left fresh air vents (Fig. 12.15).
6   Remove the right speaker grille/access panel.
7   Remove seven bolts, and on the Hatchback and Wagon an additional screw.
8   While holding the underneath of the dashboard, lift it up to free it from the guide pin and then pull it out.
9   Installation is the reverse of removal, but note the following points.
10 Make sure that the dashboard is properly installed on the guide pin.
11 Take care not to bend the heater lever and check that it moves freely before and after tightening the dashboard bolts.
12 Check to see that none of the instrument panel wiring harnesses are pinched.

22 Heater – removal and installation

1   Drain the coolant from the radiator, remove the dashboard and disconnect both heater hoses at the bulkhead. Have ready a drip tray before disconnecting the hoses, because some coolant will run out.
2   Remove the lower mounting nut of the heater on the bulkhead (Fig. 12.16).
3   Prise out the two clips and remove the heater duct. On vehicles with an air conditioner, remove the evaporator duct band.
4   Disconnect the heater control cables (Fig. 12.17), remove the heater valve cable cover and then remove the heater.
5   Installation is the reverse of removal. Take care that the heater inlet and outlet hoses are not transposed, and make sure that the hose clamps are tightened.
6   After installation, fill and bleed the cooling system and ensure that all cables are correctly installed and adjusted.

23 Heater control cables – installation and adjustment

Air mix cable
1   Set the temperature control lever to COLD.
2   Close the air mix door above the heater core by pulling the door arm up and then connect the end of the cable to the arm (Fig. 12.18).
3   Slide the cable housing back so that all slack is taken up, but do not slide it back enough to make the dashboard lever move. Snap the cable housing into its clamp.
4   While working through the heater duct opening in the right side of the heater, move the temperature lever to HOT and check that the air mix door opens fully upwards. Slide the lever to COLD to ensure that the door goes fully down and closes.

Heater function cable
5   Move the function lever to HEAT and move the heater control arm to the HEAT position in the door link slot.
6   Connect the cable eye to the control arm (Fig. 12.19) and with the cable housing pushed back to take up any slack, snap the housing into its clamp.
7   While looking through the heater floor outlet, move the function lever to DEFROST and check that the hot air door below the heater core closes.

Outside air cable
8   Move the function lever to OFF on vehicles without air conditioning, and to MAX on vehicles with it.
9   Push forward the arm of the outside air door, so that the door closes.

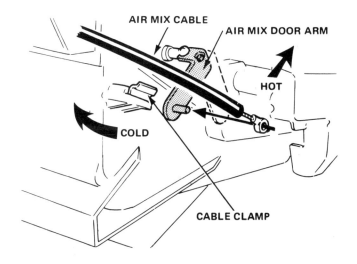

Fig. 12.18 Air mix cable installation (Sec 23)

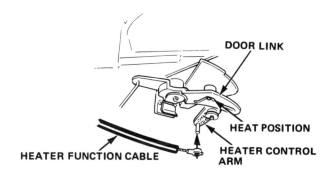

Fig. 12.19 Heater function cable installation (Sec 23)

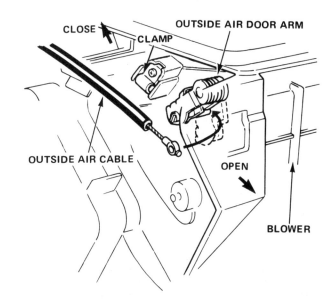

Fig. 12.20 Outside air door cable installation (Sec 23)

12

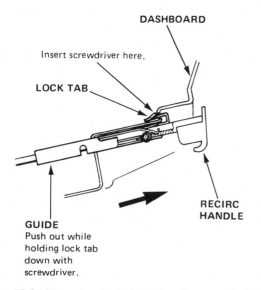

DASHBOARD

Insert screwdriver here.

LOCK TAB

RECIRC HANDLE

GUIDE
Push out while holding lock tab down with screwdriver.

Fig. 12.21 Removing the RECIRC handle assembly (Sec 23)

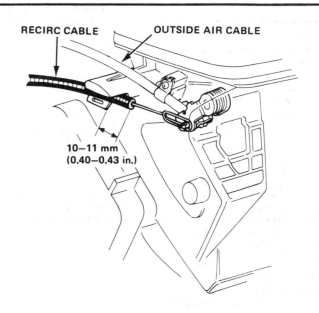

RECIRC CABLE

OUTSIDE AIR CABLE

10—11 mm
(0.40—0.43 in.)

Fig. 12.22 RECIRC cable installation (Sec 23)

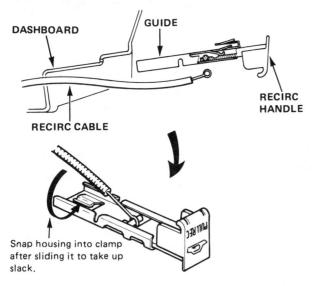

DASHBOARD

GUIDE

RECIRC HANDLE

RECIRC CABLE

Snap housing into clamp after sliding it to take up slack.

Fig. 12.23 Connecting the RECIRC cable to the handle (Sec 23)

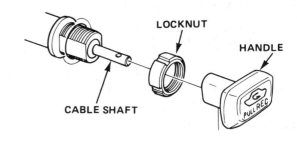

LOCKNUT

HANDLE

CABLE SHAFT

Fig. 12.24 RECIRC handle (Saloon) (Sec 23)

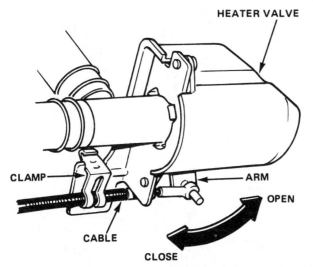

HEATER VALVE

CLAMP

ARM

OPEN

CABLE

CLOSE

Fig. 12.25 Heater valve cable installation (Sec 23)

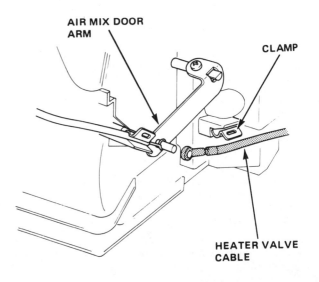

AIR MIX DOOR ARM

CLAMP

HEATER VALVE CABLE

Fig. 12.26 Heater valve cable to air mix door arm installation (Sec 23)

10 Connect the cable eye to the door arm (Fig. 12.20) and with the cable housing pushed back to take up any slack, snap the housing into its clamp.

Recirculation cable
Hatchback and Wagon
11 To remove the RECIRC handle/guide assembly, push a small screwdriver between the dashboard and the locktab on the top of the guide, and push the assembly out from behind the dash (Fig. 12.21).
12 To install and adjust the cable, disconnect the cable from the handle and connect the cable eye to the opposite side of the outside air door arm to that to which the outside air cable is connected.
13 Hold the arm in the position to close the door fully and snap the cable housing into the clamp so that 0.40 to 0.43 in (10 to 11 mm) of cable housing projects beyond the housing (Fig. 12.22).
14 Move the function lever to OFF on vehicles without air conditioning, and to MAX on vehicles with it. Pull the RECIRC handle out to its detent and connect the cable end to the peg on the end of the handle (Fig. 12.23).
15 While holding the handle in its detent position, push the cable housing back just enough to take up the slack and then snap the housing into its clamp.
16 Push the handle assembly back into the dashboard until the locktab snaps into place.
17 While looking through the access hole in the lower right-hand corner of the dashboard, pull the RECIRC handle out to its detent and check that the outside air door closes fully. Push the handle in to its limit and check that the door opens fully.
Sedan
18 To remove the RECIRC cable, move the function lever to OFF on vehicles without air conditioning, and to MAX on vehicles with it. Disconnect the cable from its clamp and from the arm on the outside air door.
19 At the dashboard end, remove the screw from the RECIRC handle, remove the handle, unscrew the locknut and pull the cable from behind the dashboard (Fig. 12.24).
20 To install and adjust the cable, first install the dashboard end of the cable and the handle.

21 Push the handle in fully and move the function lever to OFF on vehicles without air conditioning and to MAX on vehicles with it.
22 Connect the slotted end of the cable to the arm of the outside air door. Pull the handle out to the detent. Push the cable housing back from the slotted end of the cable to take up the slack and snap the housing into the clamp.

Heater valve cable
23 Close the heater valve fully, connect the eye of the cable to the valve arm and secure the cable housing in the clamps (Fig. 12.25) making sure that there is a small clearance between the cable eye and the end of the cable housing.
24 Move the temperature control lever to COLD and connect the other end of the cable to the arm on the air mix door (Fig. 12.26), ensuring that the air mix door is closed.
25 With the temperature control lever at COLD, the heater valve closed and the air mix door closed, slide the cable housing back enough to take up the slack, but not enough to cause the temperature control lever to move, then snap the cable housing into its clamp.

24 Air conditioning system – general

1 A full air conditioning system can be optionally specified on vehicles supplied to certain territories.
2 It is emphasised that due to the nature of the toxic gases in the system, no part of the system should ever be disconnected unless it has first been discharged by a professional refrigeration engineer or a Honda dealer who has the necessary equipment.
3 The main components of the system comprise a belt-driven compressor, a condenser and the cooler unit.
4 The home mechanic should limit his operations to adjustment of the drivebelt which is carried out by moving the compressor on its mounting until a total deflection of $\frac{1}{2}$ in (12.7 mm) is obtained at the centre point of the longest run of the belt.
5 On installation after discharging, the system must be re-charged by a refrigeration engineer or your Honda dealer.

12

Chapter 13   Supplement: Revisions and information on 1982 and 1983 US models

Contents

1   Introduction

This supplement contains specifications and changes that apply to Honda Civics produced for the 1982 and 1983 model years. Also included is information related to previous models that was not available at the time of original publication of this manual.

Where no differences (or very minor differences) exist between 1982-1983 models and 1981 models, no information is given. In these instances, the original material included in Chapters 1 through 12 should be used.

2   General dimensions, weights and capacities

Dimensions

Overall length	
Hatchback	148.4 in (3770 mm)
Wagon and Sedan	161.4 in (4100 mm)
Overall height (Hatchback)	53.2 in (1350 mm)
Ground clearance (all)	6.5 in (165 mm)
Curb weights	
1300 Hatchback	
1982	
4-speed	1761 lb (799 kg)
5-speed	1795 lb (814 kg)
1983	
4-speed	1773 lb (804 kg)
5-speed	1803 lb (818 kg)
1500 Hatchback	
1982	
5-speed	1854 lb (841 kg)
GL	1865 lb (846 kg)
Automatic	1878 lb (852 kg)
1983	
5-speed	1867 lb (847 kg)
S model	1898 lb (861 kg)
Automatic	1889 lb (857 kg)

Wagon
  1982
    5-speed . . . . 2002 lb (908 kg)
    Automatic . . . . 2094 lb (950 kg)
  1983
    5-speed . . . . 2033 lb (922 kg)
    Automatic . . . . 2055 lb (932 kg)
Sedan
  1982
    5-speed . . . . 1967 lb (892 kg)
    Automatic . . . . 2050 lb (930 kg)
  1983
    5-speed . . . . 1973 lb (895 kg)
    Automatic . . . . 1995 lb (905 kg)

Capacities
Engine oil (with filter change) . . . . 3.7 US qt (3.5 litres)
Fuel tank (Sedan) . . . . 12.2 US gal (46 litres)
Cooling system
  Initial fill
    1300 Hatchback . . . . 1.2 US gal (4.6 litres)
    1500 Hatchback, Sedan and Wagon . . . . 1.4 US gal (5.4 litres)
  Drain and refill
    1300 Hatchback . . . . 1.0 US gal (3.8 litres)
    1500 Hatchback, Sedan and Wagon . . . . 1.2 US gal (4.6 litres)

---

3 Specifications

Note: *The specifications listed here contain only those items which differ from those listed in Chapters 1 through 12 pertaining to 1981 model vehicles. For information not specifically listed here, refer to the appropriate Chapter.*

Engine — general
Compression ratio 9.3:1
Compression pressure (300 rpm, throttle wide open)
  Nominal . . . . 192 lbf/in² (13.5 kgf/cm²)
  Minimum . . . . 164 lbf/in² (11.6 kgf/cm²)
Cylinder head warpage service limit . . . . 0.008 in (0.20 mm)
Cylinder bore taper service limit . . . . 0.010 in (0.25 mm)
Piston-to-ring clearance (compression rings)
  Standard (new)
    Top ring . . . . 0.0012 to 0.0024 in (0.03 to 0.06 mm)
    2nd ring . . . . 0.0012 to 0.0020 in (0.03 to 0.05 mm)
  Service limit . . . . 0.006 in (0.14 mm)
Standard piston pin diameter (new)
  1300 . . . . 0.6678 to 0.6693 in (16.961 to 16.978 mm)
  1500 . . . . 0.668 to 0.669 in (16.96 to 16.98 mm)
Standard pin-to-rod interference (new) (1300 only) . . . . 0.0006 to 0.0015 in (0.016 to 0.039 mm)
Crankshaft main journal diameter
  1300 . . . . 1.9676 to 1.9685 in (49.976 to 50.000 mm)
  1500 . . . . 1.9687 to 1.9697 in (50.006 to 50.030 mm)
Auxiliary valve stem diameter
  Standard (new) . . . . 0.2587 to 0.2593 in (6.572 to 6.587 mm)
  Service limit . . . . 0.258 in (6.55 mm)
Standard valve seat width (new) . . . . 0.049 to 0.061 in (1.25 to 1.55 mm)
Auxiliary inlet valve guide diameter
  Standard (new) . . . . 0.260 to 0.261 in (6.61 to 6.63 mm)
  Service limit . . . . 0.262 in (6.65 mm)

Torque specifications	lbf ft	Nm
Driveplate mounting bolts	36	50
Flywheel mounting bolts	50	70
Oil pump mounting bolts	7	10
Oil pump gear cover bolts	7	10
Oil sump nuts and bolts	7	10

Cooling system
Torque specifications	lbf ft	Nm
Temperature gauge sender unit	20	28
Water pump pulley bolts	7	10
Water pump mounting bolts	7	10

Fuel, exhaust and emission control systems
Idle speed
  1982
    Manual transmission models . . . . 700 ± 50 rpm in Neutral

13

Fuel, exhaust and emission control systems (continued)
Idle speed (continued)
    Automatic transmission models .... 700 ± 50 rpm in gear
  1983
    1300 4-speed and all 1500 with manual transmission ...... 700 ± 50 rpm in Neutral
    1300 5-speed .... 650 ± 50 rpm in Neutral
    All models with automatic transmission .... 700 ± 50 rpm in gear
Fast idle speed (all) .... 3000 rpm

Ignition system
Ignition timing
  1982
    1300 engine .... 20 ±2° BTDC (red mark) at 700 ± 50 rpm in Neutral
    1500 engine with manual transmission .... 18° ±2° BTDC (red mark) at 700 ± 50 rpm in Neutral
    1500 engine with automatic transmission .... 18° ±2° BTDC (red mark) at 700 ± 50 rpm in gear
  1983
    1300 engine with 4-speed transmission .... 20° ±2° BTDC (red mark) at 700 ± 50 rpm in Neutral
    1300 engine with 5-speed transmission .... 18° ± 2° BTDC (red mark) at 650 ± 50 rpm in Neutral
    1500 engine with manual transmission .... 18° ±2° BTDC (red mark) at 700 ± 50 rpm in Neutral
    1500 engine with automatic transmission .... 18° ±2° BTDC (red mark) at 700 ± 50 rpm in gear
Spark plug type .... NGK BR6EB-11 or ND W20ESR-11

Clutch
Free movement at pedal .... 29/32 to 1-7/64 in (23 to 28 mm)
Free movement at release arm .... 3/16 to 7/32 in (4.4 to 5.4 mm)

Manual transmission

Torque specifications	lbf ft	Nm
Mainshaft locknut (4-speed)	43	60

Final drive and driveshafts

Torque specifications	lbf ft	Nm
Crownwheel bolts (left-hand thread)	74	103
10 mm transmission-to-torque converter housing bolts	28	39

Braking system
Minimum brake disc thickness after regrinding
  1982
    1300 Hatchback .... 0.35 in (9 mm)
    All others .... 0.39 in (10 mm)
  1983
    1300 Hatchback
      4-speed .... 0.35 in (9 mm)
      5-speed .... 0.39 in (10 mm)
    All others .... 0.60 in (15 mm)

Torque specifications	lbf ft	Nm
Guide pin bolts		
1982 Sedan	36	50
All others	20	27
Pipe and hose unions		
Rear wheel cylinder	11	15
Flexible hose-to-rigid pipe	11	15
Proportional valve	11	15

Electrical system
Bulbs (typical)
  Headlights 65/55W
  Speedometer/gauge lights 3.4W/1.4W
  Front turn signal/position lights 32CP/3CP
  Side marker lights 2CP
  Warning indicator lights 1.4W
  Interior lights 5W
  Rear turn signal lights 32CP
  Brake/taillights 32CP/3CP
  Turn signal indicator lights 1.4W
  Tailgate light 3.4W
  Back-up lights 32CP
  License plate lights 4CP
  Heater panel lights 1.4W

Suspension and steering
Front wheel alignment
  Caster
    Hatchback and Sedan .... 2° 03' ±1°
    Wagon .... 1° 18' ± 1°

Toe-out (1983 models only)
    Hatchback and Sedan . . . .   0 ± 5/64 in (2 mm)
    Wagon . . . .   0 ± 1/8 in (3 mm)
Rear wheel camber (Hatchback and Sedan) . . . .   -0° 15'
Wheels . . . .   12 in or 13 in, depending on application
Tires
  1982
    1300 Hatchback
      4-speed 600 S12-4PR
      5-speed 155 SR13
    1500 Hatchback, Wagon and Sedan 155 SR13
  1983
    1300 Hatchback
      4-speed 155 SR12
      5-speed P165/70 R13
    1500 Hatchback (except GL-S), Wagon and Sedan 155 SR13
    GL-S 165/70 SR13
Tire pressure

	PSI	kPa
1982		
1300 Hatchback		
4-speed	24	165
5-speed	32	220
1500 Hatchback, Wagon, and Sedan	26	180
Compact spare	60	415
1983		
1300 Hatchback		
4-speed	26	180
5-speed	35	260
1500 Hatchback, Wagon and Sedan	26	180
Compact spare	60	415

Torque specifications

	lbf ft	Nm
Front suspension		
Axleshaft nut (must be replaced with new nut after removal)	134	185
Stabilizer bar bracket bolts	37	51
Track control arm pivot bolt	40	55
Rear suspension		
Strut piston self-locking nut	33	45
Strut upper mounting nuts	16	24
Steering		
Steering wheel nut	36	50
Upper bracket cover bolts	7	10

4 Routine maintenance intervals

Note: *The following maintenance intervals are recommended by the manufacturer. In the interest of vehicle longevity, we recommend shorter intervals between certain operations such as fluid and filter replacements.*

Every 250 miles (400 km) or weekly
  Check the engine oil level
  Check the automatic transmission fluid level
  Check the engine coolant level
  Check the battery electrolyte level
  Check the brake fluid level
  Check the tire pressure (including the spare)
  Check lights for bulb failure
  Check the windshield washer reservoir

Every 7500 miles (12000 km)
  Change the engine oil and oil filter
  Check the handbrake operation
  Check the manual transmission oil level
  Check the clutch free play
  Check the exhaust system for leaks and loose fasteners
  Check the tightness of the engine and transmission mounting bolts
  Inspect the spark plugs and clean and reset the gaps
  Check the play in the steering rack and steering balljoints
  Check the condition of the front brake pads and caliper

Every 15000 miles (24000 km)
In addition to, or instead of, the work specified for the 7500 mile service
  Clean all dirt and debris from the radiator core
  Check the front and rear wheel alignment
  Change the automatic transmission fluid
  Check the valve clearances

Every 30000 miles (48000 km)
In addition to or instead of, the work specified for the 15000 mile service
  Check the alternator drivebelt tension and condition
  Check the condition and tightness of the coolant hoses
  Replace the air cleaner element with a new one (more frequent renewal may be necessary in dusty conditions)
  Check the operation of the throttle controller
  Replace the spark plugs with new ones
  Check the crankcase emission control system
  Change the automatic transmission fluid
  Inspect the rear brake shoes and replace them with new ones as necessary

Every 30000 miles (48000 km) or two years, whichever occurs first
  Drain the cooling system and refill with fresh coolant
  Change the brake fluid

Every 60000 miles (96000 km)
In addition to, or instead of, the work specified for the 30000 mile service
  Check the idle speed and CO level
  Check the operation of the intake air temperature system

13

Every 60000 miles (96000 km) (continued)
  Check the operation of the throttle controller
  Check the evaporative emission control system
  Change the fuel filter
  Check the condition and tightness of the fuel lines
  Change the charcoal canister (exaporative fuel control system)
  Check the ignition timing and adjust as necessary
  Check the distributor cap and high tension leads and replace with
    new parts as necessary
  Check the EGR system
  Check the secondary air supply system
  Check the operation of the choke opener

5   Engine

Engine removal

  When removing the air cleaner, additional hoses may be attached
to the top of the air cleaner cover and to the underside of the air cleaner
base. If so, before removing these hoses, tag them to simplify installation. On 1983 models equipped with a 5-speed transmission, remove
the air valve from its bracket and the control valve from its bracket.

6   Fuel, exhaust and emission control systems

Fuel filter — replacement

Caution: *There are a number of safety precautions to follow when working with gasoline. Refer to 'Safety first' near the front of this manual.*
Front
1   Remove and plug the fuel lines. When disconnecting the fuel lines,
slide the clamps back, then twist the lines off to avoid damaging them.
2   Remove the filter.
3   Installation is the reverse of the removal procedure.
Rear
4   Raise the rear of the vehicle and place it securely on jackstands.
5   Push in on the fuel filter tab to release the holder, then remove the
filter from the bracket.
6   Disconnect the lines from the fuel filter.
7   Installation is the reverse of the removal procedure.

Automatic choke — testing

Fast idle unloader — cold
Note: *On 1982 and 1983 vehicles, the unloader is vacuum controlled
rather than electrically controlled as in previous models.*

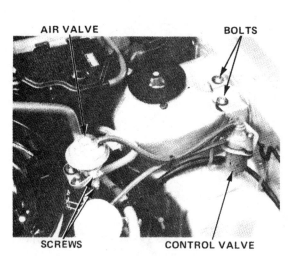

Fig. 13.1   Locations of the air valve and control valve (to be
removed on 1983 1300 models with 5-speed transmission
only) (Sec 5)

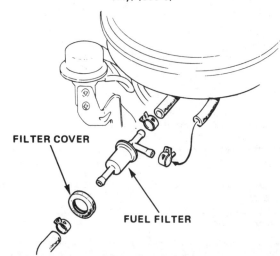

Fig. 13.2   Details of the front fuel filter installation (Sec 6)

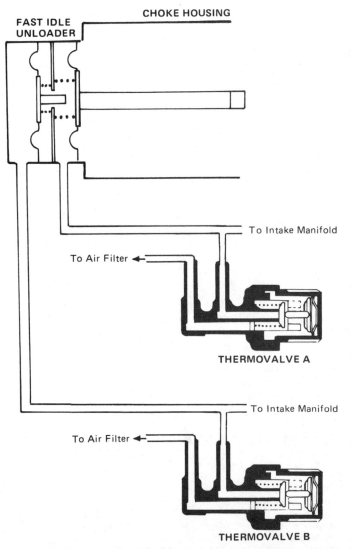

Fig. 13.3   Fast idle unloader and associated thermovalves
(Sec 6)

8 Disconnect the two hoses at the fast idle unloader.
9 Open and close the throttle to engage the fast idle cam.
10 Start the engine. It should run at fast idle. If not, go to Step 14.
11 If fast idle is attained, connect a hand vacuum pump to the inside fitting of the unloader and draw a vacuum. The fast idle speed should drop.
12 If the idle speed drops, go on to the fast idle unloader hot test in Chapter. 3
13 If the idle speed does not drop, check the unloader for leaks, blockage or a damaged diaphragm. Remove the choke cover and check the unloader rod for free movement. Repair or replace as necessary.
14 If the engine did not run at fast idle in Step 10, check for the presence of vacuum at the fast idle unloader's hoses. If vacuum is present, check thermovalves A and B as follows.
15 Locate the thermovalves by referring to the accompanying illustration.
16 Drain the engine coolant until the level is below the distributor holder.

17 Remove the distributor holder from the cylinder head, then remove the thermovalves.
18 To test each thermovalve, attach hoses of the proper diameter to each of the valve's outlets and submerge the valve in cold water, making sure the hoses are above the waterline and that no water gets into the valve body.
19 Attach a hand vacuum pump to the bottom valve outlet hose.
20 Apply vacuum to the valve, then heat the water slowly as you watch the gauge and thermometer, making sure the thermometer does not touch the bottom of the container.
21 Thermovalve A should open (not hold vacuum) below 59 plus or minus 7° F (15 plus or minus 4° C) and close (hold vacuum) above 77 plus or minus 7° F (25 plus or minus 4° C).
22 Thermovalve B should open (not hold vacuum) below 104 plus or minus 7° F (40 plus or minus 4° C) and close (hold vacuum) above 122 plus or minus 7° F (50 plus or minus 4° C).
23 If the thermovalve(s) fail any of the above tests, replace with a new one.

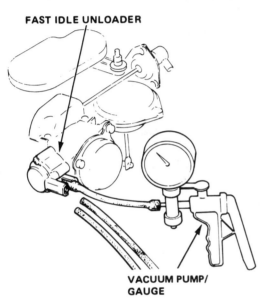

FAST IDLE UNLOADER

VACUUM PUMP/
GAUGE

Fig. 13.4 Testing the fast idle unloader (cold) with a hand vacuum pump (Sec 6)

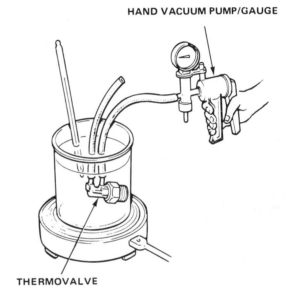

HAND VACUUM PUMP/GAUGE

THERMOVALVE

Fig. 13.5 Testing a thermovalve with a hand vacuum pump (Sec 6)

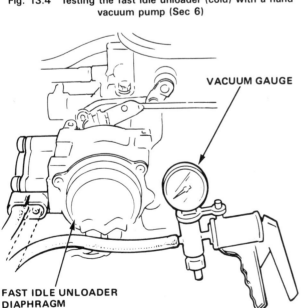

VACUUM GAUGE

FAST IDLE UNLOADER DIAPHRAGM

Fig. 13.6 Testing the cranking leak solenoid valve with a hand vacuum pump (Sec 6)

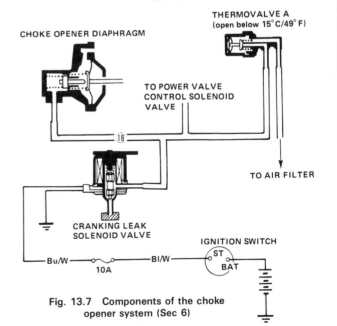

CHOKE OPENER DIAPHRAGM

THERMOVALVE A
(open below 15°C/49° F)

TO POWER VALVE CONTROL SOLENOID VALVE

TO AIR FILTER

CRANKING LEAK SOLENOID VALVE

IGNITION SWITCH
ST
BAT

Bu/W   Bl/W
10A

Fig. 13.7 Components of the choke opener system (Sec 6)

13

24 If the engine still does not run at fast idle, remove the choke cover and check the operation of the fast idle cam. Repair or replace as necessary.

25 Reinstall and reconnect any parts previously removed.

Choke opener

26 Disconnect the choke heater wires, then proceed as instructed in Chapter 3.

Cranking leak solenoid valve

27 This test should be performed after the fast idle adjustment has been made and with the engine at operating temperature.

28 Ground the secondary coil wire.

29 Disconnect the inside hose from the fast idle unloader and check for the presence of vacuum with the ignition switch turned to Start. There should be no vacuum.

30 If there is no vacuum, reconnect the coil wire. The test is complete.

31 If vacuum is present, use a voltmeter to check for voltage at the cranking leak solenoid valve (control box no. 1 — refer to Chapter 1, Fig. 1.5) with the ignition switch in the Start position.

32 If voltage is present, replace the solenoid valve with a new one and re-test.

33 If no voltage is present, check for a wiring short or blown fuse and repair or replace a necessary.

34 Reconnect the secondary coil wire. The test is complete.

Carburetor adjustments

Fast idle

35 The procedures for 1982 and 1983 vehicles are the same as those described in Chapter 3 except that there are two hoses running to the fast idle unloader. Disconnect and plug only the inside hose when making the fast idle adjustment.

Emission control systems — description and testing

Crankcase controls — description

36 Vapor emissions from the crankcase are controlled by a dual return system. Blow-by vapor is recirculated to the combustion chambers through the carburetor and intake manifold. The vapors are directed into the carburetor venturi or beneath the throttle plate, depending on available vacuum.

37 When the throttle plate is closed, at idle, or partially open, blow-by is returned to the intake manifold through breather hoses A and B

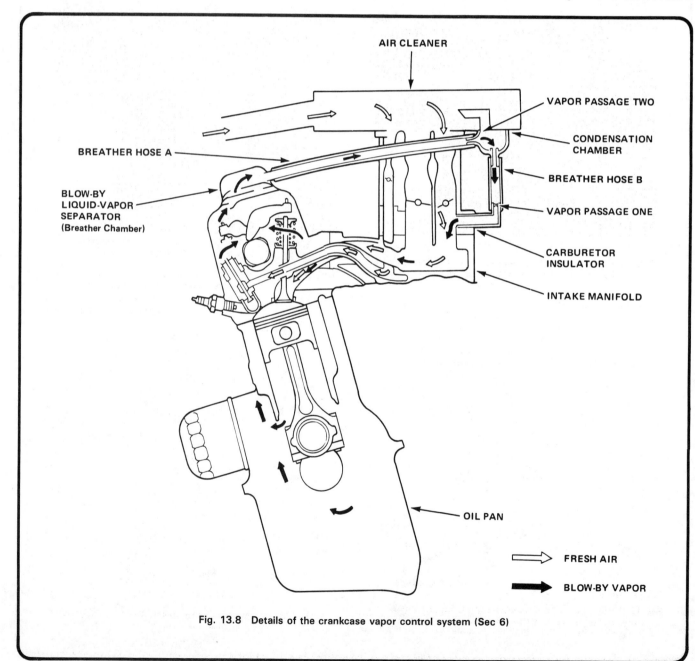

Fig. 13.8 Details of the crankcase vapor control system (Sec 6)

and through vapor passage 1 (see accompanying illustration).

38 When the throttle is wide open, vacuum in the air cleaner increases and vacuum at vapor passage 1 decreases. Blow-by is drawn into the air cleaner through vapor passage 2, from the condensation chamber and breather hose A. A small amount of blow-by is also returned through vapor passage 1.

Crankcase controls — testing

39 With the engine cold, disconnect the breather hose from the carburetor insulator and clean the fixed orifice with the shank end of a no. 57 drill bit or by blowing compressed air through it.

40 Remove the condensation chamber from the air cleaner assembly and check it for sludge or varnish in the passage. Clean as necessary. Also inspect all hoses and gaskets and replace as necessary. **Note:** *When reinstalling, the gasket must be installed in the original position to prevent breather restriction.*

Evaporative control system — description

41 The evaporative control system for 1982 and 1983 vehicles is the same as described in Chapter 3 except as follows.

42 The purge control valve is now operated through venturi vacuum by thermovalve B.

43 The information in Chapter 3, Section 22, Step 6 now pertains to all vehicles.

Evaporative control system — testing

44 If vacuum is present when performing the cold engine test, check the thermovalve as described in Step 20 of this Section, rather than checking the purge valve.

45 On 1982 and 1983 vehicles, a hot engine test of the evaporative control system is also necessary.

46 Disconnect the upper hose at the purge control diaphragm valve and connect a vacuum gauge to the hose.

47 Start the engine and allow it to reach operating termperature.

48 Once the engine is warm, there should be vacuum at idle.

49 If vacuum is present, go to Step 53.

50 If vacuum is not present, check thermovalve B by pinching off the hose running to the air filter.

51 If vacuum is now available to the canister, replace thermovalve B

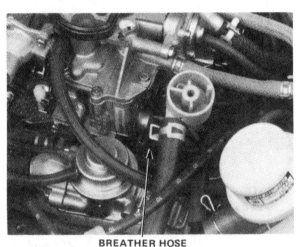

Fig. 13.9 Location of the breather hose to be disconnected from the carburetor when testing the crankcase controls (Sec 6)

BREATHER HOSE

FIXED ORIFICE   No. 57 (1.09 mm DIA.) DRILL SHANK

Fig. 13.10 Cleaning the fixed orifice in the carburetor when testing the crankcase controls (Sec 6)

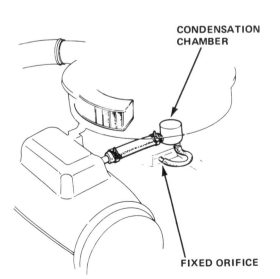

CONDENSATION CHAMBER

FIXED ORIFICE

Fig. 13.11 Location of the condensation chamber that is to be removed when testing the crankcase controls (Sec 6)

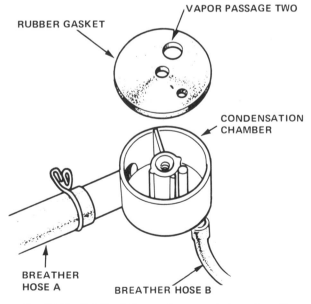

VAPOR PASSAGE TWO

RUBBER GASKET

CONDENSATION CHAMBER

BREATHER HOSE A

BREATHER HOSE B

Fig. 13.12 Details of the crankcase control condensation chamber (Sec 6)

13

with a new one.

52 If vacuum is not present, check hoses 7 and 19 for leaks for blockage and repair as necessary.

53 Disconnect the vacuum gauge and reconnect the hose.

Exhaust emission control system — general information

54 This system works in the same manner on 1982 and 1983 vehicles as described for earlier vehicles in Chapter 3. However, two additional

sub-systems, a secondary air supply system (on all 1982-83 vehicles) and a throttle closer system (on 1983 1300 Hatchback 5-speed models only) are employed. Descriptions of and testing procedures for these two systems, plus variances from the systems described in Chapter 3, follow.

Secondary air supply system — description

55 This system utilizes vacuum pulses in the exhaust manifold to draw

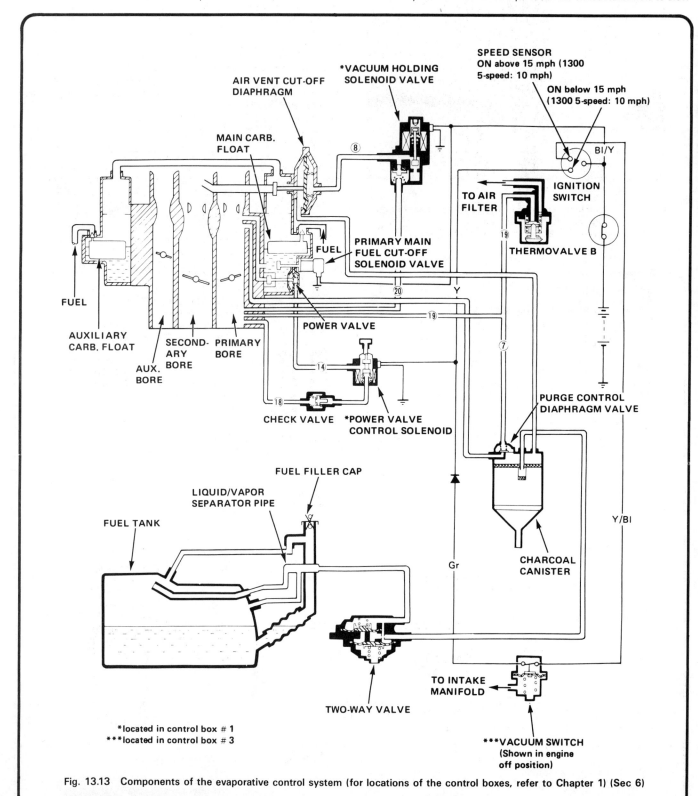

Fig. 13.13 Components of the evaporative control system (for locations of the control boxes, refer to Chapter 1) (Sec 6)

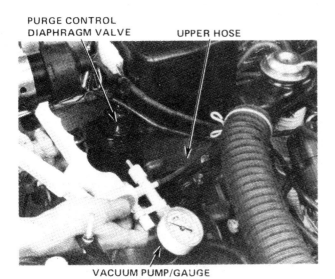

Fig. 13.14 Attaching a hand vacuum pump to the upper hose at the purge control diaphragm before performing the evaporative system hot engine check (Sec 6)

air from the air cleaner to the exhaust manifold, preventing the catalytic converter from overheating.

56 When vehicle speed exceeds the set speed of the speed sensor and manifold vacuum is greater than the set vacuum of the control switch, the control switch solenoid valve and the control switch are open and the manifold vacuum is applied to the air suction diaphragm valve to open the secondary air passage. When pressure induced by pulsations in the exhaust manifold forces the air suction reed valve open, fresh air pours into the exhaust manifold and to the converter.

57 The bellows in the control switch adjusts the switch operation in response to changing atmospheric pressure.

58 The A and B air chambers act as silencers to reduce exhaust noise.

Secondary air supply system — testing

59 Due to the complexity of testing procedures and the special equipment required, testing of this system should be performed by a dealer or auto repair facility.

Throttle closer system (1983 1300 Hatchback 5-speed models only) — description

60 This system closes the throttle valve below its idle position when the vehicle decelerates under certain conditions.

61 When vehicle speed is above 10 mph, engine speed is above 800 rpm and the clutch is not depressed, vacuum through the throttle control solenoid valve is present in the diaphragm of the throttle closer, which retracts the throttle stop screw. This causes complete closing of the throttle valve; however, the miminum fuel needed to keep the engine running is drawn from the slow speed fuel system.

62 When the throttle valve is closed, additional air is introduced into the intake manifold through the air valve.

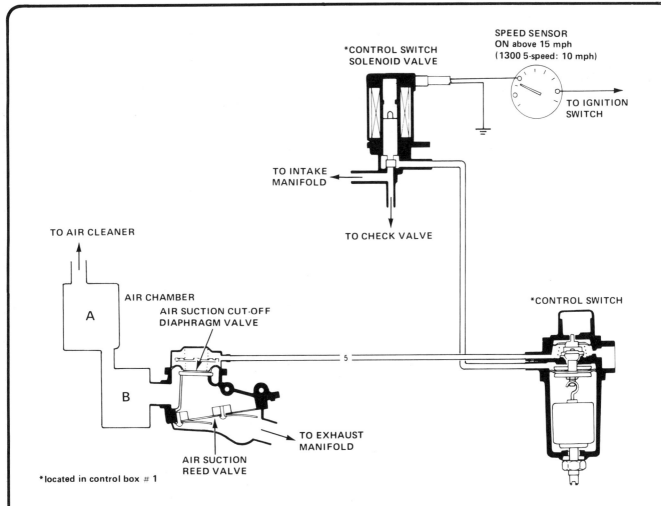

Fig. 13.15 Components of the secondary air supply system (for locations of the control boxes, refer to Chapter 1) (Sec 6)

13

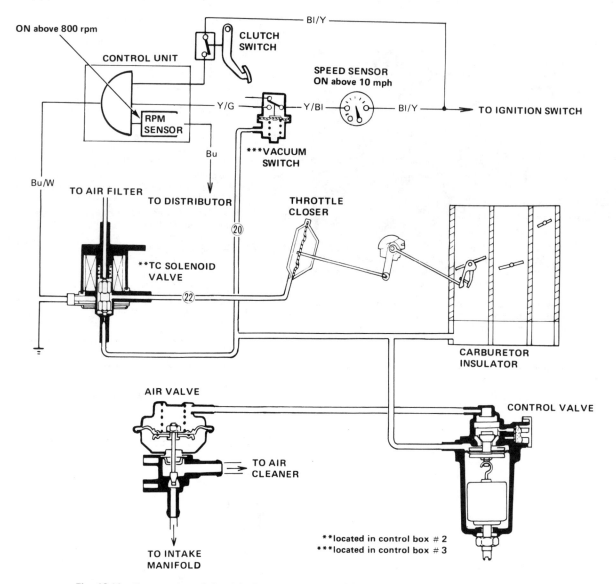

Fig. 13.16   Components of the throttle closer system (1983 1300 Hatchback 5-speed models only; for locations of the control boxes, refer to Chapter 1) (Sec 6)

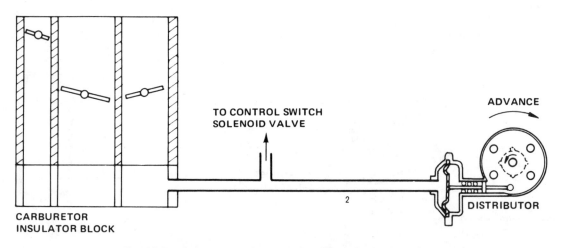

Fig. 13.17   Components of the ignition control system (Sec 6)

63 The control valve activates the air valve, depending on the insulator vacuum level in the carburetor.

Throttle closer system (1983 1300 Hatchback 5-speed models only) — testing

64 If a malfunction in this system is suspected, check all hoses and electrical connections for looseness, fraying or breaks and repair or replace as necessary.

65 Due to the complex testing procedures and the special equipment required, testing of the individual components of this system should be performed by a dealer or auto repair facility.

Ignition control system — description

66 This system works in the manner described in chapter 3 with the exception that the vacuum advance in all 1982 and 1983 vehicles responds to manifold vacuum.

Ignition control system — testing

67 Testing of the vacuum advance unit is covered in Chapter 4.

Throttle control system — description

68 Except on 49-state 1300 Hatchback 5-speed models, this system functions in the same manner as the second (dashpot) system described in Chapter 3, Section 26. On 49-state 1300 5-speed models, there is no dashpot check valve and its cranking solenoid differs slightly. Otherwise, all systems function in the same manner.

69 A throttle controller is installed in the system on all 1982 and 1983 vehicles to promote easy starting. When the engine is cranked to start,

the cranking solenoid is activated to allow intake manifold vacuum into the diaphragm so the proper throttle opening angle is obtained.

Throttle control system — testing

70 Testing of this system is as described in Chapter 3.

Exhaust gas recirculation system — description

71 The function of the EGR system is described in Chapter 3. On 1982 and 1983 vehicles, the system is composed of an EGR valve, two EGR control valves (A and B), a control switch, EGR control solenoid valves, thermosensor A, the speed sensor, a control switch solenoid valve and a vacuum switch. Component differences between the earlier model EGR system and the one used on 1982 and 1983 vehicles may be noted by referring to the accompanying illustration and the illustration in Chapter 3.

Exhaust gas recirculation system — testing

72 Testing of the EGR system on 1982 and 1983 vehicles by the home mechanic should be restricted to the procedures which follow.

73 With the engine cold, disconnect the vacuum hose from the EGR valve, then start the engine.

74 Increase the engine speed to 4500 to 5000 rpm and put your finger over the disconnected vacuum hose to test for vacuum. Vacuum should *not* be present.

75 If vacuum is present, replace the defective EGR valve with a new one (make sure you get an identical type) and re-test.

76 If problems exist with the new EGR valve installed, or if other malfuctions of the EGR system are suspected, the system should be

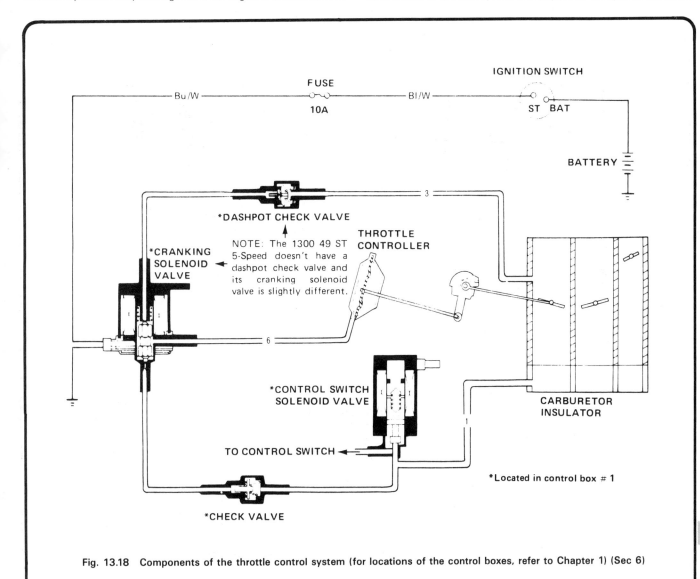

Fig. 13.18 Components of the throttle control system (for locations of the control boxes, refer to Chapter 1) (Sec 6)

13

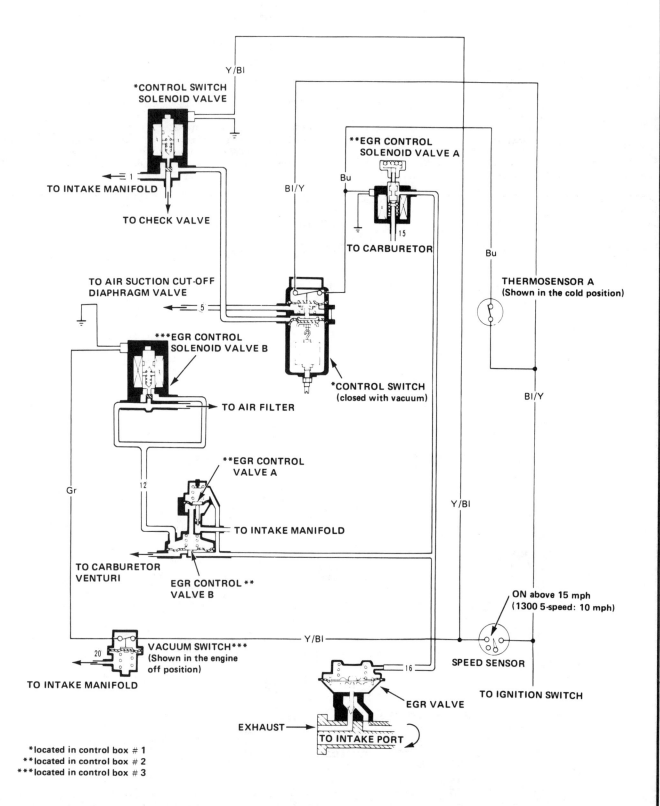

Fig. 13.19 Components of the exhaust gas recirculation (EGR) system (for locations of the control boxes, refer to Chapter 1) (Sec 6)

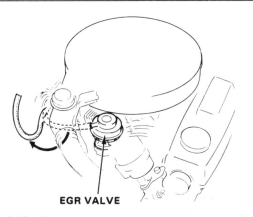

EGR VALVE

Fig. 13.20   Disconnecting the vacuum hose from the EGR valve to test for vacuum (Sec 6)

checked by a dealer or auto repair facility equipped with the special tools necessary.

Catalytic converter — description and testing

77 The description and testing for the 1982 and 1983 catalytic converter system is the same as described in Chapter 3 except that CC systems are now fitted to all vehicles.

Manifolds and exhaust system — removal and installation

78 The same manifold assembly is used on all 1982 and 1983 vehicles. It is a slight redesign of the earlier 1500 engine (US) manifold system described in Chapter 3, but the removal and installation procedures are essentially the same. Differences in the systems may be noted by comparing the accompanying illustration and Fig. 3.43 in Chapter 3.

79 All 1982 and 1983 exhaust systems employ a catalytic converter.

80 The exhaust system used on all 1982 and 1983 vehicles is a slight redesign of the 1500 engine (US) exhaust system described in Chapter 3, but the procedures and cautions regarding the system are essentially the same. Differences in the systems may be noted by comparing the accompanying illustration and Fig. 3.47 in Chapter 3.

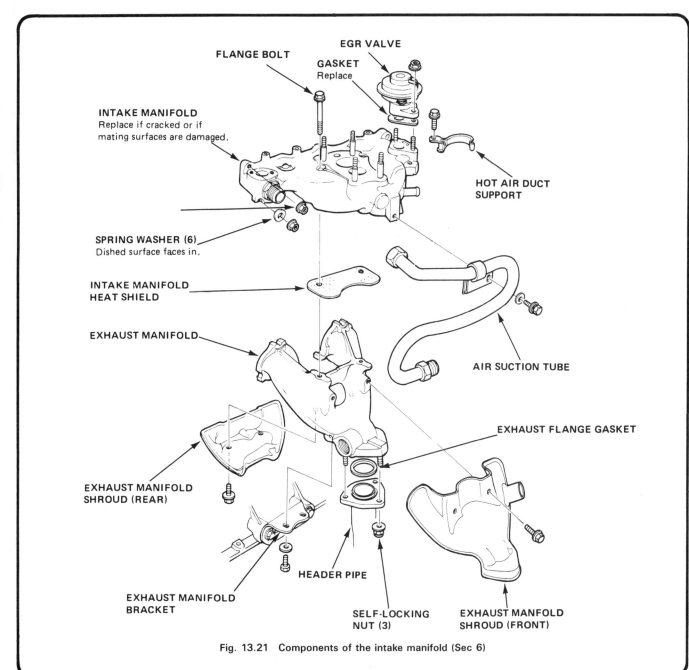

Fig. 13.21   Components of the intake manifold (Sec 6)

13

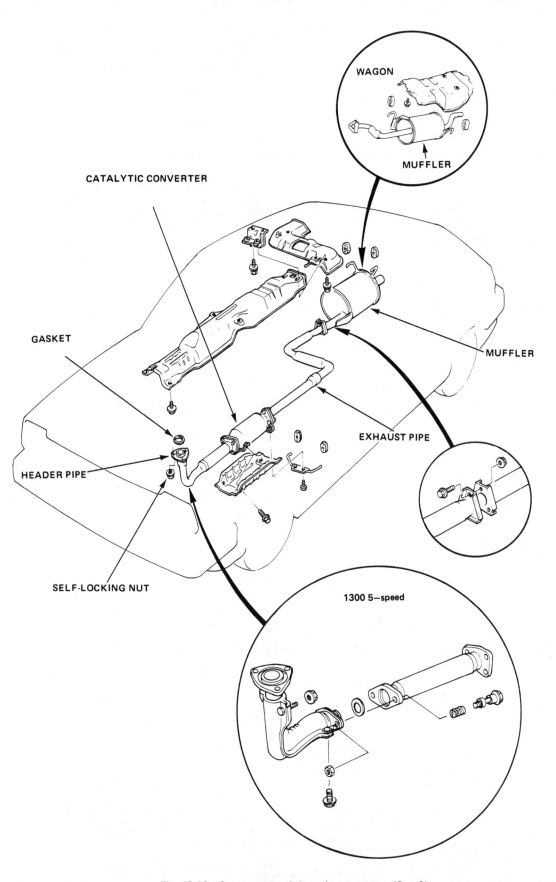

WAGON

MUFFLER

CATALYTIC CONVERTER

GASKET

MUFFLER

HEADER PIPE

EXHAUST PIPE

SELF-LOCKING NUT

1300 5—speed

Fig. 13.22 Components of the exhaust system (Sec 6)

7 Brakes

Front — general description

1   Two slightly redesigned front brake assemblies were introduced on 1983 vehicles. The first is used on 1300 Hatchback models and the second on 1500 Hatchbacks and Sedans.

2   The assembly for 1983 1500 Hatchbacks and Sedans does not use a spring plate in conjunction with the brake pads, shims and anti-rattle springs, as employed on earlier Sedan models.

3   Other slight differences in the systems may be noted by comparing the accompanying illustrations and Figs. 9.8 and 9.9 in Chapter 9.

4   Except for the differences noted above, the front disc brake systems and the service procedures for late model vehicles are essentially the same as described in Chapter 9.

Servo — general description

5   All 1982 and 1983 vehicles employ the 6.5 inch type brake servo unit.

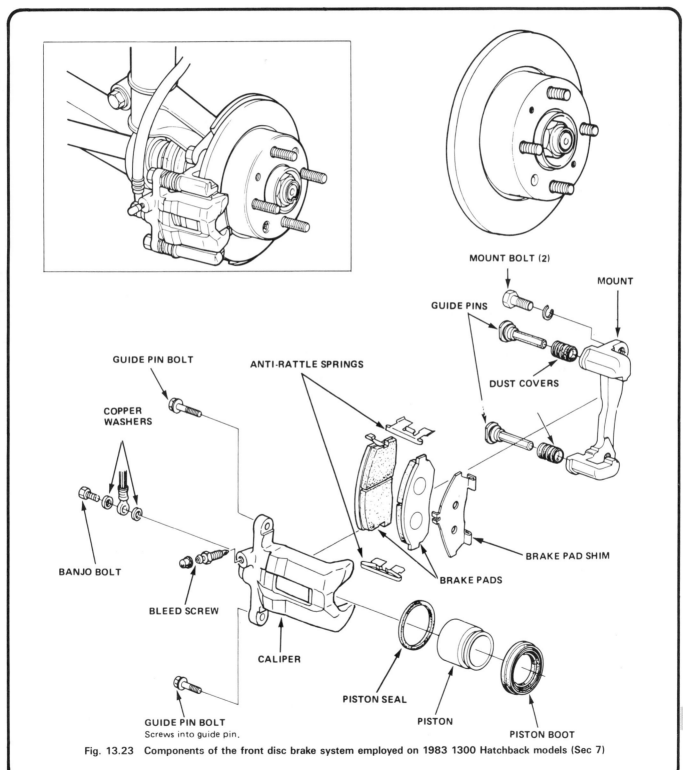

Fig. 13.23 Components of the front disc brake system employed on 1983 1300 Hatchback models (Sec 7)

13

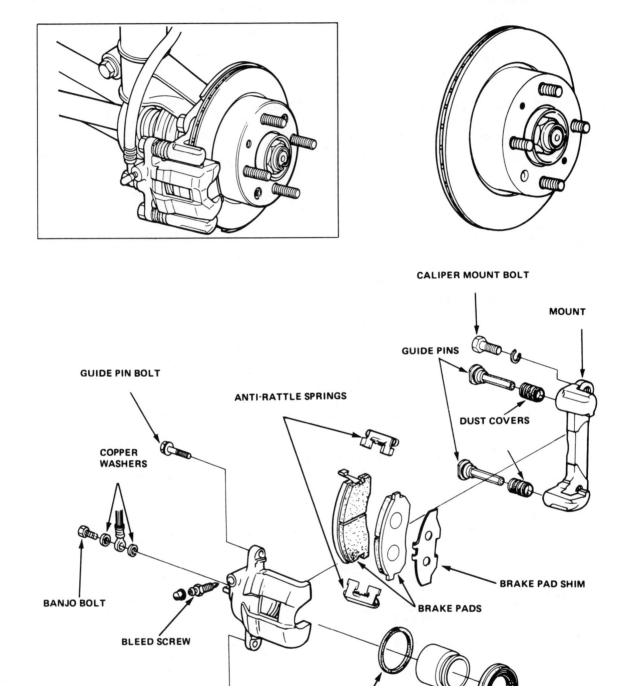

CALIPER MOUNT BOLT

MOUNT

GUIDE PINS

DUST COVERS

GUIDE PIN BOLT

ANTI-RATTLE SPRINGS

COPPER WASHERS

BRAKE PAD SHIM

BANJO BOLT

BRAKE PADS

BLEED SCREW

PISTON SEAL

PISTON

GUIDE PIN BOLT

PISTON BOOT

Fig. 13.24 Components of the front disc brake system employed on 1983 1500 Hatchbacks and Sedans (Sec 7)

8 Electrical system

Starter — general description

1   On 1982 and 1983 models, California vehicles use the standard-type starter described in Chapter 10, either Hitachi or Nippondenso, and 49-state and high altitude vehicles use the CVCC-type starter.
2   Otherwise, all descriptions and procedures regarding these starters in Chapter 10 pertain to 1982 and 1983 vehicles.

Fuses — general description

3   On 1982 and 1983 vehicles, the fuse box is located under the instrument panel on the left (driver's) side of the vehicle. Mini-type fuses are now used in all applications; fuse location assignments and ratings are given in the accompanying illustration.

Ignition switch — testing

4   As on previous vehicles, late model ignition switches may be tested without being removed; however, continuity of the switch in its various

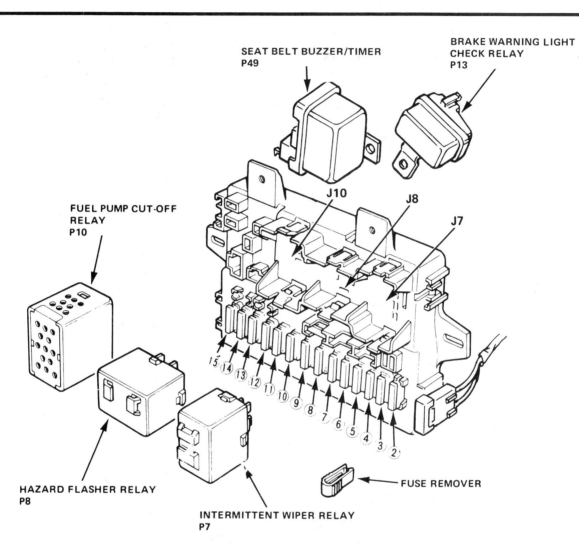

Fig. 13.25   Fuse box and junction relay panel (Sec 8)

2   Right headlight, low beam — 10 amps
3   Left headlight, low beam — 10 amps
4   Right headlight, high beam; high beam
       pilot light — 10 amps
5   Left headlight, high beam — 10 amps
6   Regulator, fuel pump/cut-off relay, primary cut-off
       solenoid valves, vacuum holding solenoid valve, EGR
       control solenoid valve A, EGR control solenoid valve B,
       speed sensor, power valve control solenoid valve,
       control switch solenoid valve, idle compensation unit
       (manual transmission only), idle compensation solenoid
       valve (manual transmission only), control unit (1300
       5-speed transmission only), T/C solenoid valve (1300
       5-speed transmission only), upshift indicator (1300
       5-speed transmission only) — 10 amps
7   Wiper motor, washer motor — 15 amps

8   Turn signal relay/lights, back-up lights, fuel gauge,
       temperature gauge, brake warning light, oil pressure
       warning light, charge warning light, seat belt warning
       light/buzzer/timer, tailgate/trunk warning light (except
       Wagon) — 10 amps
9   Interior light, trunk light, cigar lighter, clock,
       key buzzer — 10 amps
10 Brake lights, horn, hazard flasher/relay — 15 amps
11 Taillights, side marker lights, parking lights, license
       plate lights, gauge lights, ignition switch light, heater
       panel light, A/T console light — 15 amps
12 Rear window defroster — 15 amps
13 Heater motor — 15 amps
14 Cooling fan motor — 15 amps
15 Radio — 10 amps

13

positions differs from earlier models, as shown in the accompanying illustration.

Warning light bulbs — replacement
5 In order to replace the warning bulbs it is necessary to remove the instrument panel (refer to Section 10 of this Chapter).

Wiring diagrams
6 Note that wiring diagrams for 1982 and 1983 US models are included at the end of this Chapter.

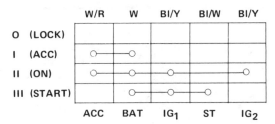

	W/R	W	Bl/Y	Bl/W	Bl/Y
O (LOCK)					
I (ACC)	o—————o				
II (ON)	o	o—————o		o	
III (START)		o—————o	o	
	ACC	BAT	IG₁	ST	IG₂

Fig. 13.26 Ignition switch continuity (Sec 8)

9 Steering

Steering wheel — removal, dismantling and installation
1 The two steering wheel types used on 1982 and 1983 vehicles differ slightly from those used on earlier models. They are now referred to as the standard steering wheel and the sport steering wheel.
2 Remove either type steering wheel as described in Chapter 11, then proceed as follows. Disconnect the battery ground cable.
Standard wheel
3 Remove the three screws retaining the upper cover and springs, then remove the cover and springs.
4 Remove the horn contact spring, ground contact plates and slip ring.
5 Clean the surfaces on the contact plates and slip ring.
6 Reassemble the parts in the reverse order of removal, then install the horn contact spring and ground contact plates so that they engage properly when the upper cover is pushed.
7 Install the slip ring in its original position.
Sport wheel
8 Remove the four screws retaining the lower cover to the upper cover, disconnect the horn wire from the slip ring, then remove the upper cover.

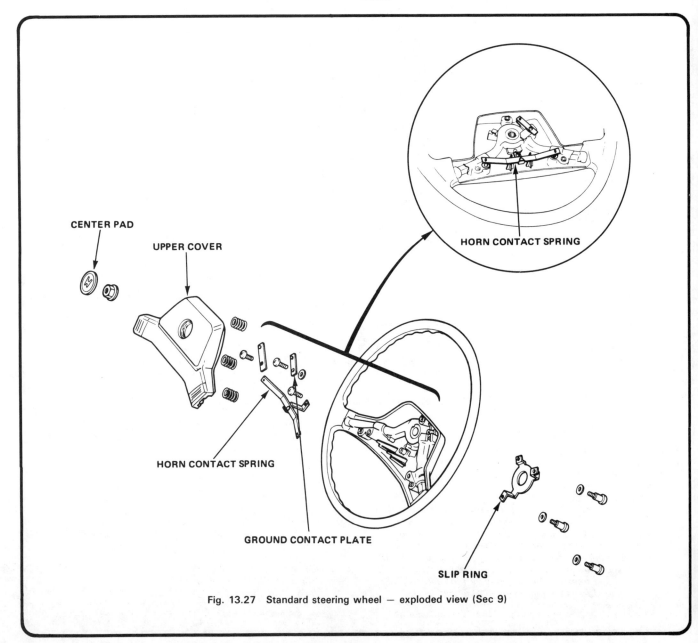

Fig. 13.27 Standard steering wheel — exploded view (Sec 9)

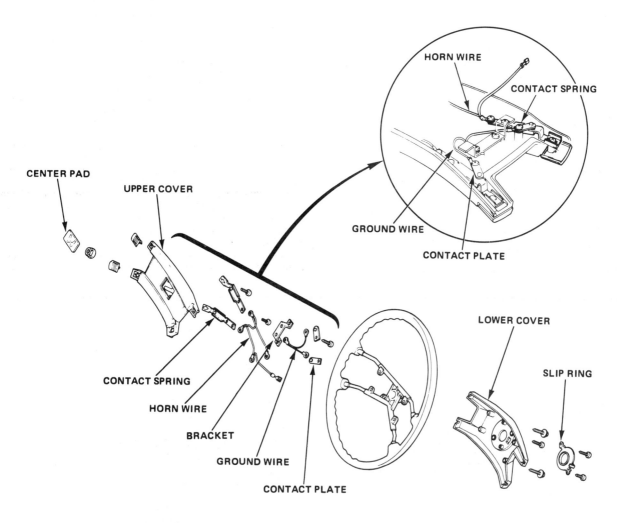

Fig. 13.28 Sport steering wheel — exploded view (Sec 9)

9   Remove the four screws retaining the slip ring and lower cover, then remove them from the steering wheel.
10   Remove the two brackets, ground wires and four contact plates.
11   Remove the horn wire and four horn contact springs.
12   Clean all contact surfaces.
13   Reassemble the parts in the reverse order of removal, then install the ground contact springs so that they engage the horn contact springs correctly when pushing the horn buttons.
14   Install the slip ring in its original position.
15   Connect the horn wire to the slip ring.

All models
16   On both steering wheel styles, reinstall the steering wheel nut and tighten it to the specified torque.
17   Install the center pad.
18   Reconnect the battery ground cable and see if the horn works.

Steering column lock — removal and installation
19   The removal and installation procedure for 1982 and 1983 models is the same as for earlier models with the following exceptions.
20   The shear screws require a 3/8-inch (9.53 mm) drill for removal.
21   Be sure to drill out the upper screw first.
22   When first installing the new switch, make sure that the key is not inserted.

10   Bodywork and fittings

Radiator grille and hood — removal and installation
1   To remove the grille, first pry out the two plugs covering the outer retaining screws.
2   Remove the four screws retaining the grille, then remove the grille.
3   If the headlight trim rings are to be removed, open the hood to gain access to the trim ring retaining screws.
4   Remove the trim ring retaining screws and remove the trim ring(s).
5   Installation is the reverse of the removal procedure.
6   Removal and installation of the hood is otherwise as directed in Chapter 12.

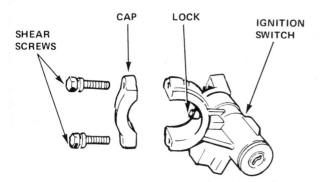

Fig. 13.29 Details of the steering column lock installation (Sec 9)

13

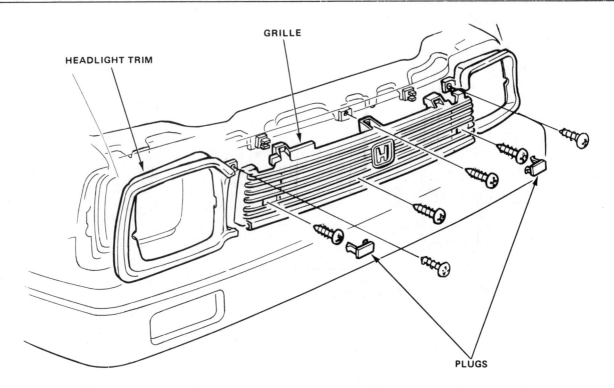

Fig. 13.30   Details of the grille installation (Sec 10)

Door interior trim panel — removal and installation

7   Other than as noted below, the removal and installation procedures for the door interior trim panel are as directed in Chapter 12.

8   After removing the dished plate from behind the door remote control lever on 1982 and 1983 vehicles, the remote control mirror on the left door must be removed.

9   Pry the plug out of the mirror control knob, remove the knob retaining screw and remove the knob.

10   Using a thin-bladed screwdriver, carefully pry the trim plate out of the door recess.

11   Remove the mirror by removing the three retaining screws.

Front door lock and glass — removal and installation

12   Other than as noted below, the removal and installation procedures for the front door lock and glass are as described in Chapter 12.

13   After removing the inside door handle and complete latch assembly on 1982 and 1983 models, remove the two screws and one bolt retaining the door mirror bracket to the left door, then remove the bracket.

Instrument panel — removal and installation

14   Instrument panel removal and installation procedures for all 1982 and 1983 vehicles are the same as those given in Chapter 12 for Hatchback and Wagon models, noting the following.

15   The procedure will be made much simpler by lowering the steering column before removal of the panel is attempted (refer to Chapter 11).

16   On 1300 Hatchback 5-speed models only, be sure to disconnect the upshift indicator connector as well as the instrument panel connector.

Dashboard — removal and installation

17   Remove the fuse box cover and the mounting nut and bolt.

18   Lower the steering column (refer to Chapter 11).

19   Disconnect the cable from the negative battery terminal.

20   Disconnect the instrument wiring harness from the fuse box, side wire harness, interior light, engine compartment wire harness, stop light switch and ground.

21   Pull the lever knobs from the heater panel.

22   Carefully pry the heater panel off with a screwdriver.

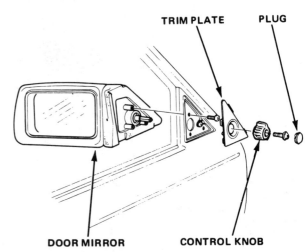

Fig. 13.31   Details of the remote control mirror installation (Sec 10)

23   Remove the heater control bracket mounting screws.

24   Remove the speaker grille/access panel from the right corner of the dashboard.

25   Disconnect the speedometer cable and, on models so equipped, the tachometer cable.

26   Remove the bolt hole plugs from both sides of the dashboard.

27   Remove the seven bolts retaining the dashboard.

28   Lift up and pull out on the dashboard to remove it from the guide pin, making sure to support the dashboard as it comes free of the pin to prevent damage.

29   Installation is the reverse of the removal procedure, noting the following.

30   Make sure the dashboard is properly engaged on the guide pin.

31   When installing the dashboard retaining bolts, install them only finger tight, then check that the heater levers move freely in both directions.

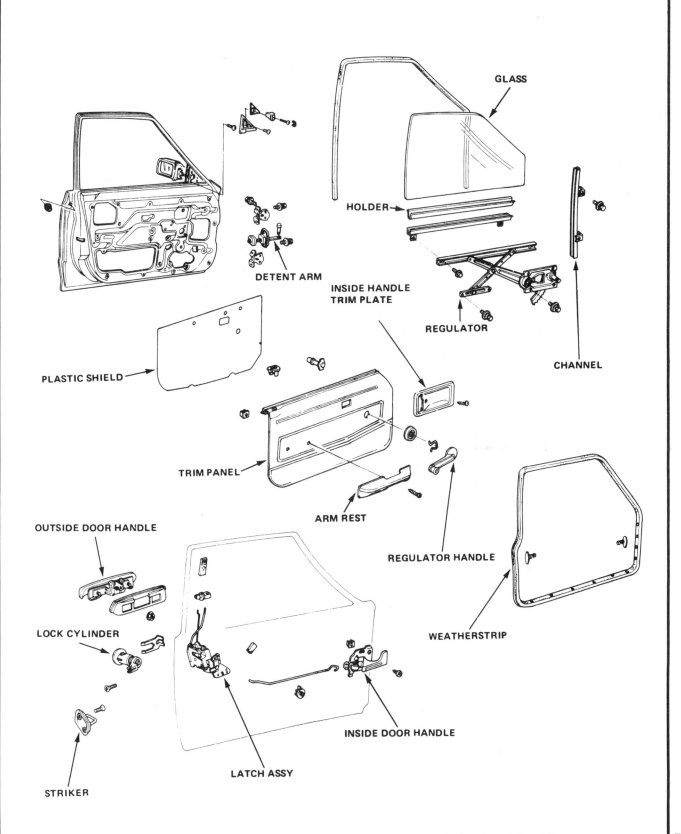

GLASS

HOLDER

DETENT ARM

INSIDE HANDLE
TRIM PLATE

REGULATOR

CHANNEL

PLASTIC SHIELD

TRIM PANEL

ARM REST

REGULATOR HANDLE

OUTSIDE DOOR HANDLE

WEATHERSTRIP

LOCK CYLINDER

INSIDE DOOR HANDLE

STRIKER

LATCH ASSY

Fig. 13.32 Front door assembly — exploded view (Wagon shown, Sedan similar) (Sec 10)

13

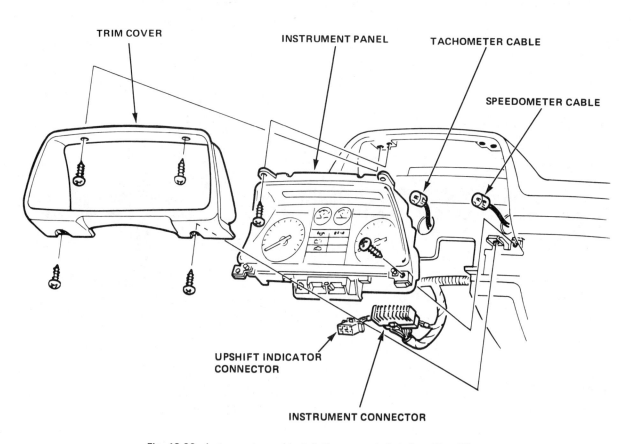

TRIM COVER INSTRUMENT PANEL TACHOMETER CABLE

SPEEDOMETER CABLE

UPSHIFT INDICATOR
CONNECTOR

INSTRUMENT CONNECTOR

Fig. 13.33   Instrument panel installation — exploded view (Sec 10)

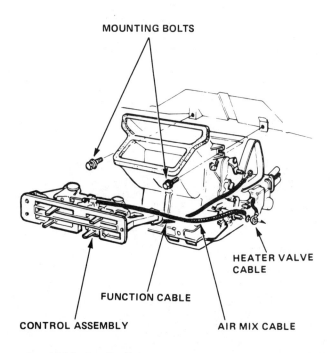

MOUNTING BOLTS

HEATER VALVE
CABLE

FUNCTION CABLE

CONTROL ASSEMBLY   AIR MIX CABLE

Fig. 13.34   Details of the heater control cable installation
(Sec 10)

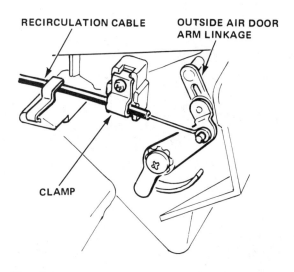

RECIRCULATION CABLE   OUTSIDE AIR DOOR
ARM LINKAGE

CLAMP

Fig. 13.35   Details of the recirculation cable installation
(Sec 10)

32 Make sure that the instrument wire harnesses are reconnected properly and that they are not pinched before final tightening of the dashboard retaining bolts.

Heater control cables — installation and adjustment
33 The procedures for adjusting the heater control cables on 1982 and 1983 models are the same as described in Chapter 12 except as follows.
34 The functions of the outside air and recirculation cables on earlier models are combined on late models.

35 To adjust the recirculation cable on 1982 and 1983 models, slide the recirculation lever to FRESH.
36 Pull the outside air door arm linkage toward the rear, closing off the inside air inlet.
37 Connect the recirculation cable to the outside air door arm linkage and secure the cable housing with the clamp.
38 Look through the access panel hole in the lower right-hand corner of the dashboard and slide the recirculation lever to RECIRC, making sure the outside air door is all the way up, then slide the lever back to FRESH, making sure that the door closes against the inside air inlet.

13

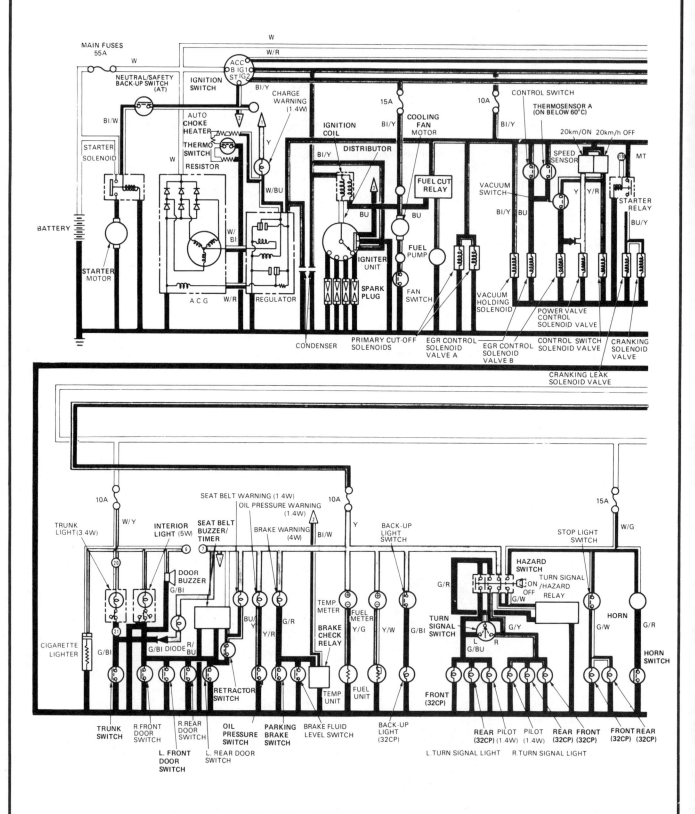

Fig. 13.36 1982 model wiring diagram

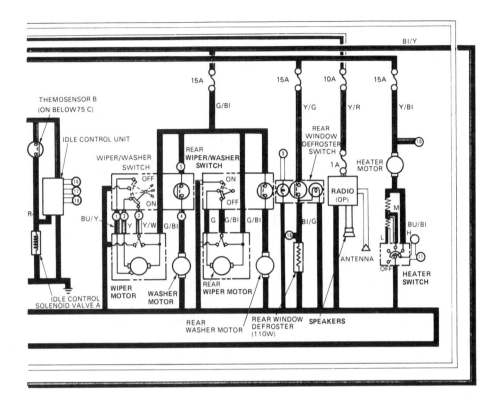

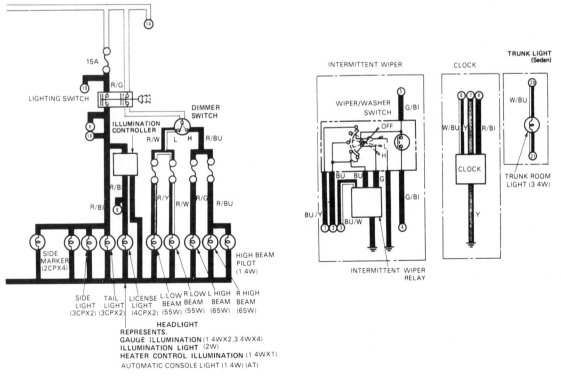

Fig. 13.37 1982 model wiring diagram (continued)

13

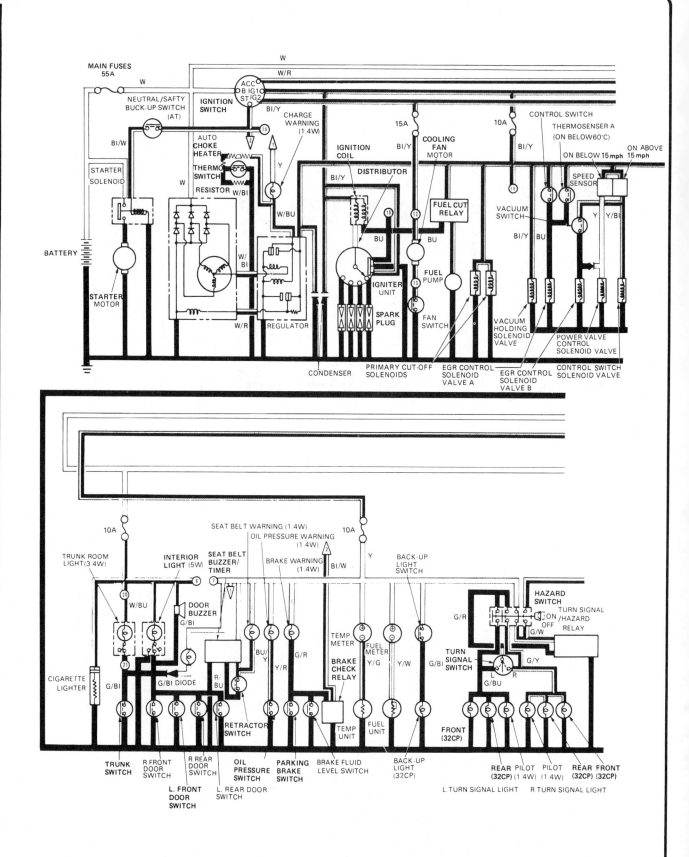

Fig. 13.38   1983 model wiring diagram

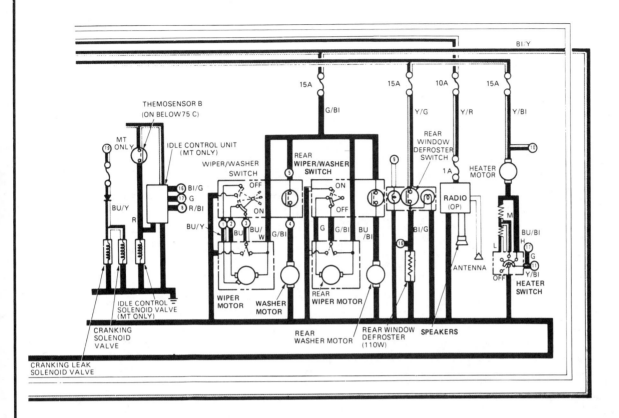

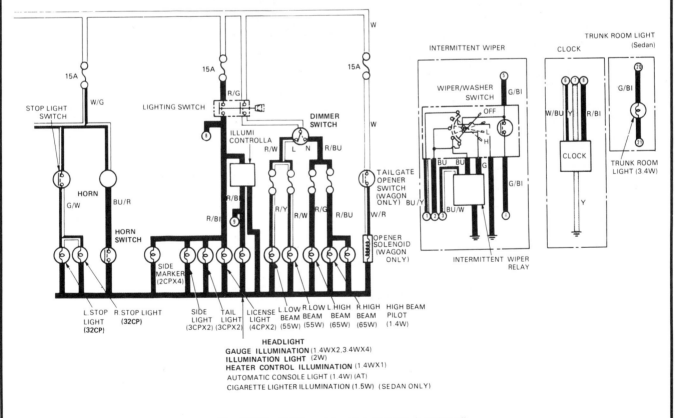

Fig. 13.39 1983 model wiring diagram (continued)

13

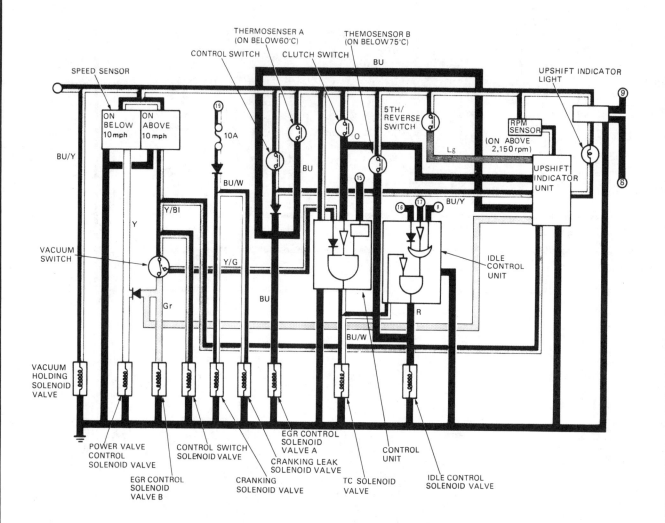

Fig. 13.40   1983 1300 5-speed emission system wiring diagram

Conversion factors

Length (distance)
Inches (in)	X	25.4	=	Millimetres (mm)	X	0.0394	=	Inches (in)
Feet (ft)	X	0.305	=	Metres (m)	X	3.281	=	Feet (ft)
Miles	X	1.609	=	Kilometres (km)	X	0.621	=	Miles

Volume (capacity)
Cubic inches (cu in; in³)	X	16.387	=	Cubic centimetres (cc; cm³)	X	0.061	=	Cubic inches (cu in; in³)
Imperial pints (Imp pt)	X	0.568	=	Litres (l)	X	1.76	=	Imperial pints (Imp pt)
Imperial quarts (Imp qt)	X	1.137	=	Litres (l)	X	0.88	=	Imperial quarts (Imp qt)
Imperial quarts (Imp qt)	X	1.201	=	US quarts (US qt)	X	0.833	=	Imperial quarts (Imp qt)
US quarts (US qt)	X	0.946	=	Litres (l)	X	1.057	=	US quarts (US qt)
Imperial gallons (Imp gal)	X	4.546	=	Litres (l)	X	0.22	=	Imperial gallons (Imp gal)
Imperial gallons (Imp gal)	X	1.201	=	US gallons (US gal)	X	0.833	=	Imperial gallons (Imp gal)
US gallons (US gal)	X	3.785	=	Litres (l)	X	0.264	=	US gallons (US gal)

Mass (weight)
Ounces (oz)	X	28.35	=	Grams (g)	X	0.035	=	Ounces (oz)
Pounds (lb)	X	0.454	=	Kilograms (kg)	X	2.205	=	Pounds (lb)

Force
Ounces-force (ozf; oz)	X	0.278	=	Newtons (N)	X	3.6	=	Ounces-force (ozf; oz)
Pounds-force (lbf; lb)	X	4.448	=	Newtons (N)	X	0.225	=	Pounds-force (lbf; lb)
Newtons (N)	X	0.1	=	Kilograms-force (kgf; kg)	X	9.81	=	Newtons (N)

Pressure
Pounds-force per square inch (psi; lbf/in²; lb/in²)	X	0.070	=	Kilograms-force per square centimetre (kgf/cm²; kg/cm²)	X	14.223	=	Pounds-force per square inch (psi; lbf/in²; lb/in²)
Pounds-force per square inch (psi; lbf/in²; lb/in²)	X	0.068	=	Atmospheres (atm)	X	14.696	=	Pounds-force per square inch (psi; lbf/in²; lb/in²)
Pounds-force per square inch (psi; lbf/in²; lb/in²)	X	0.069	=	Bars	X	14.5	=	Pounds-force per square inch (psi; lbf/in²; lb/in²)
Pounds-force per square inch (psi; lbf/in²; lb/in²)	X	6.895	=	Kilopascals (kPa)	X	0.145	=	Pounds-force per square inch (psi; lbf/in²; lb/in²)
Kilopascals (kPa)	X	0.01	=	Kilograms-force per square centimetre (kgf/cm²; kg/cm²)	X	98.1	=	Kilopascals (kPa)
Millibar (mbar)	X	100	=	Pascals (Pa)	X	0.01	=	Millibar (mbar)
Millibar (mbar)	X	0.0145	=	Pounds-force per square inch (psi; lbf/in²; lb/in²)	X	68.947	=	Millibar (mbar)
Millibar (mbar)	X	0.75	=	Millimetres of mercury (mmHg)	X	1.333	=	Millibar (mbar)
Millibar (mbar)	X	0.401	=	Inches of water (inH₂O)	X	2.491	=	Millibar (mbar)
Millimetres of mercury (mmHg)	X	0.535	=	Inches of water (inH₂O)	X	1.868	=	Millimetres of mercury (mmHg)
Inches of water (inH₂O)	X	0.036	=	Pounds-force per square inch (psi; lbf/in²; lb/in²)	X	27.68	=	Inches of water (inH₂O)

Torque (moment of force)
Pounds-force inches (lbf in; lb in)	X	1.152	=	Kilograms-force centimetre (kgf cm; kg cm)	X	0.868	=	Pounds-force inches (lbf in; lb in)
Pounds-force inches (lbf in; lb in)	X	0.113	=	Newton metres (Nm)	X	8.85	=	Pounds-force inches (lbf in; lb in)
Pounds-force inches (lbf in; lb in)	X	0.083	=	Pounds-force feet (lbf ft; lb ft)	X	12	=	Pounds-force inches (lbf in; lb in)
Pounds-force feet (lbf ft; lb ft)	X	0.138	=	Kilograms-force metres (kgf m; kg m)	X	7.233	=	Pounds-force feet (lbf ft; lb ft)
Pounds-force feet (lbf ft; lb ft)	X	1.356	=	Newton metres (Nm)	X	0.738	=	Pounds-force feet (lbf ft; lb ft)
Newton metres (Nm)	X	0.102	=	Kilograms-force metres (kgf m; kg m)	X	9.804	=	Newton metres (Nm)

Power
Horsepower (hp)	X	745.7	=	Watts (W)	X	0.0013	=	Horsepower (hp)

Velocity (speed)
Miles per hour (miles/hr; mph)	X	1.609	=	Kilometres per hour (km/hr; kph)	X	0.621	=	Miles per hour (miles/hr; mph)

Fuel consumption*
Miles per gallon, Imperial (mpg)	X	0.354	=	Kilometres per litre (km/l)	X	2.825	=	Miles per gallon, Imperial (mpg)
Miles per gallon, US (mpg)	X	0.425	=	Kilometres per litre (km/l)	X	2.352	=	Miles per gallon, US (mpg)

Temperature

Degrees Fahrenheit = (°C x 1.8) + 32

Degrees Celsius (Degrees Centigrade; °C) = (°F - 32) x 0.56

*It is common practice to convert from miles per gallon (mpg) to litres/100 kilometres (l/100km), where mpg (Imperial) x l/100 km = 282 and mpg (US) x l/100 km = 235

Index

HAYNES AUTOMOTIVE MANUALS

NOTE: New manuals are added to this list on a periodic basis. If you do not see a listing for your vehicle, consult your local Haynes dealer for the latest product information.

ACURA
*1776 **Integra & Legend** '86 thru '90

ALFA-ROMEO
531 **Alfa Romeo Sedan & Coupe** '73 thru '80

AMC
Jeep CJ – see JEEP (412)
694 **Mid-size models**, Concord, Hornet, Gremlin & Spirit '70 thru '83
934 **(Renault) Alliance & Encore** all models '83 thru '87

AUDI
615 **4000** all models '80 thru '87
428 **5000** all models '77 thru '83
1117 **5000** all models '84 thru '88
207 **Fox** all models '73 thru '79

AUSTIN
Healey Sprite – see MG Midget Roadster (265)

BLMC
527 **Mini** all models '59 thru '69
*646 **Mini** all models '69 thru '88

BMW
276 **320i** all 4 cyl models '75 thru '83
632 **528i & 530i** all models '75 thru '80
240 **1500 thru 2002** all models except Turbo '59 thru '77
348 **2500, 2800, 3.0 & Bavaria** '69 thru '76

BUICK
Century (front wheel drive) – see GENERAL MOTORS A-Cars (829)
*1627 **Buick, Oldsmobile & Pontiac Full-size (Front wheel drive)** all models '85 thru '90
Buick Electra, LeSabre and Park Avenue; **Oldsmobile** Delta 88 Royale, Ninety Eight and Regency; **Pontiac** Bonneville
*1551 **Buick Oldsmobile & Pontiac Full-size (Rear wheel drive)**
Buick Electra '70 thru '84, Estate '70 thru '90, LeSabre '70 thru '79
Oldsmobile Custom Cruiser '70 thru '90, Delta 88 '70 thru '85, Ninety-eight '70 thru '84
Pontiac Bonneville '70 thru '86, Catalina '70 thru '81, Grandville '70 thru '75, Parisienne '84 thu '86
627 **Mid-size** all rear-drive **Regal & Century** models with V6, V8 and Turbo '74 thru '87
Regal – see GENERAL MOTORS (1671)
Skyhawk – see GENERAL MOTORS J-Cars (766)
552 **Skylark** all X-car models '80 thru '85

CADILLAC
*751 **Cadillac Rear Wheel Drive** all gasoline models '70 thru '90
Cimarron – see GENERAL MOTORS J-Cars (766)

CAPRI
296 **2000 MK I Coupe** all models '71 thru '75
205 **2600 & 2800** V6 Coupe '71 thru '75
375 **2800 Mk II** V6 Coupe '75 thru '78
Mercury Capri – see FORD Mustang (654)

CHEVROLET
*1477 **Astro & GMC Safari Mini-vans** all models '85 thru '91
554 **Camaro** V8 all models '70 thru '81
*866 **Camaro** all models '82 thru '91
Cavalier – see GENERAL MOTORS J-Cars (766)
Celebrity – see GENERAL MOTORS A-Cars (829)

---

625 **Chevelle, Malibu & El Camino** all V6 & V8 models '69 thru '87
449 **Chevette & Pontiac T1000** all models '76 thru '87
550 **Citation** all models '80 thru '85
*1628 **Corsica/Beretta** all models '87 thru '90
274 **Corvette** all V8 models '68 thru '82
*1336 **Corvette** all models '84 thru '91
704 **Full-size Sedans** Caprice, Impala, Biscayne, Bel Air & Wagons, all V6 & V8 models '69 thru '90
Lumina – see GENERAL MOTORS (1671)
319 **Luv Pick-up** all 2WD & 4WD models '72 thru '82
626 **Monte Carlo** all V6, V8 & Turbo models '70 thru '88
241 **Nova** all V8 models '69 thru '79
*1642 **Nova and Geo Prizm** all front wheel drive models, '85 thru '90
*420 **Pick-ups '67 thru '87 – Chevrolet & GMC**, all full-size models '67 thru '87; Suburban, Blazer & Jimmy '67 thru '91
*1664 **Pick-ups '88 thru '90 – Chevrolet & GMC** all full-size (C and K) models, '88 thru '92
*1727 **Sprint & Geo Metro** '85 thru '91
*831 **S-10 & GMC S-15 Pick-ups** all models '82 thru '92
*345 **Vans – Chevrolet & GMC**, V8 & in-line 6 cyl models '68 thru '92

CHRYSLER
*1337 **Chrysler & Plymouth Mid-size** front wheel drive '82 thru '92
K-Cars – see DODGE Aries (723)
Laser – see DODGE Daytona (1140)

DATSUN
402 **200SX** all models '77 thru '79
647 **200SX** all models '80 thru '83
228 **B-210** all models '73 thru '78
525 **210** all models '78 thru '82
206 **240Z, 260Z & 280Z** Coupe & 2+2 '70 thru '78
563 **280ZX** Coupe & 2+2 '79 thru '83
300ZX – see NISSAN (1137)
679 **310** all models '78 thru '82
123 **510 & PL521 Pick-up** '68 thru '73
430 **510** all models '78 thru '81
372 **610** all models '72 thru '76
277 **620 Series Pick-up** all models '73 thru '79
720 Series Pick-up – see NISSAN Pick-ups (771)
376 **810/Maxima** all gasoline models '77 thru '84
124 **1200** all models '70 thru '73
368 **F10** all models '76 thru '79
Pulsar – see NISSAN (876)
Sentra – see NISSAN (982)
Stanza – see NISSAN (981)

DODGE
*723 **Aries & Plymouth Reliant** all models '81 thru '89
*1231 **Caravan & Plymouth Voyager Mini-Vans** all models '84 thru '91
699 **Challenger & Plymouth Saporro** all models '78 thru '83
236 **Colt** all models '71 thru '77
610 **Colt & Plymouth Champ (front wheel drive)** all models '78 thru '87
*556 **D50/Ram 50/Plymouth Arrow Pick-ups & Raider** '79 thru '91
*1668 **Dakota Pick-up** all models '87 thru '90
234 **Dart & Plymouth Valiant** all 6 cyl models '67 thru '76
*1140 **Daytona & Chrysler Laser** all models '84 thru '89
*545 **Omni & Plymouth Horizon** all models '78 thru '90
*912 **Pick-ups** all full-size models '74 thru '91
*1726 **Shadow & Plymouth Sundance** '87 thru '91
*1779 **Spirit & Plymouth Acclaim** '89 thru '92
*349 **Vans – Dodge & Plymouth** V8 & 6 cyl models '71 thru '91

FIAT
080 **124 Sedan & Wagon** all ohv & dohc models '66 thru '75
094 **124 Sport Coupe & Spider** '68 thru '78
479 **Strada** all models '79 thru '82
273 **X1/9** all models '74 thru '80

FORD
*1476 **Aerostar Mini-vans** all models '86 thru '92
788 **Bronco and Pick-ups** '73 thru '79
*880 **Bronco and Pick-ups** '80 thru '91
268 **Courier Pick-up** all models '72 thru '82
789 **Escort & Mercury Lynx** all models '81 thru '90
*2021 **Explorer & Mazda Navajo** '91 thru '92
560 **Fairmont & Mercury Zephyr** all in-line & V8 models '78 thru '83
334 **Fiesta** all models '77 thru '80
754 **Ford & Mercury Full-size,** Ford LTD & Mercury Marquis ('75 thru '82); Ford Custom 500, Country Squire, Crown Victoria & Mercury Colony Park ('75 thru '87); Ford LTD Crown Victoria & Mercury Gran Marquis ('83 thru '87)
359 **Granada & Mercury Monarch** all in-line, 6 cyl & V8 models '75 thru '80
773 **Ford & Mercury Mid-size,** Ford Thunderbird & Mercury Cougar ('75 thru '82); Ford LTD & Mercury Marquis ('83 thru '86); Ford Torino, Gran Torino, Elite, Ranchero pick-up, LTD II, Mercury Montego, Comet, XR-7 & Lincoln Versailles ('75 thru '86)
*654 **Mustang & Mercury Capri** all models including Turbo '79 thru '92
357 **Mustang V8** all models '64-1/2 thru '73
231 **Mustang II** all 4 cyl, V6 & V8 models '74 thru '78
649 **Pinto & Mercury Bobcat** all models '75 thru '80
*1670 **Probe** all models '89 thru '92
*1026 **Ranger & Bronco II** all gasoline models '83 thru '92
*1421 **Taurus & Mercury Sable** '86 thru '91
*1418 **Tempo & Mercury Topaz** all gasoline models '84 thru '91
1338 **Thunderbird & Mercury Cougar/XR7** '83 thru '88
*1725 **Thunderbird & Mercury Cougar** '89 and '90
*344 **Vans** all V8 Econoline models '69 thru '91

GENERAL MOTORS
*829 **A-Cars** – Chevrolet Celebrity, Buick Century, Pontiac 6000 & Oldsmobile Cutlass Ciera all models '82 thru '90
*766 **J-Cars** – Chevrolet Cavalier, Pontiac J-2000, Oldsmobile Firenza, Buick Skyhawk & Cadillac Cimarron all models '82 thru '92
*1420 **N-Cars** – Buick Somerset '85 thru '87; Pontiac Grand Am and Oldsmobile Calais '85 thru '90; Buick Skylark '86 thru '90
*1671 **GM: Buick** Regal, **Chevrolet** Lumina, **Oldsmobile** Cutlass Supreme, **Pontiac** Grand Prix, all front wheel drive models '88 thru '90
*2035 **GM: Chevrolet Lumina APV, Oldsmobile Silhouette, Pontiac Trans Sport** '90 thru '92

GEO
Metro – see CHEVROLET Sprint (1727)
Prizm – see CHEVROLET Nova (1642)
Tracker – see SUZUKI Samurai (1626)

GMC
Safari – see CHEVROLET ASTRO (1477)
Vans & Pick-ups – see CHEVROLET (420, 831, 345, 1664)

(continued on next page)

---

*Listings shown with an asterisk (*) indicate model coverage as of this printing. These titles will be periodically updated to include later model years – consult your Haynes dealer for more information.*

Haynes North America, Inc., 861 Lawrence Drive, Newbury Park, CA 91320 • (805) 498-6703

HAYNES AUTOMOTIVE MANUALS

(continued from previous page)

NOTE: New manuals are added to this list on a periodic basis. If you do not see a listing for your vehicle, consult your local Haynes dealer for the latest product information.

HONDA
- 351 **Accord CVCC** all models '76 thru '83
- *1221 **Accord** all models '84 thru '89
- 160 **Civic 1200** all models '73 thru '79
- 633 **Civic 1300 & 1500 CVCC** all models '80 thru '83
- 297 **Civic 1500 CVCC** all models '75 thru '79
- *1227 **Civic** all models '84 thru '91
- *601 **Prelude CVCC** all models '79 thru '89

HYUNDAI
- *1552 **Excel** all models '86 thru '91

ISUZU
- *1641 **Trooper & Pick-up**, all gasoline models '81 thru '91

JAGUAR
- *242 **XJ6** all 6 cyl models '68 thru '86
- *478 **XJ12 & XJS** all 12 cyl models '72 thru '85

JEEP
- *1553 **Cherokee, Comanche & Wagoneer Limited** all models '84 thru '91
- 412 **CJ** all models '49 thru '86
- *1777 **Wrangler** all models '87 thru '92

LADA
- *413 **1200, 1300. 1500 & 1600** all models including Riva '74 thru '86

LAND ROVER
- 529 **Diesel** all models '58 thru '80

MAZDA
- 648 **626** Sedan & Coupe (rear wheel drive) all models '79 thru '82
- *1082 **626 & MX-6** (front wheel drive) all models '83 thru '90
- *267 **B1600, B1800 & B2000 Pick-ups** '72 thru '90
- 370 **GLC Hatchback (rear wheel drive)** all models '77 thru '83
- 757 **GLC (front wheel drive)** all models '81 thru '86
- 460 **RX-7** all models '79 thru '85
- *1419 **RX-7** all models '86 thru '91

MERCEDES-BENZ
- *1643 **190 Series** all four-cylinder gasoline models, '84 thru '88
- 346 **230, 250 & 280** Sedan, Coupe & Roadster all 6 cyl sohc models '68 thru '72
- 983 **280 123 Series** all gasoline models '77 thru '81
- 698 **350 & 450** Sedan, Coupe & Roadster all models '71 thru '80
- 697 **Diesel 123 Series** 200D, 220D, 240D, 240TD, 300D, 300CD, 300TD, 4- & 5-cyl incl. Turbo '76 thru '85

MERCURY
See FORD Listing

MG
- 111 **MGB** Roadster & GT Coupe all models '62 thru '80
- 265 **MG Midget & Austin Healey Sprite** Roadster '58 thru '80

MITSUBISHI
- *1669 **Cordia, Tredia, Galant, Precis & Mirage** '83 thru '90
- *2022 **Pick-ups & Montero** '83 thru '91

MORRIS
- 074 **(Austin) Marina 1.8** all models '71 thru '80
- 024 **Minor 1000** sedan & wagon '56 thru '71

NISSAN
- 1137 **300ZX** all Turbo & non-Turbo models '84 thru '89
- *1341 **Maxima** all models '85 thru '91
- *771 **Pick-ups/Pathfinder** gas models '80 thru '91
- *876 **Pulsar** all models '83 thru '86
- *982 **Sentra** all models '82 thru '90
- *981 **Stanza** all models '82 thru '90

OLDSMOBILE
- **Custom Cruiser** – *see BUICK Full-size (1551)*
- 658 **Cutlass** all standard gasoline V6 & V8 models '74 thru '88
- **Cutlass Ciera** – *see GENERAL MOTORS A-Cars (829)*
- **Cutlass Supreme** – *see GENERAL MOTORS (1671)*
- **Firenza** – *see GENERAL MOTORS J-Cars (766)*
- **Ninety-eight** – *see BUICK Full-size (1551)*
- **Omega** – *see PONTIAC Phoenix & Omega (551)*

PEUGEOT
- 663 **504** all diesel models '74 thru '83

PLYMOUTH
- 425 **Arrow** all models '76 thru '80
- *For all other PLYMOUTH titles, see DODGE listing.*

PONTIAC
- **T1000** – *see CHEVROLET Chevette (449)*
- **J-2000** – *see GENERAL MOTORS J-Cars (766)*
- **6000** – *see GENERAL MOTORS A-Cars (829)*
- 1232 **Fiero** all models '84 thru '88
- 555 **Firebird** all V8 models except Turbo '70 thru '81
- *867 **Firebird** all models '82 thru '91
- **Full-size Rear Wheel Drive** – *see Buick, Oldsmobile, Pontiac Full-size (1551)*
- **Grand Prix** – *see GENERAL MOTORS (1671)*
- 551 **Phoenix & Oldsmobile Omega** all X-car models '80 thru '84

PORSCHE
- *264 **911** all Coupe & Targa models except Turbo & Carrera 4 '65 thru '89
- 239 **914** all 4 cyl models '69 thru '76
- 397 **924** all models including Turbo '76 thru '82
- *1027 **944** all models including Turbo '83 thru '89

RENAULT
- 141 **5 Le Car** all models '76 thru '83
- 079 **8 & 10** all models with 58.4 cu in engines '62 thru '72
- 097 **12 Saloon & Estate** all models 1289 cc engines '70 thru '80
- 768 **15 & 17** all models '73 thru '79
- 081 **16** all models 89.7 cu in & 95.5 cu in engines '65 thru '72
- **Alliance & Encore** – *see AMC (934)*
- 984 **Fuego** all models '82 thru '85

SAAB
- 247 **99** all models including Turbo '69 thru '80
- *980 **900** all models including Turbo '79 thru '88

SUBARU
- 237 **1100, 1300, 1400 & 1600** all models '71 thru '79
- *681 **1600 & 1800** 2WD & 4WD all models '80 thru '89

SUZUKI
- *1626 **Samurai/Sidekick and Geo Tracker** all models '86 thru '91

TOYOTA
- *1023 **Camry** all models '83 thru '91
- 150 **Carina Sedan** all models '71 thru '74
- 229 **Celica ST, GT & liftback** all models '71 thru '77
- 437 **Celica** all models '78 thru '81
- *935 **Celica** all models except front-wheel drive and Supra '82 thru '85
- 680 **Celica Supra** all models '79 thru '81
- 1139 **Celica Supra** all in-line 6-cylinder models '82 thru '86
- 361 **Corolla** all models '75 thru '79
- 961 **Corolla** all models (rear wheel drive) '80 thru '87
- *1025 **Corolla** all models (front wheel drive) '84 thru '91
- *636 **Corolla Tercel** all models '80 thru '82
- 230 **Corona & MK II** all 4 cyl sohc models '69 thru '74
- 360 **Corona** all models '74 thru '82
- *532 **Cressida** all models '78 thru '82
- 313 **Land Cruiser** all models '68 thru '82
- 200 **MK II** all 6 cyl models '72 thru '76
- *1339 **MR2** all models '85 thru '87
- 304 **Pick-up** all models '69 thru '78
- *656 **Pick-up** all models '79 thru '91

TRIUMPH
- 112 **GT6 & Vitesse** all models '62 thru '74
- 113 **Spitfire** all models '62 thru '81
- 028 **TR2, 3, 3A, & 4A** Roadsters '52 thru '67
- 031 **TR250 & 6** Roadsters '67 thru '76
- 322 **TR7** all models '75 thru '81

VW
- 159 **Beetle & Karmann Ghia** all models '54 thru '79
- 238 **Dasher** all gasoline models '74 thru '81
- *884 **Rabbit, Jetta, Scirocco, & Pick-up** all gasoline models '74 thru '91 & **Convertible** '80 thru '91
- 451 **Rabbit, Jetta & Pick-up** all diesel models '77 thru '84
- 082 **Transporter 1600** all models '68 thru '79
- 226 **Transporter 1700, 1800 & 2000** all models '72 thru '79
- 084 **Type 3 1500 & 1600** all models '63 thru '73
- 1029 **Vanagon** all air-cooled models '80 thru '83

VOLVO
- 203 **120, 130 Series & 1800 Sports** '61 thru '73
- 129 **140 Series** all models '66 thru '74
- 244 **164** all models '68 thru '75
- *270 **240 Series** all models '74 thru '90
- 400 **260 Series** all models '75 thru '82
- *1550 **740 & 760 Series** all models '82 thru '88

SPECIAL MANUALS
- 1479 **Automotive Body Repair & Painting Manual**
- 1654 **Automotive Electrical Manual**
- 1480 **Automotive Heating & Air Conditioning Manual**
- 1762 **Chevrolet Engine Overhaul Manual**
- 1736 **Diesel Engine Repair Manual**
- 1667 **Emission Control Manual**
- 1763 **Ford Engine Overhaul Manual**
- 482 **Fuel Injection Manual**
- 1666 **Small Engine Repair Manual**
- 299 **SU Carburetors** thru '88
- 393 **Weber Carburetors** thru '79
- 300 **Zenith/Stromberg CD Carburetors** thru '76

See your dealer for other available titles

Over 100 Haynes motorcycle manuals also available

7-1-92

---

* Listings shown with an asterisk (*) indicate model coverage as of this printing. These titles will be periodically updated to include later model years - consult your Haynes dealer for more information.

Haynes North America, Inc., 861 Lawrence Drive, Newbury Park, CA 91320 • (805) 498-6703